MAINE
SPORTING
CAMPS

ALSO BY ALICE ARLEN

Nonfiction

HALF A MIND: HASHING, THE OUTRAGEOUS NEW SPORT

A TASTE OF HALLOWELL

IN THE MAINE WOODS

PINE CAY

SHE TOOK TO THE WOODS: A BIOGRAPHY AND SELECTED
WRITINGS OF LOUISE DICKINSON RICH

Poetry

2096: JOURNAL OF INDIAN LITERATURE

EXCAVATION: AMERICA SINGS ANTHOLOGY

MAINE SPORTING CAMPS

The Year-Round Guide to Vacationing at Traditional Hunting and Fishing Camps

ALICE ARLEN

The Countryman Press
Woodstock, Vermont

A NOTE TO OUR READERS

Although we update this guide every time it goes to press, change is inevitable. We hope you will help us by contributing your knowledge and experience to this guide. Send us a postcard or letter with corrections, comments, or stories; or even send us a photograph. Address your correspondence to: *Maine Sporting Camps* editor, The Countryman Press, P.O. Box 748, Woodstock, VT 05091

Originally published as *In the Maine Woods*, copyright © 1994, 1998 by Alice Arlen
Maine Sporting Camps copyright ©2003 by Alice Arlen

Third Edition

Library of Congress Cataloging-in-Publication Data
Arlen, Alice.
     Maine sporting camps : the year-round guide to vacationing at traditional hunting and fishing camps / Alice Arlen.—3rd ed.
          p. cm.
     Rev. ed. of: In the Maine woods. 2nd ed. 1998.
     Includes bibliographical references and index.
     ISBN 0-88150-560-9
     1. Hunting lodges—Maine. 2. Fishing lodges—Maine. I. Arlen, Alice. In the
          Maine woods. II. Title.
     SK85 .A75 2003
     796.5'025'741—dc21

                                                                    200204138

Book design by Julie Duquet
Maps by Paul Woodward, copyright © 2003 The Countryman Press
Cover photograph of Cobb's Pierce Pond Camps © Richard Procopio
Interior photographs by Alice Arlen unless otherwise indicated

PUBLISHED BY THE COUNTRYMAN PRESS, P.O. BOX 748, WOODSTOCK, VT 05091
Distributed by W. W. Norton & Company, Inc., 500 Fifth Avenue, New York, NY 10110

Printed in The United States of America
10 9 8 7 6 5 4 3 2 1

*For all those who
work, live, and play
in the Maine woods*

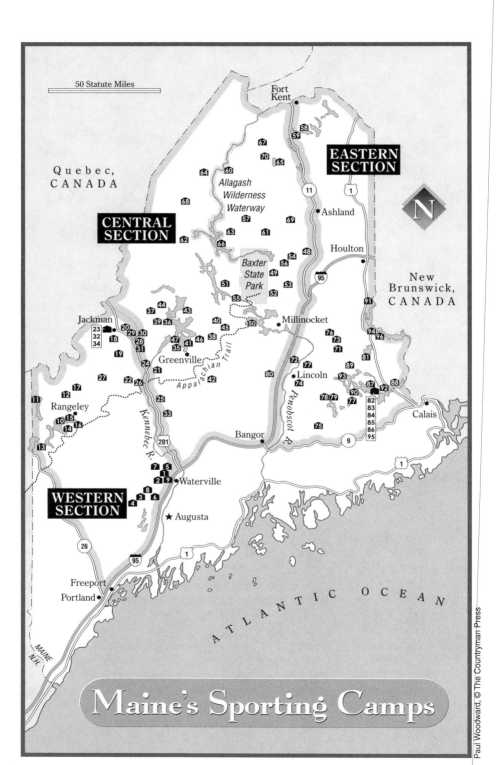

50 Statute Miles

Quebec,
CANADA

Fort
Kent

EASTERN
SECTION

N

Allagash
Wilderness
Waterway

Ashland

CENTRAL
SECTION

Baxter
State
Park

Houlton

New
Brunswick,
CANADA

Jackman

Greenville

Millinocket

Lincoln

Calais

Rangeley

Bangor

WESTERN
SECTION

Waterville

★ Augusta

Freeport
Portland

ATLANTIC OCEAN

MAINE
N.H.

Maine's Sporting Camps

Paul Woodward, © The Countryman Press

CONTENTS

Part Two **CENTRAL MAINE**

. . . none of us ever thought that there was any place in the world like that lake in Maine. I guess I remembered clearest of all the early mornings, when the lake was cool and motionless, remembered how the bedroom smelled of the lumber it was made of and of the wet woods whose scent entered through the screen . . . those summers had been infinitely precious and worth saving.

—*E. B. White,* "Once More to the Lake"

AUTHOR'S NOTE

In the fall of 1992, after a lovely stay at a Maine sporting camp, I arrived early at L.L. Bean for my author's signing session of *A Taste of Hallowell* because I wanted to purchase a guide to other sporting camps. After searching in vain, I approached a salesperson. "You know," she said, "in all the years I've been here, I've never seen a book on Maine sporting camps." Gee, I thought, if there isn't one here, there probably isn't one anywhere! (This I subsequently found to be true.)

Several months later I found myself standing before a group of strangers at a Maine Sporting Camp Association meeting attempting to share my idea of writing a book that would feature them, the sporting-camp owners, in a series of interviews. Little did I anticipate where this notion would take me. Specifically, two weeks later I was driving down a series of logging roads, miles from anywhere, seven hours from home (still in Maine!), in the middle of a snowstorm, for a rendezvous with a Maine guide at Dead Horse Gulch. This was the prelude to a wonderful few days of winter camping, a first for me.

Over the years, my sojourns at sporting camps have catapulted me into many firsts: learning to "read" rocks and really see spring wildflowers, fly-casting for bass along the misty shoreline of a pristine lake, crouching motionless, waiting for the dawn and a moose. I've had lifts in float planes with exhilarating views of the network of roads, forests, and waterways I'd just traveled. Once, flying away from a camp, our plane dipped its wings to 18 bear hunters out on the dock waving good-bye. Sheltered beaches on pristine lakes have offered midday skinny-dips; I've gazed at peregrine falcons floating in spring updrafts. Magical moments. And there are many, many more.

In all, I've traveled over 25,000 miles in Maine since my idea became a reality. And, for the most part, it's meant bumping along routes where I regularly spot (or avoid colliding with!) large and small critters, but rarely see a telephone pole or power line, tarred road, or vehicle other than a pick-up or pulp truck. Dotting this landscape are "my" sporting camps, welcome oases of warmth and hospitality.

At this point, many owners feel like dear friends and visiting their camps is like coming home, over and over again. There have been changes over the decade: new owners; new buildings; camps, vistas, and roads opening and closing. When I first started, few owners realized the extent of the industry, and communication to and between the camps was basic. By the second edition, a couple of camps had web sites; now nearly all do. And the biggest surprise and gift to me, this third time around, is the number of owners who have told me they are in the business because they read this book! It

The author at work interviewing Robin Carter at Lakewood Camps

is humbling and gratifying. Another important change, which I find hope-
ful, is the effort and success of owners, guests, and organizations to preserve
pristine land around the camps. For wilderness is at the heart of what brings
people and income to sporting camps and to Maine.

The essence of the sporting-camp experience is a deep sense of perma-
nence, continuity, and connectedness. Strangers share their hearts' desires
around tables or campfires, generations sing songs under brilliant stars or
around the camp piano. There are still these special "homes" called sporting camps, with surrounding woods and waters, that endure undeveloped.
At a time when it is easier and easier to find virtual stimulus and harder
and harder to find places where one can truly "unplug" and regain human
rhythms, we can all count ourselves lucky that a small group of hard-
working, individualistic men and women have kept the sporting-camp
traditions alive.

Maine Sporting Camps is a look at this sporting-camp world through facts
(guidebook data) and flavors (recipes), but most of all through the words of
these camp owners, which is only fitting since this book is really their story.
Guests return to their chosen sporting camp year after year not only because
the layout and location suit them, but also because the owners have created
a little community that "feels right." Camp owners really make the place for
many people: Witness the exodus of clientele after new owners take over,

The author and her vehicle, deep in the Maine woods

the migration of guests when an owner purchases a different camp, the out-pouring of affection from long-term visitors, the "camp hopping" guests do until they find the right spot and settle in. Sporting-camp owners truly know the meaning of the word hospitality, and I want to thank them here for their help, generosity, and kindness. This book commemorates the sporting-camp industry, a Maine tradition that, through the dogged deter-mination of a few individuals and their families, hasn't vanished.

So, dear reader, before you peruse these pages, I offer several overall sug-gestions. Please realize that this book is a series of snapshots. These inter-views were generally conducted during a one-hour to two-day visit. What I offer here is an image of the camps and their people at one moment in time, and as we all know from looking at family albums, things change. Sporting camps are sold, go under, rise like a phoenix. Also, they are rustic and remote, some more so than others. This book should help give you an idea of what to expect, but if, in the course of reading this book, you find camps that interest you, do contact them. It is in the owners' interest, as well as yours, that your time at their camp is a happy one and not derailed by unmet or unclear expectations.

For people who would like a cabin in the woods without having the responsibilities of actually owning it, or would like to explore remote areas in a congenial atmosphere, or "simply" regain their humanity or stretch their capabilities, this book will open up a wonderful world. Folks who love sporting camps will tell you that they are a point of reference for them—a place and time for peace, companionship, and beauty that enrich their lives immeasurably. I hope this becomes the case for you. Happy reading!

INTRODUCTION

In addition to my own thoughts, the following incorporates information from Gary Cobb's and Alfred Fenton's *The History of Pierce Pond Camps* and Stephen Cole's manuscript *Maine Sporting Camps* (see "Further Reading").

There is a grand tradition that has become an integral part of Maine's heritage: Unique to the state, and over 150 years old, it is called the Maine sporting camp. Some people think of these camps as "hunting and fishing lodges." In the spring and fall they generally are, but they are also much more: summer destinations for families, food and lodging for snowmobilers and skiers, prime spots for nature lovers, and solace for the world-weary. Nearly all sporting camps are on a lake or river, generally in a remote area of forested land. Most have buildings made of peeled and chinked logs with porches overlooking the water. The guest sleeping cabins are clustered near the shore around a central dining lodge. Plumbing was (and may still be) "out back." Primitive, and in harmony with their surroundings, sporting camps have the appearance of having grown out of the ground. New Hampshire and Vermont have private hunting and fishing clubs and game preserves. New York, in the Adirondacks, has private camps and rustic estates. But Maine sporting camps are open to paying customers and are a cultural and entrepreneurial resource distinctive to the state.

Several factors came together to produce the Maine sporting camp. The post–Civil War transition into the Victorian era saw tremendous industrial and economic expansion and the development of technologies such as the internal-combustion engine and electricity. The iron and steel industries flourished, and the railroads entered their golden age. The high economic growth rate in the Victorian era created a substantial upper-middle class. At the same time, intellectuals and writers such as Henry David Thoreau decried what they saw as society's growing alienation from nature and expressed general uneasiness about the direction of American culture. Life in polluted eastern cities during the Industrial Revolution was felt to be "undermining character, taste, morality, and the health and welfare of individuals and the family." As a result, those who could sought escape from the questionable influences and pollution of the cities, as well as from the summer heat. (Ironically, many who "took the airs" were the families of magnates and managers whose factories were causing the pollution they were escaping.)

Recreational sailing and canoeing are lasting legacies of the Victorian era. Hunting, fishing, and hiking took on a certain cachet as sporting pur-

COURTESY TIM POND CAMPS

An early Maine sporting camp

suits instead of merely functional activities. Not only did people have
motives for escape (aesthetics, expendable income, leisure time, status,
health concerns), they also had the means. It is no coincidence that the heyday of fishing and hunting in Maine was also the golden age of lumbering
and railroading. The very rail lines that were bringing trainloads of Maine
timber to fuel factory burners also carried trainloads of vacationers fleeing
back to the source of all that smog! With the growth of a national rail transportation network, an extended family vacation at one of the much-publi-
cized public sporting camps in the Maine wilderness became possible and
desirable. The Bangor, the Aroostook, and the Central Maine Railroads all
offered direct service to Brownville in 1881, to Presque Isle in 1882, to
Katahdin Iron Works in 1883, and reached Moosehead Lake in 1884. The
Somerset Railroad came to Bingham in 1890; the narrow-gauge trains got
to Rangeley and Carrabassett by 1895; and the Katahdin, Allagash, and
Fish River areas were opened by 1900. Before Henry Ford put his first automobile on the road, place-names such as Sysladobsis, Oquossoc,
Nesowadnehunk, and Munsungan were part of the vocabulary of hunters,
anglers, and vacationers from Boston to Philadelphia.

     In 1904 there were at least 300 sporting camps in operation in
Maine. But after World War II, Americans could no longer spend the
time or money on a month-long vacation at a Maine sporting camp. The

railroads were in decline and automobiles and "motor coaches" on the increase. The road system in Maine was poor and people stayed close to the tarmac, where motels and motor-coach campgrounds were now the rage. And finally, air transportation took travelers out of New England altogether. Over the years, many camps burned, some became resorts, some sold as condominiums or individual cottages, and others simply rotted away to become part of the forest.

But good things die hard. In spite of these changes and setbacks, tucked away here and there stand sporting camps whose owners proudly struggle to maintain a tradition that may very well be the only stabilizing factor in the Maine woods. Fortunately, these few hardy souls have held on long enough to witness a renewed interest in Maine sporting camps. We have come full circle. We need what sporting camps have to offer, now more than ever. There are precious few places where we can feel the fundamental connections with nature and with one another. Sporting camps still provide solace for urban refugees (meaning most of us), and a wilderness playground for those who love the outdoors. Most of all, they still provide a much-needed "port in the storm," far from the fractured, mobile, frenetic, and alienating forces that impose on our humanity.

HOW TO USE THIS BOOK

Maine Sporting Camps is largely anecdotal. Along with guidebook data is information about the region's flora and fauna, geology and history, ecological policies, and the business of recreation. The owners' comments give insights into the workings of specific sporting camps as well as impressions about the individuals who run these camps. My purpose in compiling this book is to provide a resource for the present and an oral history for the future. Some themes that came up in my interviews are specific to the sporting-camp industry, but many are universal. Thus, you can read the book purely for enjoyment—a camp or two before bed—or you can study it with the intention of finding a future vacation spot, or future sporting camp to call your own!

How to Find an Appropriate Camp

The first thing you need to decide is where in Maine you'd like to go. Then you'll need to decide whether or not you want to cook your own meals. Next, depending on your recreational interests, ask yourself what time of year you want to go. Then, consider how you feel about reading by gaslight, stoking a woodstove, or using an outhouse or central shower. How much do you want to spend? Do you want to bring a pet? The headings for each camp answer these questions and can help you narrow your search. Once you've found several camps that fit your logistical needs, the full text should help you assess other considerations.

For inclusion in this book the sporting camp must
- Have at least four guest cabins;
- Be open to the public (there are private camps);
- Be in operation during the time I was researching the book;
- Have the look and feel of a sporting camp (that is, not a campground, motor court, or individual cabin or cottage rental);
- Not be primarily transient lodging (for example, a restaurant or inn or outdoor center with cabins) or the base of operations for activities in other locations (such as whitewater rafting);
- Have an owner or manager on the premises;
- And, of course, choose to be in the book

Glossary of Terms

American Plan (AP): Three meals served as part of the price.
Housekeeping (HK): You supply the food and cook your own meals.
Modified American Plan (MAP): Two meals (breakfast and dinner) usually part of the price.
HK/AP: When a combination is noted, the first abbreviation is most prevalent (for example, the camp is primarily housekeeping but meals are also available, perhaps only at certain times of the year).
ITS: International (snowmobile) Trail System
PETS: If nothing is noted it generally means that pets are not accepted. Be sure to ask if it's important to you, since things can change.
RATES: These are simply guidelines. Check with camps for current prices.
SPORT: Traditional term for a sporting camp guest.
SPORTING CAMP: A group of cabins along with a main lodge (often log, and generally in a remote location) providing lodging (and often food), for a fee, to people interested in backwoods recreation or relaxation.
SPORTING CAMP ASSOCIATION (SCA): Founded in 1987. Members adhere to certain standards, make referrals to each other, and act together on legislative issues. Most, but not all, SCA members fit the criteria above, but not all sporting camps

in the book are SCA members (which is no reflection on their quality). For a list of members (around 55) or further information contact The Maine Sporting Camp Association, 36 Minuteman Drive, Millinocket, ME 04462.

Where in Maine?

Is there a particular area of Maine you want to explore? I have provided a map that shows the state divided into three sections, each corresponding to a part of the book: western, central, and eastern. The number for each camp corresponds to the location of that camp on the map. The camps within each geographical region are listed in alphabetical order. In addition, an introduction gives an overview of each region and indicates where you can call or write for further information. In addition, you may want to contact the Maine Publicity Bureau, PO Box 2300, Hallowell, ME 04347-2300; 207-623-0363, and ask for the free pamphlets "Maine Invites You," "Maine Guide to Hunting and Fishing," "Maine Camping Guide," and "Exploring Maine." The local chambers of commerce put out good guides to their areas, and I have listed these contacts in the introduction to each region.

How Much Is It?

The prices I've listed are generally a range of low- to high-season daily and weekly rates, either per person or per cabin. Boat rental is extra, unless I've indicated otherwise. Most camps offer package deals for hunting, fishing, off-season, and families, and some sponsor special-interest programs, so be sure to find out what is available. And finally, the rates listed in this guide are primarily for purposes of comparison and are subject to change. When you call or write for brochures, you will get the most up-to-date rate schedule.

How Do I Get There?

Once you've decided on an area, how are you going to get there? I have included general driving times under the sectional introductions and have also indicated air-transportation options. I've given general driving directions to each camp under the heading "Access." These assume you will be traveling from the south.

To drive or not to drive: that is the question. The answer is, of course, it depends. A 14-hour ordeal for a New Yorker might be a half-hour jaunt for a Canadian. A 14-hour drive, seen as part of the adventure, is preferable to flying for someone who loves back roads (or hates to fly).

It also depends on how much gear and how many people are involved. You will have more supplies going to a housekeeping establishment than to an American Plan camp. How much are you planning on using a car once

Float planes are a means of transportation . . .

at camp? If you choose a camp near population centers and cultural activities, you will probably want a vehicle (which can be a rental car from an airport if you fly in). If you plan to go to a remote American Plan camp and then return home, you can do as many do: Fly in and leave your car and worries behind.

If you drive, your chosen camp will give you detailed directions, but I recommend getting DeLorme's *Maine Atlas and Gazetteer*, which shows all the major back roads (from DeLorme Mapping, PO Box 298, Yarmouth, ME 04096; 1-800-452-5931 or 1-800-227-1656). Keep in mind that a new logging road can pop up in a matter of days and so may not be on the map. Major logging roads have mile markers—little rectangular number plates—tacked up on trees. Be aware also that there may be a logging company gatehouse along your route. You will be charged a usage fee for each person in your vehicle (a reduced fee for those going to sporting camps). There are restrictions on bringing in bicycles or motorcycles, so you'll need to check this out with your chosen camp ahead of time. Some sporting camps have private gates. Be sure to ask what time their gate closes. How hellacious to drive 12 hours only to find the gate closed and gatekeeper gone!

Be sure to check the status of your spare tire and tools, fill up with gas, carry something to eat and drink, and in all seasons have something for extra warmth (in winter I throw in a sleeping bag, small shovel, and jumper cables). Logging roads, it is important to remember, are for logging trucks, and they have the right of way. It is a convention of the back road and a smart lifesaving maneuver to pull over to the side and stop when a pulp truck comes at you. Keep alert for telltale dust clouds ahead, I actually drive

. . . no matter what the season.

with my window down and radio off so I can hear them, and don't cut the corners. If this sounds serious, it is.

In addition to being alert for logging trucks, you'll need to watch out for pedestrians—the four-legged kind, that is. It is better for everyone's health to count how many different critters you spotted, rather than splatted, along the way. Avoid moose and deer at all costs. If you're careful, driving around the back roads of Maine can be a wonderful experience. You certainly get an appreciation for how much of Maine lies beyond the coast, and how vast and beautiful are its timber resources and varied topography.

What Should I Bring?

Aside from the items mentioned above (sleeping bag, tools for emergency car repair, road map), each person will want a flashlight, warm clothes (even in summer), rain gear, bug repellent, sunglasses (even in winter), a visor hat, as well as personal items and toiletries (including shampoo). You may want a small medical kit and, naturally, any personal medication. If you bring anything that requires batteries, bring backup batteries. If you bring a radio, bring earphones (a major reason most people go to sporting camps is to get away from noise). Many camps, but not all, have libraries, and most have board games. Some camps rent mountain bikes; nearly all rent boats. For most camps, there's no point in packing a hair dryer or electric razor or anything else electrical. Most of all, don't forget to bring your sense of adventure, sense of humor, and sense of wonder!

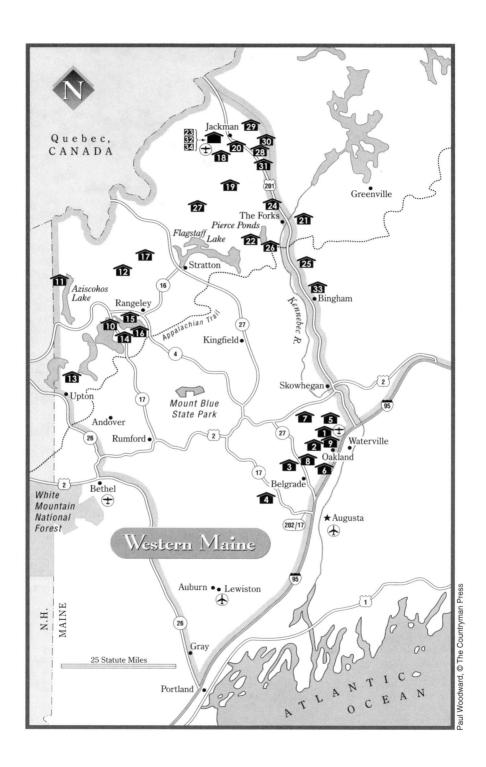

N

Quebec,
CANADA

Jackman

23
32
34

29

30

20

28

18

31

19

201

Greenville

27

The Forks

24

21

Pierce Ponds

Flagstaff Lake

22

26

25

17

Stratton

33

Bingham

12

16

11

Aziscohos
Lake

Rangeley

15

10

16

14

Appalachian Trail

27

Kingfield

4

Kennebec R.

Skowhegan

2

13

Upton

17

Mount Blue
State Park

95

Andover

7

5

26

Rumford

2

1

27

2

9

Waterville

Oakland

3

8

6

17

Belgrade

4

Bethel

White
Mountain
National
Forest

202/17

★ Augusta

Western Maine

95

Auburn

Lewiston

N.H.

MAINE

26

25 Statute Miles

Gray

Portland

A T L A N T I C
O C E A N

1

Paul Woodward, © The Countryman Press

Part One
WESTERN MAINE

This region includes the Belgrade Lakes region to the south, the Rangeley Lakes region in the west near the New Hampshire border, and the Dead River–Jackman region between ME 27 and US 201.

THE BELGRADE LAKES REGION

This region is the "southern" area of our sporting-camp inventory. Located about half an hour north of Augusta, Maine's state capital, it is made up of a chain of seven lakes and gently rolling hills and fields, and is near many cultural and tourist attractions. All the camps listed here are easily accessible by car or regularly scheduled flights.

The area was once the fishing, hunting, and farming terrain of the Abenaki Indians and was settled by Europeans in the 1700s. Belgrade mills, orchards, and farms provided goods that were carried by train to cities. By the early 1900s, those railway lines brought children to one of the couple of dozen summer camps ranged around the various lakes. Sporting camps and grand hotels popped up to service the rich and famous (and not-so-rich-and-famous). The area inspired the film *On Golden Pond* (parts of the movie were shot at Great Pond and Long Pond).

The Belgrade chain—East, North, Great, Long, McGrath, and Salmon Ponds and Messalonskee Lake—is part of the 177-square-mile Messalonskee Stream drainage, a tributary of the Kennebec River, which flows into the Atlantic. The lakes range in depth from 133 feet in Messalonskee Lake to 20 feet in North Pond. At least 20 different species of fish can be found in the Belgrade Lakes, including large- and smallmouth bass, pike, perch, brown trout, salmon, and brook trout.

Visitors to the area will find opportunities for hiking (Mount Pisgah, Mount Philip, Mount Tom, French's Mountain, Blueberry Hill), golfing, cultural events, and festivals all within a half hour's easy drive. Highlights of a Belgrade summer include a children's pet show and a loon-calling contest, a ride on the mailboat that tours Great Pond daily, and outdoor concerts at the New England Music Camp on Messalonskee Lake.

GETTING THERE: Augusta is the nearest airport to the Belgrade Lakes region (with connecting flights from Boston; rental cars available). Driving time from Augusta is 35 minutes; from Portland, 1.5 hours; from Boston, 4 hours; from New York City, 8 hours.

GUIDANCE: For further information, contact Belgrade Lakes Region, Inc., PO Box 72, Belgrade, ME 04917; 207-465-3406. During the summer, there is an information booth on the right side of ME 27 as you drive north from Augusta, about 3 miles from the village of Belgrade.

1. ALDEN CAMPS

AP, SCA
MANAGERS: Martha and Carter Minkel
ADDRESS: Alden Camps Road, Oakland, ME 04963; 207-465-7703, fax: 207-465-7912; e-mail: alden@mint.net; www.aldencamps.com
SEASON: May 17 through September 27
ACCOMMODATIONS: Eighteen log cabins: one to three bedrooms, indoor plumbing and shower, screened porch, woodstove or Franklin fireplace, electric lights, small refrigerator
RATES: $75–150 per person per day; $450–900 per person per week; motorboat $30 per day, canoes free
ACCESS: I-95 north to exit 33. Take a right onto ME 137 west and go 2 miles into the town of Oakland. Go straight through town (between the Mobil gas station on your left and Charlie's Log Cabins on your right). At the four-way stop sign, continue straight on ME 137 west. In about 4 miles, you will see the D&L Country Store on your right. Alden Camps is 1 mile past D&L on the right.

Alden's pale blue farmhouse, surrounded by flowers, sits close to ME 137, just 7 miles—but a world away—from I-95. A screened-in porch takes up the entire side of a long ell. There, white wicker chairs and sofas provide a place for guests to gather and visit. Inside is a small living room adjacent to the pine-paneled dining room and the office where you sign in. Opposite the house is a long, mowed field with a basketball court in the distance and a swing set in the foreground (baseball, volleyball, badminton, tetherball, croquet, and horseshoe equipment are available). A red barn provides the setting for weekly lobster dinners. Beyond the barn is a clay tennis court and a vegetable garden "for the enjoyment and education of the children who come here from the city," Vesta and George Putnam, heads of the family-owned business, explain.

Down the driveway, the guest cabins are set among a grove of old pines. In 1911, two years after Fred Allen, Vesta's uncle, bought the 40-acre site, he built four cabins and some tent platforms and opened up for business.

Vesta: "My uncle was killed in an automobile accident in 1922 when his family was very young. So my aunt ran the camps for quite a long time when she was left a widow. Then her eldest son ran it. But after she passed away, he decided that he didn't want to run the camps anymore. So his sister, Ellen Reed, and I started out—in 1956."

The porch at Alden's

George: "Vesta and I met at Colby College [15 minutes away], where I majored in chemistry, and were married in 1937. I then went on to MIT and became a chemical engineer working for an oil company in New Jersey."

Vesta: "We moved here full-time in 1967. We have five children and they've all worked here. Four of our grandchildren—Carter, Chris, Garret, and Melissa—have worked here. Carter and his wife, Martha, are now our managers. Alden's has seen four generations of management, guests, and staff, and we plan to keep the business in the family.

"Alden's is on East Pond, the headwaters of the Belgrade Lakes. When people are from out of state, we call it East Lake so they don't think it's a puddle. People came here to fish primarily for smallmouth bass. We have largemouth now, too."

George: "Largemouth are supposed to be the gamiest. When they hit, you know it. They're a lot of fun. We also have perch, pickerel, and bull-heads or horn pout."

East Pond is the locale of several children's summer camps, and sea-sonal private cottages dot the shoreline. Moose frequent a boggy area beyond camp, and where East Pond flows into North Pond is a meandering waterway rich with wildlife called the Serpentine. Two golf courses (one 18-hole, one 9-hole) are 15 minutes away.

Martha: "We are very aware that we're in the hospitality industry, and that people come here to relax. So we do absolutely everything we can to make people feel comfortable. The cabins are rustic and simple, but we have maid service. People come up to breakfast and when they go back they have fresh towels and their beds are made. Our cabin boys bring buckets of ice to the cabins, take care of the woodstoves and look after the guests' boats. You may pass our staff on the path and and see that they're all ready to go on their water-ski run for their break, but if they notice your water jug is empty, they'll go get you some ice. A good attitude is our number one hiring consideration.

"Our guests arrive on Saturday. They often come from an urban area, have been traveling for hours, usually in heavy traffic, maybe with screaming children, and when they get here they sometimes are stressed out, hot, tired, maybe angry. The regulars (and we have a very high return rate) hit the driveway and instantly begin to unwind. With our new guests, we do handsprings to accommodate them because we know if we can please them on Saturday night, they are, in fact, going to be happy. And usually by about Monday they start to loosen up.

"We seat our guests at a specific table during their stay (and make mental notes of where they sat for when they return again, and where everyone else was sitting as well! People look forward to their spot, surrounded by certain camp friends). And we give them the same server for the entire time. Pretty soon the server knows his or her guests and will have, say, two chocolate milks, water, and an ice tea ready and waiting on the table when they come to lunch. If there's a baby, the server helps take care of that. And all our staff take time and talk with guests.

"We now have 'kids time,' with arts and crafts, every afternoon for a couple of hours. It gives the parents a break after lunch. Then it's beach time, with water-skiing instruction (weather permitting); the cabin boys run the boat. We also have tournaments: cribbage, ping-pong, volleyball, shuffleboard.

"I first came to Alden's as a cabin girl in 1991. (I didn't have the nerve to be a waitress.) Then, in 1997, I shadowed the manager, Wendy Coons Wentworth, whose father was Vesta's first manager. After that, Carter and I took over as managers.

"It's really a fun lifestyle. We get time off in winter (although we're busy with bookings and maintaining the cabins). By April we're antsy to get our social life going again and welcome back our guests. We know so many of them, for so many years, that it feels like a family reunion each week!"

Grilled Rainbow Trout

Alden's serves not only its guests, but is open to the general public as well, by reservation.
Ellen Kiser, Alden's chef—and Martha's mother!—always prepares a vegetarian dish.

Clean the trout, sprinkle salt and pepper in the stomach cavity and fill with fresh herbs, such as dill, thyme, parsley, or cilantro. Heat the grill to medium high. Grill and splash with following sauce:

> ½ cup white wine, 2 T melted butter, ⅛ cup lemon juice, 1 T Worcestershire sauce, 1 tsp. each salt and pepper, ½ tsp. dill, ½ tsp. thyme, ½ tsp. parsley

2. BEAR SPRING CAMPS

AP, SCA

MANAGERS: Ron and Peg Churchill
ADDRESS: 60 Jamaica Point Road, Oakland, ME 04963; 207-397-2341;
e-mail: church@tdstelme.net
SEASON: May 15 through October 1
ACCOMMODATIONS: Thirty-two log and cedar-clapboard cabins: one to four bedrooms, porch, indoor plumbing and shower, electric lights, automatic heat, small refrigerator, woodstove
RATES: $625 per couple per cabin per week. Child and group rates available. Motorboats $125 per week.
ACCESS: I-95 to exit 31B. Follow ME 27 north for 17 miles through Belgrade (last stop for shopping before camp). Turn right onto ME 225 east (sign will say TO ROME, where camps are located; mail goes to Oakland). Follow ME 225 for 4.5 miles to Jamaica Point Road. Turn right. Camp is ¼ mile on the right.

As you descend the hill and round the curve into Bear Spring Camps, a pastoral view opens up before you. A rambling, white-clapboard farmhouse is set amid 400 acres of woods and lush green fields. Its red roof and pots of flowers color the landscape. Bluebird boxes and a swing set stand ready for occupants. A long dirt road leads down past a clay tennis court to dark brown cabins, each with its own dock and boat, and an expanse of lake. It was in one of the far cabins that E. B. White wrote the quote found at the front of this book. The cabins range around the North Bay of Great Pond—at 9 by 6 miles, the largest of the Belgrade Lakes. The shoreline is grassy, with about 2 feet of sand that continues underwater in a gentle slope for easy swimming.

Ron: "We have 2,800 feet of continuous shorefront. Then we own another 900 feet which goes to Meadow Stream. Beyond that is bog which

can't be developed, so this all looks pristine and will stay that way."
(Meadow Stream—a marshy area full of wildlife—is navigable, in a ribbon-
candy kind of way, for some distance.) "People fish for bass here and pike.
Pike are bony but very sweet, like a pickerel. In the early spring, if they're
not using live bait, they'll use just the biggest, ugliest lure they've got in
their boxes. They're big, so they're fun to fish for."

Peg's mother, Marguerite Mosher, offers insight into the camp's history: "My
husband Bert's father and his grandfather, George, came up here in 1910.
George Mosher went to Connecticut, made and lost a fortune, came back,
and bought the original old farmhouse here. Within a year or so they had
built a couple of camps and rented them. Up where our dining room is now
there was a summer kitchen. Probably put wood in it in the winter. I came
here in 1942. Waited tables. Back in the '30s and '40s, all the young people
in the area worked at local jobs: canning factories and sporting camps. Every
town, nearly, had a canning factory. Around here they canned vegetables.
And there were a lot of sporting camps then, an awful lot. There are housekeeping camps still around (where you cook your own meals). But the old
resorts like ours mostly have been made into condos."

Ron: "Peg and I came here in 1984 because Peg missed the sunsets and
sunrises and evenings on the porch." *Peg:* "I was literally crying to get back.
I was brought up here so I knew what I was getting in for. But Ron didn't."
Ron laughs. "No, I didn't at all!"

Ron says he trailed Marguerite's late husband around for several years
and learned on the job. Now, with two young children, up to 130 guests,
three dozen boats to maintain, and 25 staff to oversee, that early training has
proved invaluable.

Ron and Peg's daughter and son, Abby and Spencer, are an integral
part of the camp scene. *Peg:* "Families love it here. We have swings, a driving
range, tennis court, badminton, volleyball court, horseshoes, basketball,
walking trails, and the swimming and boating. Also, a lot of people come in
the spring for a month before most of our families arrive and again for another month in the fall after school starts. It's pretty much the same people from
all over New England, and recently folks from Maryland and Virginia."

Ron: "This area of Maine has a true chain of lakes." *Marguerite:* "They
used to do a tour of the lakes. Alden Camps is on East Pond, the headwaters.
That dumps into North Pond, which flows down here into Meadow Stream,
which you can portage. McGrath and Salmon Ponds come into this lake
halfway down." *Ron:* "Great Pond then flows into Long Pond, which leads to
Belgrade Stream and Messalonskee Lake, and then Messalonskee Stream,
which leads to the Kennebec River, which flows into the Atlantic Ocean!"

Peg: "It's expensive to run a camp. We've had to make ourselves handicapped accessible; we've had water regulations: and the big issue is that
property taxes are going up all the time. We are the stewards of a lot of land.

Bear Spring Camps

What with inheritance taxes and property taxes and offers of huge sums by developers, what are the incentives to keep these large parcels of land undeveloped?" *Ron:* "So we've set up a fund for unexpected expenses. It's like our kids' college fund—we're putting a little into it each year. That way, if something happens, you don't go into shock and get depressed, and you don't resent the guests or have to take out a loan or close up. But you can't focus on the bad or you wouldn't stay in business at all, because there's so much crazy stuff that happens. But so much good happens, you just go on from there."

Marguerite: "We're trying to maintain a good way of life. Our guests feel that when they come here. In 1942, when I was first waiting tables, I remember I went down to the lake to sit on a cabin porch one afternoon. Nice day, just like this. And I said, 'Oh God, I wish I could live here the rest of my life,' " she laughs. "And I guess God heard me!"

Chicken BLT Salad Bowl

Peg: "The dressing sounds a bit odd, but it really makes the salad."

> Salad: 6 cups mixed greens, 2 cups cooked chicken, 8 slices cooked crumbled bacon, 2 large tomatoes cut up, 1 hard boiled egg sliced
>
> Dressing: ½ cup mayonnaise, ¼ cup barbecue sauce, 1 T minced onion, 1 T lemon juice, ¼ tsp each salt and pepper

Place the greens in a large bowl. Arrange tomatoes, chicken, and egg slices on lettuce. Top with dressing and bacon.

3. CASTLE ISLAND CAMPS

AP

OWNERS: John and Rhonda Rice

CAMP ADDRESS: PO Box 251, Belgrade Lakes, ME 04918; 207-495-3312; www.castleisland.com

WINTER ADDRESS: 70 Pond Road, Mt.Vernon, ME 04352

SEASON: May through September

ACCOMMODATIONS: Twelve white-clapboard cabins: one to two bedrooms, screened porch, indoor plumbing and shower, automatic heat, electric lights, small refrigerator, bottled water

RATES: $70 per person per day; $483 per person per week. Child rates available.

ACCESS: I-95 to exit 31B. Turn left onto ME 27 west and go 12.3 miles to a left-hand turn, (camp sign). Go straight at intersection, then down the hill. The road narrows as it crosses the water; the camps come up quickly on the right.

Castle Island Camps nestle in a causeway between two sections of 12-mile Long Pond. Picture them in the middle of a figure 8 and you'll have the idea. Everything is within easy reach, including solicitous hospitality. The atmosphere is homey and the attention to detail evident.

John: "Castle Island Camps has been family-owned and -operated since 1929. The original owner was Leighton Castle. He pretty much built this one-acre island by hand-filling it with dirt and either bringing structures in or hand-building them on site. He built them as a sporting camp, and not much has changed since that time. All the cottages are still rustic, and many of the guests speak of them as a step back in time. Leighton owned the camps for about 17 years. Then George and Doris Weis—George was Leighton's nephew—operated the business for 22 years." *Rhonda:* "My father, Ron, was two when they moved here to run the business, so my dad grew up here. Then Leighton's two sons and their wives bought it together in 1970; after five years one couple, Horatio and Valerie Castle, ran it alone for a total of around 30 years. So, with us, this would be the fourth generation raising a family while doing Castle Island. We're only the fourth owner in 70-plus years. And I think because it's family-owned people really get a sense of being part of a family when they come here.

"Several years ago, when we were living in Virginia, we wrote a letter to Horatio and Val and just said, 'Should the time come when you want to retire, if someone in your family isn't interested or able to take over the business, would you keep us in mind.' And then we kind of put it out of our heads and went on with life. Then we got a call in the fall of 2000. They said they were in fact intending to retire and were we still interested? *John:* "We didn't feel we could put it all together by the following April, but it

Castle Island Camps

all came together. We're here at camp and we're raising our family in Rhonda's grandmother's house. She died last year, and we made the decision to move into her home."

Rhonda: "Our two girls, Lydia and Elizabeth, now 6 and 3, are in the same room my dad grew up in." *John:* "So we'll be living in Mount Vernon for six months and here six months for the camp season.

"I don't know if it's unique, but it's a testimony to Castle Island that it's family-owned. We're new owners, but the guests that come say "Oh well it's family, as long as things don't change. . . ." Because people don't want change. People here know that on Tuesday night they get fresh haddock, they know Wednesday night is turkey night. I mean, the routine is down that much. Probably if we painted the cabins a different color we could lose half our guests. It's gotta be white; it's gotta be a certain shade of white. You know what I mean? A guest's connection to Castle Island could be as long as Horatio and Val's, or our own, or Rhonda's parents, because they've been coming for a third and fourth generation." *Rhonda:* "And they have a lot of memories here. One of the guests was telling us that part of what the island has meant for him was coming here many years ago with his father. It was the only time of the year that he and his dad got together."

Castle Island Camps are located at the Narrows. On one side is the more populated shore of Long Pond, including the village of Belgrade; on the other is a section of uninhabited shoreline and marshy area for wildlife. Both areas produce trophy fish. *Horatio:* "This is one of the three best salmon lakes in the State of Maine. We often produce more record fish here than the whole state produces. We have just about everything: landlocked salmon, brook trout, northern pike, large- and smallmouth bass, pickerel, white and yellow perch, shiners, sunfish, everything, even catfish. I was talking to my brother not long ago about the fishing here when he was a kid—he's 19 years older than I am—and he said the fishing is as good, if not better, than it was then, because now the trend is catch-and-release." *John:* "The northern pike is becoming the fish of choice for anglers from all around the country. They're hearing about Long Pond in the Belgrade Lakes area." *Rhonda:* "We've heard from a lot of our guests that they've had the best fishing this year [2002] than they've had in years. In the spring we were seeing mostly salmon fishermen; now in June it's bass and pike." *John:* "That will continue through the summer, and then in the fall we'll see late-season salmon fishermen as the salmon come back up to the top.

"And we're also seeing people coming here for the Belgrade Country Club golf course, which is rated number one north of Delaware for a public golf course. We have what we call 'antiquers,' generally wives of fishermen. Even if the husband couldn't catch a fish or didn't want to come any more, the wives would say, 'Well, we're going anyway 'cause we want to go to Maine antiquing.' They leave every day, then come back and start talking about what they found and where they found it. A lot of people use this as a grounding point. They'll make day trips to Bar Harbor or other places, but they'd prefer to come back here year after year for their lodging.

"I think what makes Castle Island what it is is that we only have so much space. So we have no space to add anything. The size is what people come for, the individual attention, because we're not going to have more than 25 or 30 guests at one time. We may add a few new food items and then pay attention to the constant upkeep and maintenance of the property to keep its integrity.

"*And another thing:* We have a lot of single people who come here just because they know they can get away and they'll be treated well and it's okay to have a cabin by yourself. I notice we get a lot of people at the beginning and end of the season who come by themselves because it's quieter at that time.

Horatio: "We pride ourselves in the quality of our food, and the quantity—everyone can have as many helpings as they want."

John: "And, although we're serious about our food, we do have a few jokes up our sleeves."

And though, dear reader, John (and guests) enjoyed providing a show-and-tell, I wouldn't want to spoil the surprise!

Castle Island Fish Chowder

Horatio's father's recipe for fish chowder is served every Sunday night at the camp.

> 1 large Spanish onion, 4 baking potatoes (size 90), ¼ pound butter, 2½ pounds of haddock fillets, 1 quart whole milk

Slice potatoes and onion and add them to a pot with about 1 inch of water (too much water will make chowder too thin). Cook slowly, stirring regularly to prevent burning, and gradually blend in butter with simmering vegetables. Remove from heat when vegetables are well done but not mushy.

While the vegetables are cooking, put the haddock fillets in a second pot and cover with water. Poach slowly (just below a simmer) until the fillets are flaky and fully cooked (will take about half an hour). Remove from heat and drain off all liquid from poached fish.

Flake the fillets into small chunks and add to the pot containing the vegetables. Stir in 1 quart of milk and heat to serving temperature very slowly over a low heat. Do not boil. Add salt and pepper to taste and serve. Serves 6.

4. ECHO LAKE LODGE AND COTTAGES

HK

OWNERS: James and Eleanor McClay

ADDRESS: PO Box 528, Readfield, ME 04355; 207-685-9550 (camp); 207-362-5642 (winter)

SEASON: May through November

ACCOMMODATIONS: Fifteen white-clapboard cabins: one to three bedrooms, indoor plumbing and tub with shower, electricity, monitor heat (fireplace, woodstove available); six rooms in the lodge have private bath with tub and shower. Pets allowed ($25 per week per pet).

RATES: CABINS: $65 per person per day; $250–580 per cabin per week. LODGE ROOMS: $42 per person per day, bed and breakfast. Linens (sheets and towels) $15 per person per week. Motorboat (ski or bass boat) and sailboat rentals available; canoes, kayaks, rowboats free.

ACCESS: I-95 to exit 31A (Augusta/Winthrop). Take US 202/ME 17 west to Manchester 2.5 miles. Turn right onto ME 17. Go 10.4 miles (pass Kents Hill) to camp sign. Turn right and keep to the left; the road ends at camp.

The road passes a number of private cottages before it dead-ends at a left turn into the camp compound. A rambling white-clapboard lodge greets you on the left, and the rest of the cabins line up behind it. Trees dot a swath of lawn that slopes gently down to the dock and lake. Although there are vehicles, toys, and animals in view, there is a sense of lived-in order about the place.

Eleanor: "What's wonderful in learning about the history of this place is that a lot of it has come to me from people coming back here who were guests, guides, carpenters, or staff long ago. And they'll tell me how the place looked, how the kitchen was set up (they served three meals back in the '50s). Now I serve a continental breakfast for people who want it. And we'll cook for groups: the state has held seminars here, and residency programs send the new doctors up for the day and have a conference the next day, things like that. This main lodge was built in 1938. It was built as a sporting camp, always a family-oriented establishment."

James: "The Phaffles ran this place from the 1940s or '50s until the 1970s. They were originally from New Jersey." *Eleanor:* "They ran it for twenty-some-odd years with tour buses out of New Jersey coming in." *James:* "And this place was in mint condition then." *Eleanor:* "They'd have tours: they'd take people (on the buses) to the mountains; they'd go to the seashore. One day they'd have 'dress-up' day—we have a bunch of old costumes they had for the folks to use." *James:* "You can still see the screen they used to pull down for movies." *Eleanor:* "Down back of the lodge there's the big dinner bell they used to ring. I use it now as an emergency bell." *James:* "They had a boardwalk going down to the eight north cottages. The previous owners chopped it up. The remains of it are the porches in the front of the cottages.

James: "The camp went through two owners who didn't know what to do with it." *Eleanor:* "So little by little we're trying to bring it back." *James:* "She's been painting everything, inside and out. The place was equipped with old water heaters from the 1940 and '50s. We got rid of those. We repaired the infrastructure, like making sure the water was running all the time. Fixed roofs." *Eleanor:* "Then we worked from the inside out, replacing beds, furnishings." *James:* "Probably replaced thirty-five to fifty mattresses and box springs. It took years to clean up." *Eleanor:* "We've got it set up now so that a family of four or five, say, can come in. There's pots and pans, dishes; I try to anticipate what they'll need." *James:* "They had dumb little kitchens so I've installed new kitchens, done everything right. I've cut a lot of trees—it was overgrown in here—to let in more light. I still have a ways to go. Five years and I'll get it to where I think it ought to be."

Eleanor: "We came here May 1994. Jay wanted a business on the water. *James:* "A turn-around business." *Eleanor:* "In the winter I'm an ed-tech in special ed. When we're opening the place up in the spring, I travel back and forth morning and night. In May, my son comes down, after he gets out of college. *James:* "I hold down the fort when she's not here. We close down the main lodge in the winter and have a couple of cabins open for hunters.

James: "We're on a famous old fishing lake. Drinking water quality. Fifteen species of fish. The name was Crotched Pond, because it looks like

Echo Lake Lodge and Cottages

a pair of pants, and we're in the crotch right here. The lake's loaded with loons. It's called Echo Lake now because of the echo their call makes." *Eleanor:* "You get a thundershower here and when it starts on the other side it goes around just like you were on a mountaintop, echoes back and forth." *James:* "I count loons in August and can usually count twenty. Found 28 one year. But to sustain that many loons, and there are only about 4,000 left in the official count, I knew it was special, a clean lake. They're tame, too. Kids will be swimming, and they'll come in close, curious. The lake is 117 feet deep at its deepest, stocked with togue and salmon, a gamefish lake, so because of regulations, at the end of September fishing ends. We've got 1,000 feet of frontage, and bought back some acreage. We're the first Maine owners, and the first people to buy back acreage. There are 75 acres available up back, and I'd like to be able to buy it and put in a road in back so people won't have to drive in front of the eight north cottages.

Eleanor: "You see how quiet it is, you think you're off in the backwoods somewhere." *James:* "We're only 15 miles from I-95. Yet in here we're bringing back the habitat. We've got some beaver, otter, deer, foxes, owls, all sorts of things." *Eleanor:* "We get parents who want to go to town shopping, sightseeing, and the kids don't want to leave. We have five Siamese cats and a dog (Harry) here for them to play with, as a stand-in for their own pets."

James: "My background is in engineering, and I like remodeling. I work for an architectural firm now. Had to go back to work to keep this place running . . . my retirement business is making me come out of retirement!" *Eleanor:* "He's working on these cottages like he's building something that's going to last for a hundred years. When he fixes something, it's never going to break." *James:* "When we took over, this place was virtually empty. My wife is a big draw for this place; she's a people person. I want to pass it along to the next owners in good operating condition, with a good clientele."

5. SADULSKY'S

HK
OWNERS: Dave and Sandra Marston
ADDRESS: 499 East Pond Road, Smithfield, ME 04978; 207-362-6337 (camp); 603-472-7423 (winter); e-mail: sadulskys@tds.net
SEASON: Memorial Day through Labor Day
ACCOMMODATIONS: Seventeen half-log and tongue-and-grove redwood
CABINS: two to three bedrooms, indoor plumbing and shower, electricity, telephone hookups available; bring own linen and towels
RATES: $475 per cabin per week; seasonal rates available. Boat rentals: "We joke with folks and tell them the cabins are free but the boats and views are $475 a week . . ."
ACCESS: I-95 to exit 33. Follow ME 137 west 2 miles into the town of Oakland. Go straight through town. At the four-way stop sign, continue straight, rejoining ME 137. In about 4 miles, turn right at D&L Country Store onto East Pond Road and go 2 miles. The sign and driveway for the camp are on the left. Stop at cabin #11, office and home of the Marstons.

Dave and Sandra Marston run a low-profile operation. They don't advertise; they don't even have a brochure. But they do have a loyal clientele, and word of mouth has brought them the volume of business that suits this hard-working couple. The grounds are immaculately kept. Cabins are ranged around a central lawn area with a few chairs, swings, an old play gym, and a gently sloping beach. There is a dock and a couple of boats. There is a feeling of airiness (although the long driveway is through the woods and the cabins are surrounded by trees) and of quiet ("no loud parties," Sandra says). "This is a family-oriented camp," she explains. "We have a lot of people, mostly from up and down the east coast, who come for the whole summer."

Sandra's parents, Walter and Viola Sadulsky, are both native to the area and ran the camps for 52 years. They are still a vital presence at the place. Walter used to do trucking and road repair. Viola was a nurse. *Viola:* "When Walter was single he used to come in here fishing. Then, in the 1920s, there was just a quarter-mile path down to East Pond." *Walter:* There was an old man who rented boats for 50 cents a day. We bought it in '48 and first rented boats. Then the fishermen wanted to bring their families and we made a beach for the kids. Then people wanted a place to stay, so I started building cabins. Next thing we knew, we had a business! We built the first cabin in '54 and the last in '74."

The camps flourished in the 1970s, when nearby Colby College held a 10-week course for ophthalmologists from around the country who would come and bring their families. *Dave:* "Although shortened, the course is still running, and we still get people from around the country." *Walter:* During that earlier time we had four couples from Alabama who wanted to come and we didn't have any room. They wanted to be here so badly they said they'd pay in part to put up a building. So we made two buildings, divided in two, with bedrooms on either side. These were our last cabins. They have electric heating units because the carpenters didn't have time to put in chimneys before the couples were due to arrive."

Walter and Viola have spent all their married lives *(Walter, with a grin:* "63 years and counting!") running, or being at the camps and have seen a lot of water go under the dam—or under the docks, to be more precise. *Walter:* I was 83 when I stopped. I didn't want to sell to the outside. I wanted it to be run the same way."

Sandra: "I grew up here. Then Dave and I were in Alaska for 15 years." *Dave:* "In '95 we were transferred to New Hampshire and in '99 I retired, or thought I did! This came up—so 2000 was our first season with the camps. Walter and Viola built it up from nothing to all you see here." *Sandra:* "He blasted rocks, made the lovely protected swimming area, did everything by hand."

Dave: "Our biggest challenge is working with whatever surprises Mother Nature has waiting for us when we open up each spring. What's interesting for us is meeting people from all walks of life; they all have something to add to us."

6. SUNNY SHORE CAMPS

HK

OWNER: Marston Camps Incorporated

MANAGER: Tom Salberg

ADDRESS: PO Box 218, Oakland, ME 04963; 207-465-2572

SEASON: May through October

ACCOMMODATIONS: Thirteen log and "Belgrade" wood-sided cabins: one to four bedrooms; indoor plumbing and shower; electric light; wood, electric, or gas heat; well-behaved pets allowed.

RATES: $350–800 per cabin per week, docking space and canoes free; boat and motor rentals and off-season rates available.

ACCESS: I-95 to exit 31B (Augusta/Belgrade) Take ME 27 about 5 miles to ME 23 north. After Oakland continue 2.1 miles past the New England music camp and turn left onto Sunny Shore Place.

Sunny Shore Camps, an eclectic mix of old and new honey-colored cabins, are terraced down a hill that slopes toward Messalonskee Lake, the last in the Belgrade chain. Locals call the area's lake's "ponds," so Messalonskee also goes by the name of Snow Pond, but at nine-plus miles long it's a pretty big pond!

Tom: "This place has been in my family since 1967. My grandparents owned 25 acres next door and my grandfather had retired when this came on the market. My grandmother pushed him into buying the property. All the kids at the time were teenagers. I started here, under my grandparents' supervision, when I was 14 years old—splitting wood, bailing boats, lugging gas tanks, collecting garbage. In those days, people would put their garbage in a can outside the kitchen door, put a rock on top to keep the raccoons out. We've made a few changes since then. . . . We used to lug our own water. We had a pipe system that would pump water out of the lake—fine for showering, toilets, washing dishes, and stuff, but for the drinking water we had a spring (which was tested each year). We'd drive over and pick up that water, put it in bleached milk jugs, and leave them on the lodge porch for campers to pick up. My grandmother and her two sisters would clean cabins. We also had a couple of other cleaning women and some maintenance men around.

"The camps were originally built by a man named Clair Marston. He came in here and built one cabin at a time and built all the camp furniture. He started at the northern end of the property down by the water and built #1 in 1931. Over the course of the next 20-some years 15-some cottages got built. All unique. The lodge used to have a dining room, but it's never been used that way since it's been in my family. Every year I get someone in here who came in around 40 years ago so I get more and more of the history.

"The business is a corporation. It belongs to members of my immediate family, who are all stockholders and reside in different parts of the country. Like many Maine families whose kids have moved away and started families, we all manage to get together during the summer for a week or two. In '94, we had to make a decision as a family whether we were going to sell or renovate and develop the property. The only people interested in it were developers, so we couldn't get what we felt the property was worth. And so we decided to renovate. My folks were the ones with the deep pockets in the family, so they helped us start the common area renovations. We started with water —a 385-foot well that gives 26 gallons a minute—and sewer—a 1,000-gallon concrete holding tank and pump for each cabin. Everything pumps uphill. Our pumps down on the shore have a lot of gear to them, I mean it's got a 72-foot lift, that's a really strong pump, and an expensive pump. All the camps have new 100-amp service; all the wiring is underground. We put in a nice 55-foot marina-style pressure-treated dock with six slips, and I'm in the process of building another dock. We're coded to build up to 14 slips, which will ultimately be three docks.

"When we stared our renovation project in '94 we lost most of our clientele because we were shut down for two years. Mom and Dad finished up in 2000; cabins 2 and 12 were their last project, and 2001 was my first year back in the saddle after the major renovation. I'm still working on the cabins. If I need to put up a new building, I'll disassemble the cabin that's

Sunny Shore Camps

currently there and keep and reuse the old materials because the value of the old materials is greater than they were when they were purchased brand new years ago. And the camp will have the traditional feel and nice details.

"We've got 425 feet of frontage on the eastern shore of Messalonskee Lake. It's a man-made lake; they dammed it up 150–200 years ago. It's the deepest lake in the Belgrade chain, averaging 60 to 90 feet. The original Messalonskee river came down on our side. The northern part is sort of like a river, the southern part widens out some. It's predominantly a bass lake, there's pickerel, and sometime over the past decade crappie was introduced—a fish from the Midwest. It's a good fish, a little like a white perch, good eating. Northern pike were introduced too. They're like freshwater barracudas. I think the largest one caught so far is 24½ pounds, although the biologists say there are some in there that are 50–55 pounds. That's a big fish, and they have big teeth. They're aggressive too, I mean as far as putting a lot of pressure on the other fisheries in the lake. They're a lot of fun to fish for, but people are concerned about the trout and salmon populations. I actually don't fish much these years, and I don't visit other lakes. I'm the designated driver here at camp 24/7 for the next four months.

"Our facility here really is a set of family camps the second half of June through August, when kids are out of school. If you're a world-class fisherman, you really should be fishing somewhere else at this point. Our fishermen come late May through early June. But if you've got a family or want to get together with family, this is vintage summertime in Maine: grandparents, uncles and aunts, kids all over the place. In September I generally get childless adults (young couples or seniors). The character of the camp changes. Autumn is nice here. The sun is setting on a different part of the lake; leaves are changing and they reflect off the lake; the woods start to smell like autumn. From my perspective, I live in the State of Maine for summer and fall.

"You know, 50 years ago there were probably 50 sets of camps in the Belgrade Lakes. They became financial dinosaurs as waterfront property got more and more valuable. A lot of people who had a set of housekeeping cottages like these, their children went off to get their education and ended up working in a metropolitan area. When their parents ended up not wanting to do it any more they just sold that property off. So now what we have is a constant and increasing demand chasing a dwindling supply. From an economist's point of view (my training is in economics) that's a very enviable business situation to be in. But if this hadn't been in my family I could never have afforded it. My grandparents purchased it for $45,000, my folks sunk a ton of money into it, and there's currently no mortgage. But if I had to pay seven or eight hundred thousand dollars for the camp, I could never do maintenance and upkeep, keep up with operating expenses, and service a mortgage on top of that. And that's why there are fewer and fewer camps here. It's a lifestyle. You really have to love what you're doing."

7. SUNSET CAMPS

HK
OWNERS: Mike and Ellie Zarcone
ADDRESS: PO Box 68, Smithfield, ME 04978; 207-362-2611
SEASON: Year-round
ACCOMMODATIONS: Eighteen cabins: one to three bedrooms, screened porch, indoor plumbing, central quarter-metered showers, gas for cooking and heating; bring linens, blankets or sleeping bags, and towels
RATES: $350–650 per cabin per week
ACCESS: I-95 to exit 33. Turn left onto ME 137. Go west on ME 137 for 12 miles, through Oakland, to the village of Smithfield. Look for camp sign on the left-hand side.

Sunset Camps, a family-oriented cabin community established in 1914, is right in the village of Smithfield. While not remote or made of logs, the camp is the only one listed in this book for the Belgrade area that is open in winter for snowmobilers and ice fishermen. Convenient to supplies and food and easily accessible in winter, it is located on either side of the inlet leading into North Pond. Campers walk from one side to the other by way of a picturesque covered bridge the owners built.

In the summer, fishermen can catch large- and smallmouth bass, white and yellow perch, pickerel, and northern pike from 3-mile-long, 1½-mile-wide, 20-foot-deep North Pond.

In the winter, local snowmobile trails lead directly to the state's extensive International Trail System (ITS). An ITS trail map is available from the Department of Inland Fisheries and Wildlife, Augusta, ME 04330.

8. WHISPERWOOD

AP

OWNERS: Doug and Candee McCafferty
ADDRESS: Taylor Woods Road, Belgrade, ME 04917; 207-465-3983; e-mail: info@whisperwoodlodge.com; www.whisperwoodlodge.com
SEASON: May through October
ACCOMMODATIONS: Eleven cabins (some log): one to two bedrooms, screened porch (on eight cabins), indoor plumbing and shower, electric lights, wood and propane heat, nonsmoking and smoking cabins; well-attended pets
RATES: $80 per person per day; $539 per cabin per week; motorboats $38–45 per day; kayaks $10–15 per day; paddleboats and canoes free
ACCESS: Take I-95 to exit 31B (Augusta/Belgrade). Follow ME 8 about 15 miles. Take right onto Taylor Woods Road. Go 0.25 mile. Camps are on the left (camp sign).

Candee and Doug bought this Salmon Lake camp in 2000, but they say they've been preparing for such a move for most of both their lives:

Candee: "My parents owned Buckhorn Camps in Millinocket, so I know and this type of environment. Then I worked eight years as the Director of Parks and Recreation for the town of Millinocket, which gave me paperwork skills, budgeting, dealing with the public. And I like the hospitality business; meeting different people and giving them the vacation everyone always dreams of. I've always enjoyed cooking, worked as a short-order cook, and waitressed, so I knew the food part—I just picked up on a lot of stuff."

Doug: "I grew up in Norway, Maine, and always enjoyed hunting and fishing. I have maintenance background; I'm a plumber by trade. So the maintenance part of a camp like this is no problem. I work in a paper mill now organizing jobs and getting people set up to do specific work, which is what I do here with our employees. We use all the skills we have and all the experiences we've had."

Candee: "We balance each other, and it all came together when we decided to go into the sporting-camp business for ourselves. Doug and I went all over the state looking for a place. The hardest part about buying the business was finding the business. And finding a realtor who would take us seriously. We chose Whisperwood because of location and family." *Doug:* "We'd love a remote camp, but our kids would miss out on the social part of school." *Candee:* "Once we got here our families have been real helpful. Doug's parents are here whenever we need help with something. Doug's mother is a quilter so she does curtains and other sewing. And my father lived here at the beginning."

Rudolph Zaninetti, Candee's father and a born storyteller, kept me laughing with stories about his time as owner of Buckhorn Camps. Then he said softly: "It was a wild and remote place and I loved it. You get acclimated to the woods. I'll sit during hunting season, completely relaxed, see the growth underneath the trees, hear a noise and a little mouse pops up. And then it starts to snow. I've gotten to the point where I can tell what kind of trees are around me from the sound the snowflakes or the little icy particles hitting the trees make. With hemlock, the needles are flat and soft, whereas with spruce they're sharp and tingly so when the snow hits the spruce it just bounces off. But the hemlock has a 'shushing' sound; the snow sticks on it. Hearing that comes from serenity—from relaxing and enjoying the woods for what they are. And all my family had the experience of living in the wild. My children grew up there from the little one right on through."

Even with that background, though, Candee and Doug experienced the usual learning curves. *Doug:* "Actually, the first year was pretty much one big blur. We just rolled with whatever happened, took care of it, and went on to the next thing. We met a lot of people, which was hard 'cause you're meeting them for the first time, and you're trying to remember names and you're trying to make everything work smoothly because the bottom line is that the customer should see and feel that everything is working well. Personally, I didn't know how I was going to be at dealing with the public because I'm an introvert. Candee's an extrovert. But it worked out fine, which was a nice surprise." *Candee:* "If you ask my opinion about buying and running a place, it's not going to be the first year that's the hardest, it's the second year. Then people expect more. The first year we came in April and opened a month later! In a seasonal business like this, your money only comes in for eight months or so and you've got to budget for a full year. I had to learn all the paperwork: accounting, payroll. It's a lot.

"The camp has been here since the 1920s. We're the fourth owner in all those years. For a lot of our customers they're into fishing and they come, different times through the summer, because they know everything—the lake, the cabin, the meals, the setup. It's like going to your own camp, but you don't have to do anything.

"Salmon Lake is predominantly a bass lake—small- and largemouth. 'Salmon Lake' but it has no salmon." *Doug:* "We have beautiful brown trout." *Candee:* "It's camp policy to practice catch-and-release. It was started in 1992 by the previous owners. I would say 99 percent of our customers want catch-and-release. The others aren't sure until they see some of the five-pounders out here, and then they're convinced. We're at the top of the chain of the Belgrade Lakes." *Doug:* "Our water goes down to Great Pond; so what we do here is definitely important for the rest of the

Doug and Candee McCafferty

chain." *Candee:* "Late May and early June it's mostly big parties of men coming fishing. When school gets out, we start to see a lot of couples, because most of our guests are teachers. Then come July and August we see more families." *Doug:* "September and October we're back to couples—out to see the leaves.

Candee: "I'd like to say something about the people in the area. I wanted to volunteer in the school system in the winter because I have more time then. The teachers are great, and they all accepted me really well. Then I started driving a school bus and our family was accepted into the community. Not only that, but we've gotten to know the owners of the other three main sporting camps in the area, and they've given me tremendous referrals. Everyone's been so helpful.

"It was the dream of my parents that all three of their kids would have their own business before something happened to one of them. Being the youngest of the family, I was lucky enough to find a business and for them to help us out before my mother passed away. We bought the place in April and she passed away in June. So it was a busy, busy time . . . but we love it."

Baked Haddock with Brown Butter

Candee: "This works for any fish, really. I figure about a half-pound fillet per person, so this recipe serves two."

2 half-pound haddock fillets, ¼ cup cornmeal, ¼ cup Italian bread crumbs, 2 T plus 1 stick butter, 2 tsp. lemon juice, parsley

Take 2 haddock fillets and lightly sprinkle both sides with cornmeal and then with Italian bread crumbs. Put a chunk (about a tablespoon) of butter on the top of each, place in a baking pan, cover the fish with tin foil, and bake in a 350-degree oven for about 15 minutes.

While the fish is cooking, melt a stick of butter in a saucepan over medium heat. Keep it on there until it turns brown (not burned).

When the fish is done, place each fillet on a plate and pour the butter over to coat. Sprinkle each with a teaspoon of lemon juice and a pinch of parsley.

9. WOODREST

HK
OWNERS: Tom and Jan Barton
ADDRESS: RR 2, Box 4690, Belgrade, ME 04917; 207-465-2950; www.woodrest.com
SEASON: May through September
ACCOMMODATIONS: Nine log cabins: one to two bedrooms (one cabin with a loft), screened porch, indoor plumbing and shower, woodstove or open fireplace, gas stove, refrigerator; bring sheets and towels; well-attended pets allowed
RATES: $75 per couple per day; $555–675 per cabin per week; motorboat $35 per day
ACCESS: I-95 to exit 33. Go west on ME 137 for 4 miles through Oakland. Turn left at McGrath Pond Road. Proceed 2 miles to the Woodrest sign (with loon) on the right.

As you come down the hill leading into camp, Woodrest's rambling log lodge comes into view on the right. On the left, a line of log cabins veers off to the water's edge. Each cabin sits up on posts and has a screened-in porch and its own picnic table. A swath of lawn sports a big stone barbecue fireplace, two swing sets (according to Jan, "one for the little ones and one for big kids"), a basketball hoop, badminton net, and horseshoe pits. To the right are more log cabins.

A dock with boats floats in McGrath Pond, which, together with connecting Salmon Pond, forms Woodrest's waterway. The two lakes together are 5 miles long by up to 1 mile wide. In terms of fishing Jan says, "We have everything but pike. The primary sport is for black bass [small- and largemouth], white and yellow perch, chain pickerel, and brown trout. Black crappies [calico bass] were illegally introduced, and since they feed heavily on the smaller fish, they may be a serious threat to the smelt population in Salmon Lake. Salmon is unique among the Belgrades in supporting a major commercial fishery for smelt, which actually is a source of controversy among smelt dealers, sport fishermen, and landowners. "

The camps have been around since the late 1920s (Jan has an advertisement from 1928). Tom and Jan bought the camps in 1982. They had had a cottage "on the other side of Salmon" and were running a 200-site, 500-acre campground. *Jan:* "It was just too much to deal with and it took too much of our time away from raising our family."

Jan is from the area and her father had a hand, back in the 1940s, in constructing her present abode. "My father helped rebuild the main lodge here. Two weeks before opening day the lodge burned down. Well, they hired 40 men who worked around the clock. By the time opening day came, two weeks later, the lodge was done, kitchen and all!"

Jan is past-president of Belgrade Lakes Region, Inc., a volunteer organization that promotes the accommodation and business facilities in the area. The most visible activity of the group is its information booth on ME 27, open Saturdays 10–5 during the season, as well as some weekdays during the summer. The number for the booth is 207-495-2744. The organization also maintains a web site: www.mint.net/belgrade.

THE RANGELEY LAKES REGION

Moving inland and upland, we come to the major chain of lakes that makes up this region: Parmachenee, Aziscohos, Umbagog, Lower and Upper Richardson, Mooselookmeguntic, Cupsuptic, Rangeley, and Kennebago. Whereas the Belgrade region is primarily pastoral, the Rangeley area is mountainous. This region is bounded to the west by ME 26 and to the east by ME 27 and contains the headwaters for the Androscoggin River, which flows to the sea. The Appalachian Mountains and Trail run through it, and several ski areas can also be found here. About 100 lakes and ponds lie within the region. Half a dozen lie within 10 miles of the village of Rangeley, where a traveler can find cultural offerings and all the basic amenities. For specific information, visit or contact the Rangeley Chamber of Commerce (207-864-5364), located in the heart of downtown Rangeley at the public boat landing and parking area. Moored along the pier in this same complex are float planes available for scenic tours or lifts to remote lakes or sporting camps.

To get a stunning view of the lakes without going up in a plane, drive on ME 27 to a point called, appropriately, Height Of Land (directions are available from the chamber of commerce). Keep in mind, as you look down, that much of the waterway was originally about 20 feet lower.

Logging companies put in a number of dams in the mid-1800s in order to float logs to their mills.

The village of Oquossoc has shops, restaurants, boat and snowmobile services, a gas station, and is home to the Rangeley Lakes Heritage Trust. Thanks to the efforts of people involved with this trust, founded in 1991, more than 10,000 acres of land have been preserved, much of it adjacent to land owned by sporting camps in this area. For more information, write to the trust at PO Box 249, Oquossoc, ME 04964; 207-864-7311.

Andover is a stop-off point for Appalachian Trail hikers, and home to Telstar, one of the earliest satellite-tracking stations, which rises out of the landscape like a giant golf ball. (Trivia tidbit: On July 10, 1962, it telecast the world's first transatlantic TV broadcast.) The village of Upton sits on the crest of a hill with gorgeous views down Lake Umbagog. To get a good sense of this area, read Louise Dickinson Rich's book *We Took to the Woods.*

This is primarily trout- and salmon-fishing country. The hiking is plentiful and can be challenging, if so desired. The area is recognized as a fall-foliage destination, and in winter is popular with snowmobilers.

GETTING THERE: The Rangeley Lakes region can be reached by flying into either Portland or Augusta and then connecting with the local air service, Mountain Air Company (207-864-5307), or by renting a car. Driving time from Portland is 3–4 hours; from Boston, 5–6 hours; from New York City, 9–10 hours.

10. BALD MOUNTAIN CAMPS

AP

OWNER: Stephen Philbrick
ADDRESS: PO Box 332, Oquossoc, ME 04964; 1-888-392-0072 or 207-864-3671; e-mail: baldmtcamp@aol.com; www.baldmountaincamps.com
SEASON: May through September
ACCOMMODATIONS: Fifteen log cabins: one to three bedrooms, indoor plumbing and tub with shower, electric lights, fireplace, ice buckets filled daily
RATES: $120 per person per day; off-season rates available
ACCESS: Maine Turnpike (I-495) to exit 12 (Auburn). Take ME 4 north to Oquossoc. Continue on ME 4 to the end (just before the boat landing). Turn left onto Bald Mountain Road and go 1 mile to the camp, on the right. From exit 12 at Auburn, you can also take ME 2 to ME 17 north to Oquossoc.

Bald Mountain Camps look out on Mooselookmeguntic Lake. Stephen and I joke that we'd both heard the old saw that an Indian in the area had said, "Moose look . . . me gun: Tick!" and thus its name. Its actual translation isn't that far off: "Where the hunters watch the moose at night." The camp's

Bald Mountain Camps

red-brown cabins, with distinctive white-washed log ends, line up along a generous beach and shoreline, and, along with the honey-colored lodge dining room, are situated for sunset viewing.

Stephen: "Bald Mountain Camps was established in 1897. For our 100th birthday, former Governor Angus King came and helped us celebrate. Ed Wharf, who started this place, decided to build a camp strictly for sportsmen. Back then everybody came down to Haines Landing (around the corner) by the train and dispersed out through the lake on old steamships. You used to be able to get on a train in Baltimore at 7 AM on Friday, have three meals served to you, sleep in a Pullman car, and be here for your summer vacation by 7 AM Saturday. The trains went out in 1889 and it's a shame because it's a sensible and great way to travel.

"My grandmother's father, Charlie Jacques, worked for the Boston & Maine Railroad and was responsible for putting in the railroad from Oquossoc to Kennebago. My grandfather came up here with his dad as a logger when he was a teenager, in the early 1920s, became a registered Maine guide, and then worked here as a cabin boy and guide. He met my grandmother, and they settled in, bought the place, and ran it for 50 years. My grandparents were Mainers, French Canadian folks. Their daughter was my mother and we were here for vacations, summers. I bought it from my grandparents, and I'm only the fifth owner in all these years.

"The lake is 17 miles long, 5 miles wide, 126 feet deep, and has salmon and trout. I encourage catch-and-release. In fact, I'd go a couple of steps further. I believe that the best way to get our lakes back in order is to specifically designate areas in the State of Maine closed completely to any keeping of fish. I could sell my product as a businessman far better if I was able to say to prospective guests, 'You can't take any fish home, but you're going to have trophy fishing up here.' I can't do that now.

"Fernlyn and I have two boys, Tyler and Quinn. We have two other businesses in the area and my wife takes care of those while I take care of this. We live here on the property year-round. Even though I grew up here, I went to college for this—majored in business and hotel administration. Business has increased in a number of ways. We offer fly-in fishing trips to different ponds and streams throughout the region. I have two flying services and three guides, and I'm a registered Maine guide and pilot. When I have the time, I take guests myself. But I don't fish with them, just deposit them and then come back and do my work. I haven't wet a fly in several years. The free time I do have I spend with my boys and my wife.

"My dinner business has quadrupled. We're getting a lot of outside folks. We do one seating, 16 tables, and then sell all the tables that aren't locked up by our guests. We also do a lot of catering. Our dining room looks out to the west onto 10 miles of protected shoreline and some spectacular sunsets. On Fridays we have a real old-fashioned guide's barbecue with blueberry pancakes for dessert. Our regular menu includes meals like grilled pheasant, trout baked on a cedar plank, lobster scampi, and so forth. I've been involved with this business ever since I was a little kid and saw what it was like, at the end of the '50s, when the American Plan was on the decline. Jet travel, the ability to travel all over the world, developed about that time. Now I'm seeing the American Plan coming back. Folks are spending their dollars at places like this throughout the country where they can be served and treated like they want to be treated. It's not just rush in, rush out.

"I've considered winterizing, because snowmobiling is a big thing around here. But it's not cost-effective. The low-end cost per cabin to insulate and winterize would be $65,000. Per cabin. Remember these were all built at the turn of the century. Speaking of winter, what we offer here is ice on your porch with fresh springwater twice a day in lieu of a refrigerator. Our lakes are still very clean up here, and in the winter we cut the ice when it's 18 inches thick. We clear it off with a truck plow, shovel it by hand, and then score it so it looks like a big checkerboard. The chain saw cuts down 10 inches and then we cut down the last 8 inches with a handsaw. We chip them off as square blocks, and they come up a mechanized conveyor belt, slide down into a truck, and are hauled off to our icehouse. We'll take out as many as 2,800 cakes of ice. We have this for guests and also use it in our three walk-in coolers, which are lined with sawdust to retain the cold. We cook with gas, so if the power should go out, we have refrigeration and can cook. We just light some candles and keep going.

"I believe families want to be together more. And the things that they're looking for are rustic cabins with fireplaces, which we have; a sandy beach for the kids to play on, which we have; and sailboats and lots of water toys for big and little kids. They're not really into motorboats unless it's to use the water skis. Fernlyn and I have wanted to have horseback riding here for a long time and now provide it for our guests. I have games and books for the kids while their folks are finishing dinner. So it's a family focus. It's a nice community, a nice group of people. And as for the regulars, they've watched people come here, grow old here, and die. It's just a natural progression in places like this."

Baked Maple Chicken with Rosemary

Bald Mountain serves an extensive menu to its guests and the public. This chicken recipe is one of the Sunday entrees. It's for a single serving, so adapt according to number of people eating. Chef Meg Godaire says it's "embarrassingly easy."

half a fryer chicken, salt and pepper, half a lemon, 1 T olive oil, 1 T real maple syrup, ½ T fresh rosemary

Season the chicken with salt and pepper. Squeeze the juice of half a lemon over the chicken, then drizzle with olive oil. Bake for 20 minutes at 350 degrees. Remove from the oven and drizzle with ½ of the maple syrup and sprinkle with fresh rosemary leaves. Bake for an additional 15–20 minutes until crispy and brown. Drizzle again with the remaining syrup, garnish with lemon slice and fresh rosemary and serve.

11. BOSEBUCK MOUNTAIN CAMPS

AP

OWNERS: The McDevitt and Schyberg families
ADDRESS: PO Box 1213, Rangeley, ME 04970; 207-446-2825; e-mail: bosebuck@aol.com; www.bosebuck.com
SEASON: Year-round
ACCOMMODATIONS: Nine gray-clapboard cabins: one to two bedrooms, screened porch, indoor plumbing and shower, woodstove, gas and electric lights. Well-attended pets allowed: $10 per day, up to two pets
RATES: $140 per person per day, includes use of boats. Group, child, mid summer, and hunting rates available.
ACCESS: Maine Turnpike (I-495) to exit 12 (Auburn). Take ME 4 to Rangeley (approximately 88 miles). Continue 9 miles to Oquossoc, then take ME 16 for 20 miles to Wilsons Mills. Turn right at the sign for the camps onto a gravel road. Go 13 miles to the camp driveway on your right. By the time you've driven in to Bosebuck Camps there's good chance you've seen a deer or other wild creature and are feeling you are in the backwoods and moving toward an earlier time. As you come down the driveway and into the clearing, a cluster of cabins and log main lodge look out

over a connecting series of waterways. In the mornings, the sun comes up between far-away mountains.

Diane and Bob Schyberg were guests for years before becoming the owners in 1997. Since then, the McDevitt family, who also boast a long-term local presence, has joined them. *Bob:* "Apparently, the camp got its name in the 1920s, when a group from the US Geological Survey got caught in a blizzard late one October, with close to 4 feet of snow. They started running low on food, and it seems they had a dog named Bow that killed a deer in the deep snow. So when they started naming different places, they called this Bow's Buck Mountain. The camps were originally built in 1909 by Fern Littlehale and his partner and guide, Perley Flint. Perley won fly-casting competitions at the various sportsmen's expos and helped bring in guests. He bought the camps from Littlehale in 1911 for $500 and started building cabins, which were paid for by the more affluent regulars who used them on an annual basis.

"The camp sits on a prominent point at the top of Aziscohos Lake where the Big and Little Magalloway Rivers join. We're in a 500,000-acre wilderness area that has been protected for a hundred years or more, first by private ownership and by its remoteness, and now by restricted access and state conservation regulations, under Maine's Trophy Trout Waters Initiative. To get to the Upper Magalloway we have access to the private gate system under special agreement with the landowners.

"Aziscohos Lake was created for the logging industry in 1914. Now the lake and watershed support one of the healthiest populations of wild brook trout and landlocked salmon in the State of Maine. Many brook trout in the 3–5 pound range are caught and mostly released each year.

"Besides fishing, there are good hiking trails in this area. We have great canoeing and kayaking and our guests enjoy our little fishing boats and motors for sightseeing and exploring. This is a fun retreat for families and couples who love nature, but also like the conveniences of a private cabin and bathroom, daily cabin service, and three really delicious meals a day.

"On the hunting side, the area's famous for having trophy-sized white-tail deer and moose, but it's also the best grouse and woodcock cover in North America. We specialize in guided hunts with our bird dogs, but it's also a good place to train your own young dogs, because the abundance of birds gives them a lot of experience quickly. This is definitely a world-class destination for upland bird hunters.

"As far as winter goes, we are the only sporting camp in the area open year-round. We're just off ITS 84, halfway between Pittsburg, New Hampshire, and Rangeley. The idea of a remote camp for snowmobilers is good because it provides an emergency phone, shelter, and hot food. But the most interesting thing is that because we provide fuel, people can now take side trips and explore virgin territory. It's also a great place for backcountry cross-country skiing and snowshoeing.

One of the features of Bosebuck is its historic significance as a Native American camping area. *According to Michael Del Tufo, manager and long-time Bosebuck staffer:* "Every fall when the water's down you can pick up Indian artifacts on the shoreline, but you aren't allowed to dig. In the Maine State Museum in Augusta they have an exhibit called 'Twelve Thousand Years in Maine,' and Tom Rideout, Bosebuck's previous owner, contributed a lot of artifacts he found here." Tom Rideout: "Back in 1980 a guide named Vale was searching for his lost lure and found some Indian artifacts. He showed them to an archaeologist named Dr. Michael Gramly, who explored what's now called the Vale Site. Bosebuck is a Paleo-Indian site, 10,500 to 11,000 years old. Dr. Gramly found the oldest man-made structure in the New World on Aziscohos Lake. It's a meat cache. The Indians put meat in a rock cairn—sort of a small cellar hole—threw another rock over the top of it, covered it up, and the permafrost would freeze it so when they returned the following year they'd have something to eat until the caribou started coming through again. And that opened the door for 50 years of visitation. When they were here, the glaciers were still receding and this valley was a migration route for caribou. The hunters used the valley to ambush them. They used the natural barriers: a pond, river, or steep bank where the herds would slow down. The Indians stayed on the high banks, on the eastern shore, where the westerly wind kept the bugs off and they could observe the caribou as they migrated. In '81 they drained the lake to resurface the front of the dam, and you could see the original river channel and even the caribou trails in the lake bottom! It's the only documented place that has a habitation site and the kill site related to it. The Indians came here in the summertime. In the winter they lived on what is now the continental shelf.

"The Paleo-Indians were craftsmen at toolmaking. We look for tools like gravers used to carve designs on wood or bone made out of stone like obsidian. The next period were the Plano Indians, and they were the master craftsmen. After Plano were the Archaic, and then Woodland Ceramic, who used cheap flint and were so-called throwaway societies. They'd take any type of rock, as long as it had a flat edge to it, scrape the hide, and then cast the rock aside, whereas the Paleo-Indians here revered their tools."

Diane: "There's a women's group that comes in August—a spiritual retreat, connecting with nature and ancient ways. And we have writers and artists. It must be the isolation of this place that I love. It's so relaxing to hear the loons calling at night. We counted 17 nesting pairs on the lake. There's something about this area that seems to stimulate creative impulses."

I attended part of the women's "sojourn" sponsored by facilitator/teacher/healer Barbara Prince and "musical medicine woman"/songwriter Dawna Hammers and can attest to the fact that these women and the place itself provided a deep and meaning-filled creative experience. For retreat information, contact Barbara: 781-834-9430.

Bruce's Brown Bread

Diane: "You just can't imagine how good this bread is!"

> 1 cup whole wheat flour, 1 cup corn meal, 1 cup white bread flour, ¼ cup brown sugar, ½ tsp. salt, 2 tsp. baking soda, 1 tsp. cinnamon, ¼ tsp. ginger, ½ tsp. allspice, 2 cups half 'n' half, ½ cup dark molasses

Use bread machine, set at "cake," for approximately 1½ hours. Place in greased bread pans and bake 40 minutes in a 350-degree oven.

12. GRANT'S KENNEBAGO CAMPS

AP, SCA
OWNERS: John and Carolyn Blunt
MANAGERS: Lionell Strong and Jane Feeley
ADDRESS: PO Box 786, Rangeley, ME 04970; 1-800-633-4815
SEASON: May 23 through September
ACCOMMODATIONS: Eighteen knotty-pine cabins: one to three bedrooms, indoor plumbing and shower, screened porch, woodstove or electric heat, electric lights, private dock with 16-foot Rangeley boat
RATES: $115–135 per person per day; boats $50 per day; canoes $15 per day
ACCESS: Maine Turnpike (I-495) to exit 12 (Auburn). Take ME 4 north to Rangeley (approximately 88 miles). Go through Rangeley on ME 4/16. At the junction of ME 4 and ME 16, bear right onto ME 16 and go 3 miles to a right-hand turn, where there's a sign for the camps. Check in at the gatehouse (before 6 PM), then drive 9 miles on a dirt road into camp. The road forks uphill to the right just before camp.

When you get to the end of the road, you've reached Grant's Kennebago Camps. The honey-colored pine cabins, each with its own dock, line up along the shore of Kennebago Lake. In the central dining room you'll find red-checked tablecloths, full picture windows, and panoramic views of the surrounding mountains. The main lodge, which houses the office, has a library and sitting area with games, a TV, and a selection of fishing videos.

John: "Grant's was built in 1905 by Ed Grant and was a combination of log cabins and cedar-sided stick-built cabins. Cabins 1 through 4 were used as lumber camps. He developed a sporting camp down on the other end of the lake first, and then migrated up here. Ed Grant was a great storyteller. Ever hear about the man who kept a pet trout in a rain barrel? Well, he'd dip out a little water each day, until finally the fish was at home on dry land. It followed the man around the yard, wore snowshoes in winter, and all went fine until one day it fell in the brook and drowned. That's the kind of tall tale he'd tell his 'sports.'

"In 1977 a fire destroyed about 70 percent of the old buildings. It started in the spring when they came to open up the place. They turned on the gas, checked a few appliances, and went home. There was a tremendous explosion late in the evening and plates, saucers, wood were found halfway across the lake. Thank God no one was living or working here at the time. Nothing was saved from the original lodge except six antique chairs out for repair. Everything was charred right into the ground. Guests were wonderful. They mailed a lot of pictures, so much of the old has been re-created.

"The camps are located on 5-mile Kennebago Lake, the largest fly-fishing-only water east of the Mississippi. The upper river is for brook trout, with several deep pools that have, as one of our guests put it, 'some trout that would scare you.' The lower river has 25 pools with lots of salmon in the 1- to 3-pound range and some up to 6 pounds.

"When Grant's came up for sale, we had been guests here for about six years. I started thinking about all the facets of running a sporting camp and realized I'd had experience in every avenue. I used to race and build wooden boats when I was a teenager in Saco, Maine, and I'm redoing Rangeley wooden boats and repairing outboard motors now. I'd been in building construction for about 16 years, so nothing about the upkeep of the buildings bothered me at all. I'd been running a business, so the record-keeping end of it wasn't a problem. And I'd been fly-fishing for 15 years and had fished right at Grant's Camps. I knew the fishery and the lake and the river. It seemed almost like it was a predestined thing for us to fit right into the business here. So we bought the camps, April 9, 1988.

"Carolyn began fly-fishing at Grant's when we were guests. We were out on a boat one spring, and I was catching a fish with almost every cast. Well, she put her book down and said, 'That looks like fun. Could I try it?' And that was the beginning of it. Now she initiates fly-fishing trips out of state when Maine's fishing season is closed. And both of my children were able to cast a really tight line by age 5. So it's a family thing with us. We evolved from camping in the back of a pickup, to a tent, to a trailer that we'd haul. But it's still a lot of work to camp out. A friend of mine said, 'Have you ever considered going to a sporting camp?' And I said, 'What's a sporting camp?' I had no idea there was a whole industry out there devoted to the outdoor sport. Well, the first place he told us about was Grant's. And fortunately, we had to look no further.

"A guide from Rangeley named Walter Davenport was running Grant's at the time we bought it. The recreational aspect of the place was not being promoted, so we paid for the potential. I kept improving the fishing end of it, but I had to start from the ground up and develop a recreation plan to promote the July and August trade. Coming from southern Maine, seeing what the traffic is like on the southern coast, I knew the potential and demand was there. But people just don't realize there are facilities that exist in the wilderness like this. And you don't have to sacrifice your comfort to take a vacation in northern Maine.

"So I added hiking, sailing, windsurfing, mountain biking, all at no charge to our guests. We put in a small play area for the children, added a few pets. And we have tables on some of the beaches around the lake. Where else can you picnic and possibly be visited by a moose in the backwaters either beside or behind you? A family vacation to some people is driving someplace and then a week later driving back home and you've hardly done a thing together. When you're in our atmosphere, you are hiking together, picnicking, canoeing, fishing together. The kids will come out of the dining hall while their parents are finishing dinner, get a carrot from the kitchen, and go feed the rabbits or play on the swings. Mom and Dad know right where they are and don't have to worry about traffic or safety. We have guides that take families on nature trips, teach the plant ecology associated with the area. There definitely is a need for a real true family vacation. And it's a fun experience.

"We have a float-plane dock for private planes. For a regular flight, we drive out 25 miles to the Rangeley airport, or we have an extra vehicle for people coming into that airport with their own plane. And we have chartered flights out of Grant's all summer."

James: "We have fantastic canoe trips where we take you above Little Kennebago Lake and you can swim, paddle, fish, and picnic your way back. We also have miles and miles of logging roads for mountain biking and have some great hiking trails. For fishing, the lake has a 1A rating, one of the highest in the state. It is 119 feet deep, with catch-and-release only. It's not stocked but it has natural spawning."

The Kennebago Lake fishery was the first in the state to be declared fly-fishing-only by the Inland Fish and Wildlife Department in Augusta. *John explains:* "Fly-fishing-only means you have to be physically casting the fly, not trolling or dragging it behind the boat. Fly-fishing encompasses fishing with wet line, partial wet line sink-tip lines, and dry line.

"You really have a sense of history when you're up here in this area," adds John. "The Indians used to live on the shore of Kennebago, which means 'sweet flowing waters,' and they'd migrate back and forth to the ocean. The last caribou seen in Maine was on Kennebago Lake. I think part of the reason the caribou left is that their migratory roads were the rivers: the Magalloway, Androscoggin, the Kennebec. And they've been dammed and flooded so the habitat is gone. But the signs of caribou remain. It's nice there still is a corner of the world like northern Maine. To come to our place and actually live it and bring home pictures is a vacation that makes albums."

Grant's Kennebago Camps

Grant's Cream Puffs

Grant's is known for its chocolate chip cookies kept in a jar at the office. Here's another favorite.

½ cup butter, 1 cup water, 1 cup flour, 4 eggs (for pastry shells); 1 box instant vanilla pudding, 1½ cups milk, 1 cup whipped cream (for cream filling)

Bring the butter and water to a boil, then add the flour. Stir well. Remove from heat and add the eggs, one at a time. Mix well until the mixture is glossy and pulls from the sides of the pan. Drop by tablespoonfuls onto a cookie sheet. Bake at 400 degrees for 45 minutes. Remove the puffs from the cookie sheet and cool on a wire rack. When cool, carefully cut off the top of each puff (save the tops), and spoon out the centers. To make cream filling: Whip pudding and milk together until thick. Blend in whipped cream. Fill puffs and replace tops.

13. LAKEWOOD CAMPS

AP, SCA

OWNERS: Bill and Robin Carter, Whitney and Maureen Carter
ADDRESS: PO Box 1275, Rangeley, ME 04970; 207-243-2959 (camp); 207-864-2082 (winter)

SEASON: May through November

ACCOMMODATIONS: Twelve log cabins: one to two bedrooms, indoor plumbing and tub with shower, porch, wood heat, electric lights; pets "if you must" ($18 per day)

RATES: $130 per person per day double occupancy; child, group, and July and August rates available

ACCESS: Maine Turnpike (I-495) to exit 11 (Gray), then ME 26 north to ME 232. Proceed north to Rumford Point; turn left onto ME 2; then take your first right, onto ME 5 to Andover. In Andover, turn right onto ME 120, cross a bridge, and at the top of a hill take a left onto a 12-mile dirt road to South Arm Landing. The pickup for Lakewood (reservation needed) is beyond the landing to the left (look for the sign).

On the 15- to-20 minute boat trip to Middle Dam on Lower Richardson Lake, where Lakewood Camps is located, we progressed from sparsely populated to pristine shoreline, and I learned a bit about the camps. In 1853 a man named Joshua Rich lived near the Richardson farmstead (that the lake was named after) when a dam was put in for logging operations. It flooded both Rich and Richardson out. Rich came to Middle Dam, built a couple of cabins, and began to cater to fishermen. In 1880 another dam raised the water level again by about 20 feet.

The camps come into view. Set in a cove to one side of the dam and on a knoll, the dark brown log cabins are placed close together in a row to the left of a large main lodge. A few outbuildings and cabins spread out behind and to the right of the lodge. A dirt "Carry Road" leads through camp and along the 5-mile Rapid River to where author Louise Dickinson Rich lived. Her book *We Took to the Woods* is still an accurate description of much of the area.

From the camp's historical notes: "Lakewood is one of the oldest traditional sporting camps in Maine and the United States. The main lodge was built in the winter of 1877 by Aldona Brooks and Horatio Godwin of Upton, Maine. Godwin had previously conducted a camp, Anglers Retreat, in buildings that housed the workmen who constructed the original sluice dam. This camp stood on the knoll just south of the present camp. Brooks and Godwin opened their new lodge May 14, 1878, and operated it for one year, when it was taken over by the Androscoggin Lake Transportation Company. The name was changed to Lakewood Camps in 1920. Captain Coburn operated the camps until 1942, when Larry and Alys Parsons took over the operations until 1976. A fire in 1957 burned the original three-story main lodge ('the hotel') and six cabins. The dams were built originally to sluice, or transport, logs. The timber company had a boat named the *Alligator* that would haul the logs down the lake. The logs would go from Middle to Lower Dam into Umbagog (um-BAY-gog) Lake. From Umbagog they'd float down the Androscoggin to the mill in Berlin, (BER-lin) New Hampshire.

Maureen, Whitney, Bill, and Robin Carter at Lakewood Camps

Robin: "One of the things that we found particularly exciting about being here is that we are only the sixth owners of a set of camps that's going to be 150 years old in 2003. It's quite a marvelous thing, carrying on that tradition. Sue and Stan Milton and Janne Provencher, the previous owners, not only helped us get started, but Stan is helping us with boat driving this summer. Alys has been in and Eric Wight [game warden, author, former boat driver], the dam keeper, helps us, and we ask them all questions and everyone's been phenomenal. We have a tremendous support system. When the Miltons and Janne decided to sell to us it wasn't because we were the only people who had made an offer by any means; it had a great deal to do with the fact that they knew we wanted to own and run the camps in the traditional manner that they were meant to be operated (not as condos or a family compound or manager-run). They waited for three years until they found people who saw running a camp as a way of life. And so far, all the guests that have come back have said that 'it's just like it's always been.' And that's exactly what we intended. For example, Dave and June Berg, who came here for their honeymoon and celebrated their fiftieth anniversary a couple of years back, have helped open up camp in the past. And we wrote and asked them to come, and they came, continuing that tradition.

"I think one of the threads that weaves our story today with this history is that my father-in-law, who's been dead for over 25 years, came fishing in the Rangeley Lakes area with his family when my husband was a boy in the 1940s and '50s. (My husband now has his lovely collection of Carrie Stevens flies.) My husband and I started coming to this area about fifteen years ago, to a cabin on Rangeley Lake, because he wanted to be back here. It just felt right—all those connections. All those strands weave together and suddenly you find yourself in a place that feels like home.

"My husband is retired from the ministry after 35 years and we were looking, as we were turning sixty, for another career. A lot of people thought we were crazy. They said, 'You have no idea how much work it is.' And it is a lot of work. But it's in the most wonderful location in the world, it's varied, and has all sorts of dynamics that makes it a lot of fun. But primarily it was the lifestyle that appealed to all of us, and to be able to be host to people who have loved and cared about the area.

"When we found the advertisement for the camps, we began talking to our three children (two daughters and son). And it worked out that our son and his wife could be here. We all have a good combination of skills: my husband's in charge of the kitchen, works with the cook and manages the food, and does handyman work as well. I'm doing the baking and the financial part of it (I have my own financial business). My daughter-in-law, who's had long years of working with staff, is in charge of the front office, and our son, who's a contractor, is doing the maintenance work, the boats and buildings. We're four equal partners. So it all seems right that we suddenly find ourselves here, because we'd never been to the camps before. We've been to many camps in Maine, but never to this one. The fun of it is, my husband and I, like Alys, expect to see ourselves here for many years past our 'prime.' It was just a great decision.

"As for the resources here, the fly-fishing is renowned. One of the fabulous things about this lake is that the water is incredibly clear and pure because of the dam. The cold water at the bottom of the lake feeds through the dam and keeps the Rapid River cold, able to be fished for salmon and trout all summer. Another wonderful thing is that because we're located on the [undeveloped] west shore of Lower Richardson, we have practically no boat traffic. It remains its quiet self all summer. Of course, traditionally, sporting camps are noted for their May, June, and September fishing. What we have discovered in Maine is that July and August is the best time of all. The bugs are down, the weather is warm, you can count on nice sunny days. And we anticipate creating a way in which families can come in and enjoy this environment. It's a wonderful, peaceful place, where there are none of the usual distractions, for families to connect in a way they seldom get a chance to in their busy lives.

"In my financial business, a lot of what I do is help people find ways to use money to make their lives more enriched. It's not about having more money; it's about seeing money as a tool that helps you make other decisions. So when I knew I would be doing Lakewood Camps, one of the things that I've enjoyed is saying to my clients, 'This is an example of the outcome of a planning process, of the knowledge of where you are with your money.' It allows you to go forward into a big venture of this type, a big commitment, and not have to think, 'Oh my gosh, but that will ruin my retirement' or 'Will I have enough?' It frees you when you understand how to think about money in the context of the whole richness of your life. It's only a piece of your life; it's not all there is. So putting money in its place is the part that has enabled all of us to realize what is important and why we want to be here. And part of what can happen here for our guests is the same thing: they can clear their brains, sort things out, and think about their lives in a much broader context. We have rocking chairs on the porches, and in the evening they are all full of people just sitting there looking at the beautiful clear sunsets, smelling the fresh, pure air. All this clean air and water just does something to you; it changes something in you. I think everyone should have the chance to experience that, to be refreshed inside and out.

"We came out to see these camps on September 9th, 2001—and you know what happened on September 11th. . . . We thought about it, and then we very clearly said to ourselves, 'What more of a haven could there be than Lakewood Camps?' And what a nice thing for us to know that there are still places where people can go where they can feel safe and things stay the same. Part of the advantage of being sixty when we were making these decisions is that we can step back and see how continuing to run a set of sporting camps fits into a big picture of what the world has become. It felt like, and I don't want this to sound overly dramatic, but it felt like a certain 'calling' that there continue to be places where people can come to be peaceful. We can't assure them of complete safety of course, but we can assure them of peacefulness and serenity, a quality level of care, and a very deep connection to the nature that's all around us that we can lose sight of in the bigger cities. This is a place to regroup and regather as families and individuals, a place to feel connected to life."

Sour Cream Blueberry Cake

Robin: "This is the quantity I make for camp, but it can be easily halved."

Cake: 2 sticks butter, 2 cups sugar, ½ tsp. salt, 4 large eggs, 3 tsp. vanilla, 2 cups sour cream, 4 cups plus 2 T flour, 2 tsp. baking powder, 2 tsp. baking soda, 4 cups blueberries. Streusel topping: 1 cup flour, 1 cup sugar, 1 stick butter, 2 tsp. cinnamon

For the cake: Cream together: butter, sugar, and salt. Add the eggs one at a time and blend well. Add vanilla. Mix together 4 cups flour, baking powder, and baking soda and add to the wet ingredients alternately with 2 cups sour cream. Mix 4 cups blueberries with 2 T flour and fold into the above.

Pour into two 10" greased and floured tube pans. Chop or crumble togther the ingredients for the streusel topping and sprinkle over the cakes.

Bake for 50–60 minutes in a 350-degree oven.

14. NIBOBAN CAMPS

HK

OWNER: L. Jean Noyes

MANAGER: Shirley Turner; assistant manager: Wes Miller

ADDRESS: PO Box 770, Rangeley, ME 04970-0770; 207-864-2549; fax:
207-864-2093

SEASON: Year-round

ACCOMMODATIONS: Nine log cabins: one to two bedrooms, screened porch
(glass in winter), indoor plumbing and tub with shower, automatic oil heat,
electric lights, full kitchen with microwave and "turkey-size oven and
refrigerator"; well-attended pets ($15 per day)

RATES: $100–150 per cabin per day; $550–750 per cabin per week

ACCESS: Maine Turnpike (I-495) to exit 12 (Auburn). Take ME 4 north
through Farmington toward Rangeley (approximately 80 miles). In Sandy
River Plantation, take a left onto South Shore Drive (the Rangeley Lake
State Park road). Continue 4 miles to camp sign on the right.

From Niboban's log lodge a big field affords an expansive view of
Rangeley Lake. Down the gentle slope, honey-colored log cabins sit in a row
about 100 feet from the water's edge. Owner Jean Noyes has reached a time
in her life when most of her peers are resting on their laurels. Instead, she
has started off on a new venture as a sporting-camp owner.

Jean: "The camps are on the south shore of Rangeley Lake. North,
across the lake are the mountains, and from there to Canada is wilderness.
Behind us is Beaver Mountain and from there, all the way down to the town
of Byron, is wilderness. In other words, we may be on a paved road, but
we're in the wilderness. I have 3,000 feet on the lake and 58 acres, a lot of
which is old-growth forest. We've put paths along the lakefront so people
can walk in the open, or they can go into the woods for bird-watching, wild-
flower hunting, and things like that.

"Back in the late 1800s this was a farm. About 1899 or 1900 a Major
Harrison bought the farm and proceeded to build a summer cottage for
himself: two-and-a-half stories and three fireplaces, complete with a kitchen
and separate maids' quarters. Then he built two fairly large two-story cottages. Everything had hot and cold running water. Then he built a set of
camps with four or five cottages and a dining room. He called it Ethelwald
and operated it until sometime in the 1920s. He advertised a tennis court,
croquet, things like that, as well as fishing. At that time this was the end
of the road that came in from what's now Route 4; Route 17 didn't exist
then. So you either came in by road or you came by boat from South
Rangeley when you got off the train in Oquossoc. At the time, people were
beginning to 'motor' because he mentions 'motoring through New
England' in his advertising. The camp was only open in the summertime.

"Harrison sold the property in the 1930s to a Mrs. Mathews, who kept about the same type of operation, and she named it Niboban, which is an Indian word for the aurora borealis. She operated the camps until just about World War II, at which point motoring through New England became practically extinct. After the war people weren't as interested in renting camps; they wanted to buy their own. Many sporting camps around here were split up over a 15- to 20-year period—York's Log Cabins, Little Kennebago Club, for example—some of the old places burned (the Rangeley Lake House is gone), all that type of thing gradually was no more and only a few of the old camps still remain.

I was several years negotiating for these camps. Before I started I knew I had to put in new cabins. By the time I acquired the property all the buildings were in such poor condition there was no saving any of them. And I used your book, Alice, to read carefully about all the different camps and get ideas from what they were doing. Then I visited Tim Pond Camps and went to a Sporting Camp Association meeting and got a lot of ideas from different owners. Having been in the real estate business in Rangeley, I was well aware of plumbing issues, camp jacking, and all the things that happen to camps on the lake. That influenced the way that I built here. We started building in the early summer of 2000, and our first four cabins were open for occupancy Memorial Day weekend 2001. Then I went over to the side where the Harrison camp itself had sat and had four more cabins built by Memorial Day 2002. They're cookie-cutter cabins: two bedrooms, each with twin beds (although we can make them up into king-size). They're well insulated so we can use them comfortably all year 'round. People with a walker or cane can get into them easily. And we have our 'honeymoon' cottage, a one room with efficiency kitchen and bathroom with Jacuzzi. We haven't had honeymooners in there yet—so far people celebrating their anniversary and older couples.

"The lodge here has what I call a 'rainy day room'—it's a lounge with a ping-pong table, games, puzzles, books. We do not have televisions in the cabins, we do not have telephones in the cabins, but we have both available in the lounge, which is open until 10:00 at night if people want to use it. And we're finding people are saying, "Oh, no sound of TV or phones for a week—how wonderful!" I guess they're impressed with how quiet it is here. It's amazing—we have a full camp now, and you'd never know it! We have fire pits—one for every two cabins—and our guests really enjoy going out in the evening, sitting around the fire visiting and looking at the stars.

"In order to help the local economy, my philosophy is to use local businesses rather than compete with them. So I deliberately had the cabins built for housekeeping, because we're only seven miles from Rangeley and Oquossoc where there's everything from the bagel shop to gourmet restaurants. Then I use the area's Registered Maine Guides who specialize in fishing, upland bird hunting, deer hunting, nature hikes, etc. And the local marinas have rental boats—motorboats, kayaks, canoes—and can deliver and pick up for our guests.

"I knew snowmobilers would be a big part of my business, because Rangeley does not have enough winter beds. So in the fall of 2001 we negotiated with the snowmobile club and the state and we have a groomed connector trail that runs from right here on the property up to ITS 84. There's also access to the lake when it's frozen over. We have families, grandparents, parents and children, come up for Thanksgiving, Christmas, and New Year's. I am trying to fill a need I knew existed in Rangeley. Being the widow of a developer, I knew that the shore lots were gone. Prices for private camps and homes are going sky high. And this seemed to me a way that people could enjoy the lake without a huge investment. With the cabins I have and their weekly turnover, quite a few families can come up and enjoy the area. And they do enjoy it. They fish, swim, canoe, kayak, climb mountains. Everyone's that come so far has been very active. Fishing has been good, and we've got our first reservations for bird hunting.

"When Mr. Harrison built this property he spent a lot of money, and made a nice set of camps and attracted a very nice clientele. But who would have thought then that in fifty or sixty years it would all be gone and that you'd have to start over again! So how can I say that I've built for the future? For the present people are coming and enjoying the lake and Niboban. I've tried to offer a wilderness experience even though we're close to 'civilization' and that's what our guests say they are finding here."

15. NORTH CAMPS

HK/AP

OWNERS: Sonny and Dottie Gibson

ADDRESS: Box 341, Oquossoc, ME 04964; 207-864-2247; www.north-camps.com

SEASON: Mid-May through Columbus Day; reopens in November for hunting

ACCOMMODATIONS: Fourteen log, shingle, and clapboard cabins: one to four bedrooms, screened porch, indoor plumbing and tub with shower, woodstove, gas or oil heater, gas stove; electric refrigerator and lights; linens, blankets, and towels provided

RATES: $75 per couple per day; $395 per couple per week HK

ACCESS: Maine Turnpike (I-495) to exit 12 (Auburn). Take ME 4 north through Rangeley. Go 2 miles and turn left onto Mingo Loop Road (watch for the sign) and follow signs down the hill into camp.

When I arrived at North Camps, Dottie was on the porch of the main lodge working on plastic webbing for some deck chairs. "When you see something that needs fixing, you've just got to be willing to do it. I've done tons of these chairs, could do them in my sleep." Sonny swings by and takes me on a tour: horseshoe pits, badminton court, boat dock, sailing dock, beach, cookout area, and a clay tennis court on a knoll at center stage. The cabins are an eclectic mix of styles and sizes. One is two-storied with a screened-in porch on each floor. "It used to be the main lodge," says Sonny. "The top floor was for the help." He gestures to the water: "The camps look out on Rangeley Lake, which is 10 miles long and 3 across. Good for brook trout and landlocked salmon."

We head back to the porch of the main lodge. As the three of us talk, guests stop by, ducks wander up the stairs, and a parrot named Henry jumps up to perch on Sonny's shoulder. "I had a turtle dove once. He showed up one summer—along with the ducks. We had him seven years. Henry here talks when he's in the mood. Says 'hello, good-bye, good morning, hey come here, whatcha doin?' and if you don't answer him he'll say, 'Huh?!'

"North Camps were built by Mr. North in the 1890s. It started as three cabins and the two-storied main lodge. After North it was run by the Hernbourghs from Norway or Sweden. [Maine has the towns of Norway or Sweden, but the Hernbourghs were from Europe.] Then my dad began running the camps in 1950. My family is the third owner in all that time! My dad was an avid sportsman. In '37 and '38 he was hunting in northern New Hampshire and he happened to come over this way and decided that he wanted to make the Rangeley area his home. At the time he bought the place, we were living in Worcester, Massachusetts, and we owned and operated a dairy business. When they ran this place, my mother did all the cooking. It was straight American Plan. And she did that straight through the '50s. At that point motels and auto touring were hurting the business, and they decided in order to survive they would have to go to housekeeping. So in the early '60s he put in kitchens and we offered housekeeping for the summer, for the family vacationers, and American Plan in the spring and fall.

"In the '60s I helped Dad open and close the place and guided for the fall hunt. I bought North Camps from him in 1982." *Dottie:* "Sonny and I married in '82. I had come up here on a bus the year before. And when he introduced me to his dad he said, 'This is the woman who's going to run North Camps with me.'" *Sonny:* "It takes a certain type of person to run a place like this. If I'm chopping wood, she'll see and come out and help me. She can make curtains, fix things. Many women don't know the kind of things you need to do, or don't want to learn—just don't want to live out here and do this." *Dottie:* "I love it here. We have 20 acres and you can look out over the lake to the mountains."

Sonny: "After we bought, my dad, 'Gibby,' stayed on with his companion, Charlotte, until he died ten years later. All the time he was here he entertained the guests; he was pretty colorful and the people loved him." *Dottie:* "We were drawing spring water for the camps at that time, and water from the lake. And he helped with that, too."

Sonny: "We have 850 feet of shore frontage and we own our own land here. It's a way of life. But in this area sporting camps have mostly been bought up and made into private cottages or condos. We're the only camp left on Rangeley Lake that's run as a traditional old camp. There used to be others, and we've brought some of the cabins down lake on the ice. The real estate has become so valuable and the taxes so high that a young couple starting off just couldn't do it now. A lot of banks won't even talk to you about loans if you're seasonal. We've had young couples buy camps, would love to live here. They find out it's 15, 16 hours a day, seven days a week. They couldn't make much money; they had to work too much. So they con-doed them. It's a shame because it's a good way of life and there should be places like this for people to come to.

"We cater to fishermen in the spring, then families and fishermen, then in the fall leaf peepers and fishermen. In October and November we have hunters, which is when we offer American Plan. My two sons have been helping out over the years and are showing interest in carrying on. You like to think it will continue because it's such a wonderful place. Most people come here through word of mouth. You've got four-to five-year-olds playing with teenagers, people forming friendships that last for years." Dottie points out all the birdhouses. "One of our guests made most of these and gave them to us. Our people are like that. The swallows were perching on them before we even got them up." *Sonny:* "Each Columbus Day week-end we have a pig roast for our guests." *Dottie:* "They do pot luck for the rest of the meal." *Sonny:* "We have a big grill and cook the pig for hours. It always catches on fire and we naturally have to pour some beer all over it! It's our way of saying thank you to our guests for another great year."

16. SAM-O-SET FOUR SEASONS

HK

OWNERS: Stephen and Jacquelyn Swain

ADDRESS: PO Box 1006, Rangeley, ME 04970; 207-864-5137; e-mail: dockside@tds.net; www.etravelmaine.com/samoset

SEASON: Year-round

ACCOMMODATIONS: Five cabins: two to three bedrooms; indoor plumbing and tub with shower); electric lights, refrigerator, and stove; satellite TV; monitor heat (some with fireplace); pets welcome ($15 per week)

RATES: $150 per cabin per day; $900–1,000 per cabin per week; snowmo-bile, ATV, motorboat, canoe, kayak, water toy, personal watercraft rentals

ACCESS: Take the Maine Turnpike (I-495) to Exit 12 (Auburn). Go north on ME 4 through Farmington toward Rangeley (approximately 80 miles). In Sandy River Plantation take left on South Shore Drive. Camps are 1.25 miles on the right (sign).

Sam-O-Set's white-clapboard cabins have the look of lakefront summertime rentals, but the full-time, in-house "Rangeley Lake Guide Service" tips the property over into the sporting-camp category for this book.

Jacquelyn: "My in-laws built two of our cabins when they came here in 1925. Then they built one in the '30s and one during World War II. They had to wait for a roof until the war was over because there were no tarred goods available. We've totally redone those first units, except for the fireplaces and some parts of the log interior. My in-laws had a total of 14 cabins. We purchased a cabin in 1957 and moved it. The property was then divided, but the cabins on my in-laws' side have all been sold. We opened up a sporting camp because we wanted to live on the property, and there's no other way, other than renting.

"We sometimes do seasonal leasing—a 3- to 4-month lease; I prefer to do that in the winter. And we have two cabins that have good handicapped accessibility. We have paraplegics who use the personal watercraft we have, because they can lift themselves from the wheelchair onto them. We have people who have had hip and knee replacements who cannot step down into a normal boat, but they can mount the platform on the back of the watercraft and it supports and holds them.

"Sam-o-set was a Native American chief. He and his tribe came to this area by way of the Androscoggin River. We have about 500 feet of shorefront here at Greenvale Cove. There are geese out on the lawn. The mallards and the loons bring in their babies fairly close to shore. The loons have a celebratory cry around the Fourth of July announcing the arrival of their chicks. So we know when it's happened. The problem is the rogue loons. There have become so many single males. They will come up from underneath and spear the breast of the male loon parent and kill it. And kill the chick, and claim the female and nesting territory. The only thing they're really frightened of is the seaplanes, which, coming down at them from overhead, seem like a huge bird. And they will peck at the pontoons.

"Out back we have about 50 acres, and my son owns about 150 acres. There are trails for ATVs up there. They have to stay on the trails, which are for the most part the snowmobile trails that we paid to have put in to connect with the state park loop. My son took a group from Florida up there in early winter. They thought they'd like to see moose. He was a little dubious, but he didn't discourage them. He said there was bull moose meeting up there—six of them! He said the ladies jumped off up on top the sleds (as though that was going to protect them), and they were screaming as though they'd seen a mouse. But they ended up taking pictures and having a great time. The moose, it turned out, were very courteous. One Memorial Day we had a moose come right down to the boat launch for a drink. That was exciting; all the cabins were full and it was dusk.

"My son, Shaun, has been doing his guide service for about four years. He has an e-mail address: fishrangeley.com. He keeps meticulous records and keeps track of whether the landlocked salmon he catches are native or stocked—the stocked fish have had their fins clipped. The salmon do come down right in front of our cottages, down by the sandbar, and they spawn here. We get the big, lantern-jaw salmon in the fall. They are beautiful, and good eating. My son probably only keeps two a year. There are also brook trout, and we have some perch. He says the fishing is quite good in spite of the acid rain from the Midwest. Most of his customers practice catch-and-release. None of these fisheries are open to ice fishing, which is when many people empty their junk fish into the lakes. Like in Maryland now where they have these Japanese snakehead fish that can go across land, and have fangs; they are killing many of the small fish that the valuable fish need to eat. It's frightening what's going on with people dumping their aquarium fish. There are groups trying to bring in winter fishing here, saying ice fishing would be good for the winter business. It certainly would not. It would ruin it, and it's been proven in the Moosehead area, Greenville, other areas where they've allowed it in. It has ruined the summertime fishing. It's really upset the balance. So we hope that never happens here."

17. TIM POND WILDERNESS CAMPS

AP, SCA

OWNERS: Harvey and Betty Calden

CAMP ADDRESS: Box 22-SC, Eustis ME 04936; 207-243-2947.

WINTER ADDRESS: Box 89, Jay ME 04239; 207-897-4056

SEASON: May 15 through November

ACCOMMODATIONS: Eleven log cabins: indoor plumbing and shower, porch, woodstove or fieldstone fireplace, electric or gas lamps

RATES: $120 per person per day, includes boats. Family and summer rates available.

ACCESS: Maine Turnpike (I-495) to exit 12A. Follow ME 4 north through Farmington. Drive 2.5 miles north to ME 27. Turn right and follow ME 27 to Eustis. (From I-95, take exit 31B, then follow ME 27 through Farmington as above, to Eustis.) Call into camp from the Texaco station in Eustis (last supplies) to make sure the gate is open. From here, go north 2.5 miles. Cross a bridge and take the next left. Proceed on a dirt road 7 miles and turn left at a gate. Go 1 mile, up a hill, and follow signs into camp.

Tim Pond Wilderness Camps has a cozy feel in the midst of a vast landscape. The body of water truly is a pond: 1 mile long by ¾ mile wide, snugged up to 2,000-foot Tim Mountain and the East Kennebago Range. Log cabins branch out on either side of the central lodge, all within view of each other, forming a compact little community.

Betty has traced the camp's history back to before the 1860s: "It first started as a logging camp and then turned into a sporting camp in 1877. Back then, people would take railroads up to Kingfield, a stage to Eustis Ridge named after lumber magnate Charles Lyman Eustis, and come the rest of the way by buckboard open carriage. Once folks got here, they usually stayed for the summer." Many of the regulars had cabins named after them, like Uncle John and so on. "Back then, the cost of coming here was $2.50 a day. Now, $2.50 was a lot of money at a time when you figure most people only made $1.00 to $1.50 a day." They came to relax and fish. Tim Pond has never been stocked, and its 46-foot-deep waters still offer square-tailed brook trout.

"Our first season was 1982. Harvey and I are both from Maine and have been involved in hunting and fishing for a long time. Like most people who run a sporting camp, you start off thinking you're going to have a lot of time to go hunting and fishing. But sorry!" She laughs. "Every owner will tell you it's an adventure coming in to open up camp in the springtime. If it's going to go wrong, it's going to go wrong one thing after another. Maybe the water pump dies, or the sewer backs up, or you get every vehicle stuck in the snow and there's no way out. Which isn't that bad. I mean, what's wrong with being stranded in a place like this? Fortunately, this all happens before opening day! So one year, on top of all this, I cut my finger in the new food processor and needed stitches. I just wrapped it up. [Luckily, Betty is an emergency medical technician.] I figured it would heal eventually, and went back to work. You just take these things in stride; that's the attitude you have to have. Whatever comes along, you do what you have to do."

Harvey follows this same philosophy, when he's extracting the fish-hooks that get stuck in even veteran anglers (a daily event during some weeks). His method: "Loop the line through the bend in the hook, press down on the eye of the hook, and jerk the fly straight back and out."

Betty: "For fishing, we provide everything that people would need in one package. That way there are no add-ons. We even have fishing equipment to use—also at no extra cost—and will provide a free fly-fishing lesson. And every year since 1983 the second weekend in May has been set aside for our fly-fishing school run by Edge of Maine Fly Fishing. For around $375, a person gets the school, cabin, all their meals, boat with motor and the classes. The students learn casting, knot-tying, entomology, fly-tying, and fish indentification."

Beside fishing, hiking, and moose- and bird-watching, mountain biking has become very popular. *Betty:* "People can bring mountain bikes, or we have some to use if folks want to ride around on the back roads.

"I really like my people. We have a 90 percent return rate, so every day it's like old home week. Some of the other 10 percent, though, have never been to a sporting camp before. There's the gentleman who yelled at me one time 'cause we have a generator and I usually turn it off at 10 PM. I flipped the switch and it wasn't long before he came running. 'Lady, have you ever heard of a computer? You wiped out my whole program.' Then there's another gentleman who was angry because I didn't give him a room with a phone. I told him I didn't play favorites—none of the cabins have phones. I had two boys in here, one was about 9 and the other 11, and it was the first time they had ever picked a raspberry or a blueberry. One little boy from Texas rushed into the kitchen and gushed, 'Mrs. Calden, we've just been looking for moose and we saw one and he turned and ran into the jungle!'" She laughs. "What we see here at Tim Pond," Betty says softly, "we take for granted. But it's different for many people. Here we see stars at night. People from the cities aren't used to that. We find them sitting on their porches at night, midnight sometimes, rocking and watching the stars. We meet really nice people here. And you know, it doesn't matter what they do in life, they're up here just to be themselves."

Seven-Up Biscuits

> 2 cups flour, 4 tsp. baking powder, 1 tsp. salt, 1 tsp. sugar, ½ cup shortening, ¾–1 cup 7-Up

Mix flour, baking powder, salt, and sugar. Cut in shortening, then add 7-Up. Stir gently until just moistened. Place on floured surface and knead lightly. Roll to desired thickness and cut. Place on pan with biscuits touching. Bake at 400 degrees for about 15 minutes or until biscuits are golden brown and no longer doughy in the center.

THE DEAD RIVER–JACKMAN REGION

This section is bordered by ME 27 in the west and ME 201 to the east. The Appalachian Trail (AT) skirts Flagstaff Lake and the Carry Ponds (so named because Benedict Arnold's ill-fated band of soldiers carried—or more accurately, dragged—leaking bateaux through here). Both routes are built along scenic river valleys and offer magnificent water and mountain vistas.

ME 27 passes through Kingfield and the Carrabassett Valley, home to Sugarloaf Mountain ski resort. The AT crosses the road between Crocker and Bigelow Mountains, clearly visible along the sweep of road. Beyond Stratton, one can see marshy, shallow Flagstaff Lake; north of Eustis the drive parallels the North Branch of the Dead River to the east and Chain of Ponds in the west.

ME 201 parallels the Kennebec River and a bicycle path established on the old railroad bed from Solon to Bingham. In Moscow, the highway passes Wyman Dam (the largest in Maine) with a spectacular view of Wyman Lake and surrounding mountains. In Caratunk, the road goes directly past the wooden AT sign (on the right) and heads to The Forks, the confluence of the Dead and Kennebec Rivers. This area is command central for outfitters specializing in whitewater rafting. If you wish to catapult through Maine waters, call the Maine Rafting Association at 1-800-723-8633. The Forks also boasts Moxie Falls, the highest falls in New England.

The section of ME 201 from The Forks to Jackman is noted for moose sightings. In fact, there are so many opportunities for close encounters that the stretch has been dubbed "Moose Alley." The important thing for drivers to know is that moose are large, relatively speedy, difficult to see at night, and not too bright. A collision with a moose can be lethal to humans and moose alike.

In Jackman, the Moose Rivers' flowage branches off into many lakes and streams popular with sportsmen and vacationers. Many of the lakes and ponds in this area are at relatively high elevations (above 1,500 feet) and are spring fed. Once in Jackman you are just 15 miles from the Canadian border. The town is in a valley surrounded by mountains. High elevations also mean good snowfall, and the area is used extensively by snowmobilers. For up-to-date snow conditions, call 1-800-880-SNOW.

GETTING THERE: General driving time from Portland is 4 hours; from Boston, 6 hours; from New York City, 10 hours. There is an airport in Jackman and small planes fly in to the Gadabout Gaddis grass airstrip in Bingham. For a chartered float plane, contact Steve Coleman in Jackman, 207-668-3301.

GUIDANCE: You can get regional information from the Upper Kennebec Valley Chamber of Commerce (207-672-3702). The Jackman–Moose River Chamber of Commerce (PO Box 368, Jackman, ME 04945; 207-668-4171; e-mail: mooserus@prexar.com; www.jackmanmaine.org) has local information and snowmobile maps.

18. ATTEAN LAKE LODGE

AP, SCA

OWNERS: Brad and Andrea Holden

ADDRESS: PO Box 457, Jackman, ME 04945; 207-668-3792; fax: 207-668-4016; e-mail: info@atteanlodge.com; www.atteanlodge.com

SEASON: Late May through September

ACCOMMODATIONS: Sixteen log cottages: indoor plumbing and tub with shower, gas lights, Franklin fireplaces.

RATES: $190–225 per couple per day; $1,200–1,400 per couple per week

ACCESS: Exit I-95 at exit 36 (Skowhegan) and take ME 201 north to Jackman. As you come into town, take your first left onto Attean Road (dirt) and go 2 miles to the boat landing. There is a phone at the parking area so you can call the camp for a boat pickup.

Attean Lodge is on an island in Attean Lake, and you ferry over on the camp launch. Sally Mountain looms up on the right, and pocket-sized islands dot the lake. The dock and beach area leads up the hill to the spacious log lodge stained a warm pumpkin tone. The cottages are mostly tucked in a pine grove on a knoll to the right of the lodge. Some are connected by a boardwalk and have built-in benches so you can sit and look out on the peaceful, pristine view.

Brad: "The Coburn family was the original owner of Attean Township (36,000 acres), which they bought in the 1850s. The name comes from the Algonquin Indian tribe. Rumor has it that there was an Algonquin chief named Attean; they pronounced it At-TEE-in; today it is pronounced AT-é-in. My grandfather, Reul Holden, was an independent logger and became acquainted with Coburn because he wanted to cut some timber off Coburn's land. In those days there were no set-back [zoning] restrictions. So he bought the land and built a couple of little fishing cottages down on the back side of the island here. There were no other buildings on the lake. The island is called Birch Island and is about 22 acres. Attean Lake is about 5 miles long and 3 wide and is protected in perpetuity. Before Coburn sold it to Lowell Timber Associates, they established conveyances that stated that the land 300 feet back, all around the lake, could not be developed. Beyond 300 feet back are areas that also can't be developed either because of the Canadian Pacific Railroad or 'view sheds.' In other words, you can't look over on the side of the mountains and see any type of cutting. So the views are protected. Forever.

"My father, Langdon Holden, and his two brothers, Lyle and Roland, ran the business until my father bought them out. My mother, Violette, who lives in Jackman, was very, very involved right until we bought the place in '89. Every summer of my life I've been here. My father died in a logging accident in 1973 and I guess you could say I became the man of the family at that point.

"Back in my father's and grandfather's day the railroad was the only way to come here. There was no road access to the landing or even to Jackman. It was still horse and buggy. The automobile was slow to get here. I remember my father telling stories of how he would row across the lake— this was before outboard motors—to Attean Landing, where the train would stop and let my father's guests off. You can see the tracks from the lake here. There are still trains that go by. This is the second-longest railroad line in the world. The longest is the Trans-Siberian in Russia. This train goes all the way from Vancouver to New Brunswick.

"In 1979 there was a fire here. The dining room and kitchen were in one building and the lodge and staff rooms were in another, quite close together. The fire started in the kitchen and spread, and eventually took the lodge, too. I've done most of the carpentry and design for this new main lodge and we're really pleased with it. We've torn down a lot of the old one-

Attean Lake Lodge

and two-person cabins and replaced them with larger cabins, put in stone and brick hearths, new furniture, and new bathrooms in almost all the cottages. The oldest one now is probably the one I live in, built in 1910.

"I met Andrea because she had written to my mother for a job. I was in Florida that winter. My father was still alive at the time, and my parents said, 'Why don't you stop on your way home and interview this girl? She's from the Brunswick area, going to school in Portland.' So I was this big macho guy, you know, been in Florida, come back and interviewed her. Well, she came to work here as a waitress and has been here ever since. Need I say more! Andrea was studying education, and until a few years ago she was the third-grade teacher here in Jackman. But since we've bought this, and our seasons are spilling over into the fall and starting earlier in the spring, the business needs two people running it, really. It's become so difficult to hire people. Jackman has a limited labor pool, and those here have to go back to school before our season ends. We've had very good luck with programs that send us people from abroad. They stay through September, are great workers; it's unique, and the guests love them. They come with a backpack, that's it."

Andrea: "We like to see families together here. Some places the kids eat separately, but we have everyone eating together. That way, people intermingle. We had a very shy child last year. He announced when he arrived that he 'didn't play with other kids.' Next day, he was right into it." *Brad:* "Every school day I used to boat my son, Barrett, across the lake. A lot of mornings the fog's so thick you have to use a compass. I remember my father doing the same thing with me until I got old enough that I could take my own boat along Moose River into Big Wood Lake, right into Jackman, and tie my boat up right behind the school. Now Barrett's doing the same thing. When I graduated from high school, there were seven in my class."

I quip, "So you were in the top 10."

Brad laughs, "Yes, I was. Barrett's got it tougher—there are 16 in his class."

There are lots of beaches on Attean Lake. "Ours must be 200 feet long, totally natural," Brad says. "It's funny, you go down to the next lake, no beaches, and up the other way, no beaches at all. We have kayaks, paddleboats, and lots of islands to explore. Fishing in the area is for brook and lake trout and salmon, general law." The region also draws visitors undertaking the Moose River canoe trip called the Bow Trip, which goes around in a loop. "It's a 45-mile trip," Brad explains. "Most people take three days to do it. We have cabins we maintain along the trip. Most people bring their own gear for this. But we also have about a dozen canoes stashed away on other lakes and ponds, and we maintain trails to them for 1-day trips."

When I visited the camps there was a couple getting married the day I had to leave. Carol, the bride, had been a waitress at camp years earlier. She told me, "I came back because I had a yearning to be here. Maine does that to you: the attraction, the charm. I was first tuned in to the northern lights and loons here. It's the first place I really felt alive. You have to have a 3-day residency to get married in Maine. So we came into town Tuesday, went directly to Town Hall, signed our marriage certificates. Brad got his notary public's license specifically to marry us. So we'll get married on 2,200-foot Sally Mountain. Basically, how simple can it be? We wrote our vows; for a trousseau we both have new hiking boots! We've been to a lot of places in the States, but we haven't found one yet that matches this. We were out on a canoe trip, a chain of three lakes. Got to the last lake and hadn't seen a soul all day. One loon per lake. Quiet. The only thing you're hearing is the wind through the pines. This is it!"

As Brad deposited me back at the boat landing and my car he said, "Some guests leave here saying, 'Back to civilization.' My father used to say, 'When you leave here you're leaving civilization and heading into the jungle.'"

Apple Chocolate Chip Cake

In one bowl, mix 1 cup sugar, 1 cup oil, 2 eggs slightly beaten, and 2 tsp. vanilla. In another bowl blend 2 cups flour, 1 tsp. baking soda, 1 tsp. cinnamon, and ½ tsp. salt. Combine wet and dry ingredients, and mix well. Fold in 3 cups finely diced apple, 1 cup chocolate chips, and ½ cup chopped nuts.

Grease and flour a 10-inch tube pan or 9 x13-inch pan. Bake at 325 degrees for 1 hour.

19. BULLDOG CAMPS

HK

OWNERS: Doris and Vlad Vladimiroff
CAMP ADDRESS: HC 64, Box 554, Jackman, ME 04945; 207-243-2853; www.bulldogcamps.com
WINTER ADDRESS: PO Box 1229, Greenville, ME 04441; 207-695-4322
SEASON: Mid-May through mid-October
ACCOMMODATIONS: Six log cabins: indoor plumbing; central shower; gas lights, refrigerator, and stove; wood heat; pets welcome
RATES: $22 per person per day; child and weekly rates available
ACCESS: Take I-95 to exit 36 (Skowhegan). Follow US 201 north until you PASS the Parlin Pond rest area. Turn left onto a logging road 0.2 mile past the rest area. Follow Bulldog signs about 9 miles to a parking area and sign where you can be picked up.

Fortunately for guests, Vlad Vladimiroff operates an ATV shuttle along a 1-mile jeep trail into camp. The trail is all downhill, but the cabins are housekeeping and people bring in heavy loads of supplies, so the service (for a small fee) is welcome. The path emerges from pine woods to pass two cabins on the left. Beyond is a small clearing with a main lodge bracketed by four other cabins. Beyond this, a pond lies sparkling at the base of cliffs. You feel as though you've arrived at a hidden grotto, to a place aptly named Enchanted Pond. I sit and chat with the owners in the main lodge, surrounded by art and books.

Doris points to a quilt she appliquéd with camp scenes: "I have artwork in all the cabins, and many people do notice it. I was born in Maine, went out-of-state to college, but came back and taught writing and literature in the University of Maine system for over 25 years."

Vlad: "I grew up in New York and was also an English major. When I came to Maine in 1967, I got interested in fishing. Several years later we saw an ad for a set of sporting camps in the Jackman–Eustis area, where I had fished before. So my curiosity was aroused. And we just liked the property. It had the advantage of being a privately owned piece of land rather than on a leased lot. We figured we wanted to have the property whether we would run it as a sporting camp or not. I have carpentry experience, in fact in the winter I often work as a carpenter, and we knew we could keep the place up. So we ended up buying these camps, with my brother as a partner, in the early spring of 1973 and started running them that first season. We thought we'd just try it for a while and we've been at it all these years!"

Doris: "Our son was three years old when we came here." *Vlad:* "And now he's married, living in San Fransisco, working for a software company, and playing in a rock band. So it's not too likely that he'll want to do anything here. But who knows? I never fished until I was 25 years old, and look what happened to me!

"I think we're about the sixth owners. The camps were built in the 1920s as sporting camps. Before that there was another little settlement here used for loggers. Back at the turn of the century, all the white pines around here I guess were being cut. A big landowner in the Jackman area, Henry McKinney, called it Bulldog Camp, so it had this name before the sporting camps were even built. The natives called Enchanted Pond here Bulldog Pond, because the mountain across the water was supposed to look like a bulldog. Then it became known as Enchanted Pond, because supposedly there were a lot of mysterious things that used to happen here, like, oh, people following a deer out into the middle of the frozen lake to have the tracks disappear all of a sudden. And there are several places around here where streams just go underground, disappear, and then pop up again somewhere else. I know that in one of Maine journalist Gene Letourneau's outdoor columns years ago, about the time we bought this place, he did a write-up about the area. People have written histories of the Moose River valley, and here's a book called *Dud Dean and the Enchanted.* You've probably heard of the author, Arthur R. McDougal Jr. Another book is *The Enchanted: An Incredible Tale,* by Elizabeth Coatsworth. Unfortunately, since we've been here, no mysterious things happen anymore!

"The fishery in the pond is brook trout, general law, with the provision that no live bait be used. And it is very deep, 185 feet. It's basically glacial, and not just one big hole, but more like a big long trough.

"When we first bought the camps, there was a flying service out of Lake Parlin, where you go off at the main road. It was reliable and relatively inexpensive. So for the first four years, that's how people got in here. But then he had to retire. Some people will still fly in, maybe with Steve Coleman in Jackman, or Currier in Greenville. Our guests used to be mostly Mainers. Now many are from southern New England.

"I hate to see the intrusion of development in the areas where sporting camps are trying to exist in a wilderness setting. An outfit buys up land to cut the timber and then sells off lots to people who just want to build cabins in the woods. Usually this is something that a small timber company would do. Companies like Boise Cascade or Scott Paper didn't have a history of doing things like this. But, unfortunately, new outfits like Plum

Doris and Vlad Vladimiroff at Bulldog Camps

Creek are in the development business as well as logging. So, for example, some companies come in, get what they can from the sale of wood, and then, under the old laws, they could subdivide that land as long as the lots were 40 acres or more, to whomever wanted to buy it. With no state review or approval. We want to stay here, but a lot depends on how invasive of our little area the development becomes."

Doris: "Vlad's devotion to both the environment and fishing is enormous—and mine to the environment and ecological issues. The idea of a camp appealed to me very much. And I like the people who come in here. I like meeting people who are not only professionals and privileged, but also some regular folks."

Vlad: "It's really a mix of people."

Doris: "A very nice mix."

20. CEDAR RIDGE OUTFITTERS

HK

OWNERS: Hal and Debbie Blood

ADDRESS: PO Box 744, Attean Road, Jackman, ME 04945; 207-668-4169; FAX: 207-668-7636; e-mail: info@CedarRidgeOutfitters.com; www.CedarRidgeOutfitters.com

SEASON: Year-round

ACCOMMODATIONS: Seven cabins: two to three bedrooms, deck, indoor plumbing and shower, electric light, oil heat, carpeted, TV/VCR, phone, gas grill. One cabin is wheelchair accessible. Two firepits, hot tubs. Well-behaved pets welcome.

RATES: $35 per person per day; $185 per person per week (minimum rates apply); child, guided trip, and package rates available; motorboats $75 per day, canoes $20 per day. Optional daily cabin housekeeping $4 per person per day.

ACCESS: I-95 to exit 36. Take US 201 north to Jackman. Pass Jackman Trading Post, on the right at the height-of-land. Take the next left, and at the bottom of the hill turn onto Attean Road. Go ½ mile to camps on left.

The camp is down the road from town on a ridge overlooking Big Wood Lake. The cabins are conventionally built, with a natural wood appearance and a log main lodge set up on a knoll behind the cabins.

Debbie: "We bought this land in 1989 and built the first cabin that year,and moved up here for good in 1991. The cabins are housekeeping with a meal option from September through November." *Hal:* "If it's part of a package plan we do meals other times as well." *Debbie:* "A lot of people like it here because it's secluded, but only five minutes from town so we're near restaurants and stores, easy to get a fishing license. We have videos available for people because there's no cable service up this road."

Hal: "This area's a year-round spot. I've got canoes on some ponds and a motorboat I rent out. We're a big destination for snowmobilers. We get the earliest snow and the snow stays the latest. Even from here down to The Forks, which is thirty miles, there'll be a big difference in the amount of snow and how early it comes. Same thing about the snow for deer hunters. We do almost anything. We have beagles for rabbit hunting; do bird hunting in the fall. Do bear hunting in September. October is bird hunting and the moose season, and archery hunters. Then November is the rifle season for deer. Summer is fishing, families, and rafting." *Debbie:* "We do white-water rafting with Windfall Outdoor Center. And we have a week-long Summer Adventure package with things people can do, like rafting, canoe-ing, hiking, rock climbing, guided fishing, horseback riding, moose-watch-ing, float-plane rides. They decide what they want and we'll tailor it exact-ly to them."

Hal: "I started out as a lobsterman, down on the coast. But really just wanted to have sporting camps. Couldn't find any we wanted to buy, so we decided to build our own. I'd been coming up to these woods fishing and hunting since I was a teenager, so it was just a natural area to pick. We found a piece of land and started building. We have twenty acres here, with unlimited access for hunting and fishing. It's almost all timber lands. I got my [Master] guide's license before we came up and didn't guide until we started building this place." *Debbie:* "And he teaches a guide's class here now. And a deer clinic."

Hal: "The guide's school is for people who want to kind of get a crash course in everything they need to know to get their license. The written test is all part of it. The state does that here. It's a week-long course, with meals and lodging." *Debbie:* "Approximately 55 hours, $695. They arrive on a Sunday and the test is on Saturday." *Hal:* "We do it once a year, in the spring. And I do a deer clinic where I teach people to hunt these 'north woods bucks,' I call them. They're different than anywhere else because they don't have any boundaries up here. They're not on farmland. They travel more and you have to hunt them different. I may do two clinics: one in the spring and one in the fall. That's basically a two-and-a-half-day course; $550 with meals and lodging. I'm writing a book, *Big Woods Bucks: A Guide's Way,* based on my experience hunting here for over twenty years. There'll be quite a bit on tracking, 'cause it's my favorite thing. Most people don't understand how to tell how old a track is. There's a formula: it's a combination of the temperature at night and in the day, the type of snow it is. You've got to combine all that and come up with what the track should look like, or feel like; most of it I do by feel.

Like if it's wet underneath, or the ground's damp, and it's cold out, the track will start freezing in the bottom. Things like that. If you're tracking a deer and getting in close, half an hour means a lot in the age of a track. I can write that, but you just got to experience it."

Debbie: "I'm from the coast, the very tip of Harpswell. My father was a fisherman, and I didn't want to move up here. But now I wouldn't go back, it's too busy for me down there, after living here. Hal said that if I moved to Jackman he'd build me a house. I share it with everybody . . . but I have a beautiful house. (Laughs.) And I grew to love this life. The other part of Cedar Ridge and its success was Hal's dad, who passed away in December 2001. He was Cedar Ridge." *Hal:* "Everyone called him 'Pops.' "

Debbie: "He'd watch the place for us if we were gone, hang out with the guests, go fishing with them, hey, go down to the bar with them."

Debbie: "I'm a guide too. I took a course in '92 and got my hunting license. I don't take people out because I'm so busy in the kitchen during hunting season. Hal and I got married when we were both quite young, and he loved hunting so much I wanted it to be a part of my life too. I like hunting deer best. I've hunted with gun and bow and arrow, but I haven't done that in years. I just don't have the time, neither one of us has, really. Back when we started off, he said, 'This is going to be like a retirement.' I didn't work, by the way, before this. I raised my son, took care of my gardens, and that's what I did for a living. And he says, 'We're gonna retire up there. You wait and see, you're just gonna love it.' And all we've done is work! For the first five years I had no help. I did everything myself. I did all the cleaning, laundry, cooking, everything. Granted, business wasn't as busy back then as it is today, but it definitely stretched me. I mean, not only that, I was also helping with the building. Did all the finishing in the house. Raked and seeded the lawn by hand. So it was a tremendous amount of work. We had it all done in five years." *Hal:* "Now we sit on the couch, watch soap operas, eat bon bons . . ." *Debbie:* "Right! I wish!

"The best part of this is the people. Some of our best friends we've met because of this business. Often they'll come back in December or April (which are our 'down times,' but not really because we do a full spring cleaning in April. That's one of the things we guarantee: clean.). When people talk about their list of friends, I'm not kidding you when I tell you it's over a hundred. And we never would've met them if Hal was still doing what he was doing before."

21. C. MOXIE GORE OUTFITTERS

HK

OWNERS: Ken and Pam Christopher

ADDRESS: PO Box 40, West Forks, ME 04985; 207-663-2121 or 1-866-663-2646; e-mail: pam@tdstelme.net; www.cmoxiegore.com

SEASON: Year-round

ACCOMMODATIONS: Five logs-sided cabins: two bedrooms and loft, indoor plumbing and shower, deck, knotty pine interior, electric lights, radiant heat. Bunkhouse and a separate campsite. Well-attended pets allowed.

RATES: $32–75 per person per day; $525–650 per cabin per week; children under 10 free

ACCESS: Take I-95 to exit 36 (Skowhegan), then US 201 north for about 65 miles to The Forks. Just before the bridge into the village, take a right onto Lake Moxie Road. Camps (sign) are 2 miles on the right (just beyond entrance to Moxie Falls).

C. Moxie Gore Outfitters is a newly constructed set of cabins intended to provide the look and feel of a traditional set of sporting camps. Although not on a body of water, the lodge is off the main drag and the cabins themselves are set off farther, forming a circle in a grove of trees.

Ken: "We are located approximately 2 miles east of the confluence of the Kennebec and Dead Rivers in The Forks, and just across the street from the Moxie Falls scenic area. Moxie Falls is one of the highest waterfalls in New England, with a vertical drop of a little over 90 feet. From the cabins it is less than a mile walk." *Pam:* "We are in Moxie Gore Township, which we hope is a destination point in and of itself. We are about 3 miles from Moxie Lake. The area has an abundance of water, both within Moxie Gore and within the immediate area. There are many streams, ponds, and lakes, as well as the rivers themselves. Acres and acres of public land, and the paper companies are wonderful about letting the general public use their roadways and trails. We provide maps and general information about the area, and are happy to shuttle people to various locations. The Appalachian Trail is behind the property, so people who are hiking enthusiasts can traverse Pleasant Mountain, Bald Mountain, and cross the Kennebec River into Caratunk.

Ken: "We own 121 acres and across the street, on the Moxie Falls side, is land trust property. We're surrounded by paper-company land and state-owned lands." *Pam:* "So we're very protected and secluded. It's quiet and allows guests the feel of nature.

Ken: "We actually came here as a result of another business. My wife and sons were involved in the whitewater-rafting industry. We'd been looking at getting into sporting camps for, oh 25 or 30 years, and got a lot of ideas from your book. The last camp we looked at that we thought we might enjoy was 65 miles one-way in the woods. But at the time all three of our sons were in high school. So, we ended up here in The Forks." *Pam:* "Getting involved in rafting was secondary to our goals, but because our children were heavily involved, and I was managing the business office at the time, it gave me the opportunity to move to the area so that we could continue to explore the lodging possibilities. We've always spent our free time as a family in the woods, in one fashion or another: hunting, fishing, camping. We would stay at places like Tomhegan, which is kind of the ultimate look of a sporting camp. We've stayed at The Birches, and have spent a good deal of time in the Rangeley area, looking for an opportunity. So we've spent lots of vacations at various sporting camps and knew that it felt right, and that owning one was our ultimate goal. No matter how long it took." *Ken:* "The sporting-camp industry for me goes back to when I was 7 or 8 years old. My grandfather used to fish and hunt with Skeet Davenport, who basically operated Grant's Camps for a great number of years. He was a wonderful friend of the family. So it goes back that far for me."

Pam: "We purchased this property in 2000." *Ken:* "And we started building the house right off. I've worked in the construction business, in one way or another, for over 30 years—everything from earth work to building houses. We started construction on the cabins in December of 2001 and we had them built, the interiors finished, with the exception of some of the trim work and siding on the outside, and ready to rent the first weekend in March of 2002, three months later." *Pam:* "It was a snowmobile group and they took up all the cabins. It was very exciting to open up and have everything filled!

"We have a cabin that is fully handicapped accessible and we believe provides everything necessary for a person that has any special needs whatsoever. We're very pleased to have that. It's very needed in the area. And for people's outdoor experience, we feel we can pretty much accommodate what they want, whether it's a fishing package or a hunting package. We utilize guides within the area for that, and other resources. If we can't provide something here, we have enough knowledge of the area that we can help most people. We do have a limited capacity for boat and canoe rental, and as we move along through the process, we hope to expand upon that. That's our immediate plan.

"Within this facility we have tried to plan and situate the cabins so there is the feeling of community that happens at sporting camps. People can easily meet and get to know each other. Sort of the old school of traveling to that Maine location with your family and being together, meeting folks, and meeting up with them again in the following years at the same place. That's the kind of feel we're trying to promote." *Ken:* "I guess in bringing it all together, with the land that we have, and our trail system, we can offer wildlife photography, bird-watching, hunting, fishing, snowmobiling, cross-country skiing, hiking, biking; whatever people's interests are, we have the facility and desire to meet their needs. We've always had a real close family, with a houseful of kids and relatives, friends and neighbors. That's the way we've always wanted to be. This gives us the opportunity to be that way. In the process of doing this, it's been a lot of work, but it's been fun at the same time." *Pam:* "It's the realization of a long-held dream, and that's the best part of all: we're living our dream, and sharing our love of the outdoors with others."

22. COBB'S PIERCE POND CAMPS

AP

OWNERS: Gary and Betty Cobb

ADDRESS: North New Portland, ME 04961; 207-628-2819 (camp); 207-626-3612 (winter)

SEASON: Early May through mid-November

ACCOMMODATIONS: Twelve log cabins: one to three bedrooms, screened porch, indoor plumbing and shower (two with tub), wood heater, electric lights

RATES: $89 per person per day; $162 per couple per day; $570 per person per week; $1,020 per couple per week. Rates for nature weekend, fly-fishing school, children, and midsummer available. Motorboats $40 per day, canoes and kayaks free.

ACCESS: Lewiston–Auburn is the nearest airport; Bangor and Portland airports are equidistant. To get there by car, take the Maine Turnpike (I-495) to exit 12A (Auburn) and follow ME 4 to Farmington. From Farmington, take ME 27 to New Portland and then ME 146 to North New Portland. At Morton's General Store (last stop for supplies), go north for 23.3 miles on the Long Falls Dam Road. Turn right onto a logging road marked by a sign for the camp. Follow Cobb's signs for 4.5 miles to a gatehouse, where a gatekeeper will call to arrange for you to be picked up by boat at Lindsay Cove.

Pierce Pond Camps sit on a knoll at Lower Pierce Pond, which, together with Upper and Middle Pierce Ponds, makes up a 9½-mile-long waterway surrounded by the Appalachian Mountains. Thanks to the efforts of loyal guests, a trust was created to protect the entire 10,000-acre watershed. The spring-fed waters support square-tailed brook trout and landlocked salmon. There are 12 outlying small ponds within walking distance of the main lakes, and the Appalachian Trail and other hiking trails are within close range.

The camps were founded in 1902 and can boast of Cobb ownership since 1958. Gary Cobb's parents, Floyd and Maud, brought the family to Pierce Pond. Gary recalls, "One of my most graphic memories is of the magnificent forest and remoteness. There were no roads and very few trails until the mid-1960s. Large areas had never seen an ax." Thanks to the Cobbs' stewardship and protection efforts, the feel is still one of wildness. A booklet in the main lodge, *Birds of Pierce Pond,* states, "Birds are an ecological litmus paper. Many different species are a sign of a healthy ecosystem." The long list available for guest viewing is proof of the area's pristine habitats. *Gary:* "This place has so much to offer that each year in August we feature a special ecology and history weekend to focus on the uniqueness of the area.

"Great Northern Paper Company started in Madison and owned land in here, and with the lumbering activity, people could find the ponds. A group of businessmen secretly stocked Pierce Pond and almost immediately they were catching these huge trout and salmon. It wasn't too long before word got out and people started coming in to camp. So Great Northern got Charles Spaulding to build a camp to take care of the people rather than have them tenting—they were worried about forest fires—and it's been a sporting camp ever since. My father, Floyd, was a lumberman. But he liked to hunt and fish, so he started guiding at his logging camp. Then he went on and became a bush pilot in the Allagash area. That was wild, wild country in those days, the early 1950s, especially without a radio. The weather might be bad up there and good at home and you'd wonder why he didn't

Setting off on a fishing expedition at Cobb's

come home. So they decided to settle into a sporting camp. I was 15, and pretty excited, when we moved to Pierce Pond."

Betty: "Gary and I met our freshman year in college and got married in 1964. We then taught school in Millinocket. But every weekend and the whole summer we'd be at Pierce Pond. I was a waitress to begin with." *Gary:* "I started guiding right away but had to wait until I was 18 to be actually licensed. Then in 1969, we decided to give up teaching and go into the woods full time. My folks weren't ready to retire, so we started a wilderness boys' camp here and ran that for 17 years."

Betty: "Our son, Andy, and daughter, Jennifer, grew up at Pierce Pond and it was lucky for them, really. They both work here. Jennifer was talking about one Halloween the other day. It was before she started school and we were living in the camps for the winter. We dressed the kids all up and they went from our cottage to Gary's parents' cottage to Robert and Judy's (my sister) and that was it. 'I don't know why you even bothered,' she said to me, laughing." *Gary:* "I used to trap beaver. One day Jennifer and our niece, Katherine, set the beaver carcasses up on their tails around in a circle, gave them each a little cup, and proceeded to have a tea party!" He laughs. "And it was during that time we started building canoes. They're still being built by our guides—a Pierce Pond version of a Grand Laker–style canoe.

"We start going in to open up camp in late April. That's a real struggle: Wash all the log cabins, all the insides, sweep down the roofs, wash the windows, it goes on and on. There's no water then, of course. You have to dig a hole in the ice, pump it up, lug it up. But it's a very beautiful time of year because you're in total wilderness. You're way in here and there's not

another person or human sound. There's just something about the experience here that occupies a special place in the hearts of people who keep coming back. Even with our older guests, it's amazing how much better they
look physically after they've been here. I think a lot of it comes from the fact
that there's been very little change over the years. We had a fellow in recently that had come steady for 30 years, wasn't here for 30 years, and came
back. He saw my mother and father, the view was the same, there was nothing radically changed, and he was so pleased. That's what's really at the
heart of this place."

Cobb's Spinach and Red Cabbage Salad

*Betty: "Each week I usually use 100 pounds of flour, 30 dozen eggs, gallons and gallons of
milk." Gary: "It's a tremendous amount. You're lugging food in over miles of back roads,
across the lake, up by wheelbarrows every week." Betty: "Jennifer, our dietician daughter,
says this is a powerhouse of nutrition."*

Set out a salad plate for each serving. On each, place a bottom layer of baby
spinach leaves. Mound shredded red cabbage on top of the spinach and pile
shredded carrots on top of cabbage. Sprinkle dried cranberries and then
sunflower seeds over salad. Drizzle on the salad dressing:

Dressing: Beat together equal amounts of honey, spicy brown mustard,
orange juice, and mayonnaise.

23. COZY COVE CABINS

HK
OWNERS: Lisa and George Turcotte
ADDRESS: Box 370, Jackman, ME 04945; 207-668-5931
SEASON: Year-round
ACCOMMODATIONS: Nine cabins: one to two bedrooms, screened porch
and/or deck, indoor plumbing and shower, electric lights, monitor heat,
cable TV; linens and towels provided; two cabins are handicapped accessi-
ble; well-behaved pets welcome
RATES: $25 per person per day; $250–300 per cabin per week
ACCESS: I-95 to exit 36 (Fairfield). Take US 201 north to Jackman. Just
before town, go over the railroad tracks, take the first left onto Spruce
Street, and follow the sign for the camp.

Cozy Cove Cabins are red-wood stained a dark golden with green trim.
The long, gray-clapboard main house, with satellite dish and second-
story, full-length deck, is to the left of the driveway. Most of the cabins
are on the lawn to the right, which leads 150 feet through white birches

Cozy Cove Cabins

to the beach and Big Wood Lake with a western view of Sally Mountain beyond. The Turcottes, very new owners when I arrived, were in the early stages of settling in.

George: "It's total chaos right now, trying to get the yards set up for people coming in. The cabins are rustic, and need an upgrade, which we intend to do. We're both from Maine. I grew up in Green, she grew up in Gray, two colors getting together." *Lisa:* "We used to rent a cabin in Rangeley every year in the fall, my favorite time of year. And we were sitting on the porch saying, 'This is the life' and looked at each other and said, 'Well, why don't we do it!' It took us a couple of years to get to the point where we could look into it. Then it's taken us a couple of years from there to find a place. We looked a little bit in southern Maine, but we wanted something year-round, because we wanted it to basically be our only job. So that led to northern Maine. Greenville's expensive, Rangeley's expensive, Jackman's still reasonable.

"We've been in here eight days, and the whole moving up reminded me of the song from the Beverly Hillbillies, 'We loaded up the truck and we moved to—Jackman, Maine.' We tried to fit everything in one load, 'cause it's a long drive." *George:* "We didn't bring much air from southern Maine."

Lisa: "I was a certified nurses' aide for 19 years, and was ready for this change. George and I took classes with the Department of Human Services to become foster parents. Because of the move and everything, we haven't followed through with that yet, but we hope to. And we did think of doing a program here for foster parents and their children for a week or two in the summer so they can get away and relax. According to Leroy and Dianne Baker, the former owners, a man named Dick Spooner years ago tried to get people involved in having places and events that were handicapped accessible. He was a Vietnam vet from Vermont, and loved to hunt and fish and wanted other people who had disabilities to be able to have the same benefits of the outdoors he had. It took almost two years of planning, but a lot of people put together the Disabled Outdoor Adventure program, and now it's a major thing in the community." *George:* "So by the time we have the disabled folks and their caregivers in I will put the fireplaces together. Right now there's one central campfire area, but we think it would be great if everyone could have their own fireplace. And there's an abundance of rock, so why not?

"I have a 15-year old son, Matthew, who is very proficient at the computer. (Planning for these camps made us realize we really did need to get a computer for the web site and everything.) My son picked out the photos, changed the text, lined up the columns, and we started printing our own brochures." *Lisa:* "George has a daughter, Brittany, who's twelve, and they're both going to spend the summer with us.

"One of my favorite hobbies is crocheting; it's a nice, relaxing thing to do in the evening. I like to crochet curtains and doilies, and I make a lot of gifts for family and friends. I'm hoping to make some crochet curtains for the cabins and doilies for the tables. Right now I'm trying to learn how to sew and make some more curtains. Then the beds need quilts, and I would love to learn how to do that."

George: "I'm a millwright, and have my certification in welding. In the maintenance field, I'm a state-certified inspection mechanic, and I have a deal with a hydraulics company so I can actually make high-pressure hydraulic hose right here in the garage. So anyone needs a special fitting on the end of a certain hose, certain length, I can put the fittings on, do a factory-tight crimp, and sell it. It should be a really good, quick side job. I can also do the wiring and plumbing here, pipe work, the soldering, plus I'm doing the carpentry. And if all else fails, I've got my Class 1 CDL, my license for tractor trailers, doubles, triples, tankers, hazardous materials, the whole nine yards. And one of my first jobs, way back when, when the shoe shops were still operating in Maine, was 'little way' stitching (basically, it's stitching the leather onto the sole of the shoe). You do it with industrial-type sewing machines. So, I was able to help Lisa thread her sewing machine today. You never know what will come in handy!"

24. ENCHANTED OUTFITTERS AND LODGE

AP/HK

OWNERS: Craig Hallock and Gloria Hewey

ADDRESS: HCR 63, Box 134, West Forks, ME 04985; 207-663-2238;

e-mail: enchantedoutfitters@prexar.com; www.enchantedoutfitters.com

SEASON: Year-round

ACCOMMODATIONS: Seven cabins: one to three bedrooms, indoor plumbing and tub with shower, electric lights, renai or oil heat, two with hot tubs; well-attended pets allowed

RATES: $75 per person per day (AP); $35 per person per day (HK); hunting packages available

ACCESS: Take I-95 north to exit 36, then US 201 north through Skowhegan. The camps are 25 miles north of Bingham on US 201. From Canada, take US 201 south about an hour directly to the camps.

Enchanted's basic set of cabins, right on US 201, are tan clapboard. Craig was up on the roof, in the middle of some overhauling, when I visited. Gloria had just put new finishing touches in the cabins and was busy with the restaurant. She was gracious enough to conduct our serendipitous interview while cooking up lunch, somehow managing to be lucid and graceful, as well as efficient, all at the same time!

Gloria: "We bought Enchanted in July, 2001. Craig had his own flooring business, but he came here when he was growing up—his dad had a cabin in the area. He's a Master Maine Guide, loves the outdoors, and just wanted to come back and do this. I was an exercise physiologist, going to graduate school, and also have a degree in business administration. And I was a personal trainer and fitness/wellness director at a health club. It's interesting how things all come together. There are a lot of things we both have done that play into this business.

"The history of this complex goes back to 1952. At one point it was a motel, restaurant, and gas station. After several owners, and the discontinuation of the gas station, the rafting industry began to take off in the area, in the 1980s. But the place went through a few more hands and the previous owners got it from a bank sale.

"The main thing we want to provide for people is the opportunity to have a good time. So our big thing is customer service. We run a restaurant that's open to the public in connection with the cabins. I never ran a restaurant or bar before I came here so, I tell you, talk about a quick learning curve! But, I love it.

"The first year of course is fun. We were full every weekend that first July. In August is bear baiting and I'm trying to run this place by myself (you can see how green we were!); I had a bar full of people waiting for drinks and 12 orders waiting to be cooked. One of the guides tried to help me. Craig came in and I got him going at the bar. People realized what was going on and were wonderful. I said, 'We've got to get help!' Well, it got to the week before deer-hunting season and I had 30 men coming in—all American Plan—and no help. Then a lady up the road, the wife of an ex–game warden, calls and asks, 'Do you have enough help?' I told her, 'No!' She said, 'I'm not working this winter.' I told her, 'Get down here and we'll talk!' This wonderful woman offered to come down at 3:30 every morning (we serve breakfast at 4:30), and help me with that and then help put out all the sandwich fixings—people make their own sandwiches. She helped the whole season and wouldn't take a penny. You know what she said? 'I want you folks to succeed.' And a young lady called, a rafting guide, and asked if she could help. So, we've been very welcomed into the community."

Craig: "Hunting is a busy season for us. Bear hunting with hounds is my favorite type of hunting. We maintain 60 bait sites, which are chosen to run four specially trained hounds. Have you ever hunted with an English Cocker? Joe is our new addition, and he lives to hunt partridge. This area has an abundance of cover that holds lots of partridge and woodcock as well as snowshoe hare. And we have large populations of trophy-sized moose and deer.

Gloria: "For snowmobile season, the ITS trail goes right through our complex. We have guided trips, snowmobile rentals, gas and oil, and a rec. room with a TV, pool and ping-pong tables, and big fireplace.

"The other thing I want to mention is that I love getting groups in here. We do a big Thanksgiving meal. I had a guy come up to me afterward and say, 'I feel just like family.' I told him, 'You are family.' And I'm really excited about our womens' programs. We have several different trips. In the summer we do canoeing, kayaking, and hiking; in the winter snowmobiling and snowshoeing."

Barbecue Sauce

Gloria: "I make pork spareribs every Thursday. People just love this sauce. I'll give you the basic measurements, but I quadruple it. It keeps in the fridge for at least a week. You can use it on any kind of meat or poultry."

> 2 T vegetable oil, 1 chopped onion, 3 cloves minced garlic, 1½ cups ketchup, ½ cup cider vinegar, ¼ cup Worcestershire sauce, ⅓ cup sugar, 1 T chili powder, ½ tsp. cayenne pepper

Heat the oil over moderate heat, with the onion and garlic, for about 5 minutes, stirring occasionally. Add the rest of the ingredients and heat through. Simmer, uncovered, at least 20 minutes to thicken. Pour over meat or poultry and cook in the oven until the meat is tender and cooked through and the sauce on top is dark brown.

25. FOSTER'S CAMPS

HK

OWNERS: Lee and Paula Foster
ADDRESS: 655 Canada Road, Moscow, ME 04920; 201-672-3703
SEASON: May through November

ACCOMMODATIONS: Five log cabins: one to two bedrooms, indoor plumbing and tub with shower, porch, electric lights, monitor or wood heat, gas stove
RATES: $40 per person per day
ACCESS: I-95 north to exit 36 (Fairfield). Follow US 201 north through Moscow. Camps are on the right-hand side of the road, opposite Wyman Lake.

Fosters, a basic set of camps, is perched on a knoll several hundred feet off US 201.

Lee: "We used to be right on the edge of the big woods; now we're on the main route from Canada. The original camps were built in 1923. My grandmother, Evealina, started them. The impression was that my grandfather ran them, but my grandmother was the backbone, the brains, the heart of the business. A Mr. Best, out of Massachusetts, backed her financially. The place was all in her name. Grammy was 16 when she came here from living on different farms in Canada. She started out at sporting camps on Austin Lake waiting tables. Austin was on leased land, and the lease wasn't renewed, so she went ahead and bought the land here for the guests from there. My house (which used to be the main lodge, kitchen, and dining room) was built in anticipation of the road that would come in here because of the Wyman Dam construction. Grammy lived across the street for years and was almost 90 when she died in '96.

"My father and uncle took it over and turned the main lodge into a home. We bought from my dad in '84. Paula: "We were married in '84, and you started here before we met." Lee: "I ran it for several years for the family. It's in my blood. It wasn't smarts, wasn't the money!" Paula: "He never left here except to go to school." Lee: "Trade school, building construction, so I could fix the camps up. They didn't have kitchens in them; everything was out of plumb." Paula: " I have three kids and we have six grandchildren. My youngest son, who's in his 30s, has helped around here." Lee: "He learned a lot. He knows all the systems." Paula: "And all the grandkids have helped me clean the cabins."

Lee: "Wyman Lake runs fully through the towns of Moscow and Caratunk—2 townships long. It's used for hydropower. The dam was started in 1928 and they finished it off in the early '30s. When it was done it was one of the biggest in the country. After it was built, the fishing below the dam was phenomenal. When I was a teenager salmon and brook trout weighing 10 to 15 pounds came from Wyman Dam Pool. It's still fished all the time. We're not right on the water, but we have 20 different ponds within a half hour of here.

"Our busiest season is November, mostly weekenders. We're interested in people who want to stay in an old camp, not one of those knotty-pine, better-than-most-homes-around-here kind of place. We've had hunting parties come here since 1968 and we cater to hunters who can do things on their own. I don't have a guide, but I worked in the woods for years and can steer people in the right direction."

26. HARRISON'S PIERCE POND CAMPS

AP, SCA

OWNERS: Fran and Tim Harrison

ADDRESS: PO Box 315, Bingham, ME 04920; 207-672-3625 (radio phone at camp); 603-279-8424 or 603-524-0560 (winter)

SEASON: Mid-May through mid-October

ACCOMMODATIONS: Nine log cabins: five with toilet and sink, four share central shower houses and bathrooms, porch, gas light, wood heat

RATES: $52–67 per person per day; $335–400 per person per week

ACCESS: I-95 to exit 36. Take US 201 north to Bingham and turn left (west) onto ME 16. As you come off the bridge crossing the Kennebec River, turn right and go 4.5 miles. Turn right at a sign for the camps and follow the signs 11.5 miles to a fork. Go right at the fork, then go 4 miles to the camp driveway (sign).

Harrison's is built on a bluff overlooking Pierce Pond Stream. The final drive in takes you up one side of the bluff, and the camps nestle in an old pine grove going down the other side and into the stream. The long, low log main lodge commands the height-of-land; its wraparound porch affords views of a picturesque wooden bridge and a cascading waterfall beyond. Inside is a recreation room complete with pool table, library, and fieldstone fireplace. The spacious dining room has picture windows that look out on the falls.

Tim: "The area we're in first sold to William Bingham in 1793 and 'Bingham's Purchase' today is the entire Upper Kennebec Valley. Harrison's was originally built by Ralph Sterling of Caratunk (which means "rough, rugged country"). Ralph was a politician, surveyor, did all sorts of things, and received this land as payment for his surveying—about 10 acres in all. He started operating Sterling's Camps in 1934. The cabins were here and what are now our living quarters and the kitchen were the dining camp. The dining and recreation room were added on later. When Ralph was here the dam at Pierce Pond had already been around for almost a hundred years. I think it was 1835 when it was first used for logging. After Ralph died in the early 1950s, the place eventually got passed on to his grandson, Bob Smith, who still owns an acre of the original 10. In 1975 it was sold to Bud and Dorry Williams, of Pennsylvania, and they fixed it up and built a driveway. At the time of the Sterlings, there were no logging roads into here.

"It was Dorry Williams who started the hikers' 12-pancake breakfast, and we simply continue that tradition. The Appalachian Trail is just on the other side of the stream. And there's a blue-blazed trail [the AT is blazed white] that comes from the Pierce Pond lean-to, at the southern end of the

Harrison's Pierce Pond Camps

pond, straight to our camps. This is about the 2,000-mile mark along the AT here. As a kind of favor, because we like the hikers, we offer the breakfast. It's nothing we make any money on. We ask them at the register that's in the lean-to to come down the evening before and let us know if they want a breakfast. One pancake breakfast is with eggs, another is with sausage, another has both, and the other is just plain pancakes. I put in different types of fruit, make them thin, and sprinkle them with confectioner's sugar because hikers really love sugar. The hikers can come for dinner, but we do require a one-day advance reservation on that. A few hikers have stayed at camp just because it's a real nice spot and a good place to relax for the final push. I built a mini-replica log cabin playhouse for our daughter, Aimey, for her fifth birthday. And, when she's here, she still sells lemonade to the hikers for 50 cents a glass.

"Fran and I moved here from Massachusetts. Fran worked for a paper distributor and I was managing an actuarial-calculations department for an insurance company. Office, numbers—boring. I loved the people I worked with and it paid well, but I was unhappy. After 15 years there we wanted our own business. We had no idea what that business would be until one day Fran's sister from Maine told us how she and her husband were thinking of buying a sporting camp. We were all sitting around our pool, and Fran and I just looked at each other with a 'maybe that's it!' look. We ended up with this after almost a year of looking. We were totally obsessed with finding the right one. We looked at American Plan, housekeeping, campgrounds, general stores. We almost bought a housekeeping place, and now we wonder what we'd do with ourselves. I mean, the cooking is what we spend most of our time on here. We saw an awful lot of camps in every part of the state, but if there's a prettier set of sporting camps and setting, we haven't seen it. Fran's family never did buy a sporting camp, but we did!"

Fran: "When you're a sporting-camp owner, you don't get to be outdoors very often. But you get to be in the woods. I wouldn't do this if I didn't love being here. It's nice to be your own boss and be away from the hustle."

Tim: "With American Plan you have to love cooking, and Fran has always cooked, and cooked really well, since she was a girl. And I have always liked doing breakfast.

"We both like to hike. I've done parts of the AT in New England. Bill Erwin, the blind hiker, came through here several years ago on November 4, and that's really late. Usually once October rolls around, most of the northbound through-hikers—those doing the entire trail in a season—have come by. Bill and his dog, Orient, called themselves the Orient Express. That dog was very special. He was good to Aimey, who was just a year old at the time, just good with all people. The minute Bill got out of a chair, the dog would be right up beside him. He was a long-haired German shepherd, very smart, very surefooted. He went right across our bridge down there that has 2-inch spaces between the slats with no problem at all. Every other dog that goes across it for the first time has real trouble. When Bill came through, the water was up unusually high. At East Carry Pond there weren't any bridges and one particular end was all flooded out. Fran and I knew this because we had hiked it just a week or so before. And we were wondering how he was going to do this. Well, you know what the dog did? The dog bush-whacked him around the flooded area and back to the trail. And this was in the dark! But of course that didn't matter to Bill. He ended up coming in at 10 at night. He had climbed Katahdin first and then come back to do the rest of the trail because it would've been too late in the season otherwise."

Fran: "In the winter we live and work in New Hampshire. Aimey and our son, Tucker, spend a lot of time with Tim's mother, and seem to learn a lot from each other. At the beginning and end of the school year, we home-school our youngest." *Tim:* "All our kids know how to identify wildflowers, edible plants, the common birds. Aimey does a loon call so well the loons come to her. And we see a lot of wildlife along the stream, which has lots of pools and wild brook trout. It's general-law fishing until August 15.

"Every year in August we shut down the camps for about a week, except for serving the hiker breakfast, and we spend some of that time up at Mayor's Island, in the middle of Pierce Pond, camping with the kids. And because we're closed and the Cobbs are closed, we hardly see anybody up there, except all sorts of wildlife. We've seen a couple of golden eagles, and there are very few in Maine. I've counted 28 adult loons as we went up the pond."

Eggs Benedict Arnold

Tim: "This whole area is historically called the 'Carrying Place' because, during the Revolutionary War, Benedict Arnold took his men past the height-of-land here on to Quebec. They came up the Kennebec River, took a left turn onto Carrying Place Stream, and another left after Stoney Brook. They had boats, bateaux made of green wood and the wettest fall ever. The bateaux were a mistake—a spy had misled them—and they had to lug these heavy boats all the way from the ocean, upriver, through really rugged terrain. When they got to Middle Carry they drank some bad water and recuperated near here."

Prepare enough of the following ingredients to feed people on hand: Fry bacon and crumble. Cook spears of asparagus until tender. Make up a hollandaise sauce and keep warm. For each person, take a big, oversized English muffin and toast each half. Poach two eggs in simmering, salted water in a big fry or saucepan, and place on muffins. Top with asparagus, then bacon (you can also add ham then bacon), then the sauce over that. Sometimes I put in little chunks of tomato. Et voilà!

27. KING AND BARTLETT

AP, SCA
OWNERS: Fred and Matt Thurston
MANAGERS: Cathy and Jeff Charles
ADDRESS: PO Box 4, Eustis, ME 04936; 207-243-2956
SEASON: Mid-May through November
ACCOMMODATIONS: Eleven log guest cabins: indoor plumbing and shower, porch, gas heat, electric lights; well-attended pets welcome
RATES: $180 per person per day; $945 per person for 6 nights; boats included
ACCESS: Take I-95 to Portland, then I-495 to Auburn. Get onto ME 4 and follow it through Farmington to ME 27. Take ME 27 to Eustis. Go 3.5 miles north of Eustis. Turn right at camp sign (on the right) and follow signs 5 miles to the camp gate. (Gate closes at 5 PM.) Continue 7 miles to camp.

King and Bartlett's log cabins, stained a dark brown, are ranged around a circular drive. One cabin serves as a recreation and conference room. The main lodge is nestled by the water's edge. An old brass bell sits center stage, and there's an open grassy area that was once used as a helicopter landing spot.

Jeff: "Prior to 1991, the camps were in and out of private hands. At one point it was owned by the IT&T telephone company as their private getaway. We have a building that was once a registered post office, which we use as a conference room now. This originally was a logging camp started by Maine's first governor, William King (from Kingfield). It was his wood's boss, Bartlett, that the camps are named after.

"We're located on King and Bartlett Lake, which is 160 feet deep at its maximum depth. It contains native brook trout, lake trout (togue), and salmon. Although most of the streams and ponds are fly-fishing only, Big and Little King fall under general law and can be trolled or fished with lures. We have 14 lakes and ponds, fish 4 streams, and hunt over 36,000 acres of territory (nearly all of which is leased exclusively by King and Bartlett from International Paper Company) and we own 40 acres right around the camp. The variety of hunting and fishing opportunities around here is incredible. During the season we employ over fifteen guides." *Cathy:* "One of the things we're most proud of is that's we're an Orvis-endorsed lodge. In 2000, King and Bartlett was chosen runner-up as lodge of the year. All our guests are encouraged to practice catch-and-release.

"Jeff started here in 1996, working as head guide, and I joined him in 2001 when we became the managers. We ran a sporting camp on Sebec Lake, and when the opportunity arose to become managers here I left a 19-year teaching career to join him. For me, one of the highlights was meeting so many of the people with whom Jeff had already made a connection. Another was a weekend we had with 'Casting for Recovery.' It's a national organization that works with women who are recovering from breast cancer. For us, that was a really powerful weekend and a great time. We also host several corporate retreats throughout the year, so we have a chance to meet not only individuals, but groups of people. Each group has a different flavor. One might be here to strictly work, and the next to just fish or relax.

"Probably one of our biggest seasons after fishing is a wing shoot, the month of October, when we hunt grouse and woodcock. Last year we also hosted, for the third year, the *Shooting Sportsmen* magazine's 'Readers' Shoot.' They actually advertise in their magazine for some of their readers to come and participate with some of the editors. People came from all over the country to experience Maine grouse hunting.

"We do several moose hunts each year, usually the second week in October. Jeff, in '99, had a 'Boone and Crockett' record moose. November deer hunting is our final hoorah. What's fun for us is that the seasons change; it's what makes life interesting. A lot of work goes into preparing for the arrival of the deer hunters." *Jeff:* "We start working on our deer hunt in August, three months prior to the hunt. We set up new stands, take down old, unproductive stands. Some people want to sit in a stand, or some type of camouflaged area, and have the deer come to them. Other people like to go out and find the deer. We have a lot of people who hunt these stands early morning and late afternoon, when the deer are moving, and then will walk around on their own during the day. One of the other things I have to say about the hunting end of it is that we can offer, say a party of two hunting together, 5,000 acres by themselves. They won't see other

King and Bartlett

hunters. It's not necessarily that people come here to shoot a deer, they come here because, number one, it's a vacation for them; number two, they're from southern areas and there are too many hunters down there. So they come for those 5,000 acres to themselves."

Cathy: "At the end of November, we take what we think is a much-deserved rest. We go to Golfito, Costa Rica, where King and Bartlett's sister operation, King and Bartlett Sport Fishing International, is located. We have two sport fishing boats for charter (one 55', the other 36'), and there's a dining and lodging facility.

"What makes or breaks the pleasure of working here, and affects the pleasure of the guests, is how well the staff works together. We're very, very fortunate here. We have an exceptional cook, Donna Beloin. This is her third season, and she takes care of all the ordering as well as preparation, so that Jeff and I are free to do the other things that come up during the day. A married couple works for us: Janet Longley is our gatekeeper and Dan Longley is our handyman. They are the kinds of employees any employer would dream of having. They see what needs to be done and do it without having to be asked. The guests really are comfortable here because they know we're all happy being here.

Molasses Cookies

2½ cups oil, 4 cups sugar, 1 cup molasses, 4 eggs, 8 cups flour, 6 tsp. baking soda, 6 tsp. cinnamon, 4 tsp. ground ginger, 2 tsp. ground cloves, 2 tsp. salt

Combine ingredients and drop by tablespoon on ungreased cookie sheet. Flatten slightly and sprinkle with additional sugar. Bake at 350 degrees for 10 minutes.

28. LAKE PARLIN RESORT

HK/AP
OWNER: Jay Schurman
ADDRESS: HC 64, Box 564, Lake Parlin, ME 04945; 1-800-864-2676;
fax: 207-668-7627; e-mail: info@unicornraft.com
SEASON: Year-round
ACCOMMODATIONS: Nine log cabins: one to two bedrooms, indoor plumbing and shower, automatic heat, woodstove, electric light; well-behaved pets allowed
RATES: $35 per person per day; $85–175 per cabin per day; 4-day family package $769; boats included; snowmobiles $150 per day
ACCESS: I-95 to exit 36. Take US 201 north for 75 miles (14 miles north of West Forks). Camps are on the right side of the road.

Lake Parlin Resort has a set of classic log cabins, modernized with electricity nestled a few feet from 2- by ½-mile Parlin Lake (or Parlin Pond as it is often referred to locally). A log main lodge with cathedral ceiling, large windows, a massive fieldstone fireplace, wide-screen TV, and bar and restaurant looks out on the lake and Parlin Mountain beyond, and sits a driveway-length from a paved road.

Jay: "In 1997 we opened the place up to snowmobiling, and it was a huge success. So we're winterizing more cabins and upgrading our grooming. We groom 30 miles connecting to ITS 86, 87, and 89. Snowmobiling is as popular as rafting. We thought people would come here as a destination spot and travel from here. But now that I'm in snowmobiling, I think about 30 to 40 percent of the business is in meals, because people ride someplace to eat, so we're open to the public for food. Snowmobilers around here travel for lunch to Eustis, Rangeley, Greenville, Jackman, Pittston Farms. Pittston Farms serves around 3,000 people on the weekend during winter. Snowmobilers stay longer than the rafting clientele. They're more like the families that come in the summer. They stay for a weekend, or even for four days, and they come with five sleds and a $30,000 car and trailer. A failed ski resort, which you can see from here, has been converted to a major snowmobile route, ITS 89. It goes to the top of Coburn Mountain, 3,800 feet. And from the top you can see for hundreds of miles:

all the way to Katahdin and Baxter State Park. People fly in to stay here from as far away as the West Coast and the Southwest to see and ride that trail. And of course we get our regulars from New England, New York, and New Jersey. Snowmobilers are some of the easiest folks to deal with—they're friendly and nothing bothers them.

"We run our rafting out of a base camp across the street. We raft the Kennebec, New England's most popular rafting river, and The Dead. Our four-day family vacation package includes rafting, lodging, some meals, hiking trips. It's really popular and people get to see a lot of the area that way.

"The lake is deep—180 feet at its deepest—so it has trout and salmon. But it got overfished in the 1950s, so now it's fly-fishing-only and we encourage catch-and-release. We have sailboats and paddleboats for people, along with boats and canoes.

"I have four sons and live down in Brunswick for the school there, but come up here as often as I can. I grew up in Washington, D.C., and used to come up to Sunset Camps in the summers. I always loved sporting camps. We used to have family reunions there, 50 of us or so getting together every few years. Then, when I was in college, I answered a want ad for rafting guides. That was in 1976. I started Unicorn Expeditions in 1979, my senior year in college. I named it Unicorn because I thought it would be easy to remember and it had a good connotation. By 1986 business was so good that I was short of lodging, and I bought this place.

"This has been a sporting camp since 1947. There used to be an old hotel here, the Lake Parlin House. It was four stories with 90 rooms—huge—but it burned down and the owners didn't have insurance. The place did really well until the Depression, like most things. In the 1970s a group of nine families bought it. I got it and built this main lodge in 1993 and have been building and upgrading ever since. This is much harder as a business than rafting, a lot more work-intensive. But it's steadier work in ways. For rafting, you go from three employees to a hundred and then back to three again and it's hard to keep training new people every year. With the camps and the snowmobiling, you have year-round work. Families and snowmobiling are our fastest-growing business."

29. THE LAST RESORT

HK/AP (NOV)
OWNERS: Tim and Ellen Casey
ADDRESS: PO Box 777, Jackman, ME 04945; 207-668-5091; e-mail: caseys@lastresortmaine.com; www.lastresortmaine.com
SEASON: Early May through late November
ACCOMMODATIONS: Eight log cabins: outhouse, screened porch, gas lights, evening electricity, central shower house, wood or gas heat; dogs not allowed during July and August

RATES: July and August, $295–$425 per cabin per week, otherwise, $20 per adult per night HK.

ACCESS: I-95 to exit 36. Follow US 201 north through Jackman. Turn right at Border Trust Bank/Heald Stream Road, pass cemetery on left and turn right onto Hastings Road. Drive past the dump and follow signs 6 miles on a dirt road to the camp gate.

The camp's main lodge sits at the base of a "bowl" with cabins, a garden, and outbuildings encircling it, with a long body of water beyond.

Ellen: "How did you like the drive in? When we first got here, our road was really bad. I mean, we're talking big boulders, huge puddles that you'd have to tell people, 'Don't worry, you're not going to disappear!' We worked on that road in our spare time. I remember making a contraption with an old bedspring, weighing it down, so when you drag it the gravel gets turned up and hopefully it will get dragged into some of the holes. Then our neighbor had a York rake with big tines and so we pulled that behind our truck once a week. The better you make the road, the more people use it, and the more people use it, the more they make the holes! You've got people who fuss, 'Boy, that's some road you got there!' But then you have little old ladies who come out joyriding, so you think, well, it can't be all that bad. So I put some signs in the shape of a fish up along the way for encouragement.

"When we first came here we wanted a place as far out in never-never land as possible, because I've always loved animals and being out in the woods. We didn't name it the Last Resort, but the funny thing is we own some land in Massachusetts and I had called it the Last Resort. So it was right. We came over to see the place the day after Christmas in '86. I'd never been on a snowmobile before, and the realtor met us halfway down the lake. I got on the back of his snowmobile and away we came. Soon he gets off and says, 'You want to stop here a minute?' and I say, 'No! Keep going!' because I was afraid we'd fall in! There was about 3 feet of snow on the ground, and there were some bunnies around the camp from the previous owner. So we fed them and I videotaped the place. I had graduated as an elementary school teacher, our youngest had just graduated from high school, and Tim had just finished as a director at a computer company, so it seemed like the perfect time to do something else. That night we thought it over and said, well, we've gotta try it because we'll be kicking ourselves if we don't. And if we leave after 2 years, at least we know we've tried. So we bought it."

Tim: "This was originally called Hughey Mountain Camps in 1902 after Harry and Inza Hughey. He was a very famous guide in this area and they ran the camps until the mid-1950s. They went into a nursing home in town and even into his 90s, Harry would bird hunt. They were both 93 when they died. Inza died and Harry died the next day . . ."

Ellen: "We were very lonely our first year and actually put the place up for sale because it was getting to be a very expensive 'vacation.' But then business picked up and we took it off the market. Our niche is moose-watching. In mid-June every year I try to count the maximum number of moose I see at one exact moment. The most I counted was 18. They come to the mouth of the river because all the silt builds up there, and once the pond weeds start growing they just go out there and graze. During the summer they may be out there all day long and you can go out in a canoe or boat and just mingle with the moose. They go back in the woods in the fall. Often in the summer, if you're on your porch, you can hear them out there sloshing around in the closer coves. In the spring they're all over like crazy, eating the young buds off the trees. They won't bite the branches, they'll just 'lip' all the leaves off. Moose are good swimmers. They can swim up to 6 miles an hour for up to 2 hours at a time. And they can run at speeds of up to 35 miles an hour through the woods. In the fall, the males are out looking for mates. Gestation is about 8 months and the babies are light chocolate brown. The mother usually doesn't bring them out to the lake until the leaves have come out."

Tim: "We're on Long Pond here. It's 12 miles long and connects, by Moose River, to Big Wood and Brassua Lakes. The fishery is salmon, brook trout, perch, and chub. Even in the summer it's great fishing for the kids 'cause the chub keep them busy. We also have a little frog pond for them." *Ellen:* "You never get bored out there, that's for sure. I know logs used to come down Moose River because you can still see the boom piles. And the big white rock over there used to be called Eel Rock, because people used to catch eels and then smoke them. The eels can go from salt to fresh water, and they used to migrate up here to do their spawning. They don't come up here anymore because of the dams at Brassua Lake, the Kennebec River, and then Wyman Dam." *Tim:* "All these lakes connect, with some short portages. Several years ago, some guy kayaked all the way from Attean Lake to the sea.

"When Jackman was in its heyday, families would take the whole summer off and come in here by boat or carriage trail. Then in 1958 there was a big forest fire that started at the dump and came this way. I guess everyone in camp at the time headed out in the lake in boats. At the last minute the fire turned and went up away from the lake. But the original lodge burned down, and then they built this lodge. There have been two or three owners since then, but the place is still basically the same. We bought it in 1987 and have been loving it ever since."

Ellen: "Sometimes we've lived in the area year-round, or we go wherever there's work. But we love getting back in here. We love the wildlife: moose, deer, hummingbirds, eagles, osprey, loons . . ." *Tim:* "You can feed the rabbits by hand. And we have a lot of nature trails. Ellen and friends, like Pat Russell, are compulsive trail makers. They follow the old tote roads and game trails." *Ellen:* "We have a dry-erase board in the lodge. Each cabin is listed and people write down the wildlife they've seen during their time here. Sometimes it gets to be quite the competition." *Tim:* "One time we had a group of ornithologists and it went crazy that week! Then there's the other side where we get listings like 'something under the porch . . .' Our pets are gone now and buried in the cemetery up on the hill, but they've been replaced by all the wild critters. 'Wildness' is something that is becoming very rare and it is not something that someone can experience and fully appreciate second-hand. You need to spend some real time in nature to feel its beauty." *Ellen:* "We love it in here. It's calm, and peaceful, and quiet."

30. LONG POND CAMPS

HK /AP

OWNERS: Debbie and Randy Petrin

ADDRESS: PO Box 815, ME. 15, Jackman, ME 04945; 207-668-4872; e-mail: longpond@wtvl.net; www.connectmaine.com/longpond

ACCOMMODATIONS: Five cabins, indoor plumbing with shower or bath, electric light, monitor heat, gas grills, satellite TV; pets allowed

RATES: $20 per person per night (HK); child rates. Hunting packages (AP).

ACCESS: I-95 to exit 36 (Fairfield). Take US 201 north (approximately 2 hours) toward Jackman. Just before the center of town, take a right onto Long Pond Road and go 5 miles to camps on the left.

Long Pond Camps are in a small subdivision set well back from the road. Although there are neighbors on one side and train tracks on another, the camps look out on Long Pond and have some sense of privacy. The cabins are post and beam construction.

Debbie: "I've lived in Jackman most of my life, and I met my husband here when we were kids. This property, which we acquired in 1990, was owned by his father. Randy had become a Master Guide, he started building the cabins, and we just took off from there. We did a sporting camp because it fit the area. If you go too fancy around here, it's too much. So we basically just did the pine wood in the camps, with handmade cedar railings. We have a duplex cabin that we can open up for large parties. People from the city love it; they don't get this type of atmosphere even in town where it's a lot more crowded, the cabins a lot closer. We're 5 miles from Jackman and about 20 minutes from Rockwood. We're on five acres of land. In the cabins it's housekeeping, in the lodge meals are provided. The lodge has large rooms and living quarters and then a community and game room, laundry facilities, and kitchen. And it's handicapped accessible.

"We have a train that comes by, maybe once or twice a day, going either to Canada or toward Greenville and Rockwood. Most people like to sit there and watch it 'cause it's usually loaded with something that has to do with northern Maine, like logs, milled wood. In the summer there's full loads of army equipment—tanks and stuff—(they must be training some-where). Occasionally there are historic train rides from Jackman to Greenville. I took the tour two years ago during fall foliage. It went to the Moosehead–Greenville area and the train turned around and came back to Jackman. When we came by here, my kids stood up behind the garage on the big ledges and they all waved to me. I found out from that that I can't ride in trains 'cause I was sick as a dog, but it was fun.

"We're on Long Pond, which is about five miles long and very shal-low and narrow. We have a private boat launch, the only one on the pond, and across from us is a beautiful beach—Whipple Farm Beach. We have 14-foot aluminum boats and canoes that we let people use or rent, depending upon the status of their stay. We have paddleboats. It's a smaller lake, so you can't have really bigger boats. There's a variety of different species in the pond: brook trout, salmon, splake, perch, sunfish—giant frogs (my kids love to catch the frogs).

"For winter, we have ice fishing, cross-country skiing, a downhill ski resort forty-five minutes from here [Sqauw Mountain, in Greenville] and some of the best snowmobiling in the nation. Randy is a professional snow-mobile racer, and he has a couple of trails that he grooms to hook up to the ITS trails. He has a couple of racetracks in the field. A lot of our guests stick their kids over there if they're not feeling up to riding and the kids ride around on the racetrack and have fun. It's something a little different. My two boys, 8 and 4 years old, do it, too; they're all into racing.

"With hunting, Rick's father is also a Master Guide, and we have guides we can use from town if we need to. We book small parties; we do not overbook and leave people out in the woods for long periods of time. We do a maximum of 10 to 12 people a week so we can take care of them.

"We offer our spring and summer guests half-day canoe trips, from the Moose River under the bridge in Jackman down to here. And we'll do hik-ing trips (and actually snowmobile trips, too) up to the top of Bald Mountain, where you can see for hundreds of miles, including views of Katahdin and Canada, and there's a place where you can have picnics, bar-becues. The State of Maine is very open and accessible to mountain biking; the logging companies allow people on their roads, with certain conditions regarding four-wheelers. We have access to hundreds and hundreds of miles of biking trails (and snowmobile trails) and the paper companies are great about letting people use them, as long as they're not misused."

31. RED BUCK CAMPS

HK

OWNERS: Sandy and Tom Doughty

ADDRESS: PO Box 114, Jackman, ME 04945; 207-668-5361; www.red-buckcamps.com

SEASON: Year-round

ACCOMMODATIONS: Ten log or stick-built cabins: one or two bedrooms, indoor plumbing and shower, electric light, automatic heat, TV, some with screened-in porch; pets allowed

RATES: $18–30 per person per day; group rate $15–20 per person per day (7 or more); $170–315 per person per week

ACCESS: I-95 to exit 36 (Fairfield). Take US 201 north. Red Buck is 13 miles north of The Forks (12 miles south of Jackman) on the right side (east) of US 201.

Red Buck has basic amenities and is located right off US 201 within relatively easy access to Lake Parlin. The camp is perched on top of Parlin Mountain at 1,650 feet above sea level and receives snow earlier and longer than surrounding areas.

Tom: "It's usually about 10 degrees colder here than in Jackman [7 miles away], so we have great snowmobiling because of our elevation. We're near three ITS trails—86, 87, and 89, which are right across the street from us—and we groom our own connector trails. In fact, we've got people who've rented nine of our cabins for the whole winter, three months, so they can come up here to snowmobile. Another cabin we've got rented for an entire year. We've got a restaurant open December through March and somebody put us on the Internet as having the best burgers in Maine. We also have a store open year-round for groceries, fishing and hunting gear, and sell oil and gas from our 1,000-gallon tank. Besides the ITS, there are over a thousand miles of unplowed logging roads. Snowmobiling is a big thing around this area. We're so close to the Canadian border our trail systems connect in with the trans-Québec trail.

"And we're putting in ATV trails so you can go right from your cabin door hundreds of miles. We're offering ATV tours, like to the top of Coburn Mountain, Parlin Falls, Cold Stream Falls. We've put free canoes on 10 remote ponds for fly-fishing and they're all ATV accessible."

Sandy: "We bought this place in 1985, came up from Portland. I was working as a waitress and Tom was with S.D. Warren, a logging company. This was originally a logging camp in the 1920s. Tom got his guide's license and leads hunters."

Tom: "This western mountain region has thousands of acres of softwood forests with hardwood ridges, and logging has left huge areas of blueberries and raspberries. So there's a lot of food for bears. In the '70s, Maine eliminated the spring season for bear hunting, which has meant that the population has doubled to something over 20,000. We hunt from baited tree stands or blinds. We also have really big deer here, a lot over 200 pounds. We kind of cater to bow hunters, and allow hunting dogs in season."

While we talked, a serious game of horseshoes was in progress in the backyard, and I noticed a side table covered with trophies. *Tom:* "We have tournaments in town all the time. We play for fun. Everyone goes individually and you get teamed up with someone by drawing numbers. People come in from all over—downstate, and a lot from Canada. We play from 1 to 7 or so, and players pay 6 dollars. Everyone gets trophies, and then they split the pot up for the winners. It's at Northland, in Jackman, a place with a bar, motel, and in back it's got big horseshoe pits. The whole town plays there. We start in June and play once every month until October. The first week in February, they go and shovel the pits out for a game. It could be 20 below, 30 below . . ."

Sandy: "That's why he's got two trophies over there with a horse's ass. That's what they call the February tournament. They figure that if there's anyone crazy enough to be out there in the freezing cold playing horseshoes, that's what they should get!"

32. SALLY MOUNTAIN CABINS

HK

OWNERS: Corey Hegarty

ADDRESS: 9 Elm Street, Jackman, ME 04945; 207-668-5621 or 1-800-644-5621; www.sallymtcabins.com

SEASON: Year-round

ACCOMMODATIONS: Nine log cabins: 1 to 3 bedrooms (sleep two to ten people) with automatic heat, indoor plumbing and tub with shower; three condo-style modern lodgings; TV/cable

RATES: $24 per person per day; $145 per person per week; child rates available

ACCESS: I-95 to exit 36 (Fairfield). Take US 201 north to Jackman. After the railroad tracks, take the first left onto Spruce Street and follow the signs to camp.

Sally Mountain Cabins feature something I have not seen at any other sporting camp: three-tiered containers (visualize a green-plastic file cabinet), in each cabin, for recycling. Each log cabin has a wooden nameplate over the door with a date, such as SUNSET, 1955. A few of the interiors are painted white. The newest cabin has wood paneling with a spiral wooden staircase leading to a loft. Although the decor is an eclectic mix (as in most camps), the place has a continuity of color (dark stain and with red window frames) and feel.

Corey: "I grew up in Jackman and my parents bought the place in '74. Then it was called Guay's Cabins. My parents changed the name to Sally Mountain Cabins because we're right across from the 2,221-foot mountain. My folks run the Jackman Trading Post now." (The trading post, at the height-of-land as you head down into town, provides a few visual chuckles along with supplies. In fact, what with several other roadside spoofs in the area, you get the impression that there are a number of individuals around here with a good-natured, if not quirky, sense of humor.)

Corey: "I know that the Gilbert and Dreamland cabins and the main lodge were all personal homes. In the very beginning there were two cabins that were dragged from farther down the lake. I'm not sure if it was the Guays, or someone before them, who turned it into a cabin rental. Dreamland was built in 1936. They originally put down a beautiful wood floor and over the years covered it with newspaper and then layers and layers of linoleum. We have some of the old newspaper articles framed in the cabin to show people.

"I had the opportunity to buy this place from my parents in 1991, and I jumped at the offer. It's been great. Jackman's not very big [population around 900] but it has everything: a bank and post office, a medical center, restaurants, churches, and an airport for people who want to come in that way.

"Big Wood Lake is 6½ miles long by 2½ wide and 72 feet deep at its maximum, with salmon, brook and lake trout, splake, smelt, and cusk. In the winter I rent out ice shacks, and have the only live-bait shop in town. I say, 'Our bait is guaranteed to catch fish . . . or die trying!' I get a lot of fishermen. I'm the only one in town that rents motorboats; I also rent kayaks and canoes. Actually, it's about half fishermen and half snowmobilers. Which is good, because if the snowmobiling's bad, the camp still does well. In the fall I get small-game and deer hunters.

"The biggest challenge is having what the customers want. They expect more than people did years ago. Like they'll say, 'Oh, you have coffee pots'—the smallest thing can make a difference. And we really want to please them. They want the rustic atmosphere but with all the supplies, and they love the low rates. It's hard to do both, but in this business I find the repeat customer is what it's all about. On the other hand, we get drive-ins from all over because we're so close to the Canadian border—just 16 miles. I get a lot of people from Europe driving to Québec. There's a lot of history to the old Route 201. Around 1833, Captain James Jackman, for whom the town is named, built the Canada Road from The Forks to the Canadian border, and thereby linked the area up to civilization. We're 100 miles from Québec, a couple of hours. And people from abroad are usually doing New England. They fly into Boston and go to the White Mountains, Vermont, Québec, Niagara Falls. I even had someone from Australia a few years ago. That's what's great about the summertime—the world comes to your door!"

33. SUNRISE RIDGE SPORTING CAMPS

HK

OWNERS: Mike and Kathy Carver

ADDRESS: PO Box 435, Bingham, ME 04920; 207-672-5551; www.sunriseridgeguide.com

SEASON: Year-round

ACCOMMODATIONS: Four log cabins, indoor plumbing and tub with shower, electric lights, gas fireplace and monitor heat, swimming pool and hot tub

RATES: $100 per day per cabin (includes access to pool and hot tub); snow-mobile rentals available

ACCESS: I-95 north to exit 36 (Fairfield). Take US 201 north to Bingham. Pass Williams General Store, go to the top of the hill, and take a right onto Donigan Road to the end; continue on Dead End Street 0.6 mile to the camps.

As you come out on the ridge, the camps' two-story log lodge is on the left. The camps form a little compound in a cleared area beyond and a set of kennels is off to the left.

Mike: "We both grew up in Maine, about an hour and a half to the south. Originally we owned a camp about a mile from here. One spring, I was on a snowmobile, came up through a powerline, saw a FOR SALE sign on a tree, and decided I'd like to have this lot. The sign had been there so long most of the digits were worn off, but I could make out three of them. So I went back to our camp and started making phone calls: 7101 . . . 7102 . . . until I got to 7109 and some old guy answered the phone and knew what the hell I was talking about! Anyway, we ended up buying the lot and started building a big camp. By the time we were done it was bigger than our house and we figured we might as well sell the house and just move up. I owned a construction company too, worked all over the state, so it didn't really matter where I started from in the morning. I have a Master Guide's license and a whitewater guide's license. At the time, I was guiding people too, putting them in another set of camps. That worked out pretty well, except I didn't have all the control I wanted to have. So we built the duplex first, then we finished off over the garage, then built a camp up on the hill, and most recently did another cabin, the 'new camp'—until the next one's built! *Kathy:* "Our duplex we kind of call our 'logdominium.' There's seven twin beds upstairs, a full-sized bed down-stairs. And all the cabins have nice pine tables that Mike has made. They're housekeeping, but during hunting we do feed our hunters right in the lodge."

Mike: "We're in the foothills of the western mountains here, the upper Kennebec River Valley, overlooking Wyman Lake, which is 11 miles long. And we picked this area because it's a true four-season area. Fishing is excellent, both in the lake and below the dam. There's brook and rainbow trout, salmon, and lake and brown trout. It's general law. And there's an up-and-coming bass fishery. Rafting is huge around here in the summertime."

Kathy: "There's great hiking. The Appalachian Trail is 10 miles up the road. We're close to Moxie Falls and Huston Brook Falls, which have nice trails. There's a multipurpose trail from Bingham to North Anson for bikes, four-wheelers, horses, walking." *Mike:* "Then hunting is the main reason we did this: bear, deer, bobcat, snowshoe hare, moose. We have our own pack of hounds, so I not only hunt bear with bait, but with hounds. My hounds are primarily plotts and blueticks (which are an English breed). I also have a couple of treeing walkers up there. There's two types of walker hounds: treeing walkers and running walkers. They're registered as a separate breed. They look like giant beagles. They're tall, 55 pounds probably. Then the plott hounds vary in size. Lucy is my best bobcat dog; she's about 50 pounds. When I bought Lucy I paid $3,500 for her. I've invested over $30,000 in hounds. That's the price if you want to get into the business and be serious about it. Now I do my own breeding and raise my own pups.

"After hunting season we go right into snowmobile season; the two overlap somewhat. There's ice fishing and we rent snowmobiles. We have direct access to the ITS trails. The Valley Riders sponsor the "Wyman Lake 200," a 200-mile snowmobile race. If a family wants to go snowmobiling, I can give them a guided tour. If someone wants to go rabbit hunting for a couple of days we can do that. For snowshoe hare I run beagles. We have beagles out back, too. The hounds I run on bear and bobcats. Hunting with hounds starts the second week in September. Bobcat season is December and January. It's very conditions-oriented; you have to have the right type of snow. Can't have any crust 'cause it will cut the dogs' feet. The perfect storm is about 6 to 12 inches of fresh snow, enough so the cat bellies out— its belly drags in the snow—creating resistance. Basically, you leave by truck or snowmobile, find a bobcat track in the snow, put on your snowshoes, and the dogs trail him and get him 'jumped'—there's fresh scent and the dogs can really move on the track. Well, then the cat starts running. And they don't have the lung capacity a dog has. Plus they're breaking trail. So, in those conditions, you can be very successful. Now, if you have conditions like the snow pack has settled, a bobcat can spread its toes—that's called 'snowshoeing'—and he can walk right across the top where the heavier dog breaks through. Well, then all of a sudden, the conditions favor the bobcat. And then you have to have a bit of luck to be successful. Generally I book up to two people for a bobcat hunt and you hunt as a team. Lots of times you'll catch a cat in a particular piece of woods and you can circle that woods 'cause you know he's in there. If you know that there's two or three spots that cats generally cross you can post a guy at these spots. Even if the conditions aren't great and the cat's ten minutes ahead of the dogs, if he crosses one of those spots there's a chance of getting him, generally using a shotgun. Paper companies have gotten a lot of bad press over clear-cuts in pine plantations. Well, if you spend any time at all out in the woods you realize there's never been as many rabbits and snowshoe hares in the history of Maine as there are right now. And that's the primary food for bobcats. So the consequence is that the bobcat population has exploded. Makes for great hunting.

"As far as the dogs go, 1 in 100 puppies makes a fine bear dog and it's 1 in 100 bear dogs makes a fine cat dog. They have to be very smart. A good dog will run a cat track by sight. I mean, you can take Lucy and put her on a two-day-old track and she'll run that right through deer yards, moose yards, and stay right on that track until she gets some scent. I've put her on tracks she never did jump, picked her up eight hours later, and she's still on that track, still cold trailing. To be very successful you want to go every day because then you know what tracks are fresh. Plus you want to know where the cats are crossing. They're pretty much creatures of habit. An adult female bobcat will run 18–22 pounds, a male will run 20–40 pounds. And they'll have between one and three kittens in a litter. The males roam. The breeding season is around March. Although snowshoe are their primary food source, they can certainly take down and kill a deer. One of the problems with the cats is the mortality of the kittens from starvation is high. In their first winter they're not very good at hunting, and if something happens to the mother and they don't have good weather conditions, they'll literally starve to death. Nature's cruel at times."

Kathy: "The hunting season I think is my favorite time because you just meet so many interesting people." *Mike:* "You see them for a week and you really get to get inside their heads. I've had diesel mechanics from Pennsylvania and a guy that owns a law firm in Beverly Hills. And everything in-between." *Kathy:* "They're just the best, really appreciate everything you do."

Grouse Appetizer

Kathy: "These are like chicken nuggets only better."

> 2–4 grouse breasts, 1 cup flour, 1 tsp. garlic powder, ½ tsp. celery salt, ½ tsp. black pepper, 1 stick butter

Cut the grouse breasts into bite-sized pieces. Mix the remaing ingredients, then put in a Ziplock bag with the cubed grouse and shake. Melt the butter in a cast-iron skillet. Sauté the grouse in the hot skillet until crispy. Serve on a plate with toothpicks.

34. TUCKAWAY SHORES

HK
OWNERS: Phil and Paulette Thomas
ADDRESS: HCR 64, Box 44, Jackman, ME 04945; 207-668-3351;
www.connectmaine. com/tuckaway
SEASON: Year-round

Sunrise Ridge Sporting Camps

ACCOMMODATIONS: Seven cabins: one to three bedrooms, indoor plumbing and shower (one with tub), automatic heat, electric light, porch, cable TV; well-attended pets

RATES: $30 per person per day, $180 per person per week; child rates available

ACCESS: I-95 to exit 36 (Fairfield). Take US 201 north to Jackman. After the railroad tracks, turn left onto Spruce Street and right at Forest Street to the end.

Tuckaway Shores, Cozy Cove Cabins, and Sally Mountain Cabins are all ranged along the shore of Big Wood Lake and within walking distance of one another and Jackman's Main Street. Of the three, Tuckaway Shores is the most basic camp in terms of its facilities and cabins. The cabins and log main lodge facing the street are stained dark brown with red window frames. The Thomases live in a tan frame house they built.

Paulette: "The place started in the '20s, and we were the third owners when we purchased it in 1987. We moved here from New Hampshire. I'm a naturopathic physician and an R.N. and a P.A. There aren't that many holistic practitioners, but it's becoming more popular. I have a small client base around here."

Phil: "What intrigued us about the area was that Big Wood Lake is the third lake in a chain of six and Moose River runs through it and goes down to Moosehead Lake. It was the water, basically, that got to us. We like to fish catch-and-release ourselves, and we just enjoy boating around, looking at the mountains. These are the boundary mountains between the States and Canada."

Our side of the lake is settled and the rest is basically pristine.

"Snowmobiling and ice fishing is our busiest season. Jackman itself has over 200 miles of trails with three groomers going 24 hours a day, flattening and widening trails. If we have a group or a prior reservation, I will cook for people. I have a culinary degree and do consulting for some places around here. I was planning on getting into art. The fine-arts classes were full, but the culinary-arts classes were open, so I got that degree instead. I have my doctorate in parapsychic sciences, the study of the unknown: apparitions, magnetic fields, past-life memories. I've always been fascinated with ghost stories, miracles. It's amazing how many people have experienced a psychic phenomenon they can't explain. When we first came in and looked at this place, we just sat for a couple of hours looking out at the lake. There's good energy in this area."

Part Two

CENTRAL MAINE

This section is bounded by US 201 to the west, ME 6/16 in the south, I-95 and ME 11 to the east, and the Canadian boundary in the north. The major areas include the Moosehead Lake region, the Baxter State Park region, and the North Maine Woods. Most of the land in this region is privately owned by pulp and paper companies but is accessible to the public. Moose outnumber people in some areas. Logging roads outnumber paved. Be prepared to answer questions about your travel plans and pay tolls at the various gatehouses within this vast area. For further information, write North Maine Woods, PO Box 421, Ashland, ME 04732. Camps will send driving directions, but many owners in this region strongly suggest flying into their camps by float plane. If you drive, be aware that you need to leave ample time for the slower rate of travel, and don't expect to run into any gas stations once you're on logging roads. The driving times noted in the various regions are averages only, since some camps are farther off in the "willy wack" than others and some have rougher access roads than others.

THE MOOSEHEAD LAKE REGION

The Moosehead Lake region, although in the "southern" portion of this central section, is nearly level with the most northern area of our previous section. The camps here are in the general vicinity of 40-mile-long, up-to-20-mile-wide Moosehead Lake, the largest lake in the Northeast. The Golden Road (so named because of the expense involved in hacking out every mile of this dirt throughway for pulp trucks) forms the region's northern boundary. Another logging road, Church Pond Road, forms its eastern boundary.

Moosehead Lake drains an area of about 1,226 square miles and serves as the headwaters of the Kennebec River. Nearby are an additional 175,000 acres of water in lakes, ponds, streams, and rivers, including the Moose River and the headwaters of the Penobscot River. The town of Greenville, at the base of the lake, is the unofficial capital of the region, and can meet most provisioning, medical, and banking needs. From here, outfitters offer spring and summer whitewater rafting, and the 110-foot steamboat *Katahdin*—a last remnant of an earlier form of transportation—plies Moosehead's waters. Greenville is also home to the largest seaplane base in New England and hosts an international seaplane fly-in each fall. In the winter, a 100-plus-mile snowmobile trail encircles the lake and there is ice fishing and skiing at 3,196-foot Squaw Mountain.

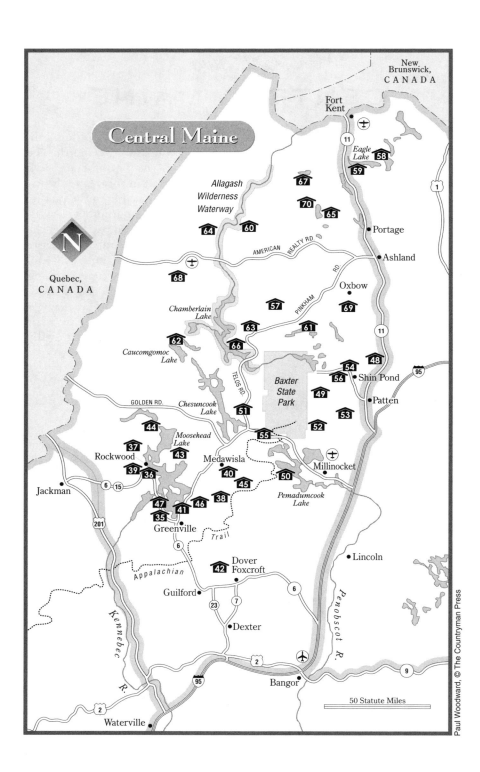

Central Maine

The Appalachian Trail winds its way through this area. Among many other hiking destinations, Gulf Hagas, nicknamed the Grand Canyon of Maine, is a 4-mile-long gorge along the west branch of the Pleasant River, with 400-foot vertical slate walls and numerous waterfalls. Moose are plentiful in this region; the area sponsors the annual Moosemainea, a monthlong series of events during the spring.

GETTING THERE: Bangor International Airport is the nearest airport (with rental cars available). Driving time from Portland is 3–4 hours; from Boston, 6–7 hours; from New York City, 9–11 hours. Float-plane services are available in Greenville: Folsom's Air Service, 207-695-2821 (Folsom's also serves as the phone link to some of the camps listed here); Currier's Flying Service, 207-695-2778; Jack's Air Service, 207-695-3020.

GUIDANCE: For a visitor's guide or a listing of summer events, contact the Moosehead Lake Chamber of Commerce, PO Box 581, Greenville, ME 04441; 207-695-2702 or 207-695-2026; fax: 207-695-3440; e-mail: moose@moosehead.net; web site: www.moosehead.net/moose/chamber.html

35. BEAVER COVE CAMPS

HK

OWNERS: Marilyn and Dave Goodwin

ADDRESS: PO Box 1233, 648 Black Point Road, Greenville, ME 04441-1233; 207-695-3717 or 1-800-577-3717; e-mail: info@beavercovecamps.com; www.beavercovecamps.com

SEASON: Year-round

ACCOMMODATIONS: Six log cabins: one to two bedrooms, indoor plumbing and shower, propane heaters and stoves, electricity, outdoor fireplace (wood for sale), picnic table; linens provided; pets allowed (fee)

RATES: $75 per day (double occupancy); child rates available

ACCESS: I-95 north to exit 39 (Newport). Go north on ME 7 to Dexter, ME 23 to Guilford, and ME 6/15 to Greenville. In Greenville, continue straight, through the flashing yellow light, on Lily Bay Road. Go 6 ½ miles to Black Point Road (big camp sign on the left, ½ mile past marina). Turn left and stay on Black Point Road for 1 ½ miles to camp. (You will veer left at two intersections.) Camp driveway is on the left.

The camps are on a side road with private summer cottages and adjacent to the former camp lodge (now privately owned). The cabins are basic, one built in 1904 another in 1905, and use the traditional French-Canadian vertical log construction; one cabin was originally a logging camp office. Situated on the east side of Moosehead Lake, the cabins look out over 2-to-3-mile-long Beaver Cove to Burnt Jacket and Squaw, now Moose, mountains.

Dave: "We took the place in December 2000. We'd been up here two years before and loved the area. Marilyn's originally from Minnesota, and her family was into hunting and fishing. I'm originally from Wisconsin. And we both wanted to get back into the country. We didn't find anything in the Midwest like the sporting camps here. We already had our eye on this place when we found your book, and it gave us a really good idea what it took to run a sporting camp. Instead of turning us off, it really made us feel much better about going ahead with this because we were going in with our eyes open." *Marilyn*: "Although, we were five months into my pregnancy, and wondered, do we go in the middle of nowhere, leaving doctors behind? But I said, 'Let's do it.' I didn't meet the doctor 'til we moved here. I called and she was willing to take a patient on that late in the pregnancy. No problem. The doctor's wonderful and the hospital, Mayo Regional in Dover-Foxcroft, about a 45-minute drive, was great. Our steepest learning curve was figuring out what the place had to offer for our guests: how thick the ice was, where the best fishing was, the nature of the ski and snowmobile trails, the distance to some point—luckily we knew all the restaurants because we'd tried them all). And for us, it also was things like where to make photocopies (the hardware store or the pharmacy, turns out)."

Dave: "This place, actually the whole shoreline up to Black Point, was leased from the paper company and run like a health resort." *Marilyn:* "This was in the early 1900s." *Dave:* "In order to get in here you had to go by steamboat from Greenville. Not until the 1970s did it become private land. The previous owner put a few cabins up on concrete posts and leveled them, and we re-did two of them last year. Fortunately, my dad taught me carpentry, plumbing, wiring because now this is part of my job." *Marilyn:* "We've had pipes freeze. You think you've drained them and come to find out there's a hole in the pipe. So you have to fix it. This year, he's taught me how to shut them down. Being that I'm not, well, 'plumbing inclined' it's taken me a while to figure it out." *Dave:* "Not only shut them down, but also start them up in case she gets a reservation on short notice and I'm not here. We also have a backup generator and have gotten proficient in starting that up." *Marilyn:* "We haven't had to use it all that often. There was a fire in town, then our neighbor hit a telephone pole; the longest we had to use it was for 19 hours just before J.D., the baby, was born." *Dave:* "Beaver Cove is powered from the one line out of Greenville. If there's any problem our power goes off. We've learned to call the power company immediately because we're not sure anyone else is going to tell them. There's very few people around, especially in the winter. (The ITS system is only a mile and a half from here, though)."

Marilyn: "We're off the main road so you don't hear the logging trucks, and away from town so it's quiet." *Dave:* "Actually, you can hear the train from the other side of the lake go by in the middle of the night." *Marilyn:* "When we first moved in, I was up with the baby, like 2:00 in the morning, and heard this noise. I went door to door looking for a vehicle 'cause it sounded like one was coming down the driveway. We finally got talking with the previous owner and he said, 'Oh, that's the train.' *Dave:* "Said it took them a while to figure it out, too. We liked that this was a safe environment for the kids, but one of our concerns was how would it be for them if they made friends with someone for a week and they then went away. But we're finding that with repeat business they will be able to see their friends. Plus our daughter, Kianna, is in daycare in Greenville and has a lot of friends now."

Marilyn: "We're close enough to town for people to go in for meals. And yet cooking here is different than if you're at your own home. There are no microwaves, and no TVs, clocks, or radios. People don't seem to mind. We see them relaxing on the dock, or in their cabins, watching the sunset. We rent canoes and have canoes on some remote ponds. The marina next door rents kayaks and boats. For fishing, we have the brook trout and the lake togues, there's salmon, and cusk. Brookies, from my understanding, aren't usually more than 14 inches; togue can get up to, from what we've seen, 29 inches; and then cusk, which is usually something that ice fishermen fish for, mostly at night, have ranged from 20 inches to about 3 feet. They're not a pretty fish—not something you ooh and ah over when they come up out of the hole, but people tell us they make an excellent fish chowder." *Dave:* "It's got the name of 'poor man's lobster.'"

"People find it real easy to talk with Marilyn and end up unloading all sorts of stuff. She's almost like a therapist." *Marilyn:* "I don't offer too much advice. You just sit there and listen 'cause you know it's what they need. Originally I taught high school business courses (which comes in handy now). My master's was in educational technology. My goal was to teach in Texas for five years (which I did) and move up the West Coast, teaching in different states, eventually landing up in Alaska. But instead of going west, I went east." *Dave:* "And I was vice president of research and development for a high-tech company in Rochester, New York. Part of living here is that I've gone back to doing software development out of my office upstairs. And I do consulting work. (Having at least two jobs is pretty much the way things work around here anyway.)

"The Internet is a good tool because we do have our web site and get requests from people from all over the world. You're marketing travel destinations basically. That's one of the reasons we liked getting into this business, because we were already prepared to handle web sites. We had a guy in here who wanted to check his e-mail every day. He was the one that gave us the idea to set up a wireless Internet connection." *Marilyn:* "We're not encouraging them to bring work, but if they see a bird or something we can't identify, they can look it up on the web right away." *Dave:* "We may be the only sporting camp with a wireless hookup." *Marilyn:* "Actually, we met on-line in '96, and I believe we're pioneers in Internet marriages. We e-mailed for about nine months, about four months later we were engaged, another six months later we got married, and two years later we moved here! There were about 7,000 members of the dating service when I joined, and less than 200 people had married at that point. It's now becoming much more common." *Dave:* "The Internet has definitely played a major role in our lives."

36. THE BIRCHES RESORT

AP/HK, SCA

OWNER: John Willard

ADDRESS: Box 81-SC, Rockwood, ME 04478; 207-534-7305 or 1-800-825-9453; e-mail: wwld@aol.com; www.birches.com

SEASON: Year-round

ACCOMMODATIONS: Eighteen log cabins: one to four bedrooms, indoor plumbing and shower (central bathhouse in winter), electric and gas lights, woodstove or fireplace; twelve "cabin tents" with outdoor firepits; three yurts; central lodge with TV, bar, and living-room area

RATES: $80–125 per person per day; $525–795 per person per week (AP); $40–115 per cabin per day (HK)

ACCESS: I-95 to exit 39. Go north on ME 7 to Dexter, ME 23 to Guilford, and ME 6/15 to Greenville. Continue on ME 6/15 to Rockwood. After the Village Store, turn right across a bridge and then right again at the camp sign. The Birches driveway is several hundred yards farther on the right.

The Birches Resort is located about halfway up the west side of Moosehead Lake and looks across to Mount Kineo. It has the look of a traditional sporting camp, but at the main lodge, which quietly bustles with staff and activities, it has the feel of a resort. The State of Maine has purchased Mount Kineo and 21 miles of shorefront beyond the mountain, "so," John Willard smiles, "the pristine view you see is what will be there in the years to come.

John: "The Birches was built in the 1930s by a man named Oz Fahey, a logging contractor up in this area. When the Depression came along, the logging industry fell off but he had crews still willing to work, basically for room and board. So he made his house the main lodge, built cabins on either side, and went into the sporting-camp business. Each year he would build another cabin. The last one, as far as we can tell, was built in 1945–1946. We did some new roofing and found boards from shipping crates that said FAHEY, ROCKWOOD, MAINE on them from when they were rationing lumber. He had wealthy guests that would come here for the summer—spin-offs from the Kineo Resort. Some of the guests liked it here so much he would let them design their own cabin.

"Fahey ran the place during the '40s and early '50s. A man named Telford Allen, the president of a cosmetics company, bought it in 1960 and sold in '64. He had a Spanish manager because he lived in Central or South America somewhere. He built a swimming pool, a marina, a new lounge—spent a lot of money and then went broke. So from '64 to '69 the camps were closed. Then my dad was looking around for a place for a kids camp. He was in the construction business and decided he wanted a change. Well, he found The Birches in 1970, and he and I and my brother decided not to open for kids but to try it as a sporting camp.

"The summer of '78 my father had a heart attack. It rained just about every day that summer. Even the customers left early; it was pathetic. There was nothing for him to do really; so he picked names for our cabins from a Henry Mancini album, found pieces of driftwood, dried them out, and painted the names on the driftwood. We've got Ramblin Rose, In the Mood, Days of Wine and Roses, and so on. A lot of people will call back and say, 'I want September in the Rain,' or something. Most of us who've been here a long time will automatically know which number cabin that is.

"I felt there was no way I could make a living here just renting out cabins. So that's how we ended up doing canoe trips and whitewater rafting, which grew into our Wilderness Expeditions outdoor-adventure programs. We now have Moose Cruises twice a day, flat-water and whitewater kayaking, mountain biking, challenge courses, sailing lessons, interpretive hiking, ski trails, and snowmobiling. We're dedicated to offering the largest activity-based resort in the country: 11,000 acres of pristine, private wilderness.

"There's a pattern to our year. March is the end of ice fishing. April we'll do our spring cleaning. First part of May fishing season starts up for lake and brook trout and salmon. Also in May the white-water rafting season comes in. We've got a base camp at The Forks on the Kennebec River and one on the Penobscot near Baxter State Park. People stay at the base camp or we have a shuttle from here. It's about a 50-minute drive.

"The end of school starts our summer season. Summertime we're maxed. Sometimes we'll have a hundred people in the lodge for dinner. People come by boat and we can feed them outside by the dock. We have about 10 full-time staff then. Resort America sends employees to us from foreign countries, college kids. They'll work here for a month and then go back home. We have people here now from Germany, South Africa, England, and Russia. They're here to brush up on their English, get college credits and work experience. In the winter I get kids from Australia and New Zealand 'cause that's their summer. It's fun, a great way to staff the place, and the guests love them.

"In the summer we also have what we call cabin tents. They're sort of between a cabin and camping: four beds in each one, lights, a door, windows. They're cheap to build and great for weekenders. Then I have land over at

Brassua Lake where I keep sea kayaks and canoes. I fly people over in the morning, let them paddle around all day, give them a lunch, and pick them up in the afternoon. They love it—the beaches, driftwood, wildlife—they never see anybody all day. And I do some scenic flights. I've been flying since 1994, and in 2000 got a float plane so people don't have to go all the way down the Greenville. They just step over to the marina.

"September and October is fall foliage. And then hunting is in November. Most of our winter business comes from snowmobilers, cross-country skiers. We have three yurts in the woods people can cross-country ski to. And people can ski back to the main camp to use the hot tub, eat if they want to. I have a fellow out in the woods all summer long just working on trails. We rent skis and snowmobiles and have a separate, 40-kilometer system of trails for skiers. We groom with a 9-foot wide groomer; it's just like a carpet.

"When I first came up here I went to the University of Maine and studied forestry. Then I lived in here in a trailer and one of the smaller cabins two or three winters with no running water and dug holes in the ice just to get my water out. I know what it's like to live hard. Some people come up here and say, 'Geez, you got it made.' And I say, 'Hey, if you stick with the same job for 30 years, you'll have it made, too!' This is the accumulation of a lot of plain old hard work.

"I'm at a crossroads now. I don't want to develop my land or clear-cut, but I have to keep the machine moving. I've put in a 20-lot subdivision near The Birches. I wouldn't have to develop more than 1,000 acres and would try to keep the rest as a park. There's been a big change in land ownership around here in the past year or so. There's huge money out there, private individuals who want to buy 5-, 10-, 20 thousand acres. And they're doing it. Unfortunately some of them are gating their property and putting up NO TRESPASSING signs all over the place. We try to keep land remote, but there are no NO TRESPASSING signs on my land.

"What's exciting is that there's a big movement now to use federal land, water, and conservation money from offshore drilling and leasing to buy development rights on a lot of the land up here. I think they just got $12 million, but they really need about $30 million more to do it right. If they can do that, I think Moosehead will be okay."

Baked Stuffed Onions

4 big sweet onions, peeled, cut in half, ends cut flat to sit up; 4 slices Muenster cheese

Stuffing: 1/3 cup Parmesan cheese, 2 cups bread crumbs, 1 cup chopped mushrooms, 1/2 cup chopped onions, 1/2 cup chopped celery, 1/2 cup melted butter, 1 tsp. chicken base, salt and pepper to taste

A moose-watching expedition at The Birches Resort

Sauté vegetables in butter, chicken base, salt and pepper. Mix with the Parmesan cheese and bread crumbs. Place a handful of the stuffing on each onion half. Cover with Muenster cheese slices. Place in pan, loosely covered. Bake at 375 degrees for 20 minutes.

37. BRASSUA LAKE CAMPS

HK, SCA

OWNERS: Dale and Pat Tibbetts

ADDRESS: PO Box 187, Rockwood, ME 04478-0187; 207-534-7328; www.brassualakecamps.com

SEASON: Year-round

ACCOMMODATIONS: Four smoke-free cabins: one to two bedrooms, indoor plumbing and shower, refrigerator, electric lights; linen supplied; pets allowed (fee)

RATES: $65–105 per cabin per night. Weekly rentals receive one night free. Motorboat, canoe, kayak, and paddleboat rentals.

ACCESS: I-95 to exit 39 (Newport). Take ME 7 north to Dexter, ME 23 to Guilford, and ME 6/15 to Greenville.

Brassua Lake Camps are down a hill and ranged in a cozy, tree-enveloped line beyond the main lodge.

Pat: "When we first bought the camps there was no business here whatsoever. We'd been 15 years trying to find camps that, well basically, suited me. We'd gone down the coast of Maine, Chesuncook, Greenville, you name it. And I didn't want them. Some of them were too remote, some, everytime we'd go back and talk to the people they'd raise the price, or the place just didn't work for me. So we came down here in end of February 1995, I skied in, he snowshoed in, and I took one look at the view across the lake, loved it, and said, 'These are the ones. But before I make any commitment, I want to see inside.'"

Dale: "We have four children and were in the family dairy farming business. Then I went into the logging business, where originally I spent a good deal of the time up in this part of the country. Eventually I started logging closer to home, but we decided we wanted to find a set of sporting camps for our retirement business. I had an airplane and used to fly around whenever I'd have some spare time and we'd look at different places. Just by chance one day, when I was trucking for some other people, I stopped and picked up a *Maine Sportsman*'s magazine, happened to run through the real estate ads, and found these camps." *Pat:* "We were told they've been here since the '40s." *Dale:* "I knew where they were 'cause I'd hauled wood by here for years, even used to sleep in the turnout to the camps in my truck. I thought we could use the airplane in the business; I've had four of them over the years. The funny part of it is, once we got this property, we couldn't afford to keep the plane any longer. It's a nice attraction, but it really isn't a money maker." *Pat:* "We actually had a lot of work to do here on the grounds and cabins. So time-wise, money-wise, we couldn't keep it."

Dale: "Brassua Lake is ¼ mile off the main road. Very quiet, very few people on the lake, although we're only 2 miles from a store. A lot of people come here for that reason." *Pat:* "A lot of people just sit on the dock, look at the scenery, and watch our beautiful sunsets." *Dale:* "The lake is 9 miles long, 4 miles wide, about 65 feet at the deepest—averages about 35–40 feet deep. It's partly man-made with a dam down around the corner. We have native brook trout and salmon that are stocked and a lot of native salmon, too, along with yellow perch and cusk. At the northwest end of the lake you can see Boundary Mountain toward the Canadian border. There's a point that goes into Little Brassua Lake, and there's an island on it called Fossil Island. An Indian tribe used to come here and make arrowheads. There's artifacts to been seen when the tide is low. Nobody knows what tribe or where they came from, but the flint they used came from as far as California." *Pat:* "We're getting a tour boat so we can take people on guided trips around the lake.

"We're open all year round and are the first owners to do that." *Dale:* "It took a lot to make the camps livable during the winter. We had to put in underground water, heating systems, insulation. We have gravity-feed spring water into all of the camps. We're accessible to the snowmobile trail to Rockwood because we put in our own connector. And we have hunters in here. I'm a Master Guide and my specialty is moose hunting. We're in the south-central zone, and can hunt right from the camps. We've had 100 percent success up 'til now. I had one man in here that had very specific requests for his moose hunt: wanted a good-eating cow, didn't want to wake up early, and so forth. We left the camp after a nice breakfast, and 45 minutes later he had his good-eating cow. At the same time, there was another guy in camp that had been trying for two days to get a moose. He was leaving the following day and was desperate to get something. Well, we went out that next morning and 20 minutes later he had his moose. I do deer hunting on demand, but don't do bear hunting at all. I'll do rabbit hunting though. I never was much of a rabbit hunter 'cause when I was a small kid, I used to hunt rabbit for our family to eat. And it was always late in the winter when times were hard and we needed the food. Sometimes we'd trap them or hunt them, but it was always the end of the season. And rabbits never appealed to me because the flavor of the rabbits then was strong. Partridges are the same thing, now the season extends into December, they feed on the seed pods of the birch trees so the meat's stronger and not so good. But I shot some rabbits early in the fall and they're very good eating. They aren't into their winter diets, which is mostly bark and buds off the trees, twigs and stuff, not the grasses they feed on in the summer. One time I was out with a friend and we spotted a rabbit. I got out my side of the truck, took his rifle, put in a shell, and fired at the rabbit. Apparently the shell was old and didn't work because there was only a little 'pop' and we assumed that the bullet didn't go off. I put in another shell and got ready to shoot again when all of a sudden the rabbit fell over. I don't to this day know what killed that rabbit. There was no blood. And Ray said, 'I think the rabbit just died from laughing!'

"I was appointed a director on the Maine Sporting Camp Association, and I'm very concerned about what our future is going to be in the sporting-camp business what with people and companies buying up land, and what will happen to people who are on leased land and whether their leases will be honored. . . . I think some very good sporting camps may be in jeopardy."

Pat: "I have people who plan surprise getaways, like birthday gatherings and anniversaries. This one couple came for the first time last year and they liked it so much she came up as they were leaving and booked for her husband's birthday for this year, without him knowing it. And we kept it a secret for the whole year, between us. She kept making the deposits without him knowing it, and sending along a return envelope with her writing not mine. When he went to the airport he thought he was picking up some executives for his boss. Instead his brother walks up to him and tells him he's going to Maine. Even then he couldn't hardly believe it! Every year on our anniversary of buying the camps, August 7th, I give anyone who's here a big feed, because we're so happy to be here. Sometimes it's a five-bean supper. And at Christmastime, I make all the guests that have booked that year a handmade Christmas card, which is my way of saying 'Thank you for your business.' Dale and I take care of the grounds, we clean the cabins, take care of everything ourselves. We do all of our work after our people are up so they have it quiet here. My mother always said, 'Hard work doesn't hurt anybody.' Any you know, it doesn't."

Dale: "We've gone through an awful lot to get here, but today we've got a reasonably successful business. And six years after we bought, we've built a home here. So now we're here for good, I hope. I think you've got to look for God all around you—in nature. There's so many things in nature that can't be duplicated by man, from the tiniest seed to a beautiful plant or tree. Therefore I believe that God's all around me, and closer to me here than anywhere else."

38. LITTLE LYFORD POND CAMPS

AP, SCA

OWNERS: Arlene and Bob LeRoy
ADDRESS: PO Box 340, Greenville, ME 04441; 207-280-0016;
www.littlelyford.com
SEASON: Year-round
ACCOMMODATIONS: Ten log cabins, (eight in camp): one to two bedrooms, individual outhouses, running spring-fed water, camp sauna, open-air shower, gas lights, woodstove. One remote cabin, one housekeeping cottage.
RATES: $85–100 per person per day, includes use of boats
ACCESS: I-95 to exit 39 (Newport). Go north on ME 7 to Dexter, then take ME 23 to Guilford, then ME 6/15 to Greenville. In downtown Greenville, turn right onto Pleasant Street (uphill) toward the airport, past Moosehead Farms, past Rum Ridge, and follow LLPC's blue-and-white signs 13 miles to North Maine Woods gate (fee). Proceed another 4 miles to the LLPC driveway on your right.

You drive into Little Lyford down a gently sloping hill, past chicken and llama huts and the owners' home, to the low log main lodge and its covey of honey-colored log cabins. Under a conifer canopy, lined up behind each cabin are log outhouses. Half a dozen sheep and a goat scurry away; three dogs scamper to greet you.

Arlene: "I think we're doing things a little differently than other sporting camps. We're not doing any hunting. And we brought the llamas in for llama trekking. So what we're really concentrating on is ecotourism and nonconsumptive recreation. And we're getting a whole different type of guest in here: people who may be intimidated by going into a camp full of fishermen or hunters. They come here and it's a kinder, softer kind of sporting camp. If they don't know about fishing, Bob can bring them out and do one-on-one fly-fishing lessons. We had a gal come in here and learn to fly-fish; she's now a guide on the Connecticut River.

"We have animals here. At this point: six sheep, a goat, four llamas, three dogs, three cats, and a rabbit that lives in the house. My dream is to run a nonprofit farm animal sanctuary. Our animals have all been rescued from neglect or cruel situations. We have chickens and a rooster and we get fresh eggs. We have an organic vegetable and herb garden. It's a nice education for kids. They help us with the garden; they help us collect eggs. They'll go in, watch the hen lay, and hold this warm egg that just came out of her in their cupped hands. Parents can come here and not worry about their kids. We've got child-sized kayaks on the pond. One year we watched a five-year-old girl walk out onto the dock, get into a kayak for the first time, and go paddling off. We don't have a childrens' playground; they really have to use their noodle and think of what they want to do next."

Bob: "I still remember clearly the first time I came in here. I've been to a lot of different camps in Maine, participated in the operation of a couple of them, but walked in here and there was just a different feel. It felt like you were truly walking back in time. We've pinned down the start date to between 1870 and 1875. It began as a logging camp. It was more or less a depot; this camp here fed other camps that were farther out. They'd bring food up from Bangor, probably via rail to Katahdin Iron Works and then by ox cart up to here. Plus they grew food here. You can wander deep into the woods and see old fencing and chicken coops, and where they had live-stock—the hay fields, old barn foundations, and equipment like ox carts." *Arlene:* "A man named George Bliss started coming up around 1913. He brought his typewriter in and kept a daily journal, year after year: what he did, what he ate, everything. We have his journals and pictures." *Bob:* "It's all on our web site; every page of the journal. They're called the Bliss Journals. We don't know the exact transition from logging to sporting-camps, but from the early 1900s until now we've got all the sporting camp records. It's probably averaged out to a 10- to 12-year time frame for each owner.

"We found out these camps were for sale in August of '97 and moved in Halloween night. Drove down the driveway around 10:00 PM with about eight inches of fresh snow, pulling a U-Haul, fired up the lights, got the woodstoves going. . . ." *Arlene:* "And our first guests came in that Thanksgiving." *Bob:* "I've been in the business before, but this set of camps is a whole different ball game. The learning curve was huge—we're still on the upswing on that." *Arlene:* "When you serve meals, it's a whole different thing. You spend a lot more time with your guests; it's a lot more personal. It's good because you can watch the interaction among the guests and before long they're trading phone numbers, e-mail addresses. It just brings people together. People who come here all have the same values, I think. They're really concerned about the environment, belong to similar organizations."

Bob: "We're surrounded by Indian, Elephant, Baker, and White Cap Mountains—the camps are basically in a small alpine valley. Directly behind the camps is the West Branch of the Pleasant River, which runs from here 2 miles below us to Gulf Hagas, near the Appalachian Trail. Gulf Hagas is called the "Grand Canyon of the East." It's got a whole series of 30- to 40-foot waterfalls; it's got the Rim Trail all the way around it. It's one of the main drawing cards for the camps, especially in the wintertime. In summer, access is fairly easy. Winter you can't get in there, look at it, and get back out in a day's time. So people will come in here, spend the weekend, and on one of the days ski or snowshoe down to the head of the gulf and hike around looking at the waterfalls and 100-foot granite cliffs."

Arlene: "The camps were opened for winter activities for the first time in 1978. In winter, we have an extensive trail network for skiing and snow-shoeing. You can follow the river five miles upstream to Big Lyford." *Bob:* "When conditions are right, we hop right on to the river and ski that. It is strictly backcountry skiing: we keep the trails clear of brush, sign them, and have a map, but we don't set track or go out and groom them.

"For spring and summer activities there's First and Second Little Lyford Ponds, and several other little ponds above us. They're all filled with wild, native brook trout. It's a unique fishery, never been stocked. We have an outpost cabin: the only cabin on a beautiful little spring-fed trout pond called Mountain Brook Pond. It's surrounded on three sides by mountains. Hike-in only. Carry in—carry out. And from there you can hike into Lost Pond." *Arlene:* "We have canoes and rowboats on other remote ponds in the area." *Bob:* "You could come in for two weeks and fish a different pond every day." *Arlene:* "We're within the 100-mile wilderness corridor behind the North Maine Woods gate system, 17 miles or so from Greenville, and this pocket we're in is part of 400,000 acres of undeveloped land."

Bob: "Basically what we're trying to do here is bring back the traditions of of these sporting camps. The way it was. No electricity, woodstoves (I cut around 24 cords of wood a year), outhouses, gardens, and livestock. We've recreated the late 1800s wilderness camp."

Summertime Scrambled Eggs

Arlene: "I serve vegetarian meals and fish; homemade breads and desserts. I think we're the only camp that's totally vegetarian. Our organic eggs come from our flock of free-range laying hens." The following makes four servings:

> 4 eggs, 3 T water, ¾ tsp. salt, ¼ cup (½ stick) butter, 1 cup cubed cooked potato (1 medium), 3 T finely chopped onion, 1 small zucchini (halved and sliced), 1 tomato (chopped)

Little Lyford offers cabins like this for cross-country skiers.

Beat eggs, water, and salt with fork. Heat butter in 10-inch skillet over medium heat until melted; cook and stir vegetables in butter 2 minutes. Pour egg mixture into skillet. As mixture begins to set on the bottom and sides, gently lift cooked portions with a spatula so that the thin, uncooked portion can flow to bottom. Avoid constant stirring. Cook until eggs are thickened but moist, 3–5 minutes.

39. MAYNARD'S-IN-MAINE

AP

OWNERS: Gail and Bill Maynard

ADDRESS: PO Box 220, Rockwood, ME 04478; 207-534-7703; e-mail: gmaynards@hotmail.com; www.maynardsinmaine.com

SEASON: May 1 through December 1

ACCOMMODATIONS: Twelve cabins (each sleeps one to six people): indoor plumbing and shower, woodstoves or automatic heat, electricity; pets accepted

RATES: $55 per person per day

ACCESS: I-95 to exit 39 (Newport). Go north on ME 7/11 to Dexter. Continue north on ME 23 and then take ME 6/15 through Greenville to Rockwood. After the Village Store, turn right across a bridge and then take the first left (sign) to Maynard's on the right.

Maynard's is on the north side of the Moose River right past the village of Rockwood's general store. A circular drive leads up to a lodge and cabins along an expanse of lawn. Set back high and far enough from the road, the camps have the feel of an enclave. It's pretty hard to miss Maynard's. A huge white wooden sign sits atop a classic main lodge, taking up much of the roof area. Morning glories twine around porch posts; a long row of weathered rocking chairs faces out to Moose River and Blue Ridge Mountain. Inside, old fishing paraphernalia and photos, stuffed animals, and exotic African artifacts grace the office and living room area. One group of cabins is within a grove of trees, the other set makes a gentle arc down along the lawn. Behind is a working farm with chickens, pigs, cats, a dog, and a big vegetable garden for the camp kitchen.

Gail: "I married Bill in the late '60s, and with him came this. We started a family early, so I was waitressing and carrying a baby on my hip day after day at first. The good thing was we weren't open all year round so I had a little bit of time. My father-in-law, Roger, was doing the cooking. Previous to that my mother-in-law did it, but she had a stroke and Roger had to learn in a hurry. Then Roger had a bad heart attack in 1990 and after that I was doing everything."

I had interviewed Roger in 1994, before he died, and Gail asked that his comments be included here. *Roger:* "Well, my father, Walter, was born in Massachusetts, and as a kid he heard Mr. Wilson, of Wilson's Camps here at East Outlet, talk about running camps and decided that's what he wanted to do. When he bought this place, nothing was here. This was just an old farm, but it had burned down. One of our cabins was built, painted, and occupied by guests in a day and a half! By 1919 it was a real sporting camp. The main lodge was built in 1932. I remember there were a lot of guides here, as many as 42 guides at one time; one for each person, basically. I figure around the mid-1930s were the golden years for this place. My father was running it then, and my mother, Vivian, did all the cooking. As for me, I remember running around as a kid mostly steppin' on nails!

"We had seven or eight governors together here at one time. We had the leading contralto of the Metropolitan Opera with us for three seasons and the leading cellist. And the manager of the *I Love Lucy* show. Chet Huntley was here. When I was growing up, this side of the river was all farms and cleared land, with very few houses. My father died in his 70s, so I started running the place in the 1940s. When we first started we was getting $2.50 a day, including meals. But in the early 1900s you were making money. You didn't pay over a dollar for a loaf of bread. Loins of beef were 15 to 18 cents at that time. It was easier getting fresh produce then, because the Maine Central train was running in here daily from Portland, coming out on the wharf down to Rockwood. The Mount Kineo Hotel [a huge resort hotel at the base of Mount Kineo in the middle of Moosehead Lake] was operating then. We had a garden here and two cows and 67 chickens, so all our milk and eggs were taken care of. Plus we had homemade ice cream. We'd think nothing of taking 3 quarts of cream and making ice cream so rich that when you ate it, it stuck to the roof of your mouth. We put up the ice ourselves, cut it in the cove, and put it in the icehouse."

Gail handed me Walter Maynard's typed memoir. It starts: "The Autobiography of Walter Maynard: Maine Guide, Trapper, River Driver, Game Warden, Deputy Sheriff, Camp Owner and Builder, Big Game Hunter, commercial fisherman, Captain of Commodore's Yacht at Moosehead, collector for American and British museums in the jungles of South America, agent for public schools, Harbor Master." And it goes on to relate just how one man did, in fact, do all these things! Walter Maynard was born in Rutland, Massachusetts, in 1885. His mother died when he was 8, and he was sent to an orphanage. He then became a "bound-out boy," from which servitude he shortly escaped on a passing train. In March 1911, after an incredible number of jobs and escapades, he "bought fifty acres of land from Harry Johnston on the north bank of Moose River about one mile from its mouth. The natives called it 'a pile of brush.'" His son, Roger, "was born premature, only weighing 3¾ pounds, but turned into a healthy boy." Healthy enough, indeed, to carry on the Maynard tradition into future generations.

Gail: "We have three children—Bill, Missy, and Kristy—and they all help a lot—shovel roofs in the winter, cut wood, help my husband plow, whatever else has to be done. In the wintertime, I usually work somewhere and Bill plows 80-some-odd driveways. We try to budget ourselves in the summertime to carry us through the winter.

"We own 99.9 acres here, and we've been lucky in one respect that this whole place has been in the same family generation after generation. So much in this town depends on our type of business. There are no factories

Maynard's-in-Maine

around. If the camps go under, what are people going to do? If you're in this kind of business, you can't collect unemployment. We're seasonal, so my crew work for four months, or whatever, and then they have to look for work somewhere else. And insurance, forget it! I've got insurance for the place, and workmen's comp, but as far as medical insurance for my family, I haven't had it in years.

"Each year we do a turkey shoot every Sunday during the month of October. And every Labor Day weekend for years we've had a pig roast as a fund-raiser for cystic fibrosis. In 2001, we raised over $10,000, which is really pretty good for a little town like Rockwood. Something else is that the fishing around here has improved. We have a lake coalition trying to help things, and I've never seen so many salmon brought in as I have this year. The stocking helps, and a lot of people are doing catch-and-release, so there's more for everyone. It's a good sign, and I hope it keeps up."

Frozen Pumpkin Dessert

20 crushed gingersnaps, 1 cup canned or fresh pureed pumpkin, ½ cup sugar, ½ cup chopped pecans or walnuts, 1¼ tsp. pumpkin-pie spice, ¼ tsp. salt, 1 quart rich vanilla ice cream

Butter a 1½-quart oblong glass baking dish. Sprinkle with half the gingersnaps. In a medium-sized bowl, stir ice cream until softened, but not melted. Blend in the remaining ingredients. Pour into a baking dish. Sprinkle with the remaining crumbs. Cover with foil. Freeze for 3 hours or until firm. Cut with a sharp knife. Serve with whipped cream and chopped nuts.

40. MEDAWISLA ON SECOND ROACH POND

HK (AP IN WINTER), SCA

OWNERS: Shannon and Larry LeRoy

ADDRESS: Route 76, Box 592, Greenville, ME 04441; 207-695-2690 (radio phone) or 207-695-2821 (Folsom's Air Service); www.medawisla.com

SEASON: Year-round (closed December and April)

ACCOMMODATIONS: Seven log cabins: one to three bedrooms, indoor plumbing and shower (two with running water in winter), gas or electric lights, woodstove

RATES: $60–100 per cabin per day (double occupancy); $420–700 per cabin per week (double occupancy)

ACCESS: I-95 to exit 39 (Newport). Take ME 7 to Dexter, then ME 23 to Guilford, then ME 6/15 to Greenville. Go straight on Lily Bay Road, 20 miles to Kokadjo. At Kokadjo Trading Post (last supplies), keep left on Baxter State Park Road and go 1.25 miles to the big camp sign on the right. Turn right and go 5.75 miles. Cross the wooden bridge. Turn left. The camp is within 1,500 feet.

Getting to some camps is part of the adventure. This is the case with Medawisla as you drive deep into timber lands and turn the corner into their small compound of dark log cabins. Biologist Shannon LeRoy walks the woods, pointing out tracks of martin and mink.

Shannon: "The camp was built in 1953 by Ray and Louise O'Donnell. He was a bush pilot and had his own flying service. Ray died in the mid-'60s and Louise married Freddy Rogers, then they ran the camps. Freddy's still around." *Larry:* "He's been a real help. We bought the place in 1992 from our friends Russ and Mimi Whitten.

"In the early 1900s, the timber industry backed up the waters of Second Roach Pond to run pulp. The flow starts at Moosehead Lake, then up to Spencer Bay, which is the outlet of the Roach River. Then at 7 miles

you run northeast up Roach River, which is famous for salmon fishing, to First Roach, a lake 7 miles long. Then the run from First to Second Roach is about 1½ miles, to Second Roach, a lake 3½ miles long. We're the only camp on it. It's 48 feet deep with salmon and square-tail trout, no togue, and lots of smelt. It's a great breeding ground, so the entire Roach River drainage is closed to ice fishing. Beside fishing, we offer some guided canoe trips. They go down the West Branch of the Penobscot to Chesuncook village. It can be done in one 7-hour day or they can stay in the village and Louisa and Dave Surprenant, at the Chesuncook Lake House, will feed and put them up for the night. Folsom's Air Service then flies them back here."

Shannon: "We also have great hiking. We're 8 miles from the Appalachian Trail. The hike up Whitecap Mountain is wonderful, with great views. We also have a couple of trails right out of camp. There's the new Turtle Ridge and Debsconeag trail system in the Nahmakanta Preserve—the nicest I've ever seen—with some hikes 15 miles long."

Larry: "During the summer we're booked mostly with moose watchers. You see, we have a unique setting in that we have both a lake and a river environment here. The deadwater out front is a fabulous habitat for wildlife." *Shannon:* "We've had as many as 12 moose at one time out there." *Larry:* "Occasionally we have to change the Energizer batteries in one of them!" *Shannon:* "But seriously, we get a tremendous number of loons and eagles, too. They recorded the loon sounds for the movie *On Golden Pond* here. We get some pretty interesting wildlife questions from our guests, like, 'How old does a deer have to be before it turns into a moose?' To which I replied, 'I haven't seen it happen yet!'

"We raised three children here: Stoney, Lacey, and Skylar. We home-schooled them until high school, and they're off now." *Larry:* "I'm pleased with how well they've adapted, which I see as a success story for all of us."

Shannon: "Larry and I got married in the church in Chesuncook. Flew the minister in by bush pilot. And I fell in love with Maine. I never realized there was a place with water and trees like this. I was born and raised in the deserts of Wyoming, which is where we met. Larry was born in South America." *Larry:* "Dad worked for Mobil and Texaco on an overseas oil project. I lived there until I was 13—actually spoke Spanish better than I did English at an early age. In 1960 my folks, Frank and Jean, came to Maine and traveled by canoe and plane up Moosehead, across and down the West Branch into the Eagle Lake area. My dad said he wanted to go to the most remote spots in Maine. So they hired an old Indian guide and picked out a spot near Caucomgomoc Lake, just north of Chesuncook Lake, and explored all around that area. And when they got to Chesuncook Village they just fell in love with it. Dad ended up buying one of the camps and then building his own place. We spent all our summers there as kids. I was up there for the first time in 1961. We were on a canoe trip, and it took

Dogsledding on Chesuncook Lake with Medawisla Camps

my older brother, Tom, my dad, and myself three days in a 20-foot canoe to get down Chesuncook Lake in a bad storm. In the summers I worked for Bert and Maggie McBurnie at the Chesuncook Lake House, and then at Pray's cottages back when Charlie Pray was in his first year as senator. But I was not making a living in the woods.

At that point we lived in the mountains in Wyoming, and it was a 13-mile drive to town and snow lasted seven months of the year. It was a survival environment, and we've always enjoyed that. Dad raised us like that, and Shannon's father raised her that way. So we figured the sporting camp was probably the best way for us to go."

Shannon: "In '97 we decided to stay in for the winter. Since then, our business has evolved around backcountry cross-country skiing." *Larry:* "We have a network of about 60 miles and groom 30. And we work closely with Steve Madura, of Song in the Woods, for our popular dogsledding trips. In the 2000–2001 winter we got a lease on a winter camp area out between Trout Pond and Fourth Roach, on an isthmus. We set up two four-wall outfitter tents. It's a 7-mile ski from camp to either warm up or actually spend the night, or nights, there. We had a family from Israel that went dogsledding with Steve, on about a 19-mile trip, and I met them at the winter camps and set up this gourmet lunch. (We feed our winter guests, usually at the lodge.) We had tablecloth, china, home-cooked biscuits in the reflector oven, even dried flowers on the table. They loved it!"

Shannon: "There are only four full-time residents in Kokadjo, our nearest outpost. Carol Stirling Kealiher, and her late father, Cliff, over at West Branch Pond sporting camps have been like family." *Larry:* "Actually, Shannon's got her own business because of Cliff. It got started when I made myself an ultralight fly-rod and Shannon asked me to build her one. I said, 'I'll teach you how to build one yourself.' Then she made one for Cliff, a 9-foot, 5-weight, and gave it to him for his 80th birthday. He shed a tear— we all did. His was number 1, and he was so proud of it he showed it off all over town and people started asking her to build rods. So now she has the Roach River Fly Company and makes her rods right here at camp." *Shannon:* "I've built over 40 to date, all numbered and with names on each. They've gone to people all over the country.

"A lot of our people are coming up here primarily to relax. So we've equipped camp with a nice collection of books. With the pressures of modern-day city life, people need a place to escape and unwind. They hear about wildlife in the cities, but they don't get a chance to touch that in their lives. I tell our guests that wristwatches aren't allowed in here. Eat when you're hungry, sleep when you're tired. And I'll tell you when it's time to go home."

41. MOOSEHEAD HILLS CABINS

HK
OWNERS: Bill Fowley and Sally Johnson
ADDRESS: PO Box 936, Greenville, ME 04441; 207-695-2514; e-mail: mooseheadhills@ctel.net; www.mooseheadhills.com
SEASON: Year-round
ACCOMMODATIONS: Four cabins: two bedrooms, indoor plumbingand whirlpool tub with shower, fireplace, electricity, automatic heat, full kitchen; one out-cabin
RATES: $125 per cabin per day; $750 per cabin per week; child rates; pets $5 per pet per day
ACCESS: I-95 north to exit 39 (Newport). Go north on ME 7 to Dexter, ME 23 to Guilford, then ME 6/15 to Greenville. In Greenville go straight through the blinking yellow light and continue on the Lily Bay Road for 3 miles. Moosehead Hills Cabins are on the left.

Moosehead Hills Cabins sit tucked off the main road on a bluff overlooking Moosehead Lake. As one drives down the circular driveway, the view is expansive. The new log lodge, where Sally, Bill, and their children live, and the newly constructed guest cabins give one a sense of what Maine's older sporting camps must have looked like in their just-felled and -fashioned infancy. Although the cabins' modern touches stretch the limits of what could be termed traditional, Sally and Bill's intentions and attitudes toward their place is right on target.

Sally: "You won't find manicured lawns here. We very purposefully left our 50 acres in a very natural state. It is wooded, and we put the house and cabins in the upper-middle part of the property and left the rest wild for people to enjoy. We have nature trails all around the property. And when you go down to the waterfront, you'll see that it's in its natural state. It gives you the feeling of unspoiled wilderness, which I think is what most people want when they come here.

"Up until recently, we were kind of the typical corporate, living the rat-race in the suburbs, dual-income couple. But we both had roots in rural areas. Bill grew up in the White Mountains of New Hampshire, and I grew up in western Massachusetts and spent all my summers on a lake in a little camp that my father had built, with no electricity or running water. And I really developed an appreciation for the creativity and purposeful interaction you have as a family when you don't have television, those crutches to rely on that put you into a vegetative state. Bill and I had gone to college together in Maine and had loved it up here and wanted to find a way to get back up. We were planning a family and wanted our kids to grow up in a small town, less focused on material things with more participation in nature. Another thing that affected me very much is that I lost my mother about five years ago. My parents had been tremendously hard workers; always planning and working and saving for their retirement. And they never were able to experience it. Bill and I talked a lot about how if you have a dream and a way you want to live, if you don't do it now, you probably won't be able to do it. So we came to the decision that time and lifestyle was more important to us than money. And that decision was something that gave us courage to make the move."

Bill: "We came here May of 1998, took a year to build our home, started on the cabins, and finally opened for business in July 2000. I had worked carpentry for two summers growing up and then did a bit more to support myself when I was getting my MBA, which was all part of the corporate plan at the time. But I gotta tell you, I was in shape for a desk job when we got here. I'd get out seven or eight in the morning and I could work until maybe one, and then I'd have to go in and lie down." *Sally:* "We were lucky in the beginning in that we had a neighbor that was 75, Junior, who would come over to plow our driveway, mow our lawn." *Bill:* "I finally had to ask him to stop 'cause it was embarrassing to have this old guy mowing our lawn! Plus, I wasn't lying down anymore! When I started in on the cabins we chose logs because they fit the area and what we wanted the place to look like." *Sally:* "We really wanted simplicity—no TV or phone, but wanted a fireplace in each one, quilts, special all-natural soaps and candles, a full bath with whirlpool tub because we wanted people to be out in nature all day long and come back to a little luxury and comfort. Bill really has a talent for carpentry. Not only can he put up a good sturdy structure, but there's something creative and artistic in what he builds. So many people have commented on the wonderful . . ." *Bill:* "toilet paper holders! (Laughs.) It's fun. And this summer I concentrated on the grounds, built a play area for kids, and a nature trail. That was a labor of love for Sally . . . she didn't labor much, but she really loves it! (Both laugh.) We have three cabins here, one over at Wilson Pond, Sunrise Lodge, and we bought a really nice private piece of property over on the other side of the pond. That will be cabin #5.

"When we found this property we felt it was so nicely situated. It's only 3 miles from town, so people can go in for dinner, but when you're here it can feel very removed and peaceful."

Sally: "People outside of Maine don't generally think of a 'camp' as a cabin. Initially we called ourselves Moosehead Lake Camps, but after answering questions from people like, 'How many campsites do you have?' or thinking it was a kids' camp, we finally just got tired of it and said Moosehead Lake Cabins so people could understand what business we are in." *Bill:* "And the decision to be housekeeping rather than American Plan was simple—we didn't want to cook!

"We've put out guest books this year in all the cabins and found that our people were increasingly mentioning our shepherd-lab, Hoser, in them. Turns out we would let him out in the morning and he had this 'gravy run' where he'd go have breakfast in the cabins with people—and then go back and have dinner with them! One entry says they'd been here for a week, had fabulous weather, had a great time, saw umpteen moose, bald eagles, but the highlight of their vacation was breakfast with Hoser! That was our surprise." *Sally:* "Many of the places don't allow pets, but we do. We love dogs. It's really a perfect setting for someone to come with a pet.

"We talked long and hard about what we wanted this business to be. We decided we wanted to focus on a few adventures that could really give people a sense of what it feels like to be here. One of the things we try to promote is hiking. I've hiked all over New England and have never been anywhere that has better terrain for all levels of hikers, such lovely views of lake and hills. We put together a list of descriptions and directions to a whole bunch of area hikes which we give to our guests who want to go out and explore the beauty of this region. There's also in-process a cooperative effort between the Maine Appalachian Trail Club and some local Moosehead people to create a hiking loop around the whole lake. It will be around 150 miles long. Another thing is that we coordinate moose safaris. We have a registered Maine Guide come up here and take people out to a very remote pond for a nice four-hour canoe or kayak experience. We also do kayak and canoe trips out the West Outlet to the Kennebec, which comes out of Moosehead Lake and goes into Indian Pond. It's about a five-hour trip you can do all by yourself. We can provide the boats, shuttle cars, and you just take yourself down this meandering river. It has a few little rapids, lots of wildlife. In the winter, snowmobiling is a huge focus here. There's a trail

Bill Fowley and Sally Johnson at Moosehead Hills Cabins

right from the cabins that hooks in with the main trails. Snowshoeing is another thing. For cross-country we point people to two very good places locally. Our guide can take guests to several places where they can experience several hours of dogsledding. That's a real novelty. The last one is massage: we have a person who can come right to your cabin—which is great after a day outdoors. Oh, and it's so much fun around here during fly-in time: the international seaplane fly-in in Greenville, which is the weekend after Labor Day. We're both pilots so we love planes and flying, although we haven't had any time to do that since we've been here! There's really a lot of fun things to do around here."

42. PACKARD'S CAMPS

HK, SCA

MANAGERS: Jerry and Laura Packard

ADDRESS: RFD 2, Box 176, Guilford, ME 04443; 207-997-3300; e-mail: lrp@kind.net; www.packardscamps.com

SEASON: May through November

ACCOMMODATIONS: Fifteen log cabins: one to three bedrooms; screened porch; indoor plumbing and shower; electric range, lights, heat, and refrigerator; a few full hook-up campsites available; post office and tackle shop during summer; no jet skis

RATES: $35 per person per day; $375–650 per cabin per week; campground rates available
ACCESS: I-95 north to exit 39 (Newport). Follow ME 7 north to Dexter, then ME 23 to Guilford. Take ME 150 north out of Guilford 13 miles to Sebec Lake (the road ends at the camp).

Jerry: "In 1894, my great-grandfather started this place. The family were shipbuilders in Searsport. Marlborough Packard, my great-great-grandfather, helped build a lot of those big schooners. His son was kind of a rebel—didn't want to build ships. He liked to fish and hunt, so he came to this area and that's how it all started. This was an old farmhouse, and he started taking in a few log drivers and fishermen in the spring. One thing led to another and within two or three years he began building cabins. My grandfather took over from him, then my father, then me, and my children are the fifth generation. In 1900 they started a post office here, and it's been here ever since, open June 1 through September 15. This is the end of the road, so people around the lake come by boat or on foot to get their mail.

Years ago you'd get to the camps by boat and train. Transportation was available by steamboat up the coast from New York or Boston on up to Portland and then to Bangor along the Penobscot River. From there you could get a train to Greenville, Dover-Foxcroft, and Guilford. There was a narrow-gauge that went through Monson and then everything—the mail, the passengers—would come up Sebec Lake by steamboat. And people bought all their things locally. Until about the late 1960s, this was the old store right here. I used to tend store when I was a kid, cut ice for the soda. All the people in town walked down to get vinegar for pickling. That's the old molasses barrel, still half full of molasses. There's the old kerosene pump—turn the handle five times and you had a gallon of kerosene for lights and things. We keep everything.

"My grandfather was born right in this room, now the dining area, my father was born in one of the cabins, and my grandfather's sister was born in another one of the cabins. My mother came up here to work, just for the summer, met my father, and never went home. Same thing with my grandmother. And Laura and Jessica's mother, Amanda, came up here as a waitress and stayed here until we sold the place in 2000.

"Sebec Lake is really unique. We're an excellent cold-water fishery, which means salmon and trout, but we're also an excellent warm-water bass fishery. Very few lakes are good at both. It's a very deep lake, 165 feet at its deepest, but it's also got some large bodies of shallow water. It's 12 miles long by 4 miles wide, a natural lake.

"When this was an American Plan camp, we'd have a hundred people for supper sometimes because we ran it kind of like a restaurant. We had 10 or 11 employees just in that part of it. But costs went up and it became hard

Jerry Packard and his daughter Laura

with all the government regulations, so we started going to housekeeping back in the late '50s, when people with families just couldn't afford to do American Plan. My grandfather rented our first housekeeping cabin in 1917, and the guy who ran the steamboat up here told him he was crazy, no one would pay to rent a housekeeping cabin. At that time he got $14 a week for it, which was a lot of money. He settled on that because he said, 'My dog's 14 and that's what I'm gonna charge.' And when we started our campground everyone said, 'You're crazy—you're gonna ruin your place.' Well, that campground pays the taxes and the hired man's salary. Now if you wanted to build it, they wouldn't let you. So we've been kind of ahead of our time.

Laura: "More and more, we're focusing on nonconsumptive recreation. People enjoy kayaking, canoeing, bald eagle– and moose-watching, and mountain biking. The Appalachian Trail's nearby and so is Baxter State Park for hiking, wildlife photography, mushroom- and berry-picking. And we do have good fishing and hunting."

Jerry: "We used to be remote geographically. Now we live one-day's drive away from 60–70 million people. Years ago at least 98 percent of our business came from outside Maine. Now it's probably 70 percent. That's one thing that's changed noticeably in just the last five years. There are more people coming into southern Maine, and it is economically more like Massachusetts than the rest of Maine north of here."

Laura: "Our biggest clientele are families looking for a getaway where they can appreciate the outdoors. They come looking for the atmosphere we provide. Here people treat them well and take care of them, and they can have not just lodging, but an actual experience. It's an interactive time where they're learning about their surroundings, the heritage and culture. I'm lucky to be here doing what I love in a place where my family's been living and working for well over 100 years." *Jerry:* "I think I read somewhere that only 2 percent of family businesses last 100 years. We're happy to be in that 2 percent." *Laura:* "We have all the bookkeeping records from before 1900. So if I knew your name, I could tell you what cabin you, or your grandparents, stayed in, what guide you had, how much money you spent, and everything. A lot of people don't have roots that are that strong—everything's so transient—and I think people like to be part of the continuity here, and I like being part of it. It's a powerful experience."

43. SPENCER POND CAMPS

HK, SCA

OWNERS: Bob Croce and Jill Martel

CAMP ADDRESS: Star Route 76, Box 580, Greenville, ME 04441; 207-843-5456 (camp) or 207-695-2821 (Folsom's Air Service)

WINTER ADDRESS: PO Box 580, Holden, ME 04429; 207-843-5456

SEASON: May through November

ACCOMMODATIONS: Six log cabins: one to three bedrooms; outhouse; gas stove, lights, and refrigerator; woodstove; hand-pumped water

RATES: $17–50 per person per day

ACCESS: I-95 north to exit 39 (Newport). Take ME 7 north to Dexter, then ME 23 to Guilford, then ME 6/15 to Greenville. At the blinking yellow light, continue straight on Lily Bay Road, 20 miles to Kokadjo Village. At Kokadjo Trading Post (last supplies), keep left on Baxter Park Road. Go 1 mile; at camp sign turn left onto a dirt road. Follow signs 12 miles to camp.

Spencer Pond Camps looks like a family compound (a few of the cabins are out of sight in the woods). There are vegetable and flower gardens, a small wire-mesh enclosure for poultry, and a cozy, lived-in main lodge. Spencer Mountain rises up behind the lodge. Guests drop off supplies upon arrival and then deposit vehicles in the parking area by the gate. With this, the sense of having stepped back in time is complete.

Jill: "We've been coming to the Moosehead Lake region for 31 years. We visited the camps for the first time in 1983 and bought Spencer Pond Camps in 1994 from Anne and Chick Howe. Anne was just in here the other day looking after things while we were off briefly visiting family. We see ourselves as stewards of the Spencer Pond traditions that they, and others before them, started."

Not surprisingly, Bob and Jill asked that I use Anne's account of the history of the camps, from my first edition of this guide.

Anne: "The original cabin was built in 1901 by Mose Duty, a guide who was born on one of those 200-acre homestead farms on Moosehead Lake. He guided for a Mr. Stetson, who owned this entire township. Mose told Mr. Stetson that he always wanted to have a cabin on this lake. So Mr. Stetson said, 'Go pick out your land, son.' He picked out this spot and started building the big cabin in the center of camp. He called it Sabotowan, the Abenaki Indian name for Big Spencer Mountain. The name for Little Spencer, the one that's right handy here, is Kokadjoweemgwasebemsis, so it's understandable he didn't use that!

"Well, in 1944 he became ill. His wife, Lillian, put a sheet out on the side lawn so that the next plane that went overhead would see it. This was their only means of communication. And Ray O'Donald, who was the third bush pilot in the State of Maine, and was stationed out of Greenville, flew over and saw the sheet, landed, picked up Mose, and took him to Greenville hospital. Meanwhile, Lillian had to contend with the cow and horse. She let the horse go loose. But the cow had to be milked. Well, there was the added problem that Lillian was blind. So she hung on to the cow's tail, attached a little bucket to her own waist, and away they went down the blazed trail to Kokadjo. And every time she was hungry, she'd milk the cow. I don't know how long it took her to get there. It's 12 miles now, and the way she went was considerably longer, with several brooks to go across, rivers actually. There were no logging roads, of course, no roads at all. She left the cow at Kokadjo, hooked a ride with the mail carrier into Greenville, and got to the hospital in time for Mose to die. Well, of course she couldn't come back in here. So Lillian sold the camp to George and Louise Dulac; Louise was from the next-door 200-acre parcel. And it wasn't until 1948 that the lumber company—the Stetson lands had sold out to Oxford Paper Company—permitted them to open it as a sporting camp. And we then bought from them in 1970.

"Little Spencer Mountain was a volcano. It erupted three times that we know of. It was formed before there was any life on earth. The ocean was halfway up it, right where the cliffs are. The lake itself is very shallow, about 10 feet on average, and is a hundred million years older than Moosehead Lake, which was formed by a fissure, a breaking away of rocks. This has a beautiful, smooth bottom, but it also has at least 2 to 3 feet of silt over the bottom because it's in the last stages of natural eutrophication (filling in).

"We have a large moose population around here, and I may be the only person in the United States that has raised a moose from birth. What happened is, some dogs chased the mother away. The people walking the dogs mistakenly attended to the newborn. Eventually, realizing they had a problem on their hands, they called the local wildlife biologist, who asked me if I would take him. And so we did. We raised him with no information at all except for a small text from the University of Alaska, which I later grew to disagree with. Also, what we didn't know was that a moose, if you get him in the first three days of his life, imprints on humans. So he never becomes a moose; he stays a 'people.' And we got him within the first three days. It was an amazing experience. Amazing. This was in 1983, and it has deeply affected our lives. He wasn't able to live in the wild, and so we were forced to have him put down. Chick still needs to talk about it. For me, putting together my book, *Bully*, was a real catharsis. It took seven rewritings to get it out of my system."

Bob: "The first year we came here we met Bully. Right outside our cabin. It really was an amazing thing, part of the 'magic of Spencer' we talk about."

Jill: "Previous to becoming caretakers of Spencer, we looked at other sporting camps. We wanted to work and live in the outdoors, rather than just visit. When this became available it was a 'Eureka!' experience, something I've wanted all my life."

Bob: "We have a desire to preserve what we've loved here over the years and help others have the same enjoyment. That's an important part of our personal satisfaction, seeing the enjoyment our guests feel being here. The rewards are intangible more than financial in a place like this.

"We've added a few of our own traditions since we've been here. Every Saturday we bake up a batch of Maine-style yellow-eyed baked beans. When supper time comes, the guests come over and help themselves."

Jill: "I also maintain a small flock of laying hens for the children to gather fresh eggs. It's very popular and it gets back to our homesteading legacy. Also, I have animal-shaped cookies I give to the guests when they leave that they can eat while they're on the road. Each year it's a different theme: So far we've made moose, bear, loon, and trout. Now I'm looking for a deer, fox, or eagle cookie cutter. One thing we have continued is the tradition that our guests can come right into the vegetable garden and get whatever they like to eat for their meals."

Bob: "We continue to offer excellent self-maintained hiking trails from around camp, and now we also have mountain biking, bird walks, and canoeing. The moose-watching is incredible." *Jill:* "We're on their feeding route, and we don't have a generator, so it's quiet. The other night we had the coyotes and owls yipping and hooting back and forth to each other. Then a moose came along, feeding on the water grasses by camp in the full moon. What a special night that was!"

Bob: "Since the Howes have been here, the forests have begun to grow back and there are more boreal birds: spruce grouse, black-backed three-toed woodpeckers, boreal chickadees, and wildlife that's more common in the deeper woods, like martins, which are a bellwether for healthy old-

Gulf Hagas, one of many good hiking destinations in the area

growth forests. We also have fishers, coyotes, and bobcats, and guests have reported seeing wolves." *Jill:* "If people show even a hint of interest in the outdoors, we have reference books we show them." *Bob:* "We want to promote guests discovering the magic on their own, like we did. With our encouragement. We can help by sharing our knowledge and experience, but we want them to have the satisfaction of active involvement. There's too much already that's passive: TV, theme parks, guided tours. We like to promote the rewards and learning that come from self-sufficiency."

Jill: "The magic of Spencer really does get down to our spiritual side. It's a real connection to our heritage, our natures, which feeds the soul. We have journals in each cabin for guests to share their thoughts with other guests. And we hope people walk away with a better understanding of our place in the real world. As Anne always said, and it's true, 'We don't deal with people's pocketbooks here; we deal with their souls.'"

44. TOMHEGAN

HK

OWNERS: Tomhegan Camps Association

MANAGERS: Leona and Norman Harding

ADDRESS: PO Box 310, Rockwood, ME 04478-0310; 207-534-7712

SEASON: Year-round

ACCOMMODATIONS: Nine log cabins: one to three bedrooms; indoor plumbing and tub with shower; wood heat; gas stove, refrigerator, and grill. Four lodge rooms with private bath, hot-water baseboard heat, electric lights, central kitchen and dining area, and living room with fireplace. Linens and towels provided.

RATES: $120 per cabin per day; $1,010 per cabin per week; lodge rooms: $85 per day (double occupancy); entire lodge (17 people maximum): $375 per day, $2,250 per week

ACCESS: I-95 north to exit 39 (Newport). Take ME 7 to Dexter, ME 25 to Guilford, and ME 6/15 to Greenville. At Greenville, turn left at blinking amber light and stay on ME 15 for 20 miles to Rockwood. Turn right at bridge and follow signs for the 9-mile dirt road (5 miles public, 4 miles private) into camp.

Tomhegan is stretched along a mile and a half of shorefront, and adjacent to a wildlife reserve, on the northwest end of Moosehead Lake. One feature, unique in my experience, is Tomhegan's boardwalk, which extends the length of the cabins. Another innovative feature is its owners' association. When I was doing the research for my first Maine sporting-camp book, back in 1992, I saw a huge FOR SALE sign along the water's edge and learned, from a very sad and sickly Margaret McBurnie, daughter of the original owners, that the rundown camps were to go the way of so many others: sold to individuals and removed from the public domain. (The camps were thus not in my book.) Ten years later I found a very happy and healthy Tomhegan, as well as Margie, who still lives a few steps from the cabin in which she was born.

Margie: "I was born in #4 cabin, Diana, on April 13, 1916. 'Course there wasn't any road into here then. There wasn't even a road from Greenville. People came by railroad to Kineo Station they called it; that was Rockwood. The doctor came up to Kineo Station and snowshoed up 6 miles on the lake to here, but I came before he arrived. My mother, Lilla Blanche Spinney, pretty-near died, and the doctor told her not to have any more children. The camps opened in 1912, and my father, Russell Parker Spinney, died in '39, Fourth of July, dancing, heart attack. That was an awful shock. Mother and I then ran them until mother died in '51. I was married in 1950 and my husband, Keith McBurnie, and I started running them (we had our honeymoon in cabin #1, Hemlock). I ran them for some time myself, but stopped in 1977 because I had cancer. They gave me two to five years to live, so I thought I'd better sell the camps. But I kept this cabin for as long as I live. There's no number on it, they just call it Margie's Cabin.

"My father was from New Hampshire, didn't like office work, so he went to Rangeley Lakes, Captain Barker's Cabins, to learn how to guide. He met my mother there; she was the camp secretary. One day he met Governor Rollins up there, the governor of New Hampshire, and he had a son, Douglas, who he wanted to get into the woods where he couldn't get anywhere near liquor; have his son go into partnership with my father in a set of sporting camps. So he bought 3,000 acres and my father came up here with my mother in February 1910. They came by horse-drawn sled with a barrel of molasses, 2 barrels of flour, and 1 barrel of salt pork. My mother had never been this far into the woods. They built a lodge, then they built #2 cabin, the one with a loft. Then, young Douglas went to Monte Carlo, where he died. My father bought the camps and 127 acres from the Rollins, which he made into a game preserve. The Rollins family still owns the rest. The story behind the name goes: there was an Indian guide, a Penobscot— I used to go to school with several and down to Yankee Point there's still some living. He and his son came out on the lake and their birch-bark canoe capsized because a squall came up. The father swam ashore, but the son Tom, he couldn't swim. So he said, "Tom, he gone." He was drowned, you see. So we call it Tomhegan. Actually, that's the name of a real Indian.

"Those first years, my parents had to lug all their water from the lake, and they just had outhouses. They were here five years before I was born. When I was a kid, there weren't any other children here, all I had to play with were the animals. I always thought that when I got old I'd take care of the animals 'cause they were my playmates when I was young. I played with woodchucks and chipmunks, squirrels, deer. I named them. My father took me, by boat, half an hour, to Rockwood to grammar school. I was there eight years. During this time, my father made maple syrup in the spring and sold it to the Kineo House [a hotel], which was in full swing. By high school there was still no road to Greenville so he sent me to a Quaker girls' boarding school, Oakgrove, in Vassalboro [Maine]. I was there four years. I was very homesick at first, only 13 years old, never been away from home before, but 'course when I graduated I cried and cried 'cause I loved it down there. My father asked me what I wanted when I graduated from high school in '34, and I said, "a little deer." The game warden found me one and I named her Diana. She lived to be 18-and-a-half years old, and she had triples five times, 35 offspring in all.

"When I was running the camp dining room, we had three cows, until you had to have your milk pasteurized. And we had pigs. We have two islands: one is called Spinney Island; the other, in back, used to be Pig Island, where we kept three pigs (now it's called Isle of Man). The pigs swam off. Then I had a pen full of pheasants, thought guests would like them for dinner, but weasels got in. They don't eat them, just suck their blood. We always had a cook and served lobster every Friday night and a buffet every Sunday. Mother cleaned the cabins and I waitressed from when I was 14 years old. The camp was only open for fishing, for families summering, then. They used to come and stay a long while. Many famous people. They came by boat from Rockwood Landing—we had three boats going back and forth—until I had the road built in '54. There were 8 or 10 guides. One guide, his wife cooked so he was here all the time; the others would come and go. There was no hunting, no vegetable garden, because we had tame deer. People would show home movies, play billiards. The lucky thing is we've never had anything burn down here."

Owner and association president, Mike Shidlovsky: "In 1993 the lodge and all the cabins, with the exception of numbers 4, 5, and 6 sold at auction. To own property, you have to be part of our association. One of the pluses of having multi-ownership is that after the auction the camps really needed a lot of repair. Working as a collective, we have more to contribute toward the expenses. All the cabins have new roofs, have good wells, have new or functional septic systems—there have been many inside and outside improvements. We have nine owners. All the owners are part of the rental pool and have committed to repairing our unique boardwalk. Actually, Tomhegan is unique physically and organizationally. It's a very special place and we're all trying to work together to assure its long-term health."

Managers Leona and Norman Harding: "We're here because I just got sick of the whole work force. The work ethics were going down and down. I looked in the papers one day, saw this job, and we interviewed the next day. We were standing out front, talking with Jeff, the former owner, it was the first day of hunting season, I knew this was a game preserve around here, but he's talking and a deer came right over, nuzzled him, and Jeff never even flinched. I'm thinking, 'What's going on?!' Before we were done there were about 14 deer around us—Jeff had carrots in his pockets, had been feeding them all summer. We're driving out the driveway and I says to Leona, "We've gotta have this job!" From our point of view it's great—we're running a business, but not spending our own money. We got the job and moved here November 2000." *Leona:* "December it's closed and then it all started right off in January with the squirrel, the first place I rented. Seems a squirrel had crawled underneath and eaten through the mattress, mattress cover, both sheets, and the blanket! It wasn't very big so I said, 'Well, we'll just put a little hand towel in there and flip it over.' Which we did. I made up a new bed for them, and we all had the best laugh over that! Then in February we lost the power one weekend. We were full: the lodge and every cabin. And it was bitter cold. So we're running around making sure everyone's got the woodstoves going. I'm giving them all candles, passing out decks of cards and cribbage boards. So we learned real quick!

"The history of the boardwalk is that Margie's parents put it in, but there was no handrailing then. Then Alice Statler-Hilton, longtime guest, was getting on in years, and she paid to have the boardwalk redone with a railing. People sit out on their porches or walk down the boardwalk toward the marina and visit with each other. We walk down it, hand in hand, each evening to make sure everything's okay."

Norman: "I've got a story about guests and the deer. We had a couple from Florida here and they'd never seen deer up close. The lady held out a carrot and the deer ate right out of her hand. She wanted to know what they eat and I told her just about anything. Strawberry twizzlers are their favorite, but peanuts in a shell, vegetables. So she was feeding them everything out of their refrigerator except the meat. Her husband said he only got a steak for dinner, nothing else, one night once she started in. They went to Greenville twice—an hour plus each way!—got grocery bags full of stuff for the deer. Another couple came in the next week and that woman saw the other one feeding the deer, and it turned out the two women were having contests to see who would get the deer! Those deer learn from week to week which cabin has the best pickings. *Leona:* And we have ducks and geese; they come back the middle of May when the ice goes out. By fall we've got around 50 ducks out here. We had 11 rabbits we turned loose this spring and we must have about 30 in here now. It's fun to watch them play leapfrog with each other out on the lawn. Margie told me one time she had three bear cubs. They grew up, of course, and one day, after Keith had just varnished the lodge floor, she was in the kitchen making donuts. The kitchen swinging door kept moving back and forth so she went to see what was going on. Well, here was this big bear. He'd come right into the lodge, step, step, all over the varnished floor, and headed right for the smell of those donuts! Margie said she went out the back door and shut it tight. They always say that bears go out the same way they came in. 'Well, that's true,' she said. He ate, turned around, and went right back over that varnished floor!"

45. WEST BRANCH POND CAMPS

AP, SCA

OWNER: Carol Stirling Kealiher

ADDRESS: PO Box 1153, Kokadjo, Greenville, ME 04441; 207-695-2561

SEASON: May through September

ACCOMMODATIONS: Eight log cabins: one to two bedrooms, screened porch, indoor plumbing and shower, woodstove, electric light; pets accepted

RATES: $68 per person per day, includes boat or canoe

ACCESS: I-95 north to exit 39 (Newport). Take ME 7 to Dexter, ME 23 to Guilford, and ME 6/15 to Greenville. At the blinking light, go straight on Lily Bay Road 19 miles. Take a right onto Frenchtown Road (camp sign) and go 10 miles on a gravel road to camp sign on right. "The telephone line ends here!"

As you reach the end of the road and come into the camp yard you see a set of log cabins and log lodge that almost say aloud, "We have stood on this spot and have withstood time and weather, and plan to stay standing long into the future." A horse wanders by, munching placidly. At the main lodge, a porch wraps around the clear evidence of the lodge's former outside walls and roof. Inside, the bookcases are filled with vintage reads, there's comfortable old furniture, and a piano that still plays tunefully enough that the camp waiter sits down and people come by and sing. This is one of those places where time has stood still.

Carol: "The camps were started in the mid- to late 1880s as a logging camp. Then Charles Randall sold to my great-uncle, Lewis Chadwick, in 1910, and it's been in our family ever since. When my grandparents were ready to sell, they first offered it to their oldest child. But he was in the Marines and wanted to make a career out of that. So they offered it to my mother, and it wasn't a matter of 'Well, maybe we'll give it a try.' It was just expected that that's what she would do. So my parents took over in the spring of 1950 when I was 2½ years old. And then I took it over, so it's been through two generations in the female line. One way or the other, the family's been running it a long, long time.

"West Branch Pond here is the source of the West Branch of the Plea-sant River. The West and East Branches converge just north of Brownville Junction and eventually drain into the Piscataquis River,

West Branch Pond Camps

which flows past Milo, where my parents are from. At Howland it reaches the Penobscot River, which flows to the sea. This is a different watershed from Moosehead Lake.

"We're a summertime camp for vacationing and fishing. The pond is fly-fishing, with nice pan-sized brook trout. To go with those breakfast trout, we plan on having our own eggs and milk cow once again, and to expand our garden. We have the horse, and our camp dog, TARI-2, is named for where we are on the map: Township A, Range 12. They did the surveys around the time of the Civil War.

"Each generation in my family has handled education for their children differently. My grandparents sent their children back to Milo to live with relatives when school was in session and they were working here. My folks wanted us all together, so my father built a house in Greenville, and my sister and I started kindergarten there, worked our way through high school, and went off to college. Our three boys, Jack, Nathan, and Eric, were home-schooled. Two went on to college and graduated summa cum laude. People come in here and marvel that children from out here in the backwoods can do so well out in the world. Our oldest went to Montana and became a wildlife photographer. He had an injury, and I lost him in the fall of '95. It's something, I imagine, that you never get over. But these camps have helped in a way. I talk to friends, and relationships come and go, people move, bad and good things happen, but the camps are the one constant in my life. They are a precious thing to me, and to our guests. I think one of the boys may take over eventually. It's too much of a family heritage, too unique to let it go. These places generate quite a story."

West Branch Pond Camps' Breakfast Trout

Carol: "I think good, home-cooked food is getting harder and harder to find. People sure appreciate it here."

> 6 slices bacon, six 8- to 10-ounce trout, cleaned (heads and tails still on), 1¼ cup yellow cornmeal, salt and lemon pepper to taste, ⅓ cup canola oil, 4 thinly-sliced pieces of lemon for garnish

Fry the bacon in a cast-iron pan 'til crisp and brown. Drain on brown paper and set aside. Reserve the bacon fat for next step. Rinse the fish, then dredge in cornmeal. Salt and lemon pepper both sides to taste. Add the canola oil to the bacon fat. Heat pan until very hot, but not smoking. Fry the trout for about 3½ minutes per side. Use spaghetti tongs or a wide spatula for turning. Shake the pan frequently to avoid sticking. Trout should be golden and crisp on the outside, moist and tender on the inside. If your pan is too small, cook fish in batches and keep warm in a low oven. Serve one trout per person. Garnish as you wish with lemon and crumbled bacon.

46. WILSON POND CAMPS

HK
OWNERS: Bob and Martine Young
ADDRESS: PO Box 1354, Greenville, ME 04441; 207-695-2860; e-mail: info@wilsonpondcamps.com; www.wilsonpondcamps.com
SEASON: Year-round
ACCOMMODATIONS: Seven cabins: one to three bedrooms, indoor plumbing and shower, screened porch, woodstove and automatic heat, electric lights, stove, and refrigerator. One remote cabin. Pets accepted only at remote cabin.
RATES: $80 per couple per day; $550 per cabin per week
ACCESS: I-95 north to exit 39 (Newport). Go north on ME 7 to Dexter, take ME 23 to Guilford, then ME 6/15 to Greenville. In Greenville, turn right opposite the cruise ship *Katahdin* onto Pleasant Street and go 3.5 miles to camp.

The Youngs' camps are the only set of housekeeping cottages on Lower Wilson Pond. Five cabins are right on the water; the other two are a short walk away. The Youngs have owned the camps since 1995.

Martine: "My husband and I are from Maine originally and have always loved camping and being in the outdoors. We spent a lot of time with our children in the Moosehead area and at Fish Creek Pond in the Adirondacks. These experiences made such an impression on us all—no TV or phone, learning how to water-ski and do outdoor things. My husband was helping his brother try to find a cottage to buy in the area. They had been looking around

Wilson Pond Camps

when the realtor told them there was a sporting camp for sale. Well, I could just see his ears go 'ding!' Now, we had just built our dream house. From scratch. It had taken us two years. My husband came home and said, 'Martine, you've got to hear what happened!' and I knew, somehow, just by looking at him that we'd be losing our beautiful new home.

"Bob at the time was head of the maintenance department at the Hathaway Shirt Company, and he'd heard all the rumors about the company closing up. So he knew he might be losing his job and he said this might be our opportunity to go into a business that was a lifestyle as well. We could live our dream. I asked him how we could possibly afford it, and he said we'd have to sell our brand-new home. I knew we'd be able to operate a camp because my husband holds all the licenses—electrician, plumber, boiler operator—and we'd both had a lot of camping experience. The other thing is that between the two of us we had lost three parents in three consecutive years. We knew how short life is and how important it is to try to follow your dreams. So we put our house on the market one Friday and on Saturday it was sold! I'm a strong believer that there's a reason for everything."

Bob: Wilson Pond is almost 7 miles long and over 32 feet deep, with lake and brown trout, salmon, and some white perch. The fishing is good because we have a lot of people who catch-and-release. Our remote camp is on Upper Wilson Pond. It's accessible by boat only, and tricky even by boat at times!

"We're open year-round because we're close to Squaw Mountain for skiers and the area's good for snowshoeing. Also, it's a big hobby for people around here to go out on snowshoes, snowmobile, or skis and hunt for sheds. Every year the moose and deer shed their antlers and people go around and pick them up. I've seen some in stores that go for over a hundred dollars.

"We have fixed the place up considerably since we've been here. All the former guests comment on it. One woman used to come in with her son and his family. And she'd get a motel room in town and visit them on the pond. She was just floored at how clean and neat everything was and said, 'I think I've died and gone to heaven.' We stayed in each cabin at first and every time I needed something I'd get seven. So they're fully equipped. One time when we were first here a man came driving in and I introduced myself. He didn't say his name, he just said, 'How much for the place?' I looked at him and said, 'Excuse me?'

" 'How much?' I shook my head, 'It's not for sale.'

" 'Everything's for sale. Name your price.'

"I'm thinking, we've only owned it for two years. You have no idea how hard we've worked to bring it to what it is now. I said, 'There's no price that could ever repay that.'} We have an editor from *Sports Illustrated* who comes for what he calls 'total mental relaxation.' As we say, 'Come once and you'll come again and again.' "

47. WILSON'S ON MOOSEHEAD

HK
OWNERS: Wayne and Shan Snell
ADDRESS: Greenville Junction, ME 04442; 207-695-2549
SEASON: Year-round
ACCOMMODATIONS: Fifteen log cabins: one to five bedrooms, indoor plumbing and tub with shower, screened porch, electric lights and refrigerator, automatic and wood heat (four cabins have fireplaces), gas stove, TV hook-up; well-attended pets accepted
RATES: $75–300 per cabin per day; $425–1,500 per cabin per week
ACCESS: I-95 north to exit 39 (Newport). Go north on ME 7 to Dexter, take ME 23 to Guilford, then ME 6/15 to Greenville. Wilson's is 6 miles past Squaw Mountain on Rockwood Road (ME 15).

Wilson's is about halfway between Rockwood and Greenville, within walking distance and view of the East Outlet Dam at the headwaters of the Kennebec River. The half-mile driveway passes over railroad tracks that brought guests to the camps and fish back to Boston in the latter part of the 1800s and into the 1900s. One can tell that this was once a thriving hub. An ocher-colored building with maroon trim looms large and somewhat Victorian. Hotel-sized, with a square tower, the structure is sagging and may not be long for this world. The cabins spread out on the lawns under gracious old trees and span the outlet into the Kennebec and its entrance cove in Moosehead. The white-clapboard main lodge houses the tackle shop and office.

Wilson's on Moosehead

Shan: "Wilson's started in 1865, built as a sporting camp, and is the oldest continuously running sporting camp on Moosehead Lake—and probably about the oldest in Maine. Henry I. Wilson left Massachusetts after the Civil War ended, in 1865, to come up and build a sawmill and dam here on the Kennebec. He said that this area was a 'sportsman's paradise' and built the first 'long house' for his sports. The hotel was originally called the Outlet House. We have the old register and one of the guests was Ulysses S. Grant. One year President Eisenhower's staff came up, checked the place out, and selected Wilson's for the President's vacation. They told Don Wilson he'd have to clear out all the guests so the President could stay. Mr. Wilson answered, 'I'm not refusing my guests for anyone.' So they went to Rangeley that year. His guests came even before the President.

"We are on the widest part of the lake, and from here you can get a 120-mile view out across the lake and islands to Big and Little Spencer Mountains, Squaw Mountain, and even Katahdin. Moosehead is 40 miles long by 20 wide and from here you can see 20 miles across, the widest view of Spencer Bay. Each of our cabins has a great view.

"The East Outlet is fly-fishing only. You can get salmon or square-tail trout in one of the eddies below the dam or cast into the big pool above the dam, just in front of the sucking water of the spillway. We've got great hunting and fall foliage. In the winter Squaw Mountain, for downhill skiing, is just down the road, cross-country skiing is out the back, and we have a thousand-foot frontage on the lake for ice fishing. There are hundreds of miles of well-groomed snowmobile trails around Moosehead that you can get onto right here at our entrance.

"My husband and I have been here since 1983. He was a school principal down in southern Maine and we just wanted to get away from it all. But we're still working hard, harder than ever, up here! It's a big place to take care of, there are a lot of rules and regulations and expenses, and there's always something that needs fixing in an old camp. We've seen a lot of changes over the years. At the end of the '80s we were losing some of our families because of the economy. In the '90s we're getting more couples. And it used to be that 90 percent of our guests didn't want TV. Now I'd say it's about 50 percent. Sporting camps were never meant for sitting inside and watching TV; it's a time for family bonding and adventure in a beautiful wilderness spot. These camps have a long history, and hopefully they'll be here a whole lot longer."

THE BAXTER STATE PARK REGION

This region includes the land and waters surrounding 250,000-acre Baxter State Park, a forever-wild wilderness area left to Maine by former governor Percival Baxter. The Golden Road and Church Pond Road form the southern boundary, with ME 11 to the east and the Canadian border to the west. The northern boundary of the park serves as the northern boundary of this region as well. Looking at this area in terms of physical features, you find Chesuncook Lake to the west, Shin Pond area to the east, Grand Lake Matagamon to the north, and the town of Millinocket in the south. Millinocket is the major city and gateway to most of the camps in this region, and has most of the facilities a traveler might require. East Millinocket is home to a large papermill, currently up for sale. Farther north, the town of Patten serves as the focal point for the village of Shin Pond and its group of camps. It is also a center for lumbering operations. You might want to visit the Lumberman's Museum (207-528-2650), which features the history of Maine's lumbering industry.

Within the park, the northern terminus of the Appalachian Trail is atop "mile-high" Mount Katahdin—at 5,267 feet, Maine's highest peak. About 45 other peaks and ridges provide additional hiking opportunities. There is a perimeter road (narrow, windy, and dirt) around the park leading to public camping sites (reservations required). The park does not allow motorcycles or pets.

GETTING THERE: The closest airports are Bangor International Airport and Presque Isle (rental cars available at both). Driving time from Portland is 4–6 hours; from Boston, 7–8 hours; from New York City, 10–12 hours. Float planes are available through Scotty's Flying Service, Shin Pond, 207-528-2626; Katahdin Air Service, Millinocket, 207-723-8378;

Folsom's Air Service, Greenville, 207-695-2821; and Currier's Flying Service, Greenville, 207-695-2778.

GUIDANCE: For further information, contact Baxter State Park Headquarters, 64 Balsam Drive, Millinocket, ME 04462 (207-723-5140).

48. BEAR MOUNTAIN LODGE

HK/MAP/AP, SCA

OWNERS: Carroll and Deanna Gerow

ADDRESS: Moro Plantation, RD 1, Box 1969, Smyrna Mills, ME 04780; 207-528-2124

SEASON: Year-round

ACCOMMODATIONS: Five cabins: one to two bedrooms, indoor plumbing and shower, electric lights, oil or gas heat; two outpost cabins have outhouse, woodstove, gas lights, and cookstove

RATES: $18–30 per person per day, $120–175 per cabin per week (HK); $250 per person per week (MAP); $50 per person per day, $350 per person per week (AP).

ACCESS: I-95 to exit 58 (Patten–Sherman). Take ME 11 north through Patten. Bear Mountain Lodge is 12 miles beyond Patten on the left (east) side of ME 11.

D*eanna:* "These camps were built prior to 1955. Carroll and I used to run it in the summers during the 1960s for a man named Ray Lorentz. Then we bought the place in 1970. I'm from Patten, 12 miles away, and Carroll is from Knowles Corner, only 4 miles away, so we joke that we didn't go far in life! Since Carroll's from right here and he was trained as a forester, he knows where to guide people. November is our busiest time, when the trophy-size deer around here are in rut. Rifle season in November is bucks-only with doe by permit only, and we have application forms. In fact, our place is the local game-inspection station. The season for natural-feed areas not baiting for bears is the same as the rifle season for deer, so it gives people a chance to hunt bear along with deer, which is why we're so busy. During that time most guests eat their meals in the lodge.

"We're not on a lake or stream, but there are a lot of fishing options in the area. We're right on Route 11, which is very scenic during fall-foliage time. For a two-lane highway, it's a pretty important road. I read the other day that the North Maine Development Commission figured out that $7 million worth of commodities go by on this road. Daily!

"After hunting season is over, we get snowmobilers. Clubs and individuals make reservations to stay with us, or just eat a meal at the lodge. To reach us by snow-sled you go on ITS 75—which is groomed—from Patten, Island Falls, and Oakfield (20 miles south), or north to ITS 85 and Oxbow (30 miles) or west to ITS 85 and Shin Pond (20 miles). And from these areas there are trails heading out in all directions."

49. BOWLIN CAMPS

AP/HK, SCA
OWNERS: Bowlin Camps, LLC
OWNER/MANAGER: Lt. Col. Ken Conaster
ADDRESS: PO Box 251, Patten, ME 04765; 207-528-2022;
e-mail: bowlincamps@ainop.com; www.bowlincamps.com
SEASON: Year-round
ACCOMMODATIONS: Nine log cabins: one to three bedrooms, indoor plumbing and shower, porch, three with kitchenette, gas range, wood heat, gas and electric lights; well-attended pets allowed
RATES: $75–85 per person per day, $475–595 per person per week (AP); $70–145 per cabin per day (HK)
ACCESS: I-95 to exit 58 (Patten–Sherman). Turn left onto ME 158, then right onto ME 11 and go north to Patten. From Patten, take ME 159 west to Hay Lake. Turn left at the sign, just beyond the ranger station. Follow the dirt road and signs 8 miles to camp.

As you pull into camp, you see the East Branch of the Penobscot River to your right and a small pond on a knoll to your left. The driveway leads up a hill past the log main lodge, nestled in the hollow surrounded by maples and pines. To your left, on the top of the knoll, a cluster of honey-colored log cabins spreads out toward the woods. A large garden and cleared field stretch out behind the cabins.

Ken: "The camps were started in 1895 by Charles McDonald. He bought the property from the logging companies who were using it in the 1850s to bring logs down the river. We have two of his original cabins; the rest burned down in '48. After that the Chapmans had it, then Jon and Betty Smallwood came in 1968. They're the ones that raised four boys back here with no running water; they were the first and only kids in Maine who took a float plane to school each day. Then we bought in '99, so there have been only four owners over 100 years! And the road in has only been here since '86.

"The way that my partner and I found the camps is that we were up in Maine bear hunting. I'm a pilot by trade, and Maine Guide, and after I'd shot a bear we went flying. We were looking for a camp. We have a camp in South Carolina, but I like the North better; I'm from the North, my partner's from Virginia. We looked at one farther north, but didn't like it, and on the way back just happened to fly over this one, having no idea it was for sale. And we said, 'Now there's a beautiful place. Right on the river, gorgeous, well maintained. We landed and drove in, just to visit, and lo and behold, found out they were retiring. We negotiated and a year later owned the place.

"It's one of the most secluded places in northern Maine, yet accessible by vehicle. Baxter Park is very close on our western side. From the dooryard you're looking at Traveler Mountain and Katahdin. According to Jon and Betty, there was a huge fire in the park in 1912, and families living in the woods near Grand Lake Matagamon all moved out. But the fire never jumped the lake. Most of Baxter burned. It started sometime in the fall, and it was still smoldering in the spring. Some places it burned 10 to 12 feet deep in the ground.

"We've kept the place just like it was, only now every cabin has a bathroom and shower. So you can have what we call a 'soft adventure.' You're in the deep woods, but you're not going to an outhouse. We've added tin roofs to the cabins to make them heat easier, and put in insulation. We want them to be comfortable for families. We cater to people fishing, hiking, vacationing, hunting, snowmobiling.

"For hiking we have numerous trails—any compass point you choose I can give you trails you can hike, and usually you won't see another individual. One thing about here is that it is posted for four-wheelers. Most everything around the camp is owned by Irving Corporation, which doesn't allow four-wheelers on their property.

"In the last 10 years the snowmobiling industry has grown so much in northern Maine. When Jon and Betty had it they could feed 20 people; we've expanded that so we can feed 48 now. And at lunchtime, from 10:00 until 2:00, we're full—a thousand sleds a day. We're 30 miles from Millinocket and the first gas stop. I keep 2 to 3 thousand gallons on hand. We also have something I don't think you'll see at any other sporting camp. In 1990, with the help of the Matagamon Snowmobile Club, Jon and Betty built a suspension bridge to get snowmobilers over the river. It's 122 feet long, all on cable. It comes right through the yard and goes on to Shin Pond Village. In September 2001, we all got together and at another river crossing about 3 miles from here, across the Seboeis, we built a 165-foot bridge that we can take the groomer across. So now it's actually an ITS trail (85A) because there are no water crossings. In the winter you can drive pretty-much any vehicle in here because we keep it plowed.

"One of the things we're expanding upon is the river. This is one of the most pristine rivers in the State of Maine. We probably see 15 to 20 canoes, in addition to ours, go down it the whole year. We have a two-day, 36-mile trip here that has no portages whatsoever. We can pick you up in Medway at the end. Or, if you want a one-day trip, we can pick you up at Whetstone. It's just a gorgeous piece of wilderness water that a novice can do. There are wilderness campsites all along the route. You don't have to pay for them; all you have to do is get a fire permit from the forest service at Shin Pond Village.

"We cater to basically all types of hunting: bear, deer, partridge (ruffed grouse), and varmint (coyote in the late winter and early spring). The coyote population is continuing to grow in Maine, so we're offering a coyote hunt where we use electronic calls (which are legal) and mouth calling and kill them with a high-powered rifle, small caliber—something that's fast and flat-shooting. The only time you can really call them in is when there's lots of snow. And for bear hunting, I have about 120,000 acres I lease and I run 50 active bait sites (the first one's about ½ mile from camp; the farthest's about 13 miles away). At Bowlin's you're not on a highway getting in a vehicle to hunt, you're right in the middle of the hunting area. Thirty-three years under the different owners we've never been below 50 percent success rate. We take 12 hunters a week, at the most. We pride ourselves here that you're not a number but can get the individual attention you deserve.

"The bird hunting is usually the month of October, when the leaves are at their best. And we have lots of birds. To flush four to six coveys a day is not uncommon. There are two kinds of grouse: ruffed and spruce. Ruffed is a little bigger than spruce with a red mark over the eye, and the tail is darker. The spruce is almost tame and isn't hunted.

"Fishing is something we're building on here. This is probably one of the best fishing rivers I have ever seen. You can literally float this river down to Whetstone during the spring run and catch 100 trout. You can stand on these banks out here early May to mid-June and catch 5 or 10 trout without moving. It's pristine, clear, and because there's only one road into it, it's not fished that much. Only people that come to the camp can get to this part of the river."

Fiddlehead Soup

"All the guys take turns cooking, we all like to cook. We'll even feed people coming in to just look around. (Normally of course I like to have advance bookings, but drive-ins are no problem.) There are acres of fiddleheads in the spring and this soup is a real favorite."

First you need to have ½ gallon of homemade chicken stock. Season that to taste with adobo seasoning, McCormick's seasoning salt, and salt and pepper. Then you add ½ cup crushed garlic, 1 quart heavy cream, and 1 quart coarsely chopped fiddleheads and bring almost to a boil. Reduce heat and simmer for 30 minutes and serve.

50. BUCKHORN CAMPS

AP/HK, SCA

OWNERS: Leon and Linda Jones

ADDRESS: PO Box 639, Millinocket, ME 04462; 207-745-5023; e-mail: buckhorn@kai.net; www. Buckhorncamps.com

SEASON: Year-round

ACCOMMODATIONS: Seven log cabins: one to two bedrooms, porch, indoor plumbing and shower (showers in lodge during winter), gas and kerosene lamps, wood and propane heat, gas stove and refrigerator. Bunk room. Lodge rooms: electricity, indoor plumbing, and shower.

RATES: $60–85 per person per day (AP); $25–50 per person per day (HK); customized meal plans and child rates available

ACCESS: I-95 north to exit 54 (Howland). Take ME 6/155 west to Milo and then ME 11 through Brownville Junction to Jo-Mary Campground sign on left. Stop at the Jo-Mary checkpoint (call ahead to arrange boat pick-up). From the gate, follow Jo-Mary Road 6 miles. Take a right at the intersection. The cut-off road is 8.8 miles from the gate on the right. Follow camp signs and take a left at 12.9 miles to the landing site.

If a drive in on dirt roads isn't enough, the boat ride and view of Buckhorn Camps sitting alone on the pristine lake should give you the sense of having arrived back of the beyond. Log cabins are ranged around a long peninsula on a 2-mile island. A large, free-standing fireplace and long log building overhanging the water dominate the foreground. Huge pine trees form the background.

Leon: "The history of this place is that a man named Albert Haynes was scouting phone lines for the loggers in around 1889. From what I understand he started the place as a private sporting lodge—dues were 25 cents a month. And then, I've been told it was in 1897 that he started a commercial operation here. Bert was known as a caribou guide on Katahdin. Bert and his son, Jasper, owned the camps. Bert and a doctor from Brewer drowned in the lower lake (Lower Jo-Mary) on Memorial Day, 1927, and Jasper took over. At that time people came in by railway; up the Pemadumcook chain of lakes into Pemadumcook where they were met by canoe and brought up through Lower Jo-Mary, which most of this island is on, through to the lodge. After Jasper took over, he became a pilot so then there was air access into here. From what I hear, he was pretty infamous as a pilot. I understand he flew refrigerators in—tied them on to the pontoons— but his daughter says the story of him flying a cow around isn't true. Then, right around 1960, Jasper crashed his plane and died of injuries a week later. And at that point Rudy Zaninetti, and some other folks, bought the camps in a partnership. They were run commercially, maybe 10 years, and then there was a boy's camp in here for a short time, and then they became private around 30 years ago.

Buckhorn Camps

"We bought them in 1998. I'd been in the previous winter by snow-mobile. But every time I'd try to bring Linda in it rained and we couldn't travel the lakes. So she got to see them in May and we owned them in June. And then the adventure began.

"We had talked about doing something like this for a long time. I'd already acquired my Master Guide's license, so I was geared that way. It was one of those jump-in-with-both-feet things. We came here from mid-coast Maine, but had a camp on Ambajejus Lake prior to this. I started coming up to this general area almost 25 years ago. I just like the Katahdin area, like guiding on the West Branch of the Penobscot River.

"Salmon fishing's what I really enjoy, although I don't get much chance these days. I think they're the hardest fish to land, got the most fight, most acrobatics. The only other one's the smallmouth bass, but the salmon's smaller and more powerful, I think. I really prefer them in the fast water, but I'll take them in the lake if I have to. Here I have a different type of fishery, but a good fishery. For instance, we have a great spring run of white perch within walking distance.

"We're on a lake that borders two lakes and the flowage runs right by the lodge into the lower lake. The waters actually flow north here, which is rare in Maine. We're the drainage of the Jo-Mary Mountain area. The point the camps are on is only 200 feet wide at the widest, so all the cabins have a water view. Middle Jo-Mary is roughly 2 miles by a mile and a quarter and about 24 feet deep; Lower Jo-Mary is around 65 feet deep, roughly 5 miles long and a mile or so wide, and holds salmon and lake trout year-round. There's no public access; it will never be developed, no roads in. The Appalachian Trail goes along one shoreline; Antlers Campground is there. It does get fished pretty hard in the winter. These lakes have good feed: a lot of chub and some smelts.

"The prime moose-watching is usually mid-May through mid-July and most years we see half a dozen moose a day during that time. They feed either side of the peninsula. Then when the weather gets hot they fade away. The Cooper Brook deadwater is a big draw for them. It's a thousand acres of marshland. Full of wildlife. Nice place to kayak and canoe."

Linda: "Every season is so different and special. In the spring, the wildflowers are blooming all around. The moose often come on the island to feed on the wild azaleas. And we often see newborn calves from the living-room window in the mornings. In the summer people come from out of state and see the wildlife for the first time. Children get to fish and swim and enjoy life as it should be. In the fall I canoe over to pick cranberries at a bog not too far from here. There's nothing like the taste of wild cranberries. Leon guides deer, bear, and moose hunters during this time. They hunt, I feed them. I've had hunters leave saying, 'How am I gonna explain to my wife that I gained 5 pounds!'"

Leon: "I'm in the middle of putting in a new kitchen and totally refurbishing the Sports Lounge, which overhangs the water, and was the old dining hall. That's where I'll be doing my snowmobile feeding. In the winter, the Jo-Mary road is a major connector from ITS 83 to 86. I'm also working on Nellie's Camp—Nellie was Bert's wife; there's also Nellie's Island across the way. During Bert and Nellie's time they had a hired man named Amos Archer and he hand-hewed the cedar shakes for the cabins. They're actually cedar boards, a Haynes trait, 4–5 feet long. According to the book *A Museum of Early American Tools*, by Eric Sloane, a good man could 'rive' a thousand shingles a day using a 'froe' (which looks like a long metal knife, for slicing) and a mallet.

"In the winter, I carry water to the cabins. I place a 55-gallon barrel with a spigot in the showers, we have jugs of drinking water, and use buckets to flush the toilets. The lodge has year-round bathroom facilities. The distances between places are cut phenomenally in winter: it's 8 miles over the lake to the dike at Ambajejus versus 40 off the lake. All these logging roads that aren't plowed are open to riding. And for us, that's the time we bring in most of our supplies. I try to get ahead as much as I can in the fall. I have an old pontoon boat I've converted into a barge, with a wheelhouse so I can get out of the weather. I move propane and wood, everything I can over open water with that. Then during the winter, everything comes in by snowmobile—mostly food, for the restaurant, and supplies like extra propane and fuel for the generator."

Linda: "The winter of 2001, I started working at the Millinocket hospital four days a week and coming in here weekends. I'm a Certified Nuclear Medicine Technologist and a Registered Radiologic Technologist. Balancing Buckhorn and the hospital makes life quite interesting at times, especially during the winter. But, so far, it's been do-able." *Leon:* "You gotta be a jack-of-all-trades around a sporting camp, and you've got to be fairly proficient. You've got to be in good shape physically because it's hard work. It's hard to find help. They think the woods life is so romantic and don't realize just how much work is involved. I find sporting-camp owners have a real good appreciation of what the others are doing because we all know."

Deviled Fish Fillets

3 cups soft bread crumbs, 1½ T grated Parmesan cheese, ½ tsp. salt, ½ cup melted butter (divided), 1½ T Worcestershire sauce, ½ tsp. dry mustard (1 tsp wet), 2 pounds fish

In a mixing bowl, mix ¼ cup butter and remaining ingredients, except fish. Place fish fillets in a single layer in a greased shallow baking pan. Spoon bread crumb mixture evenly over fillets. Drizzle remaining ¼ cup butter over bread crumbs. Add water up the sides of the fish (approximately ½ cup). Cover with foil. Bake in 325-degree oven until fish flakes when tested with a fork. Remove foil. Put under the broiler and lightly brown the bread crumbs.

51. FROST POND CAMPS

HK, SCA

OWNERS: Maureen Raynes and Gene Thompson

CAMP ADDRESS: HC 76, Box 620, Greenville, ME 04441; 207-852-4700 (voice mail); e-mail: frostpondcamps@msn.com; wwwfrostpondcamps.com (phone calls and e-mail answered within three days)

SEASON: Year-round

ACCOMMODATIONS: Seven log and frame cabins: one to two bedrooms; one cabin with indoor plumbing and shower, six with private outhouse; central water and shower; porch; gas lights, stove, and refrigerator; woodstove; ten off-site campsites, no utilities

RATES: $22–28 per person per day; motorboats $42 per day, $252 per week; canoes $17 per day, $102 per week; child rates available

ACCESS: I-95 to exit 56 (Medway). Take ME 11/157 to Millinocket. Follow Baxter State Park Road for 9 miles. At Northwoods Trading Post, the last source for supplies, cross over to the Golden Road. Continue in the same direction, but do not follow the signs for Baxter State Park. Look for signs to camp and Ripogenus Dam after about 20 miles. Cross the dam and continue 3 miles on a dirt road along Chesuncook Lake to camp.

Getting to sporting camps is part of the adventure, and the Frost Pond Camps access offers a drive over a dam and along a meandering road within several feet of Chesuncook Lake. The well-graded entrance drive has a long allée of shade trees. The main lodge and camps to the left of the road lead down to Frost Pond, 1 mile long by 1 mile wide and 40 feet deep.

Gene: "We're the only place on the pond except for a secluded private cottage. People fish here for square-tail trout and on the West Branch of the Penobscot for world-class landlocked salmon. We have a canoe at Little Frost Pond and are right by Harrington and Chesuncook Lakes. For guests who like to hike, we have a couple of trails. One goes along Ripogenus Dam through the gorge along the river. In October we have excellent grouse hunting, in November we gear up for deer hunting, and for moose we're in zone four, which has an excellent success rate.

"Most of what we know about the history of the camps has been handed down by word of mouth. Rick and Judy Givens, the former owners, said Ripogenus Dam was completed in 1916, and a road built 3 miles to Frost Pond, where there was a lumber camp for about 10 years. Eventually they pushed the road in about 3 miles farther and built what was called Duck Pond Storehouse. A lot of the lumber camps were portable and they'd move them around on skids. So Frost Pond was discontinued as a lumber camp. Harry Bowe and, supposedly, Al Nugent took it over and ran it as a sporting camp. They built four cabins, but it wasn't too long before Al Nugent realized there wasn't enough money there for two. So the story is that he migrated north and started Nugent's Camps. This took place around the late '20s. Then Flossie and A. E. "Boot" Levensellar owned it. Boot worked on the telephone lines for Great Northern Paper Company and he built canoes and traded horses for the logging operations."

Maureen: "I know, from talking to the game warden that used to have this district, that Boot would go out and 'clean worms' (this pond at the time was fly-fishing-only). If he was out there and Flossie saw a game warden coming, she'd go down to the dock and yell, 'Boot, telephone!' and he'd know that he'd have to dump his worms overboard. That was their code! Boot built a log cabin, three frame cabins, a workshop, woodshed, and garage.

"I used to work down in Bangor. We lived up here part-time and part-time in Bangor for work. After I started getting comfortable being up here I decided I liked it pretty good. And we talked about a lot of different options on how we could live up here full time. We wanted to home-school Jed. As he got close to going to school I realized I wasn't going to see him that much because I was working long hours. I wanted out of the office lifestyle. I wanted my own business so I could have complete control over the service, make my own decisions, do things from the heart. So that was a real driving factor, and being with Jed all the time. I grew up in a rural setting in Maine. We're both from Maine, so that's why this move worked for us. A lot of people were shocked when I left a corporate environment to come here, but this lifestyle is much more me. I was just working before, now I'm living.

"And this just kind of came together. We called Rick and Judy late February 2000. We came in the first week of March and moved in June first. Fortunately June wasn't overly busy so we could get a handle on things. In the fall especially we had some regulars. Ever since one cabin was finished in the late '60s, the first group to use it has been coming back here."

Gene: "This is a quiet area. There's not a lot of traffic going by. Radios and stuff like that, well, most people don't bring them, and if they do they understand that as long as you can hear it in your cabin, that's fine. But I don't want other people listening to your radio (and that goes for the camp-sites, too). A lot of the folks that come up here, especially in the summer-time, come up to listen to the loons, the owls, the sounds of nature. And we're getting people saying they're here because it's getting too noisy other places they've been staying. They really need some peace and quiet. And another thing they love are the stars. When it's dark here, it's dark. There's no ambient light. So we have people out laying on the lawn seeing how big and close the stars look.

"We're upgrading around here all the time, starting with the bottom and working our way up. I've jacked up one cabin so far, and I've got anoth-er one set up to go.

"I started out doing mechanic work and then worked at a mill up in Houlton where I did electrical work, was a machinist, carpenter, mechanic, and millwright. Whatever needed to be done, I was the guy that did it. When I was talking with Rick about buying this place, he said, 'Well, of all the people who've looked at it, you are definitely the most qualified because there's nothing you can't do.' Except tie flies; I can't tie flies. But all of my background has been very helpful. I did work for the town of Millinocket for four and a half years, and that's when I started working with the public. Then in '88 I opened my own garage and was working with the public all the time. By the time Maureen and I married in '94, and my son was born, I owned a place on Chesuncook Lake and was working in Millinocket. While I was at Chesuncook of course I got to know Bert and Maggie McBurnie, the former owners of the Chesuncook Lake House. I sold Bert his first telephone for the Lake House, because I also have a contract with Unicell selling and installing cellular phones. I've been very poplar out in this part of the world for a number of years because whenever their cell phone doesn't work they look me up and I do custom antennaes for them and all that. Keep them working.

"Some friends of ours, another game warden that used to be at Rip Dam, said, 'Why don't you buy Frost Pond?' I happened to be doing maple syrup—I have my lines down by the dam—and I met Rick. Maureen took a day off from work. Jed set there at the table, leans over, and says, 'Dad, tell that guy that he can be all done and we'll come live here.'" *Maureen:* "He

MAUREEN RAYNES

Frost Pond Camps

was only four at the time." *Gene:* "Already made up his mind. At this point he's seven and if I was to go outside and say, 'Come on, Jed, we've got to go to town,' he would be very upset. Not on his list of things to do. More fun right here than it is in town.

"There are no ITS trails near here so we don't get into a lot of heavy-duty snowmobiling. We have a few folks that come out and do what we like to call 'bushwack' snowmobiling, which is riding the old unbroken trails on the old logging roads. What we get most is people who want to do a little cross-country skiing, snowshoeing, and hanging out. The birds will come and eat out of your hand in the wintertime. Here again, quiet activities." *Maureen:* "I break a lot of snowshoe trails open along the ridges so if people want to go up and enjoy the view it makes it a little easier. We have snowshoes available with the cabins and additional ones to rent. We do have a 10-mile loop from the camp yard that we keep open with a snowsled. Our access is plowed in the winter. We do suggest, however, that a four-wheel-drive vehicle is a good idea." *Gene:* "It's always plowed; never sanded."

Maureen: "I've got to tell you a story. I'm a notary public and a Maine Guide and was toying with the idea of doing weddings out here, putting the two together. Well, we had a couple in late last August who spent the whole time out on the pond canoeing and fly-fishing. They came off the pond one gorgeous evening, a beautiful sunset, and he said, 'We just got engaged!' He was beaming. And I said, 'You know, I'm a notary and can marry you if you decide you want to come back and get married here.' They said that sounded great and we left it at that. Sure enough, I got an e-mail in the winter: 'Can you marry us in three weeks time?' I said, 'Sure!' And we put it together. It was really a beautiful wedding. They took our largest cabin. She brought all kinds of beautiful flowers. There was still snow on the ground and everything was just gorgeous. There was no schedule for the day. Whenever they felt ready was going to be it. We had some friends of ours stand up for them because they came by themselves. Gene took the snowsled and the shovel down to the campsites and shoveled out some stairs over the snowbank and packed down an area. And we did the ceremony right there on the edge of the pond. It was just incredibly special for all of us."

52. KATAHDIN LAKE WILDERNESS CAMPS

AP/MAP/HK, SCA

OWNERS: Al and Suzan Cooper

ADDRESS: Box 398, Millinocket, ME 04462; 207-723-4050 (camp radio phone), 207-723-9867 (winter); e-mail: t3r8lake@ime.net; www.katahdin-lakecamps.com

SEASON: Year-round

ACCOMMODATIONS: Ten log cabins: one to two bedrooms, outhouse, gas lights, woodstove

RATES: $100–125 per person per day (AP); $50–60 per person per day (HK); motorboats $40 per day; canoes $20 per day; pack-in with mules $25 per person ($50 minimum)

ACCESS: I-95 to exit 56 (Medway). Take ME 157 north through Millinocket and follow signs to Baxter State Park. Just after the Togue Pond (Park) gatehouse, take the right-hand fork (Roaring Brook Road) to Avalanche Field. Park your car and walk 3.5 miles in to camp, or call ahead to reserve packhorses to bring you and your gear in.

By the time you leave your car and walk, cross-country ski, fly, or pack in by horse to Katahdin Lake Wilderness Camps, the buzz of a plugged-in world is far behind. Log cabins and outbuildings form a thin oval around a clearing (think of an open exclamation point with the lodge as the dot). Down the embankment is 1½-mile-long by ½-mile-wide Katahdin Lake. Turner Mountain and Katahdin are so close they are reflected in the spring-fed waters, which hold square-tail trout. Sandy beaches ring most of the shoreline. The camp has 200,000-plus-acre Baxter State Park as its next-door neighbor, and there are no other public camps within 11 miles in any direction.

Suzan: "Oliver and Della Cobb were the previous owners. They owned it from the late '20s to the early '60s—44 years. I had the honor of knowing Della before she died in 1977. She had a diary for every year she was here, and that woman could keep you right at the edge of your chair with stories about the camps. Oliver Cobb Jr. remembers coming in here by buckboard when he was a child. And he said you could drive it through the woods anywhere because there were such massive virgin trees they blocked the sun, and there was no understory. Back in the 1800s, before Baxter Park became a park, people would come by train to Stacyville and then walk and ride the buckboard 11 miles to camp. Millinocket wasn't even on the map until 1903. They call it the magic city because, with the pulp mill, it popped up overnight.

"We've been here since 1975. My dad was originally from Maine, but was 25 years a dairy farmer in Massachusetts. And when I was in college in '69 my folks, Embert and Josephine Stevens, bought these camps and moved away. It was empty-nest syndrome in reverse. I mean, your parents aren't supposed to up and leave after you've lived in the same house 20 years! They lived here 5 years, but then Dad was thrown from a horse—he fell 13 or 15 feet and broke his back on the rocks. So Al decided he'd like to try to buy the camps, and we did. And it was pretty miraculous, really. The paper company had never given a 10-year lease before and we had to have that in order to get a mortgage from the bank. So we prayed and said, 'Lord, if you want us to have these camps, You're going to have to do this.' And, lo and behold, we got the lease! So we knew it was right.

"When we came here we were newlyweds. Our son, Alfie, was just a year old, and we didn't have much of anything. I was a schoolteacher; Al had no experience running a business. But Mom and Dad said, 'Work here with us for one year. We'll put all the wages you make toward a down payment.' So we went back to Massachusetts, had a big yard sale, and sold everything except our bed, a bureau, and Alfie's crib.

"These camps have been here since about 1885. Always sporting camps. They say that Teddy Roosevelt hunted caribou around Katahdin from right here. The original owner, to the best of my knowledge, was John Cushman. And his great-great-great-grandson sometimes guides for us! Al is a registered guide, so we hire only one other guide. Dana and Ruth Cushman used to come in to Sandy Stream Pond when they were in their '80s and she had to use two canes. It took them two hours for what is normally 15-minute walk. I see that determination in the generation that came before us. Like my mom and dad starting a new adventure in their 60s. My mom drew her second moose permit for the hunt when she was 90 years old—and she went! Now that's motivation. I've got a quote up in the kitchen we found at a flea market that pretty much says it: 'A wishbone ain't as likely to get ya someplace as a backbone.'

"Katahdin is the northern terminus of the Appalachian Trail and Alfie went to college in Georgia, a short distance from the southern terminus. I joked if he didn't like college, he could walk home! Our sons have all been home-schooled. Alfie went to high school at Lee Academy, east of Lincoln, because they had a five-day dormitory. He had to leave at 4:30 on Monday morning to get to school. Now he's married and we are expecting our first grandchild. Al and Val are slowly moving state by state toward Maine."

Al and the Coopers' second son, Sam, comes into the kitchen from a provisioning trip with the horses. It is pitch-black outside. Suzan introduces us. *Suzan:* "Our boys have all learned how to tie flies, and they sell them to our guests. It's a way for them to learn about business and money. They can't have a paper route."

Sam: "I really like to tie nymphs. Now, a nymph would be like any kind of larva that would hatch out before it changed into whatever it was going to be. I also like to tie dry flies, but they're a little harder. On a dry fly you have a hackle. And hackle is usually dyed or natural-colored rooster-neck feathers. And you also have saddle hackles, the hackles on the back. They should be stiff, long, and not fuzzy. You tie it onto the hook. Then you take your hackle pliers and you wrap it around the hook so it sticks out and makes a wing—it looks like a wing to a fish, anyway. And then you tie on the body for that particular fly. You follow a pattern. All my flies are $1.25 apiece, but you have to sell quite a few to make up for your supplies." As of this writing, Al and Suzan's third son, Chris, has taken over the fly-tying business, while Sam "has acquired his dad's love of guiding and sharing the outdoors with people."

Al: "We used to have a nice hovel here to keep the horses in, all hand-made with logs, a beautiful thing, but it fell in. And to get that back is going to be almost impossible. Just one log weighs eight, nine hundred pounds! You're not talking about a two-by-four. It's an arm-wrestling match between humans and Mother Nature. Some people think humans have conquered nature, but that's a joke. Just look at the abandoned black-top roads with the cracks in them and you'll see delicate flowers growing out of the blacktop."

Suzan: "Della Cobb spoke of a time when they got 8 feet of snow. In one storm. They climbed out of the upstairs window, and it took them two days to get down to the horse hovel to feed the horses." *Al:* "There's always been horses here. We used to have Belgians, now we have Appaloosas, and we'll be getting mules again. Yesterday was my birthday and I have a head-lamp my wife gave me. It really helps when you're hauling in the dark. The good thing about our getting mules is they're not balkish of bears. We had a bear in 1990 that was 265 pounds. Dressed. There were four of us out in the wilderness trying to put it on the mule, and the mule took it back to camp about 10 miles away.

"For bear, if they don't get a mast crop of either beechnuts or acorns, their systems are triggered to go into their dens early. If they don't get enough food, they'll die. Females den first in this kind of situation. The boars and females never den together. The reason for that is the females have their babies in January. They breed in June, but the egg doesn't implant until she goes into the den, because her condition when she goes in determines how many eggs will implant. And she doesn't want the male in the den because he would kill the babies. And for the whole six months they don't defecate or urinate in the den at all. As soon as they're in the den, the

ALFRED J. COOPER

A view of Mount Katahdin from Katahdin Lake Wilderness Camps

urine that would ordinarily have been expelled is automatically transferred to a special system where it all changes over into protein and is reused to help them survive the winter. This system has put the scientists in great awe. They cannot figure it out, and they cannot duplicate it."

Al: "You know what saved this place? The difficulty of getting here. People have access to Maine wilderness now more than any other time in history. They never had logging roads, ATVs, or snowmobiles before the '60s. We've been so lucky to live out our dream here at Katahdin Lake. Now, after nearly three decades, we're ready to sell the camps. We think the sporting-camp life would still appeal to many! We are looking for a younger couple who would love to continue, as we have, to serve the public and keep the sporting-camp tradition alive. A traditional set of sporting camps like this only comes up for sale every 25 years or so. We feel the right couple is out there somewhere." *Suzan:* "As time marches on, the camps have a time-lessness about them. We are very aware of the brevity of life and the necessity of passing the baton to the next 'runner,' especially since fybromyalgia has now limited my 'go power.' If there's a quiet and secluded wilderness, it ought to be preserved. Because there's not going to be that many left. What's that Maine motto? 'Maine—The Way Life Should Be.' Well, the sporting camps are 'Maine—The Way Life Used To Be.'"

Bear Roast

4–6 pounds bear roast (from hindquarter), 4 strips bacon, 1 onion (sliced into rounds), 3 garlic cloves (sliced), pepper

Remove all fat from the bear and bone it out. Roll and prick the meat and insert slivered garlic. Tie with cotton string if necessary. Sprinkle with pepper. Arrange onion rounds and raw bacon strips on top, securing with toothpicks as necessary. Roast, uncovered, in a 325-degree oven for 35 minutes per pound, or until internal temperature is 185 degrees. Internal temperature is very important, as with pork. Remove from oven and serve.

53. LUNKSOOS

HK/AP, SCA
OWNERS: Lee Bertsch and Janet DeGraw
ADDRESS: PO Box 252, Sherman Mills, ME 04776; 207-365-4548; 207-551-4189 (mobile); e-mail: lee@lunksooscamps.com; www.lunksooscamps.com
SEASON: Year-round
ACCOMMODATIONS: Four log and board-and-batten cabins: one to three bedrooms, indoor plumbing and shower (in three cabins), central showers, screened porch (one cabin), gas lights, woodstove and propane heat, fully equipped kitchens with gas stove and refrigerator
RATES: $60 per day double occupancy; $450 per cabin per week for three people (HK); $40 per person per day additional (AP); hunting package rates available
ACCESS: Take I-95 north to the south entrance to Baxter State Park in Millinocket. Go left at the end of the exit ramp, back over the highway, and turn right onto ME 11 north. Follow ME 11 about 20 miles until it comes to a T and go left (right would take you into Stacyville). The road becomes dirt. At any fork, go straight. Follow the river a few miles. Camp driveway is on the right (sign).

When I arrived, Lee and Janet were in the midst of a million projects to get Lunksoos (LUNK-eh-sue) up and running. Lee was making shelves; Janet staining chairs. I even got to lend a hand with the chairs. Turned out, here was another couple that had used this book to get into the business. The camps perch up on a hill, on either side of the main lodge, and overlook the river and the camp's small, relatively hidden, campsite by the bank.

Janet: "We'd been talking for years about having a business up in the woods, because Lee loves hunting and fishing and has been coming up to the north Maine woods for 30 years. The thought of having a business was always enticing, but it was in February 1999, when we came up here on snowmobiles, that we decided we just had to do it. In the process of look-ing for sporting camps to buy, we kept getting disappointed. The things we could afford, that were on the market at the moment, were too close to civilization for us. We had stayed at many sporting camps that were deep in the woods, and that's what we wanted. This came along, and it was like a mini-miracle. We closed on June 14, 2002. Now it's August and we're preparing for bear season. We've already done a lot of work: Lee's located contractors to put in septic systems and dig an artesian well." *Lee:* "I make more phone calls now than I did at my work in Boston." *Janet:* "He was working for a computer company." *Lee:* "We liked this place because we were familiar with the area, knew people up here, and knew that there are a lot of snowmobilers up here." *Janet:* "We love to snowmobile." *Lee:* "We're near ITS 83, 86, and the local Route 70. They're only 2 miles away. And the snowgroomer's going to come right to our door. The Baskahegan Company will let me cut a trail from the local loop and bring it down over the moun-tain right to here. And we also had to get permission from John Hancock's timber division. We own 13 ½ acres here, and that's unusual—owning the land versus leasing it."

Janet: "We're in T3R7, (township 3, range 7, unorganized territory) on the side of Lookout Mountain. It's on the East Branch of the Penobscot River and just south of where the Seboeis comes in to the East Branch, and just north of where Wassataquoik Stream comes in. Looking out the window here in our log lodge you can see the Knife Edge and the North Basin of Mount Katahdin. And I believe that's Hunt Mountain straight ahead of us.

"The word *lunksoos* means "a mountain lion" in Algonquin (there's a Lunksoos Mountain near here), but the word connotes something fearsome." *Lee:* "I think historically there were mountain lions here 'cause there have been sightings of mountain lions now." *Janet:* "I grew up in northern New Jersey, and my father had seen mountain lions there even, so certainly they were here at one point.

"This is the camp where the Fendler boy arrived—Don Fendler, you know his book, *Lost on a Mountain in Maine?* Well, he arrived on the other side of the river after his nine days of being lost in the Katahdin wilderness. He was spotted by someone here at the camps. They shouted to him to stay put and they went across the river and rescued him. At that time there was a telephone line in here. They called his parents and it all worked out from there. The building that was here then was different, in fact there have been several lodges." *Lee:* "This one was built in '65.

"There was an established hunting business here, and we're going to build on that, bear and deer hunters. There's 55 bear sites, and it's an out-standing area. Then there's the fishing: bass, trout, and salmon." *Janet:* "Lunksoos Lake, just north of here, has been stocked with brook trout." *Lee:* "We have a clearing on the river for canoeists who make the trip down. It's a good stopping-off point from Matagamon. It takes two days to get down here and you can stay overnight. There's a privy, showers, a tenting area by the landing. And then you can take out at Whetstone Falls." *Janet:* "There's a good boat landing here, and people are welcome to bring their own boats to use the river. Canoe trips on the East Branch are popular—it's a milder river than the West Branch—and the Seboeis is even milder yet. People doing the Seboeis can also use this as a stopping-off point." *Lee:* "We're planning on putting in two or three lean-tos down there eventually for them to sleep in." *Janet:* "Included with that tent or lean-to rental is use of the shower, and the campers can come up here for free dessert! One of the things we offer at Lunksoos for our guests is free dessert in the evening because we like to encourage people to come into the lodge and meet each other and, if it's cold, have a chance to relax by the fire."

Lee: "We'll be doing all sorts of advertising for snowmobilers, and will be offering them healthy food, not just hamburgers and hot dogs." *Janet:* "We hope to have a small restaurant here in the future, where we'll offer a salad bar, fresh fruit, and will also be able to cater to people with special food needs or allergies. We know there are a lot of people out there who have to watch their diet for whatever reason, and we intend to accommodate those folks by having food they can eat and enjoy.

"This is a real adventure for us because we are in our fifties. Lee's retired, and I'm still working in the computer industry. I figure I'll need to keep my day job for at least a year to help get this off the ground. There's some difficulty in that because I work 300 miles from here. When we first came, we had seen the place with 6 feet of snow on the ground. After we purchased and started to look around more closely, we saw that there were decades' worth of things that had been tossed into the woods in back of the camps and forgotten. It took six pickup truck loads to get rid of it all. Initially it took many, many phone calls to learn that we could recycle virtually everything in Millinocket, which is about 40 miles from here. There's a lot to do. You come in and you have new ideas and want to make things prettier than they were before. You want more light in the cabins, more gas lights, which means more propane, and running gas lines, what lamps do you buy and how do you get them here? Then getting prices on lumber— we're refinishing the interior of two of the cabins—that's a lot of wood to bring in. We threw out all the pots and pans, the utensils, and bought new ones. It's only been eight weeks and Lee's already refinished the kitchens in three of the cabins.

One of the things that was a surprise to us was how many licenses and insurances are needed: easement insurance on the road in here, the state licensing that's involved for just having a rental cabin. You have to have a lodging license, then one for food, then of course there's the Land Use Regulation Commission that has to approve of everything that happens on the land. Our septic system had to be designed and the plans went to the state for approval, same with the well." *Lee:* "Everything we do is a separate permit. Each separate permit is separate money." *Janet:* "And all the various regulations forces us to make certain decisions. The thing that made it difficult this first couple of months is that all the work with the legal stuff and the contractors and regulations took time away from actually doing the physical work that was needed on the place. We want our place to be very environmentally friendly. We're looking into alternative sources of energy and certainly will recycle. So it is quite a project getting started. Still, we really do recommend it!" *Lee:* "I'm just looking forward to meeting new people, seeing them have the fun I've had in places like this over the years, and sharing my experiences and local knowledge with them." *Janet:* "And for my part, I find coming to the woods very restorative. We hope to provide an environment where people can come and re-center themselves and have a peaceful, happy experience that refreshes their souls."

Venison Chili

Janet: "We make a relatively mild version, but you can add whatever hot seasonings you want. By the time you're done with this it's very thick and rich."

> 1 pound kidney beans, 20 medium tomatoes, 3 cans tomato paste, 1 tsp. each salt and peper, 2 T chili powder, 3 pounds venison (ground once), 1 pound sausage meat (hot, if desired), 6 medium onions (chopped), 3 cups chopped green peppers, hot peppers (optional)

Soak the kidney beans overnight. Drain and rinse. Add water to cover and bring to a boil. Reduce heat and boil gently until soft, about an hour. Crush the tomatoes in a large pot. Add tomato paste and simmer until thick, also about an hour. Add 2 T chili powder, salt and pepper as sauce thickens. Sauté venison and sausage with onions and pepper. Add hot peppers if desired. Mix all the ingredients together and serve warm over rice.

54. MOUNT CHASE LODGE

AP/HK

OWNERS: Sara and Rick Hill

ADDRESS: 1517 Shin Pond Road, Mount Chase, ME 04765; 207-528-2183; e-mail: mtchaselodge@ainop.com; www.mtchaselodge.com

SEASON: Year-round

ACCOMMODATIONS: Five log cabins: one to three bedrooms, indoor plumbing and shower, wood and propane heat, electric lights; three cabins are fully HK, two have coffeepot and refrigerator; main lodge has eight guest rooms, fireplace, TV, hot tub

RATES: Cabins $70–80 per couple per day (HK); $70 per person per day (AP); $400–525 per cabin per week. Lodge rooms $65 per person per day (MAP).

ACCESS: I-95 to exit 58 (Patten). Take ME 159 ten miles west to Shin Pond Village. Pass the store and campground and head up the hill, to the camp sign and driveway, which will be on your right.

The Hills' camp compound is focused on the white main lodge; the cabins are off to either side among the trees. The main lodge has a big central living room with a fireplace and a music area. A glassed-in room serves as a dining area with tables pushed together into one long seating arrangement. The windows look out to what appears to be a river; it is actually the thoroughfare leading into Upper Shin Pond.

Rick: "The pond is 2 miles long by a mile and a half wide and 70 feet at its deepest, 45–50 feet average, with landlocked salmon, bass, and brook trout. It's at the base of Mount Chase, which got its name because of an American-Canadian skirmish back in the 1800s, maybe the 1820s or '30s. The town of Patten wasn't settled yet. A man by the name of Jim Chase, I believe, affiliated with a Bangor logging enterprise—although this is hearsay—came up from Bangor. He was supposed to burn the hayfields where the Canadians were staying, since hay was the prime feed source for the horses they used in logging. This was so the Canadians would move out back across the border and relinquish cutting. The day he came here was a brisk August day with the prevailing wind out of the west. Windy day. And the fire got out of control. It forced him into the highest area, and, as I'm told, he subsisted on berries on top of the mountain [Mount Chase] for three weeks. The fire burned many thousands of acres, encompassing as many as seven townships, each of which is 6 square miles! After the fire, the woods grew back to hardwoods and softwoods, which is what it is today. And, as the story goes, Shin Pond gets its name from this same Jim Chase, who thought the lower pond had that shape as he was sitting looking down on it from up on the mountain.

"This lodge was built in 1959 by Henry and Mary Schmidt. At one point there were three places in Shin Pond owned by Schmidts, none of them related. Henry and Mary built three cabins and owned the place from '59 to the spring of '76, when we took over. My family had roots in the Patten area, my grandmother and her family—her father was a sheriff there in the early 1900s. This great-grandfather came over here and built a cabin on Lower Shin Pond as a summer place. The camp still remains in the family. My mother and father brought us up here summers.

"Prior to buying the lodge, I worked as a computer-parts designer for Digital Equipment in Massachusetts, which is where I grew up, on a farm. Sara was a corporate buyer there, bought office supplies. We had originally looked at another place, but as luck would have it, the previous owners asked if we were interested in this place and we knew it was what we had in mind. When we got it, it was primarily a bear-hunting and fishing camp. But that changed in 1981 when the state eliminated the spring season on black bears. Our business had to transition to a recreational base, and we are a year-round operation now. More people are getting involved in winter recreation than ever before. We're right on ITS 85, and there's ice fishing out the back door.

"I've been a registered Maine guide since '76 and an active member of the Professional Maine Guides Association, holding the offices of president, vice president, chairman of the board of directors, and now I oversee the legislative-action committee. There's a structured procedure for becoming a Maine guide now. The Department of Inland Fisheries and Wildlife gives a comprehensive written test and there's an oral exam administered by a registered guide and two members of the warden service. Our association was formed in 1978 for the purpose of educating legislators about the issues and concerns affecting the guiding industry. There are around fourteen hundred registered guides on the books. Most are 'patch holders' and don't guide for a living. About four or five hundred are people who derive at least 50 percent of their income from guiding services. The rule of thumb for guides is $100 to $250 a day, depending on the services. The high end is the striped-bass guide, who provides the fishing boat, motor, lunch, and equipment, versus someone who might do a half-day canoe trip. There are several different categories of guides: hunting, fishing, whitewater rafting, and recreational (which includes hiking, cross-country skiing, snowmobiling, and naturalists).

"The most important thing for today's Maine guide is that they be a good communicator. You need to be an educator about the woods and waters, be a good businessman, but most of all be good with people. It's extremely important when you're taking people into situations out of their comfort zone that they can trust the guide's ability to take them safely through their experience. People should not question a guide in a safety situation. People who haven't done much hiking should really consider getting a guide if they're planning to do Katahdin. More people get in trouble there, and become problems to the park service, because they aren't properly equipped. The old, scruffy guy with a plaid jacket is no longer the image or the case. Today's guide is a professional, safely and effectively working with people for their own benefit—1997 was the 100th anniversary of registered Maine guides. And the first registered guide in Maine was a woman, 'Fly Rod Crosby,' out of the Rangeley area."

The address for the Maine Professional Guides Association is PO Box 336, Augusta, ME 04332; 207-751-3797; e-mail: guides@midcoast.com; www.maineguides.org.

Sara's Toll House Pie

Sara: "People always say how beautiful it is in here, and how lucky we are. Well, we've never gotten 'rich' in here, but then it's your definition of wealthy. We feel enriched by our surroundings and by the people who come in. This is something our guests seem to like a lot."

1 pie crust, unbaked

1 cup melted margarine, cooled; ½ cup flour, ½ cup white sugar, ½ cup brown sugar, 2 eggs (beaten), 1 cup mint chocolate chips, 1 cup walnuts

Mix ingredients together in order given. Pour into prepared pie crust and bake at 350 degrees for 1 hour.

55. PLEASANT POINT CAMPS

AP/HK
OWNERS: Mardi and Clif George
ADDRESS: PO Box 1505, Greenville, ME 04441; 207-422-6826 or 207-460-5226 (cell); e-mail: mardi@pleasantpointcamps.com; www.pleasant-pointcamps.com
SEASON: Year-round
ACCOMMODATIONS: Five log cabins: one to two bedrooms, porch (one screened), private outhouse, shower and bathroom in lodge, inside hand pump for water, propane and kerosene lamps, woodstove, propane cook-stove, and refrigerator. Well-attended dogs welcome for $5 per stay ("Lance, the resident golden, likes company.")
RATES: $75 per person per day (AP); $40 per person per day (HK); motor-boats $30 per day; canoe and Sunfish free
ACCESS: I-95 to exit 39 (Newport). Take ME 7 to Dexter, ME 23 to Guilford, and ME 6/15 to Greenville. Go straight on Lily Bay Road 20 miles to Kokadjo (last supplies). At 1.8 miles turn right (loon sign). Go 17 miles (staying left at forks) to Jo-Mary Road (this is a landmark, don't turn). One mile beyond Jo-Mary Road take a right at the fork and go 4 miles to parking. Either ring the ship's bell for boat pick-up or walk a mile along the shore path to camp.

The rustic, maroon-brown log cabins of Pleasant Point Camps are built along a peninsula on Fourth Debsconeag Lake at the base of a 1,400-foot cliff. The upper three-quarters of this lake is owned by the state—the Nahmakanta Unit Preserve—and the other quarter is owned by the paper company.

Mardi: "Our involvement with the camps started one wonderful March day in 2001 when my husband and I snowmobiled in here. Clif said he wanted to show me some camps he'd seen four years ago. We found the camps, went down on the ice, but nobody was there. I fell in love with the spot. We heard they were for sale but that they were going to be fairly expensive and there were lots of people waiting to buy them, so it wasn't the right time for us. Later in the fall we were visiting our friends at

Nahmakanta Camps nearby—we were going to take care of the camps while they were away—and they told us that a deal to buy Pleasant Point had fallen through. Well, we went back over, called in our bid, and 48 hours later our bid had been accepted.

"My grandfather, Hal Hunt, was a North Pole explorer and Maine Guide, and I spent my childhood trotting along behind him as we went into camps and lakes all over the north woods. He was quite well known from his time, was quite a character. My mother wrote a book about him called *North to the Horizon*. Well, as I was sitting at camp that second visit, I felt that my grandfather had been in to that lake. This could be in my own imagination, but it's the kind of place he would go.

"Clif has run two sporting camps before: Tea Pond and Penobscot Lake Lodge. I met Clif after a summer of skippering my own 28-foot sailboat to the Atlantic side of Nova Scotia, which is quite wild, wilder even than the Maine coast. I decided that was pushing the envelope a little bit. It was about meeting my fears and concerns and saying, 'Yes, I can do this.' I have a great sense of adventure, but I know I'm not as physically strong as a man. During that trip I thought, 'I really would like to have a partner, someone to be with, but not someone to control me.' After putting the boat to bed for the winter, I joined a dating service, and that's where I met Clif. I found out about his love of the north woods and the ocean. In 1976 he had taken a 97-day canoe trip, solo, from Maine to New Brunswick. He had actually camped 25 feet from where my father kept his sailboat! So we had a lot in common. We're partners and friends and got married to honor each other.

"The camp has quite a history. Our oldest cabin is from the late 1800s and was built by a trapper who lived here with a Native American woman. She spent a year decorating the inside walls and ceiling with birch bark, the inside of the bark, all cut out and tacked up in a mosaic. Included in the mosaic are some oil paintings in the ceiling. We call it Indian Camp. The other thing that's interesting about Indian Camp is that Roosevelt stayed there during his presidency. And he hunted bear on the cliffs. There are blueberry barrens up there and I guess that attracted the bears.

"Some of the trees still have signs of the telegraph wires that were put in because of Roosevelt. The President always had to be in touch, just like nowadays. So they strung telegraph wire in from Millinocket to the camps.

"Part of what's hard is that there's no written history of the camps. We've found some letters in the walls as we've reconstructed Moose Lodge, so little things are showing up. It's sort of like an archaeological site." *Peter Garland (Clif's grandson):* "When we were replacing the floor in Indian Camp we found a newspaper from 1906 that was used for insulation." *Mardi:* "Right now we're taking down Moose Lodge, which was in terrible shape, and leaving Moose cabin. We're building a new main lodge up on the ridge, on the peninsula, where the camps are, so starting in 2003 we'll be able to offer American Plan as well as housekeeping. Clif loves to cook, I'm a good cook, and one of our joys is having guests and talking. Clif and I have had a lot of life experiences. I'm the daughter of a foreign service officer, Clif's been in the north Maine woods a long time, so we look forward to swapping stories and welcoming guests May through October.

"The camp's lake, Fourth Debsconeag, is one of the most pristine, clear lakes in Maine. It's about 2 miles long by about half a mile wide. We have various boats for our guests' use, and will be willing to give them a sailing lesson on the Sunfish if they need it. There are lake and brook trout, casting and trolling are allowed, and the lake is 160 feet deep. It sits in a glacial bowl, so it has bluffs on one side and cliffs on the other. And there are adjacent lakes for people to fish. Sixth Debsconeag, which has a path up to it, is stocked in the fall. On the cliffs we have turkey buzzards, hawks, bald eagles, and perhaps a few peregrine falcons.

"We're going to be fairly conservative in the off-season and we will open up for hunters or snowmobilers —if they've been our guests in the summertime. It's so remote it will be difficult for people to get in in the winter if they don't have a snowmobile. But I've cross-country skied and snowshoed all over the lake and it's lovely. We were in here when the ice was breaking up and Clif still teases me about when I went out and said, 'Where did you buy the wind chimes?' He laughed and said, 'Mardi, that's the ice crystals rubbing together.' It was wonderful. That evening we were sitting down having dinner and three loons arrived. The lake was only one-third open. It fascinates me: how do they know the lake's open enough for them to land? I mean, they're smarter than we are. I've gotten so I can talk to them. I don't know what I'm saying, but they will answer me, which is really fun.

"My background is that I am a licensed clinical therapist and worked with dysfunctional families and abused and neglected children for 35 years. I retired on July 4, 2002 to become the co-owner of the camps. And one of our dreams is to have some womens' groups, especially in the month of August, when the swimming is great but the fishing is off because it's too warm.

"We're both at Pleasant Point because we love people, but we also love the solitude that the north woods brings. And we want to give people the chance to fall in love with the backwoods."

Swedish Meatballs

Mardi: "This recipe can be made ahead and warmed up in the oven."

4 T butter, ½ cup minced onion, 2 cups bread crumbs, 2 cups milk, 1½ pounds lean hamburger, 1 pound ground pork, 2 eggs, salt and pepper, ½ cup flour, 1½ cups cream or evaporated milk

Sauté onion in butter. Soak bread crumbs in milk, then add the onion, hamburger, pork, eggs, and salt and pepper to taste. Make meatballs and roll in the flour. Use

Pleasant Point Camps

more butter to brown the meatballs and then put them in a serving dish. Add 3 T flour to pan drippings and then add cream or evaporated milk and stir with a wisk until combined. Pour gravy over meatballs.

56. WAPITI CAMPS

AP/HK

OWNERS: The Frank Ramelli family

ADDRESS: Patten, ME 04765; 207-528-2485 (camp); 978-928-5878 (winter); e-mail: Ifly@ainop.com

SEASON: May through November

ACCOMMODATIONS: Seven log cabins (two to three bedrooms) with indoor plumbing and shower, wood heat, electric lights and refrigerator (not on generator), porch

RATES: $55 per person per day (AP); $295 per family per week (HK)

ACCESS: I-95 to exit 58. Take ME 11 north to Patten and turn left onto ME 159. Go 10 miles west to Shin Pond. Cross the bridge and take the next left. Go 2 miles on a dirt road into camp, at the end of the road.

Wapiti's brown-stained log cabins, with orange-painted oars for window shutters, spread out to the left of the driveway. A well-cared-for lawn slopes down toward the lake with its view of Katahdin in the distance. You pass a healthy pocket-sized garden with a sign that reads GARDEN OF

EATIN', a swimming pool and covered barbecue area, and (a hint of Frank's Italian background) a bocci court.

Frank: "We are the only cabins on Wapiti Lake, or Davis Pond, as it used to be called. It is a spring-fed lake 1 mile long by half a mile wide and 72 feet at its deepest, and is stocked with brook trout. You can see Katahdin, at the end of the lake, from the porch of every cabin. We like to say, 'This is where the road ends and the trails begin.'

"These camps have been around since 1912. The history is that there were two women, a librarian and a schoolteacher from Bangor, who came up and stayed at what used to be a big hotel called the Shin Pond House. During their stay they would hike in here with friends for a picnic. It was a field with cows—they just liked the gorgeous view. Well, they went to the owners, the Webber family, who were the largest exporters of hardwood in Maine in the early 1900s, and got permission from them to lease the land. They built the lodge first, then tent platforms, and then it was so popular they built cabins on top of the platforms. And it has been serving sportsmen ever since. In fact, we're the oldest bear-hunting camp in the Patten area.

"My wife, Anita, and I bought the camps in 1985. We're from Massachusetts, although we spent 23 years based in Austria, traveling around behind the Iron Curtain. I used to go hunting with my father at Maynard's and loved sporting camps. I retired when I was 50 and bought these. It was with great sadness to the family that Anita passed away in March 2002. She was from Germany and liked cooking, and so was fine with the idea of doing this. We used to come to Maine together, and she said she always wanted a little nest, and this was the closest thing to it. I'm now running the camps with our daughter, Karen, and son, Tony, and their families."

Anita's German Cucumber Salad

2–3 cucumbers, ½ cup mayonnaise, ½ cup sour cream, parsley, dill, salt and pepper

Slice the cucumbers very thin and store in the refrigerator to chill. When ready to serve, take them out and squeeze all the water from the cucumbers with the palm of your hand. Add mayonnaise and sour cream. Season with parsley, dill, and salt and pepper to taste.

THE NORTHERN REGION

For the purposes of this book, this region includes "everything else" north of Baxter State Park, bordered to the east by ME 11 and by the Canadian boundary to the north and west. (Maine is surrounded on three sides by Canada.)

Many of the sporting camps in this book are located in remote or pristine spots. I suspect, to visitors from major urban areas, that the State of Maine itself seems remote. It is, to some degree. That is its charm—it is one of the last outposts of the American wilderness—and that is why so many people are drawn to sporting camps in the first place. But it is here, in the North Maine Woods, that even the Maine resident comes head-to-head with the concept of "vast wilderness." You can drive around for days and for hundreds of miles without seeing streetlights, telephone poles, or paved roads. Mileage is posted on small metal or wooden rectangles in trees, wildlife meanders on or beside the right-of-way, pulp trucks and pickups outnumber cars. Piles of logs, lumber camps, and busy loggers attest to the fact that this region is a huge network of tree farms, Maine's largest cash crop. When you venture into this region, it is best to remember the old Boy Scout motto—and be prepared. Please refer to the sections "How Do I Get There?" and "What Should I Bring?" in the introduction of this book.

GETTING THERE: Many of the sporting-camp owners in this region suggest flying in to their camps. A number of owners are pilots themselves and can pick you up at a set rendezvous and fly you directly to their dock. The closest airport is in Presque Isle (rental cars available). Float planes are available from Bangor International Airport through KT Aviation, 207-945-5087; or contact Katahdin Air Service, 207-723-8378, near Millinocket; Northstar Outfitters, Portage, 207-435-3002; or Scotty's Flying Service, Shin Pond, 207-528-2626; as well the services in Greenville. Driving times vary wildly depending on the location of the camp. Generally, driving time from Portland is 4–6 hours; from Boston, 7–9 hours; from New York City, 10–13 hours.

GUIDANCE: For further information, contact North Maine Woods, PO Box 421, Ashland, ME 04732; 207-435-6213.

57. BRADFORD CAMPS

AP, SCA

OWNERS: Igor and Karen Sikorsky

CAMP ADDRESS: Box 729, Ashland, ME 04732; 207-746-7777; e-mail:

maine@bradfordcamps.com; www.bradfordcamps.com
WINTER ADDRESS: PO Box 778, Kittery, ME 03904; 207-439-6364
SEASON: May through November
ACCOMMODATIONS: Eight log cabins: (one to two bedrooms), porch, indoor
plumbing and shower, woodstove, gas lights; two outpost cabins
RATES: $120 per person per day, $775 per person per week; child and family
rates available.
ACCESS: I-95 to exit 60. Turn left onto ME 212 west and go 10 miles to
Knowles Corner. Go right onto ME 11 north, 31 miles to Ashland (last
gas). Go left at the four-corners (staying on ME 11 north), go 1 mile, cross
the Aroostook River, and turn left at the T intersection. Drive 0.75 mile to
the Gateway Store. (You can call the camp from here.) Take the right-hand
fork onto a dirt road. Go 5 miles to the North Maine Woods gate (fee: $18
per person). From the gate, take the left fork. Go 10 miles, cross the
Machias River, and take the left fork. Go 15 miles and take a right at the
sign for the camps. Follow signs about 19 more miles into camp.

After driving a maze of logging roads through vast tracks of forest, you
reach Bradford Camps by emerging onto a spacious lawn with a quarter-acre
of gardens lush with flowers and vegetables, surrounded by picturesque log
cabins. Smoke rising from the chimney at the main lodge in the distance
and the no-cars-in-camp policy all contribute to the traditional sporting-
camp feel and the sense of having come to a place set apart.

Igor: "Bradford's was started in 1890 by Will Atkins, who came up here
from the Rangeley and Moosehead Lake areas. The camps are named after
Governor Bradford of Massachusetts, an ancestor of Milt Hall, the third
owner. We're located at the headwaters of the Aroostook River watershed on
Munsungan Lake. It's a mile by 4 miles long and 123 feet deep, with lake
and brook trout, landlocked salmon, and smelt, and is bounded by 1,400-
foot Munsungan Ridge on the south and 2,300-foot Norway Bluff on the
north. You should see these hardwood ridges in the fall-foliage season with
the sunset hitting them. It's magnificent! They're the dividing line between
the Aroostook and Allagash watersheds. The Aroostook empties into the St.
John River, which heads north and east into New Brunswick. Most rivers
everywhere else flow south, but the waters in northern Maine all flow north.

"At one end of Munsungan is a thoroughfare with a path to Chase
Lake, where we keep a canoe for our guests. We also have two fly-in-only
outpost camps: Big Reed Pond and Bluffer Pond. The Big Reed Pond camp
is special to us for a couple of reasons. First, it's in the middle of a 5,000-
plus-acre preserve owned by The Nature Conservancy, with the largest old-
growth forest in New England. Second, the pond has blue-back trout,
Salvelinus alpinus oquassa, and this fish is found in only 10 other lakes in the
world, all of them in Maine!

"For our first-time guests, especially, we really want them to be guid-

One of the cabins at Bradford Camps

ed. Not only will they learn how and where to fish here, and have a little history and lore of the area, but they'll also be able to get to some of the outlying fly-fishing ponds. Munsungan is a smelt-driven fishery, which means the fishing is primarily trolling. And we have 50 waters within a 20-mile radius of us. With a guide, our guests can have a total fishing experience, plus guides are a sporting-camp tradition we believe in upholding.

"From the 1930s, as soon as float planes were a business around here, Bradford Camps was serviced by them." (*Karen:* "Around half of our guests fly in.") *Igor:* "But from that time on every owner of Bradford's has owned a plane. When we took over we basically completely over-extended ourselves to purchase the camps. It has taken us five years to get our feet on the ground enough to completely over-extend ourselves again and buy a plane. It certainly has been one of my lifelong dreams. At this point I do not have a commercial rating, so will not be flying guests around. But eventually I'll be able to come over to a guest at the breakfast table and ask, 'Where do you want to go today?' and walk down to the dock and fly them there.

"The way I got into this is really a lifelong thing. I started when I was 10 going to Gary and Betty Cobb's boys' camp. I went there for 12 successive summers and eventually helped run it. When that closed, I helped at the Cobbs' Pierce Pond sporting camps next door. I took architecture in college and spent 12 years in the building industry, but those early experiences were pretty well ingrained. I built Karen her first fly-rod, and our honeymoon was a fishing trip to Alaska. Our honeymoon suite was a 16-foot Winnebago; our first vacation was a canoe trip down the Allagash. We kid each other that we have yet to take a vacation where we haven't had to buy fly dope and long johns."

After spending four years staying at different sporting camps, we knew what we wanted: classic, historical camps in good condition and in a remote, pristine location. We were invited to some Maine Sporting Camp Association meetings and almost everyone tried to talk us out of buying a camp, said it was no place to make any money. But in February of 1996 we called the Youlands, the former owners, and it all happened in one breath. Less than six weeks later we closed on the place and we were in here opening up camp on April 26, having left our jobs the week prior. I had been with a roof-truss manufacturer and Karen had worked eight years in the clothing industry—product management. And here we were owners of a sporting camp and in less than two weeks we had full ice-out, 20 guests, cabins cleaned, water running, food on the tables!"

Karen: "Igor and I didn't fall into the traditional roles of what sporting-camp owners used to be with the wife in the kitchen cooking and the husband doing all the outdoor things. We had to create a new way for us to be sporting-camp owners together. The reason that it works for us is that we both have very strong opinions, but we are both able to be flexible on how to get something done. Igor and I have completely different strengths and skills, but what keeps us working well together is our shared sense of humor."

Igor: "I'm in the midst of creating some hiking trails around here. I've put in about 10 miles so far, and we're offering some family trips in the area. We have some canoe trips, like on Munsungan Stream or the Allagash 15 miles away. We can also arrange a whitewater rafting trip on the Penobscot River." *Karen:* "Several years ago *Outside Magazine's* Family Guide included our camp as a place that would be a good vacation destination for families. After that we started filling up in the month of August. Then word of mouth spread as well, so our family time is pretty much booked well in advance now."

Igor: "So there's a lot to do in addition to the fishing or hunting. For hunting we have thousands of acres of excellent cover for grouse, deer, and bear. And at camp we have a 10-station sporting clays course. We have a 20-year lease with Seven Islands Paper Company, which has a 'green company' international certification for good cutting practices and policies." *Karen:* "In 1999 we became members of the steering committee to help the New England Forestry Foundation and the Pingree family succeed in putting together the largest conservation easement, to date, in the United States. It's a complex topic, but it's very important, and it set a precedent. Over the years that we've owned this camp, many trusts and foundations have been established in Maine to have conservation easements over large tracts of land. Ours is three-quarters of a million acres. Seven Islands is the land management corporation for the Pingree heirs. Unlike the other paper companies, they are not just logging the land and feeding a mill. They have diversified interests and the foresight to set aside this land to never be developed. And they were able to satisfy two very diverse groups with different aims: logging and recreation. Traditional use will still be upheld, so this was pleasing to groups that don't generally see eye-to-eye in the forest. The New England Forestry Foundation is a nonprofit organization, and the Pingree family sold the development rights to them. They raised $30 million in a very short period of time." *Igor:* "The fun part of it for us is that not only do we benefit from the windfall assurance that we won't have development around the lake, but we also served as the ambassadors to the fundraising effort. So we would have people from all walks of life coming here and then going out for the day to get a picture of what's happening to the woods (good and bad) and what could be done with the conservation easement."

Window-Cleaning Recipe

Igor: "Our food's so good, I don't know why we're putting this in, but it is a recipe of sorts that we've tinkered with." Karen: "We've debated on how to best wash our windows. I used to prefer paper towels, but that wasn't good ecologically, plus it leaves lint. Igor believed in newspaper, but was harder to handle and used up what little newspaper we got in." Igor: "Now we use a sponge to apply the cleaning solution, a squeegee to dry wipe after each sponge stroke, and wipe the four edges of the window with a clean cotton cloth."

1 gallon hot water, a squirt of liquid soap, 1 cup white vinegar, 1 cup rubbing alcohol. Combine and get scrubbing!

58. EAGLE LAKE CAMPS

AP/SCA

OWNERS: Ed and Paula Clark

ADDRESS: PO Box 377, Eagle Lake, ME 04739; 207-752-0556; e-mail: EdwEClark@aol.com; www.EagleLakeSportingCamps.com

SEASON: Year-round

ACCOMMODATIONS: Thirteen log cabins: one to four bedrooms, indoor plumbing and tub with shower, gas and electric lights, propane heat; pets welcome

RATES: $75–95 per person per day; $475–620 per person per week (double occupancy); child, group, and special rates available, as are boat rentals

ACCESS: Take I-95 north to exit 60. Turn left onto ME 212 west and go 10 miles to Knowles Corner. Go right on ME 11 north for 60 miles to Eagle Lake Village town landing for (pre-arranged) boat to camps.

A number of years ago I took a boat trip around Eagle Lake and saw a classic but unoccupied and deteriorating set of camps out on a peninsula. I've seen this situation a number of times over the years and it never fails to make me a bit sad for those abandoned cabins, silent and uncared for.

Fortunately, as is the case with Eagle Lake Camps, it is not a foregone conclusion that they will sink into oblivion. Light honey-colored camps bracket the main lodge, complete with a massive stone fireplace. The interior walls of nearly all the cabins are partially covered with birch bark. The camps were in the final days of readiness prior to opening, and there was an air of quiet expectancy. Over a delicious lunch, Ed told me I was his first official guest. The first of many, I'm sure.

Ed: "At Eagle Lake we're in the northern part of Maine, in Aroostook County. The lake is 18 miles long, shaped like a reverse L. The north–south portion runs down into the village and then the east–west portion runs about 12 miles. The camps are just about in the middle of that—we're 6 miles to the village and 6 miles to the other end of the lake. We pick up our guests at the landing in our 1954 wooden boat and bring them up here. We're also almost in the geographic centerof a public reserve lot of about 24,000 acres. So for 3 to 4 miles in any direction there's literally just woods and water. In the public reserve land there's only three small private cabins and a couple of primitive campsites. Other than that, Eagle Lake Camps is the only thing on this end of the lake. At nighttime, when you sit here, it's just like you're in the middle of absolutely nowhere. You don't see the village, because we're around the corner from that end of the lake, you don't see the lights, or the reflections from the lights.

"These cabins were built about 130 years ago, as sporting camps, by a businessman from New York City, a Mr. Titus. They were built, all about the same time, I believe, by either Swiss or Swedish craftsmen who came in. Back then, in the early 1870s, they would have done it all with bucksaws, axes, and horses. The birch-bark wall lining is a very traditional and unique thing here, and the fireplace is billed as one of the largest stone fireplaces in Maine. Like the camps, it had gone downhill to the point where it had split open and was totally unusable. It was taken down and rebuilt to the original size and shape by craftsmen from Montana. Another incredible resurrection—this ought to be the 'Phoenix Camp' I suppose! Actually, for the longest time they were known as the Michaud Camps, from about 1920 to 1960. And if you look at some topographic maps today, you'll see this noted as the Michaud Camps. The old brochures are real interesting because they talk about how to get here by train. And, in some ways, it might have been easier 60 to 80 years ago to come here. For example, you could get on a train in Baltimore at 7:00 on a Friday morning, get a sleeper car, wake up and be here 7:00 Saturday morning. And the old brochures talk about going back down to the village, getting on a train with a guide and canoe, and going to several of the other lakes out here.

"That's another interesting thing about Eagle Lake: there are two drainages that come in here. One comes via the Square Lake thoroughfare, right by the camps, and that includes Square Lake, Cross Lake, Mud Lake, and

Long Lake. And on the other end of the lake, Fish River comes in, and that has St. Froid Lake, and several other lakes, that all drain into Eagle Lake, and then out to the St. John. So you can generally go from one lake, to another, to another. The thoroughfare itself is 3½ miles long, so if it's windy you're always protected there. It has a famous salmon pool. This is all cold-water fish: brook trout, salmon, and togue. Some of the biggest fish in Maine have been caught here on Eagle Lake. It's relatively deep: about 126 feet. There are some 17 brooks, or tributaries, that run into the lake. There's also ice fishing.

"We're going to be open for snowmobilers. I understand ice comes in here late December, so we'll have snowmobiling January probably into April. We came up for the first time, I think it was the first week in April, and drove across the lake in a truck. Did that a couple times in April.

"As for my being in here, I didn't wake up one morning and say, 'I want to own a sporting camp and spend a chunk of money.' I've been working at finding a camp of the right type, that suits my personality and finances and so on, for 12 or 13 years. I've made some offers on others, but I'm glad now that I couldn't get them at the time. And then 12 or so years ago I got my guide's license in preparation for being in this situation. I researched nearly 200 camps; everything I saw advertised or heard about. I've always been an outdoors person ever since I was a kid growing up in Connecticut. I hunted and was a Boy Scout, loved being at camp, loved camping. We've had our own private cabin in the Milo–Brownville Junction area for over 25 years. I love deer hunting—not necessarily for the taking of the animals, but just being out there—and especially like bird hunting—which is one of the things I'd like to develop here. Bird hunting and fly-fishing on small ponds are two of my favorite things to do.

"People say to me, 'Oh, you've retired now?' Sure, I've retired from an 8-hour work day five days a week to a 14-hour work day seven days a week! That's one heck of a retirement! If I'd known that I would've kept working! But seriously, I have no illusions, never did, that owning a sporting camp was the thing to do if you wanted to relax and do twice as much hunting and fishing. Five years ago my wife and I spent our honeymoon at the Milo camp and she loves these places just as much as I do. But Eagle Lake is very far north, a good seven hours for her to travel back to see her grandchildren. Not only is it seven hours, but if you go by road access (which is limited to supplies, services, and emergencies only), you start out with (or end with) 20 miles of very difficult, gated road that takes at least an hour and a quarter to travel. So for my wife it is difficult to handle the logistics of being here, someplace she really loves, and still visit with family fairly frequently.

"Before I bought this place I worked for 30-something years in a variety of manufacturing positions, two very large companies. And basically I did that for the usual reasons: income and raising a family. I graduated college on the 2nd of June, married my first wife on the 7th of June, and started working for GE on the 23rd of June. My idea was that: you go to college, get married, have children, buy the house, the station wagon, the picket fence, the dog, and then you die. You know. I think it was reasonable to do what I did, but if I'd been truer to myself I would have been an earth scientist or even better, a game warden, and forget the money. I love the saying the philosopher Joseph Campell has: 'Follow your bliss.' And I've tried to tell my son, and other folks, that's what you have to do in life. I have a bunch of clichés, one of which is: 'You only live once, and you're dead a long time.' Finally, after raising a family and working hard, I've had this great opportunity to come here and really do what I somehow should have done 30 years ago. I really feel now that I'm at the stage of doing what I was meant to do. I love to build things—I'm a finish carpenter—and that's another way I would've gone if I hadn't done this. So I love the thought of bringing back six of these cabins. But sometimes I do feel like Howard Hughes on Long Beach Bay trying to get the *Spruce Goose* into the air.

"I heard before I even got here that this was one of the 'gems' of Maine sporting camps. And it fortunately was brought back far enough that it can and will be saved. I like to think of this as a new 130-year-old sporting camp. My dream is that it will be competing with the 5 or 10 best camps in Maine. This is one of the most abundant areas I've seen for wildlife. I've seen more bears here, for example, in the last two months than I've seen in the last 12 years. There's moose right here, otter, lots of deer, and the lake's well named because the eagles are literally on our treetops. I open the door in the morning and an eagle will fly out of the trees. I would like to have a genteel place for fly-fishermen, and for bird hunters to come with their dogs. A dream place to go."

Apple Spice Cake

Ed: "Our kitchen has turned out great! I have two people working with me. Together with my two daughters, one each weekend, we've run dinners the past two weekends: 29 people the first week, 64 the second. We're definitely started!"

2½ cups flour, ¼ tsp. baking powder, 1½ tsp. salt, ½ tsp. cloves, 2 cups sugar, 1½ tsp. baking soda, ¾ tsp. cinnamon, ½ tsp. allspice, ½ cup shortening, 1½ cups unsweetened applesauce, ½ cup cold water, 1 large egg, ½ cup chopped walnuts, 1 cup raisins (lightly coated with flour)

Sift together the dry ingredients in a bowl. Add the shortening, applesauce, water, and egg. Beat well and stir in nuts and raisins. Bake at 350 degrees about one hour (until tester comes out clean).

59. FISH RIVER LODGE

HK/AP, SCA

OWNERS: Jim and Kathy Lynch

ADDRESS: Box 202, Eagle Lake, ME 04739; 207-444-5207; e-mail: frlodge@ainop.com; www.fishriverlodge.com

SEASON: May through November

ACCOMMODATIONS: Eight cabins: one to three bedrooms, indoor plumbing and shower, gas heat, electric lights and refrigerator, gas cookstove

RATES: $80 per couple per day, $400 per cabin per week (HK); $90 per person per day, $375 per person per week (AP)

ACCESS: I-95 to exit 58 (Sherman Mills–Patten). Go north on ME 11 to the town of Eagle Lake. In the middle of the village, at the Eagle Lake grocery store, turn right and go 1.5 miles on a paved road to the camps.

By the time you've reached Eagle Lake, you are only 18 miles from the Canadian border and 6-plus hours north of Portland. Almost as far north as you can get in Maine. The camps, a set of dark brown cabins and log main lodge overlooking Eagle Lake, are at the dead end of a paved road, but just 1.5 miles from ME 11 and the conveniences of Eagle Lake village.

Kathy: "Don't confuse us with the Eagle Lake in Acadia National Park or Big Eagle next to Chamberlain Lake. We had a woman call us once, 'I'm here in Bar Harbor and I can't seem to find you!' Our Eagle Lake is part of the Fish River chain of lakes in the St. John Valley. It's 18 miles long. Being on a lake is great for family vacations, and we're very family oriented. That's our biggest growing sector. Sporting camps aren't just for hunting and fishing. The photographic opportunities are great, for example, and we just had a couple who got engaged while they were here."

Jim: "For beginning canoeists, a good trip would be the Fish River from the head of it and down. It's a two- or three-day trip meandering down through the North Woods with no whitewater."

Kathy: "We're fortunate here because over 9 miles of lake beyond the camps are all Maine Public Lands, which can never be built on. Our guests have access to about 26,000 acres of public lands. Eagle Lake was settled in 1840 by Sefroi Nadeau, a Canadian Frenchman, and Richard Woods, an Irishman. The town was incorporated in 1911 and was given its name because of the eagles in the area."

Jim: "The camps themselves were started in 1928 by Charlie Wiles, a lumberman. They were built for his wife because she wanted to start a business. She did very well, and they kept adding on to the lodge and building cabins. They called them Charles Wiles' Lake View Camps. When we bought them, in 1993, they were called Camps of Acadia and we changed it to Fish River Lodge because, like we mentioned, it was getting confused with Acadia National Park.

"I taught for 13 years at a vocational school. Then I started my own outdoor-equipment business in Cumberland. We decided when the kids were out of high school we'd do something in this business. We looked around until we found camps that were reasonable, plus we wanted to be easily accessible and have a good lake. We're at the very end of what they call Old Main Street here, so we have a paved road into the camps. We're on public utility, public electricity. Eagle Lake here is 18 miles long, 2½ miles wide. It is the last lake on the Fish River chain of lakes from Fish River Lake, Portage Lake, St. Froid Lake. In an easterly direction, we can go to Long Lake, across Square Lake, and back into Eagle Lake.

"If anyone came to me saying they wanted to purchase a set of sporting camps, what I'd tell them is manage a place for a year, see what it's all about, the ups and downs of the business. Then make your decision. And instead of going to a bank, have the seller finance it if possible. That way you're going to get a better interest rate, plus you won't have the headaches. A survey is worth it, but that should be the seller's expense. The majority of camps are on leased land. But we couldn't do that. We wouldn't be able to sleep at night."

Kathy: "When we first got here I was fishing off the dock one day and people coming by said, 'You can't catch any fish off the dock.' Well, a couple weeks later we had a 10-year-old boy who caught a 17-inch salmon off that dock. He was beside himself!"

Jim: "Basically Eagle Lake has landlocked salmon, brook trout, and togue. In the wintertime they catch cusk. We also have white suckers, chub, and jack smelts—the large smelts. For ice fishing, they plow a two-lane highway right down the lake from the center of town. And there'll be anywhere from 30 to 40 ice shacks right in front of the camps here. The lake is 80 feet deep in front of the camp, and the deepest part is between 140 and 180 feet, depending on the time of year. It's fly-fishing-only, artificial lures, the month of September on the Fish River and the thoroughfare between Eagle and Square Lakes. At any other time of the year it's whatever you want to do: trolling, plug fishing, worms, whatever.

"Hunting is great in the fall, good bear hunting, very good moose hunting. If a guy can't get a moose up here, he shouldn't be moose hunting. Deer hunting—there are some big deer. It's not uncommon to get a 250-pound buck, but you have to be a hunter because the territory's so big. There are thousands and thousands of acres with nothing. Plenty of logging roads for partridge and woodcock, or 'timberdoodles' is what we've always called them. You're almost guaranteed a bear. We have three guides available, plus I'm a registered Maine Guide.

"We're very fortunate that rabies hasn't come this far north, or heartworm problems, or Lyme disease. There is a strain of rabies coming in being carried by raccoons that there is no cure for yet. So if you see a raccoon walking around in your yard that's lethargic, chances are it's got rabies. Fox and coyote also carry rabies. With all the antitrappers and fur people, pelts aren't

Jim and Kathy Lynch of Fish River Lodge

worth anything. So the trappers aren't trapping them, and the hunters aren't shooting them. Pine martins, fisher, and skunk don't usually have rabies."

Kathy: "Hunting does have its uses. For every deer that's shot by a hunter, the biologists say 10 starve during the wintertime because of the cutting and the building, especially in southern Maine. I mean, when you build a house or mall in the middle of their field where they spend the winter, where do you expect them to go?"

Jim: "Do you know there are probably more moose killed on the highway than they take during the hunting season? And it happens in the deep woods by the logging trucks. They can't stop, no way, and the moose dies."
Kathy: "If a deer comes out of the woods, it'll stop by the road, look, and then jump out. So if you're paying attention, you'll see a deer first. A moose comes out of the woods, takes four or five steps out of the trees, gets in the middle of the road, and stops. There's no warning. I came back from Cumberland one night and I had three of them come out in front of me. One of them was a fairly close call—for the others I was able to slow down. The lights make them blind and totally unpredictable." *Jim:* "Not only that, but a moose, being dark, is very hard to pick up. You've got to watch

for the eyes to glow, to reflect the light. But moose eyes don't glow as much as deer eyes for some reason. One thing about a moose, he could be jogging alongside the road right beside you and all of a sudden, he'll just turn in front of you. And they trot right along at 35 miles an hour." *Kathy:* "We had friends come up here. The wife was in the passenger seat and there was a moose running right beside them. Her husband kept going faster and faster because he was afraid the moose would get ahead and dart in front and he wouldn't be able to stop the car in time. And the moose kept right up with him! Finally, they just stopped and let the moose go. She said she couldn't believe it—she's looking out her window and there's a moose right there!"

Cabbage Delight

Kathy: "You can use any meat, but it calls for kielbasa in the original recipe and that's what we like best. I'm giving you ingredients, and people can just figure how much they need based on how many they're going to feed. This is really delicious."

Onion, green pepper, olive oil, carrots, cabbage, kielbasa

Cut onion and green pepper into small pieces and sauté in olive oil in Dutch oven or pot until soft. Shred carrots and add to onion–pepper mixture and cook about 5 minutes. Core cabbage, cut in large chunks, and add along with the meat.

Turn down the heat and simmer, covered, until tender. Serve alone or with rice or potato.

60. JALBERT (WILLARD) CAMPS

AP/HK, SCA
OWNER: Phyllis Jalbert
ADDRESS: Phyllis Jalbert, 312 State Street, Brooklyn, NY 11201; 718-858-4496; e-mail: riverat@rcn.com; or Dana Shaw, 6 Winchester Street, Presque Isle, ME 04769; 207-764-0494
SEASON: Year-round
ACCOMMODATIONS: Six guest cabins, three log cabins in the main camp: one to two bedrooms, central outhouse, screened porch, gas lights, woodstove, sauna, rustic hot tub; one cabin has a full kitchen; also outpost cabins along the Allagash with gas lights, wood heat, and plumbing "out back"
RATES: $100–125 per person per day (AP), includes use of boats; $50 per person per day (HK); group rates available for groups of five or more
ACCESS: I-95 to exit 58. Take ME 11 north to Portage. At Dean's Motel in Portage, turn left. Follow the signs and pay at the gatehouse. Follow the main logging road south of Portage Lake. Turn left at Dead Horse Gulch and continue to the bridge at the base of Round Pond, where you need a boat pickup to get to the camps.

I visited Jalbert Camps in the middle of winter and participated in one of their winter-camping expeditions. Jalbert's (pronounced JAL-bear) is on a 2-acre peninsula in Round Pond along the Allagash, and most people come upon the cabins while canoeing the wilderness waterway. In winter you get to walk on water while trailing a toboggan-load of gear, sleep in a cotton tent with a portable woodstove, make an outdoor privy, learn how to keep water and the body from freezing, see a coyote chase a herd of deer across a frozen lake, reach the luxury of log cabins, and generally have an incredible adventure.

Phyllis: "In the late 1930s my grandfather, Willard Jalbert, used to come up here for hunting, guiding parties, and fishing. He was a lumberman." *Maine guide Dana Shaw continues:* "He was born about 15 miles downriver and spent most of his life on the Allagash. 'Moosetowner' is the name that's given to people who live in the Allagash area." *Phyllis:* "They're mostly of Scottish and Irish ancestry, perhaps mixed with French, too. My grandfather was considered to be a real Moosetowner." *Dana:* "After the war, Willard and Willard Jr., Phyllis's father, and her uncle Bob decided they needed to build a camp here, and that's how the camps started in 1946."

Phyllis: "This was true wilderness in those days. It's 35 miles to Allagash Village from here. We used to put in below Allagash Falls and sometimes we could make it here in a day, if nothing went wrong. Otherwise, my father would leave us along the river somewhere and go back to town and get what he needed. We have another camp downriver. It was one little cabin at first and they kept adding rooms on and now it's the Hilton of the Allagash. There were a lot of other log cabins along the river, which have since burned down because of the Allagash Waterway protection."

Dana: "The reason we're able to offer camps in a state preserve is as a result of Supreme Court Justice William O. Douglas. He took a trip through here and Phyllis's grandfather and father and I were on that trip. This was back in 1960. He said to us, 'This will be destroyed unless it's preserved.' So he went back to Washington and sent Stewart Udall, secretary of the interior at the time, up here to investigate. They really wanted this to become a national preserve." *Phyllis:* "But the state didn't want to lose control of the area." *Dana:* "So the state bought these buildings and burned down all the structures along the river except Nugent's up in Chamberlain Lake. This was in 1966. And they allowed the Jalberts to lease them back for a percentage of the gross income. And that's how we were able to hang on."

Phyllis: "My father and brother died in 1976, in a car accident together, and then my uncle died in a plane crash coming up here in 1980. My cousin ran the camps for five years, but he just wasn't of the nature to do this, so he gave it up. I was the only person in the family who came forward and tried to keep it. I was terrified—terrified. The grunt work that went into this place is unbelievable. That huge stove over there came up in a canoe! I mean they dumped it in the river several times, they portaged it across the falls. It was a major operation. I was nine when this cabin we're in was built. I remember them putting in the 'picogee,' the top log. And then, all of a sudden, it wasn't going to be part of us anymore? I spent a whole year putting together a proposal. There were people who wanted this place, and some who felt it should be burned down and returned to wilderness. And our position is that this has always been a working river, a log-driving river with log cabins along it. Anyway, we presented the proposal, the governor had to sign off on it, and I got it. We started in '86 with a 10-year lease and a 10-year option. The state is happy because the cabins are in much better shape now. We're not open like many of these other camps; people don't just drop in here. They only come in by special appointment."

Dana: "We start our fishing groups around May 1, ice-out. We feed people, and some bring their own food. The fishing is all wild brook trout, and it's actually pretty good still. We have fishing until mid-June, when the water starts warming up, and then we start our family-type groups."

Phyllis: "We organize guided Allagash canoe trips. The classic trip starts at Telos Lake and ends up at Allagash Village and takes 7 to 10 days. Or you could do shorter sections. For the most part, the Allagash has flat-water and Class I and II rapids, making it ideal for a wide range of canoeists. Then in the fall we have hunting both at base camp here and at Whittaker Brook, a camp 8 miles upriver. We have coyotes in the area, and you can hunt for them after dark.

"We started our winter camping in 1988, and 1992 was our pilot year for taking off from here on foot, with no snowmachine backup and no dogs. From here to our tent site is about 4 miles. Then we go 4 miles above that and stay in a cabin, then 2 more miles, and then we swing back and stay in the tents again. We'll pull our made-to-order Egyptian-cotton tents and gear behind us on special easy-run toboggans Dana made.

"It's so beautiful here in winter. Here's how you can sleep outside, even if you don't have a tent: You make a snow cave. First, you want to have some snow! Then you use a snowshoe or shovel and heap up an elongated mound of snow about 10 by 7 feet long and about 4 or 5 feet high. As you heap the snow on, really pack it down. The weight of the snow will keep pushing down and it will settle. When it's set, in about 2 hours or so, you can just dig it out. Be careful not to dig too close to the outside or it will collapse. Keep about a foot of snow all the way around. You can measure some twigs or boughs to a foot and place them around the top of the cave, so when you dig it out and come to a stick inside it means you've gone to the foot mark. The secret is to make the opening very small—just enough to crawl down into, and with the inside having just enough room to turn over and move around some, but not so large that your body heat can escape. And it actually warms up to a little below freezing when you're in there, even if the temperature outside is 10 or 20 degrees below zero."

Dana: "In the old days, this river was run in 20-foot Old Town guide-

The author winter camping at Jalbert Camps

model or E. M. White double-ended canoes that were good for poling and paddling. Then they brought in a 2.5-horsepower motor. But you put that on and the stern would tend to drag down. So over the years the canoes kept getting broader in the stern, with a flare in the bow and midsection so the water would roll out, not in. My first canoe was a Gallup canoe built in Fort Fairfield, Maine, and it just worked so much better than the old canoes. But I broke it in two trailering the thing, and I was heartsick. So I built myself a mold. I wanted my canoe to be bigger, longer, deeper, wider, with the same general features of that Gallup canoe. And my canoe came out much better than I expected. The material on the mold is cedar covered with sheet metal. The reason for the sheet metal is when you drive the little tacks in and the tacks hit the metal, they clinch. Now I had a hauling canoe which could work well with a 10-horsepower motor and float over bars at maximum speed without hitting rocks.

"Back when I was beginning to guide, a young fella in my 20s, the 'Ole Guide' was talking about giving these people a bear scare." *Phyllis:* "My grandfather was called the Ole Guide because he didn't want to be called the O-L-D guide!" *Dana:* "Well, these guests were egging to see a bear. So he got me to one side and says, 'Hey, go get that bearskin hanging alongside the cabin and drape that over you and go rutting around out there by the woodshed. And then we'll grub around with a flashlight and when you see the flashlight,' he says, 'you duck.' So, of course, I was out there grubbing around and he says to these people, 'Did you see him?' And everybody says, 'Oh yeah, I saw him.' Well, the Ole Guide, unbeknownst to me, had a shotgun. And he loaded that thing and he fired a shot. Can you imagine! I didn't know who fired that shot, and here I am with a bearskin draped over me! Now that's a Moosetown story, and trick!"

PJ's Oatmeal Sundaes

Phyllis: "Cereal provides powerhouse nutrients—paddle power. But you first have to convince people to eat it! This does the trick."

> 2 cups water, ¼ cup raisins, 1 cup rolled oats or five-grain cereal, 2 T oat bran, 2 T wheat germ, 2 apples (precooked with ½ cup water, 1 tsp. vanilla, ½ tsp. cinnamon, and 1 T maple syrup)

Combine water and raisins in a saucepan. Bring to a boil. Reduce heat and add oats, wheat germ, and oat bran gradually while stirring. Add the apples, vanilla, and cinnamon. Reduce heat and cook for about 5 minutes. Spoon into bowls and top with any combination of nuts, seeds, fruit (fresh or dried), and milk or yogurt, along with real maple syrup, if you have some.

61. LIBBY CAMPS

AP/HK, SCA
OWNERS: Matt and Ellen Libby
ADDRESS: PO Box 810, Ashland, ME 04732; 207-435-8274 or 207-435-2462 (radio phone); e-mail: matt@libbycamps.com
SEASON: May through November
ACCOMMODATIONS: Eight log cabins at the home camp (sleep two to six) with indoor plumbing and shower (two have a tub), skylight in roof, gas lights, woodstove; ten HK outpost cabins; well-behaved pets welcome
RATES: $130–360 per person per day, includes boats, flights, and guide
ACCESS: I-95 to exit 58. Take ME 11 north approximately 40 miles and turn left at the sign for the camps, onto a road that will take you through the town of Oxbow. Continue to the North Maine Woods gate ($25 fee). Continue on a dirt road about 20 miles, following signs. For quicker access, camp seaplane pickup is available at Presque Isle airport or at Matagamon Lake near Patten. Van pickup at the airport is also available.

Libby's is tucked in the forest with some old and some very new cabins built of massive spruce and balsam fir logs. Matt Libby has been handcrafting log buildings as long as he can remember. Inside, homemade quilts add warmth and skylights add light.

Matt: "The Libby family came to Maine from England in the 1660s. Two of my great-grandfathers were original settlers of Oxbow, the closest village to camp down the Aroostook River about 35 miles. In the 1850s C. C.

Libby moved to Oxbow, which only had a number for a name. Here, miraculously, he met a woman, Melissa Trafton, daughter of another original settler, Eben Trafton. They had farms and supplied the loggers during the 1880s. Then, around 1885, they started Libby Hotel. At the time, there was a man named Will Atkins who was running sporting camps on an island here on Millinocket Lake. Will's customers would come and stay at my grandfather's hotel on the way through. Then in the 1890s my grandfather, Ike, and his brother Will decided to get into the sporting-camp business, and they bought the island camps and Munsungan Lake camps from Will Atkins. They also bought several other sets of camps including Spider, Musquacook, and Churchill Lake camps. The saying was, '50 camps [cabins] in three counties, half a million fish waiting for your line,' or something like that. The dining room on the island was twice the size of this one here—70 feet long. And back then they thought it was too rustic to have your lodge look like logs, so they sawed them in half to make them look like boards. They'd have a cow they would swim over in the spring. The chore boy, my uncle Charlie, used to walk the cow up the trail from Oxbow 25 miles, cross the river, and then swim across the lake, leading the cow, so the guests would have fresh milk.

"Then the two brothers decided that Ike would run the town end and Will would run the camp end. Will died in 1938 and left what he had to his sisters. Well, they came up, and to make a long story short, we lost all the camps. So in 1938, my dad, Allie, and three customers from the island bought a new set of camps here on the mainland, which were built by Will Atkins' son, 'Sleepy.' After two or three years the camps on the island were sold to Maine Public Service Company. They wanted to flood every lake on the Aroostook so their dam in New Brunswick could save the spring high water to use in the summer and the fall high water to use in winter. They flooded the lake with about 7 extra feet of water and let us have some of the cabins on our island. I was on the raft in the late '50s when we moved them across the lake, just a 4-year-old kid.

"Dad started with three cabins here and built River Camp, a two-day paddle upriver, and then built Chandler Pond Camps. In 1950 he bought his first seaplane, because he wanted to get to the little ponds. He got a lease to build a camp on Big Caribou Pond just before he died. This was in 1959. He was 46 and Mom would have been 42. Here she is, a lady back in the wilderness, no communications, four sons, with me as the youngest. All her supplies had to be flown in by Ray Porter, a pilot out of Shin Pond. Before Dad died she'd bought a new washing machine, a boat, and a tractor, which they brought in by cutting the footpath wider. So here she is, the first winter after he dies, and all she's got is bills. And no husband. So she sold the plane—for $700!—and the farm equipment. Then after another year, she got her spirit back up, kept running the camp, and built the one Dad had planned to build at Caribou Pond. In '68 she built the dining room. My brothers and I did the work. She took out a small-business loan for $10,000 to do it. That was a lot of money back then and everybody, especially guys, said a woman would never be able to do that, no way, leased land and all. But she did it. She paid it all off." *Ellen:* "Early. She's an amazing woman, really." *Matt:* "Mom did it all and sent four boys to college. She remarried in '69 to John Gibson, who managed half a million acres for Seven Islands Land Company, which included land for one of our outcamps.

"In '68 we got our first 'road.' I can remember the last 3 miles took an hour—just crawling. You could walk ahead faster. Everybody'd get out and walk while the guy drove the stuff in. We had that right up until '89.

"I went to the University of Maine at Orono, like all my brothers. And my sophomore year I met Ellen. Best thing that could ever happen to me." *Ellen:* "You've got that on tape!" *Matt:* "And I guess probably our first date I told her about the camps." *Ellen:* "The first 5 minutes after I met him." *Matt:* "Yeah, well. I didn't appreciate camp until I got away from it. Growing up you think this is just an old camp in the woods. And then when you find out that everything else is just an old town with a lot of people, you start to see what you have. So our junior year Mom was talking about selling and we decided to buy her out. We got married in college." *Ellen:* "Because we had guests coming in here the day after graduation!"

Matt: "I started flying in 1977, the first year after we took over and in '87 I got a float plane. That's one of the special things about our camps. We have a vast area we cover, but the plane can get us to our remote outpost lakes in 10 minutes. The big lake here [6 miles long by a mile wide, 60 feet deep] is fished in the winter—brook trout and landlocked salmon—so the smaller lakes and streams are better for fly-fishing. We can fly you out to our Chandler Pond, Mooseleuk, Clear Lake, or Lower Hudson Pond camps. They're housekeeping and we limit those to a three-day stay." *Ellen:* "Everyone wants to go to there."

Ellen: "We spent the winters of '81 and '82 in here. The kids didn't get sick until we went to town to do a few sportsmen shows. Matthew was 1 and Alison 2½ . A few years ago we had a family reunion. It was the first time in 15 years that the four boys had been together."

Ellen: "The first hunting season I was here a fellow brought in this deer liver that filled the bottom of the sink. I looked at this thing and thought, How do you cook it! Well, the old fellow who worked for Elsie, Matt's mother, said, 'You know, liver and onions.' Well, I'm sure if it didn't taste just like the bottom of your shoe, it wasn't even that good by the time I got through with it!"

Matt: "Deer season takes a lot of preparation. For one thing, you're heating uninsulated camps that time of year, which takes a lot of wood. I get up at 3:30 and we'll have breakfast at 5 AM. We'll head out the door probably 5:30, so they'll be in the woods 15 minutes to a half an hour before daylight. Hunting has been getting better over the years. The only problem now is they've cut down too many of the deeryards, so the limiting factor is the wintering areas. The hunters go on a deer run [trail], or on a deer 'scrape

Matt and Ellen Libby

line,' which looks like a patch of open dirt. The buck will usually break a limb above the scrape and put a scent there from around his eye or by his ear and that will key some deer to what is there, and then a doe will come by and urinate there. So that's an active spot. There may be several of these scrapes within half a mile. You build the hunters a little ground blind, for cover, and then they'll wait. Usually 2 or 3 hours is all they can stand in the cold. During this time the guide is looking for new areas, maybe trying to get deer out of their beds and running down their natural runs. We'll come back, pick hunters up, maybe show them the new areas, try to stalk some deer if they're quiet enough, which they seldom are, and have lunch. The first hour and a half is prime. The deer may be moving out of their bedding area into their feeding area, or vice versa. But if there's a full moon, a lot of times the deer will feed at night and bed all day.

"A trophy buck here would be over 190 pounds. In Maine, if a hunter gets one over 200 pounds, he gets into the Big Bucks Club. There are probably 800 to 900 a year taken that are over 200 pounds. A lot of guys could care less about weight. Their first trip up they want horns. And they aren't interested in just the deer meat. Most of them come from great hunting states like New Jersey and Pennsylvania. Their deer may not be much bigger than a German shepherd, but it's good eating. Down there the bigger deer are culled out by the hunters. Up here, 10 or 15 percent of the big deer are killed by hunters. We have about as many deer in our area as we can hold. Any more and one harsh winter could wipe out 50 percent of them, because there's no place for them to winter. They don't winter in a clear-cut, or on a ridge, no matter how many trees are on it. They have to have 'black growth.' A deer-yard is mostly black spruce. We call it black growth because you have such a heavy overstory of conifers that it's dark in there. It keeps out the snow. If you go on a hardwood ridge, you'll be up to your waist, say. Down in the black growth, you're up to your knees, or less. There's a lot of food down there for them—lichens off the trees, mosses, and as the season gets harsher they'll start on the tips of cedar trees. If they can't reach the cedar, they're probably going to die. They'll eat hardwood buds. And in a logging area, the deer will come in and feed on fallen birch tips. When a tree falls, all the tops are available to eat and it's also great cover. Summertime, deer feed on just about anything that's green—moss being the least preferred, to ferns, raspberry leaves, and water plants being the most favorite. In the fall they like old-man's beard, which hangs on spruce and fir trees and looks like Spanish moss.

"I think northern and southern Maine is like black and white as far as hunting, trapping, and outdoor issues in general. You find a lot of people moving into Maine from cities where there are no deer or moose who think, 'You can't kill them.' But come on up to northern Maine and stay here for a whole season and see if you have the same feeling. I think that if there's to be no hunting in an area, it ought to come from the people who live in the area. Let us use our own judgment and our biologists—we hire biologists to look at the herd—and let's listen to them. Every single human has in him the need to provide for his family. People must realize that. Here you need to harvest against fire and disease, and it's a renewable resource."

In 1990 the Libbys expanded with Riverkeep Fishing Lodge in Labrador, Canada, and in 1993 Libby's became an Orvis-endorsed lodge, the first one in New England.

Whole-Wheat Biscuits

Matt: "Ellen's fresh-baked breads and pastries have saved the day many times when the fish decided not to bite or the deer decided not to appear. Without the long line of talented Libby women, the repeat customer list would undoubtedly be short."

2 cups all purpose flour, 1 cup whole-wheat flour, 2 T sugar, 4½ tsp. baking powder, ¾ tsp. cream of tartar, ½ tsp. salt, ¾ cup cold butter or margarine, 1 egg, 1¼ cups milk

Combine dry ingredients. Cut butter into slices and combine with dry ingredients, using pastry blender until mixture is crumbly. Combine egg and milk, stir into crumb mixture just until moistened. Turn onto floured surface and knead 10–15 times. Roll out to 1-inch thickness and cut with biscuit cutter. Bake on greased baking sheet at 450 degrees for 10–15 minutes. Watch carefully. Makes 12–15 biscuits.

62. LOON LODGE

AP/MAP/HK

OWNERS: Michael and Linda Yencha

ADDRESS: PO Box 404, Millinocket, ME 04462; 207-745-8168 (please leave message); e-mail: relax@loonlodgemaine.com; www.loonlodgemaine.com

WINTER ADDRESS: PO Box 2469, Wilkes-Barre, PA 18703; 717-287-6915

SEASON: May through November

ACCOMMODATIONS: Five cabins (one log outpost cabin): one to three bedrooms, porch, no running water in cabins, central bathroom and shower house, wood or propane heat, gas stove, gas refrigerator, and gas lights; bring blankets or sleeping bags and towels; pets welcome

RATES: $30–65 per person per day; $150–375 per person per week

ACCESS: I-95 to exit 56 (Medway). Take ME 11/157 through Millinocket. Follow signs to Baxter State Park and go 10 miles to the North Woods Trading Post (right side; last phone and gas). Cross over to the Golden Road and head west about 18 miles to the Telos Road (sign). Turn right and go 13 miles to the North Maine Woods gate (fee). Continue 8 miles and turn left (sign). Go 26 miles, following signs to camp.

Mike and Linda mail out three pages of directions with accompanying maps for people driving into camp. Loon Lodge is 90 miles from Greenville, 78 from Millinocket, and 91 from Ashland—or, as they explain it, 3 hours from any town. The cabins, basic with a cozy, attractive log lodge, are set on a knoll overlooking 1½-mile-long by ½-mile-wide Round Pond.

Linda: "Round Pond mostly has white perch, and surrounding ponds have lake and brook trout, salmon, and muskie, a large member of the pike family and the largest freshwater fish in Maine. One advantage of our remoteness is that we're the closest sporting camp to Allagash Lake, which is hard to get to and totally pristine. Round Pond is near the headwaters of three of the most famous rivers in New England: the Allagash, the Penobscot, and the St. John. We have a wide variety of terrain and lots of wildlife. The alder swamps and beech ridges attract upland birds such as ruffed grouse, woodcock, deer, and bear. The shallow ponds and swampy lowlands attract ducks like black ducks, teal, mallards, wood ducks, mergansers, as well as loons, bald eagles, Canada geese, and moose, right to the shores of the pond. There are over 5,000 acres of water you could fish or explore without getting out of your boat.

"Since the nearest paved road is over 50 miles away, and then you have to go almost another 30 miles to get to a town, this place is for people who really want to get away from it all. That's what happened to us. Mike was doing Boy Scout trips when we found this area, and we fell in love with it. We had a hard time getting the lease from Seven Islands because they thought we were too young. But we got it in '84, stayed in a tent that first year while we built the first cabin, and have been here ever since.

"One of the things we did was to put in a thousand-foot driveway to make it easier for guests to get in. The other thing that's made a big difference is our new shower house, so people can have electricity and hot and cold running water."

Mike: "Deer, bear, and moose hunting are my specialities and we make every effort to give our hunters the best trip they can have. We only take a limited number of hunters a week and hire experienced guides to take care of them. Deer hunts in northern Maine mean big bucks. Granted, we don't have the numbers you can find in southern New England, but we make up for that in size. Bucks that dress out over 200 pounds are taken out of camp every season.

"Over the past few years the business has been evolving and now we're getting more and more families and nature lovers, ecotourists, staying with us. We like to call them our nonconsumptive guests. They're great to have and all they want to see is wildlife for pictures, and to just kick back and relax.

"Our lodge and cabins are a work in progress since we built everything from scratch and are constantly adding and improving things. One nice touch we've done is put a theme to each cabin, and then over the winter I design and build all the furnishings for the cabin. People love this. Our guests that come year after year are always wanting to see what's new. Their enthusiasm and support give us both real pleasure."

Chocolate Pecan Cheesecake Bars

Linda: "My menu is basic, simple, hearty, homestyle cooking. Our meals (except lunch) are served family-style and all you can eat. About 90 percent of the time my guests complain of gaining weight at the end of the week. Of all my jobs in this business, I love cooking the best."

Crust: 1 package Pillsbury Plus dark chocolate cake mix, ½ cup margarine or butter (softened), 1 egg, ½ cup chopped pecans

Filling: 8 oz. package cream cheese (softened), 14 oz. can sweetened condensed milk, 1 tsp. vanilla, 1 egg

Heat oven to 350 degrees. Grease a 9" x 13" pan. Combine cake mix, margarine or butter, and egg. Stir in pecans—reserve 1 cup of mixtue for topping. Press remaining mixture into the bottom of the pan.

Beat cream cheese until fluffy. Add remaining ingredients and beat until smooth. Pour over crust and sprinkle reserved topping over this.

Bake for 35–40 minutes or until edges are lightly browned. Cool completely. Cut into bars. Makes 36 bars.

63. MACANNAMAC CAMPS

AP/HK/MAP, SCA

OWNERS: Jack and Josie McPhee

ADDRESS: PO Box 598, Millinocket, ME 04462; 207-757-7097; www.macannamac.com

SEASON: Year-round

ACCOMMODATIONS: Seven HK log cabins; newer cabins have full utilities, older or more remote cabins have outhouse, no running water, gas lights, woodstove, porch. Main lodge: AP or MAP, three rooms, all utilities.

RATES: $25–48 per person per day (HK); $120 per person per day (AP); $75 per person per day (MAP)

ACCESS: I-95 to exit 56 (Medway). Take ME 11 through Millinocket to the right-hand fork for Ripogenus Dam. Cross the dam onto Telos Road and go 38 miles. The Telos gate fee is currently $18 per person for Maine residents, $25 for nonresidents. A sign for the camps is on the left.

Macannamac Base Camp has a spacious main lodge surrounded by luxurious gardens. Inside is a fieldstone fireplace, and sliding doors lead to a deck that looks out on Haymock Lake. There are guest accommodations on the second floor, and the place has a bed & breakfast feel to it. Nearby are new and airy log cabins. Pilot Jack McPhee provided one of the highlights of my research by flying me, in his Piper Cub, to outpost camps on Cliff and Spider Lakes, where guests have a lake to themselves.

Jack: "One of the first questions people ask us is, 'Do you live here year-round?' Yep, this is home. It's a great reminder to us just how fortunate we are to be here. I did this all because I wanted to live here in the backcountry and, in figuring a way to make a living here, Macannamac Camps came into existence. We're located on three lakes: Haymock, Spider, and Cliff, all of which are part of the Allagash River watershed. They have brook and lake trout and whitefish. All the cabins are on their own lot and have their own dock to the lake, which gives people privacy and the feeling of enjoying their own private camp. That's our philosophy—that people can treat the camp like their own.

"We have the full-service lodge here at Haymock, along with what we call full-utility housekeeping cabins (a full bath and running water to the kitchen). We're able to do this because of our generator power. No other camps in this area fit the criteria of full-utility housekeeping. Our outpost camps at Spider and Cliff are more remote and basic.

"My father and I had the first camp built at Spider in 1973, which we used as a personal camp for many years. It was also a great backwoods camp for me during my years on patrol as a game warden pilot. I officially started in the sporting-camp business in 1983 and built our cabins and the main

JO MCPHEE

Macannamac Camps

lodge from then until '87. We lost two cabins to fire, but rebuilt both of those along with the cabin that my wife, Josie, and I live in.

"The name Macannamac is the Abenaki Indian word for Spider Lake. We lease from Seven Islands, and our cabins are on property controlled by an organization of landowners called North Maine Woods. Visitors coming here register and pay fees to pass through their gates. There are a number of these gates around the North Maine Woods. Our gate system is operated from May through November. In the past, our landlord has been bombarded with people who want to own a private camp on perhaps an otherwise pristine lake. Our camps alleviate the potential for wilderness sprawl. Really, it makes no sense to spend thousands of dollars a year to own and maintain a camp that spoils a wilderness setting, when you can come to Macannamac, have your own remote cabin, and only spend $400 a week.

"Now that I'm retired from my job as warden pilot, I seem to still get in a lot of flying time. Most of what I do is airborne radio tracking, called felonics, which tracks critters that have radio devices on them. I cover bears, Canadian lynx, coyote, fisher, and fox. With black bears, we've been mapping out their dens. We have a ground crew that goes around from January through March and checks out the dens. We've been doing this for over 20 years. Actually, I've been at it so long I kind of get attached to some of the animals I track. I followed one bear for 15 years who was live-trapped and given the ID number 283 and a radio collar. (Those who fly, though, call the bears by names.) I tracked another bear that covered 75 miles in 48 hours, and that's for me, in a straight line, in the air. Imagine what the bear did! It's hard to stalk a black bear—so even if I were to tell a hunter where I saw one, it would still be hard to get. So our tracking is for research, not for game hunters."

Josie: "Our only 'off' months are December and April, and that time is spent getting ready for the coming season. Other than that, the camps are open and available to anyone wishing to come this far north, whether it's a hard-core sportsman or a family group. In spring we have beautiful wildflowers: fairy calypso orchids, the size of your thumb; pink, white, and yellow lady's slippers, and hepatica, a white flower that blooms here very early, before the grass. Actually, the first flower out is coltsfoot, or dandelion flower. It's the same yellow as a dandelion and the flower blooms in the snow before there are any leaves. The leaves come out in late summer, strangely enough. We also have bog orchids, along with red trillium—gorgeous wildflowers. Even our driveway is flanked by purple fireweed and goldenrod.

"It's amazing to me to look at what Jack's done, right from the ground up. He's had a lot of help along the way, but he deserves most of the credit. We know our excellent clientele has been the key to our success and we hope to enjoy this place for many seasons to come."

Apple Oatmeal Crisp

Josie: "Seems like some of the best tasting, most favorite 'eats' are the simplest to make."

1½ pounds tart cooking apples, ½ cup butter or margarine, ¾ cup brown sugar, ¾ cup quick-cooking rolled oats (uncooked), ½ cup flour, 1 tsp. cinnamon

Core and slice apples into a baking pan. Melt butter in saucepan. Take off the heat and stir in rolled oats, brown sugar, flour, and cinnamon. Sprinkle over apples. Bake at 350 degrees for 35 minutes or until golden brown and apples are soft. Serve with whipped cream, or ice cream.

64. MCNALLY'S CAMPS

AP, SCA
OWNERS: John Richardson and Regina Webster
ADDRESS: HCR 76, Box 632, Greenville, ME 04441; 207-944-5991; www.nugent-mcnallycamps.com
SEASON: Year-round
ACCOMMODATIONS: Six log cabins: one to two bedrooms, indoor plumbing and shower, gas lights, wood heat; bring sleeping bags and towels
RATES: $80 per person per day; child rates available; canoe (with motor) rentals

ACCESS: I-95 to exit 56 (Medway). Take ME 11/157 through Millinocket, bear right onto Baxter State Park Road, and go 10 miles to a left-hand turn for the West Branch Region. Continue up Golden Road 18 miles, then take a right onto Telos Road. Go 15 miles to the North Maine Woods gate (fee if over 12 or under 70). Go 8 miles to Chamberlain Bridge. Continue north on Telos Road 11 miles. Pass Pinkham Road and take first left past Haymock Lake (1.5 miles). Five miles past John's Bridge take right at Poulin Road. Go 11 miles to Cut Over Road. Turn right and go 2 miles and bear left at T. Go 4 miles (past American Realty Road) to Clayton Lake. Continue 1 mile to a right turn (camp sign). After 4 miles turn right and continue another 4 miles to the camp's gated road on right and another 1.5 miles to camp.

John: "Will McNally, who many consider to be the father of North Maine Woods sporting camps, had a son, Dana, who built this place in 1951. Both men had a flair for designing and building. We bought these camps in 1997 from Mycki, Dana's wife. We're on Ross Stream, originally called Chemquassabamticook (Sebemsicook) or 'place of many fish.' And there are a lot of trout. It's a classic fly-fishing stream: general law with a one-fish limit in the fall. And there's whitefish and togue in the lake. The stream is on the north end of Long Lake, 500 yards outside the Allagash Wilderness Waterway. We offer a 30-mile motorized canoe trip from Nugent's, our other camp, to here. It's a great way to see remote Maine and still sleep in a bed with a roof over your head. And did I mention ice fishing, cross-country skiing, snowmobiling, snowshoeing, and great hunting? We've got it all covered!"

Mycki McNally offers another definition for Chemquassabamticook: "Friends once sent us a sign with the Indian name and I asked Dana, 'What does that mean?' Without skipping a beat he turned to me and said, 'Squaw, you no-good cook—go home!'"

Dana's manuscript, *Bush Happy*, is typed on the back of letterhead that lists Will McNally's holdings: Big Fish Lake, Round, Ferguson, Island, Moccasin, North, and Beavertail Ponds, and First, Second, and Third Chase Lakes. Mycki notes that was 100 years of continuous operation of McNally camps—quite a North Woods empire. Three of McNally's camps are in Dana's book: Zella Island (Wilderness Island in this book), Red River, and McNally's.

As Dana writes:

"Mose McNally, Dad's father, was one of the finest lumbermen in this section. He came from Fredericton, New Brunswick, and made his way up the St. John and then Aroostook Rivers to settle in Ashland. He got driven out of Scotland for stealing chickens, according to Dad, William (Will) Parker McNally, next to the youngest of five boys, who became the camp hunter. Dad remembered that at that time, in the early 1900s, there was no such thing as game laws, and there were no deer, but plenty of caribou.

"During the years while I was away from Maine, I had learned to hunt ducks, and after coming home and going into business with Dad, the thing I missed above all else was good duck hunting. I got Wilfred Atkins, the local game warden, known as 'Sleepy' around here, interested in duck hunting around Portage and Fish River Lakes. In the fall of 1950 we had a hard freeze early in October and most of the ducks left our hunting grounds. One of our guides, Herber Umphrey of Fort Kent, had also become somewhat duck conscious. So one afternoon he and I and Sleepy loaded the Pacer with a tent, sleeping bags, and a bit of grub and flew into the Allagash country to try and locate a few. When we flew over the marsh where Chemquassabamticook Stream enters Long Lake, hundreds of ducks flew up out of the many small pot holes. So we landed, carried our duffel ashore, tied the plane down for the night, and set out for what turned out to be the fastest duck shooting any of us have ever experienced before or since.

"It was a beautiful, clear afternoon, just cool enough to be comfortable walking. We set out abreast and about twenty to thirty feet apart, walking toward the pot holes. A small bird flushed ahead of us and from the view I got of it in flight, it looked to me like a woodcock. I had never hunted any woodcock, but the markings on the back of its head and rump pretty well matched pictures I had seen. Sleepy said, 'What kind of bird was that?'

'A woodcock,' I answered. 'Is the season open on woodcock?'

'Yes, but are you sure it was a woodcock?'

'Sure,' I said. 'Didn't you see the markings on its back?'

"About that time another one took off and within the next five minutes we must have seen at least half a dozen. The more we saw, the more convinced I became that they were woodcock until I finally shot one. We picked it up and decided it was indeed a woodcock. During the next few hours we ended up with an even bag limit each. Also, the marsh was literally alive with Black Ducks that day. They would flush out of the tall grass only fifteen to twenty feet ahead of us, circle around unperturbed by our shooting, and fly straight back over us as though they had never seen us. It was like shooting Pheasant in a corn field! By the time we had hunted back to where we had left our duffel, we each had our limit.

"The sun set on three very happy hunters that evening. And what a beautiful evening it was, too. The surface of the lake was as calm as a mill pond, the air was warm and it felt more like an evening in June than mid-October. As we boiled coffee over a driftwood fire, we decided that there was no sense in bothering to pitch the tent. We would just put it over us to keep out the dampness and lay under the stars. We laid there for hours after supper, watching the fire, telling stories, and listening to the ducks talking out in the marsh in front of us—one of those evenings that come but once in a lifetime!"

There's more to the story. Dana and pals were awakened by a deluge and eventually had to take off into the teeth of a gale out of the north, "colder than a banker's heart." They landed in Portage, where

"Sleepy piled out, taking only his woodcock as a gift for his supervisor. When Herber and I walked into the cook camp at Fish River, Mycki took one look at our 'woodcock' and wanted to know what we were doing bringing home a bunch of jacksnipe when the season had been closed on them for years! A few days later, I landed at Portage and Sleepy was waiting for me on the dock with a copy of Roger Tory Peterson's *A Field Guide to the Birds* in his hands and a most unkind expression on his face. It seems that our warden's gift to his supervisor had definitely been a mutual surprise!"

During the following winter they made plans to build at the stream.

"We chose a site on a high bluff overlooking the lake and what had been the marsh. There was a good spring nearby and plenty of the right sized spruce logs not too far away. Above the campsite, about three quarters of a mile up the stream and on the same side, Cunliffe Brook leads back half a mile into Cunliffe Lake, a wild, remote little body of water that provides some of the best trout fishing in this part of the country. At the junction of Cunliffe Brook and the stream there was a burned over area of roughly one hundred acres very sparsely grown up into white birch and patches of wild raspberry. An old tote road passes just behind the campsite and runs up the stream and through the burn to Cunliffe Lake. This looked like a good bet for bear, deer, and grouse and so it has proved to be. About July we had been granted a lease on the chosen campsite by the International Paper Company and were ready to start building.

"There seemed no easy way to get a horse in there so our plans were to make only a simple cabin with logs small enough to be carried on our backs out of the woods. What we call a 'post camp' or cabin made from short logs standing on end. Except for the sills and plates, all the side logs are about six feet six inches long and not more than eight to ten inches in diameter. Three or four of the guides, with me and Dad, who was doing the cooking, flew in and landed in front of the campsite. We pitched a tent up on the bank, cut a supply of wood, made ourselves some bough bunks on the ground, and staked out the base of the camp. By that time it was getting late, so we launched the eighteen foot aluminum canoe I had flown in previously and caught ourselves a mess of brook trout for supper. When we climbed the bank after cleaning the trout, we could smell the coffee boiling over the open fire and Dad had a batch of biscuits browning in the outdoor baker. Trout never taste the same as they do when freshly caught and cooked in the open. After we cleaned our few dishes, we sat around the fire and Dad got to reminiscing about his early days in the woods."

The next day they started building the cabin. They cut long-lasting cedar logs for sills and rigged a parbuckle to get them up the high bank from the stream. A parbuckle in this case was a long rope with each end fastened to a stake about opposite the ends of the logs, but up on the bank.

The center of the rope is then dropped down the bank and under the log and the rope is long enough so that this middle can be dragged back up the bank before it brings up around the log. Three or four men then pull on the middle of the rope and the log rolls up the bank on the rope. This is also the method used to get the ribs and other long logs to the top of the cabin from the ground.

"The next job was to hew off the floor sills, place them over the mud sills, and notch and lay the floor timbers over them. Now we cut four plates, hewed off one side flat and notched in the ends so all four surfaces would be at the same level. We then put a good big post upright on the floor sills at each corner and hoisted the plates on to them and spike the posts, plates, and sills in place. Then you need to cut, carry in, and spike the upright logs, which will be the walls, between the plates and sills, leaving the openings for the door and windows. After we had filled in the walls, we determined the pitch of the roof and layed and spiked the two gable ends and put the ridge pole in place on them. We then notched rafters into the ridge pole and the plates and were ready to board in the roof. We had now been away from Fish River for five days and had to leave for home camp. But during the summer, two or three of us would fly over and work on the cabin and by the middle of September it was about ready for the hunting season."

Thus started McNally's Camps. Eventually five more cabins, a main lodge, and an enclosed garden and outbuildings were constructed. In the main lodge, a well-appointed kitchen looks out on a dining area where guests eat family-style at long tables. A living room with a fireplace is off to one side. Overlooking the stream outside, the Indian-name sign—Dana's "Squaw no-good cook"—remains. Of course this description of Mycki as a cook runs counter to all reports. She asks, "Do you know the only sandwich that won't freeze? Peanut butter and bacon."

Raspberry (or Strawberry) Jell-O Pie

Current guests continue to enjoy good cooking at McNally's under Reggie and John.

Combine 1 cup water, 1 cup sugar, and 3 T cornstarch in a saucepan and bring to a boil, stirring constantly. Remove from heat and add: 3–4 T raspberry (or strawberry) Jell-O. Stir well to blend and dissolve Jell-O. Add to precooked pie shell filled with fresh raspberries (or strawberries). I use a graham-cracker crust. Cool and enjoy.

65. MOOSE POINT CAMPS

AP, SCA

OWNERS: John Martin, Patricia Eltman

ADDRESS: PO Box 170, Portage, ME 04768; 207-435-6156

SEASON: Mid-May to mid-December

ACCOMMODATIONS: Ten log cabins: one to two bedrooms, indoor plumbing and shower, gas lights, wood heat, porch; pets allowed

RATES: $85 per person per day; $385 per person per week

ACCESS: I-95 to exit 58. Take ME 11 north to Portage. Turn left at Dean's Motel and left onto Toll Road (camp sign). Pay a fee at the gatehouse and continue 17 miles to the camps, following signs (black lettering).

Moose Point Camps is a set of classic, honey-colored log cabins ranged around a peninsula jutting into Fish River Lake. The cabins form an irregular T shape with the low main lodge at the top-left portion of the T. There is a comfortable sitting area with sliding glass doors, and a main hallway leading through the kitchen into a sunny dining area with long tables. Native American drawings and artifacts grace the walls and shelves, gifts from participants of a tribal gathering.

John: "The original camps were built in 1906 and were purchased in the 1930s by Dana West, who had them for 25 years or so. Then in the late '60s they were bought by Rose and Bill Mitchell, who occupied them for 23 years. I ended up with them in the fall of '91. I worked in a sporting camp as a kid, Camps of Acadia (now Fish River Lodge), at Eagle Lake. My uncle and aunt owned those camps for some 20 years. And I worked there from seventh grade through high school. I mowed lawns, brought in wood. I always wanted to own a set of sporting camps after I retired as state legislator from Eagle Lake [including 19 years as Speaker of the House].

"The place was called Moose Point Camps when I got it. It was the Mitchells who put up the wooden moose out on the point. It's actually just two pieces of wood: The body of the moose, the front leg, one back leg, and the head are all one piece. One leg in the front and one in the back and the antlers are add-ons.

"We're open until black-powder season, for muzzle-loading guns. Remember Davy Crockett? His gun was a muzzle-loader. We've had black-powder season in Maine since the mid-'80s. For the fishery, we're located on the shore of the west wing of the Fish River chain of lakes. We've got trout, landlocked salmon, togue, and whitefish. It's called Fish Lake by some and Fish River Lake by others, and it's 5 miles long. Fish runs into Portage, which runs into St. Froid, and then into Eagle. And if you start at the other end, on the east side of the chain, there's Long Lake, then Mud, then Cross, then Square and Eagle. There's only one portage, at a falls, and that's after you leave Fish. Otherwise you can canoe the whole thing. You

Moose Point Camps

could put in at Carr Pond, which is the headwater of Fish Lake, and go down to Eagle Lake in about two days."

Pat: "I do marketing and advertising, and I oversee the kitchen and food operation. I go in to the camp as much as I can, but I live 312 miles away and it's easier for John." *John:* "I live only 36 miles away, in Eagle Lake. I can literally go 1 mile from my house and be on woods roads the rest of the way." *Pat:* "People forget it's a big state. I go practically from one end to the other when I go back and forth from Portland. I have been doing sportsmen's shows and mailings; I do a lot of that some years."

John: "The camps were in pretty good shape, but there's always work to be done. We put in underground gas lines for propane, put in the internal water system, dug a well, leveled the road in. We built an icehouse in the fall of '92 because that summer we used about $1,200 worth of ice. Every time people would come in, I'd say, 'Bring ice.'"

Pat: "John gets to oversee everything. He's the CEO."

John: "I've never understood that title at all. I mow lawns—"

Pat: "We all chip in. Whatever needs to be done, we do it."

Boiled Dinner

One 8- to 10-pound ham with bone, 1–2 large onions (quartered), carrots, turnips, potatoes (all in large chunks)

Place ham with onions in a large pot, cover with water, and bring to a boil for 1 or 2 hours at steady low boil. An hour or two before serving, add carrots, turnips, more onions (if desired), and potatoes, enough to feed the number of people being served. Potatoes go in last. Cook until the potatoes are done. Place the ham in the center of a platter and arrange the vegetables around it.

66. NUGENT'S CAMPS

AP/MAP/HK, SCA

OWNERS: John Richardson and Regina Webster

ADDRESS: HC 76, Box 632, Greenville, ME 04441; 207-944-5991; www.nugent-mcnallycamps.com

SEASON: Year-round

ACCOMMODATIONS: Twelve log cabins: one to two bedrooms, porch, individual outhouse, central showerhouse, two hand-pumps for drinking water, gas lights, gas stove, and gas refrigerator, woodstove; bring sleeping bag and towels for HK; well-attended pets welcome

RATES: $80 per person per day (AP); $45 per person per day (MAP); $25 per person per day (HK). Boat shuttle from Chamberlain Bridge landing: $25 one way.

ACCESS: I-95 to exit 56 (Medway). Take ME 11/157 through Millinocket, bear right on Baxter State Park Road, and go 10 miles to a left-hand turn for the West Branch Region. Continue up Golden Road 18 miles, then take a right-hand turn onto Telos Road. Go 15 miles to the North Maine Woods gate (fee if over 12 or under 70). Go 8 miles to Chamberlain Bridge parking area (boat launch). (In winter, continue across the bridge and drive 8 miles to Nugent's 2.5-mile snowmobile trail.)

Nugent's Camps are located along the Allagash Wilderness Waterway, a world-renowned destination for canoe enthusiasts in summer and snowmobilers in winter. The cabins, nestled on a knoll on the north shore of 2½- by 18-mile-long Chamberlain Lake, offer respite for weary travelers, no matter what their mode of transportation. The camps are rustic, and state rules require that they be kept that way. They have dock facilities for boats up to 26 feet. (Note: Before camp, there's a bridge with a 7-foot clearance.) Guests come to troll for lake and brook trout and whitefish or to hunt in the remote woods.

John: "In 1936, Al and Patty Nugent came here on a homemade raft and built these camps together out of the wilderness. They built them specifically for hunting and fishing. This was, at the time, a public lot they

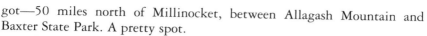

got—50 miles north of Millinocket, between Allagash Mountain and Baxter State Park. A pretty spot.

"We're both from central Vermont. Our house there was in the woods, but it just wasn't a big enough patch of woods, so we began looking for bigger patches."

Regina: "I had worked for the state of Vermont as an office manager for 10 years, so it was kind of a career switch for me, going into the sporting-camp business. But I grew up in a rural area, at the end of a dead-end road, so it was not a big switch in that sense."

John: "We happened to see an ad from Webber Oil in the *Maine Sportsman* for someone to run their private camps. We looked it up on the map and it was right around Mount Katahdin, which is where we'd decided we wanted to be. So we started at Rainbow Lake Camps and, oddly enough, that's where Patty Nugent started, too. She must've been there in the late '20s, early '30s. We stayed there close to 5 years. Then we went to Lake Clark in Alaska to work, but everything fell through on that. Meanwhile, a friend saw a notice in the Bangor paper that said the State of Maine was putting Nugent's up for bid. You see, the state owns these camps. They bought the Nugents out, basically forced them to sell. Al and Patty took the money and leased the camps back from the state for $20 a month, I think it was. All the years it was assumed that Parks and Recreation would burn these buildings when Patty was gone, because they wanted just wilderness. But Nugent's Camps were so well established, as were Jalbert's, that people pushed to save them. So the state passed a law and the camps were protected.

"The state awarded the lease of the camps to us in 1987 with one 10-year lease and two 5-year extensions. The Bureau of Parks and Recreation determines what we can and cannot do. Any improvements we make on these old log cabins have the same codes that apply for a new building in Augusta! And I have to follow strict rules about where I can cut. There's a lot of red tape and rules now, for all the sporting-camp owners. There are people who say Alaska's different, or northern Québec, but it's the same everywhere probably.

"When we came in here, Patty was getting too old to run the place by herself. And it was sad she had to go. I mean, she loved this place, but she just couldn't physically stay here anymore. When she left, she was an unhappy soul till the day she died, because this was her home."

John and Regina became the owners of McNally's Camps in 1997 and have thus become, as Regina puts it, "stewards" of two camps that were run by women who were legends in their own time, Patty Nugent and Mycki McNally. Indeed, sporting camps owe their longevity to the fortitude of women like these—other names include Alys Parsons (Lakewood Camps), Violette Holden (Attean Lake Lodge), Elsie Libby (Libby Camps), Margie McBurnie (Tomhegan)—wilderness women all, who kept the camps running long after their husbands had died.

John: "I suppose wilderness is relative. I mean, you can drive up here

from a major city in a day's time and think, gee, this is nice, nobody's
around. There are still some nice remote areas in Maine, and I think this
happens to be one of them. The whole Waterway's a good concept and I'm
glad it's run on a state rather than a national level. It is one of only a few
run that way. It was established in 1971, the first federally designated
wilderness and scenic river. It has a 15-member advisory board, which I'm
on. When it started out, it had a lot of use. Big groups of 30 or 40 kids from
summer camps, for example. Now we get campers, but in smaller groups.
The Allagash flows north, which is somewhat unique as far as rivers go. The
Waterway is 92 miles long, and it begins at Allagash Lake and ends
upstream from Allagash Village.

"We have a canoe trip we offer. You leave Chamberlain in the early
morning, go to Lock Dam, and from there to Allagash Stream, Eagle Lake,
Churchill Lake, and Chase Rapids, where your gear is portaged by the park
rangers. Ice-out up here doesn't happen until the middle of May, so in June
it's fairly exciting water. And it's so beautiful. You start with big lakes and
wide green areas, views of Katahdin. At Churchill it starts to close in to
ridges and hills. Boats are allowed on Telos and Chamberlain Lakes. On
Eagle Lake you can have canoes with up to 10-horsepower motors, but no
boats, and Allagash Lake is canoes only, with no motors. Most people start
their trip at Chamberlain Bridge or Churchill Dam. There are several outfitters in Allagash Village that rent canoes and shuttle people around." One
is Allagash Outfitters, Box 149, Allagash, ME 04774; 207-398-3277.

Regina: "We also host naturalist groups in the summer, like for the
Audubon Society. But by the same token, John and I are not anti-hunting.
We get a lot of hunters and fishermen. We like to see the people who at least
give some thought to where they are and what they've got around them.
And we really do get a lot of people who appreciate it."

John: "We're open year-round: January–March, May and June, and
November are our busiest months. We don't close down and we generally
don't take a vacation somewhere else because we find that there are very few
places we'd rather be than here."

Reggie's Togue "McNugent's"

1 large togue (or whitefish), 1 cup stale beer (or water), 1½ cups Bisquick,
1 egg, sprinkle of pepper, 1 tsp. garlic salt

Fillet togue or whitefish (this should be done when the fish is freshly caught). Chunk
the fillets up into 1-inch cubes. Combine ¾ cup Bisquick with pepper and garlic
salt. Mix the other ¾ cup Bisquick with egg and beer (or water). Dip fish chunks
into the dry ingredients first, then dip into beer batter. Deep-fry in 2 inches, or
more, of oil, four or five pieces at a time. Cook 2 minutes or until golden brown.

67. RED RIVER CAMPS

AP/HK, SCA

OWNERS: The Brophy family

ADDRESS: PO Box 320, Portage, ME 04768; 207-435-6000 (summer); 207-528-2259 (winter); e-mail: redrivercamps@direcway.com; www.redriver-camps.com

SEASON: May through October 15

ACCOMMODATIONS: Nine log cabins: one to four bedrooms, indoor plumbing and shower, wood heat, gas lights; three cabins are HK equipped—linens included (bring towels). Pets welcome; Mike (laughing): "If they sleep on a bed, I charge the same as I do a person."

RATES: $85 per person per day (AP), motorboats and canoes included; $37 per person per day (HK); child rates available

ACCESS: I-95 to exit 58. Take ME 11 north to Portage. Turn left at Dean's Motel and then fork left at the Great Northern Paper Company road (dirt). After the North Maine Woods tollgate, take a right-hand turn (sign) and go 12.5 miles. Bear left all the way in, going another 8.2 miles. The camp driveway, on the left, is steep and rocky.

Most of the cabins at this classic sporting camp form a gently rising horseshoe around the mowed hill to the left of the main lodge. Tucked down by the water's edge at the end of the slope, the lodge has a cozy feel. The logs for the buildings have a reddish brown stain. There are a couple of cabins right at the water's edge, and another cabin awaits guests on the island for which Island Pond was named, an easy paddle away.

Mike: "Around 1886, a man named Chapman married a woman with a lot of money, took all her money up here into the woods, and built a set of camps, a private retreat. He built on the island first, in 1887. The main lodge, the cabin on the hill in back of the lodge, and the guide's cabin were built prior to 1900. Actually, the guide's cabin was originally a schoolhouse. Families would come in here, and while the adults went out fishing, the kids would stay in school. They'd hire a tutor to teach the kids. When I redid the walls in there, I found slates with math problems and things like that.

"The bell in the dining room was originally the schoolhouse bell. And there was a two-chair barbershop up on the hill. The camp on the island was just one big room, nothing there but a fireplace and a piano; that was the dance hall. No sign of the piano around today. Throughout the years, all the previous owners have taken a little bit with them each time they left.

"After Chapman built it, the story goes, his wife got tired of him spending her money and the place got sold to the Whitman family. They owned several textile mills in Massachusetts. And they bought it as a family compound. Herschel Currie bought it right after World War II. He had worked here as a caretaker for the former owners: the Christies and McNallys.

"The people coming in here came to Portage on the B&A [Bangor and

Aroostook Railroad]. They got off the train, got in a canoe at Portage Lake, canoed 20 miles up the lake and up Fish River as far as Fish River Falls. The following morning they would either walk or come in by horse and wagon the 10½ miles to here.

"We're in the southeast corner of Township 15, Range 9 (T15R9), which is Public Reserve Land. The camps sit on the north shore of Island Pond, which is roughly half a mile long by a quarter mile wide, and 44 feet at the deepest. It's fly-fishing-only for brook trout. Most of the ponds around here are fly-fishing-only. We have 25 lakes and ponds to fish within a 5-mile radius of camp. We're one of the very few places in Aroostook County that have areas restricted to fly-fishing-only. We've got canoes spread all around for people who come in here and want to go to these other lakes and ponds. Several are within walking distance, others you go to by boat. The state has done a good thing blocking off some of the roads in the area to make the ponds a little harder to get to, which cuts down on the fishing pressure and on the poaching. Plus it's a good walk. The state does have a cabin in the area, but other than that, we're the only taxpayers in town!

"This Reserve Land has four ponds that support a population of arctic char [blue-backed trout] that came down in the Ice Age. Only 10 bodies of water in the whole state support a population of arctic char, and we've got four of them here: Gardner, Deboullie, Pushineer, and Black. It's a rare fish, but not endangered. They don't get very large, but just the fact that they survived that long, and are still surviving on their own, is amazing. They were trapped here when the glaciers receded. They look a little like brook trout, but they're a separate species.

"When we first started driving in here, we used what Pete and Chris Norris, the previous owners, had used, which was the North Pond Road. But the bridges kept washing out and you'd have to drive down the riverbank and up the other side. In the fall, if it was the least bit icy, I remember getting stuck in those rivers. The more you tried to get up on the other side, the more the water would splash and freeze, and you were basically just building an ice valley. So we stopped using that and went up through the village of St. Francis at the Canadian border [the camps are only 20 miles from the border]. We used that maybe a year. It was about 22 miles long and probably a 2-hour drive. The earlier road was 29 miles in and took an hour and a half. [These are all just tote or logging roads.] Then the state bought this township from the paper company, so instead of leasing from the paper company we were involved with the state. And the state started talking about an access road. They wanted the general public to be able to get into this state-owned land, the public camping spots. This was 1986. They surveyed campers and published the results, and 75 percent of the population surveyed said, 'Leave it the way it is. The rough access adds to the adventure and keeps it remote.' So the state put the road in from St. Francis anyway! But we did have an easier way of getting in

In the kitchen at Red River Camps

and out. Now access is the easiest it's ever been, due to the logging operations, as they have been harvesting near this area.

"We got involved with the camps because I started working here as a guide in 1975 when the Norrises owned it. I'd work during deer season, and was here at camp when my first child was born. Then, in 1979, Pete and Chris were looking for someone to run Red River Camps until they could find a buyer. I grew up in this type of life and loved it and thought it would be great for the kids, too. (Jennie was nine months old and Matthew was about 1½). And I guess it was 'cause 20-some-odd years later, Matt is working here and Jennie would love to be here, too.) So we came in the spring of 1980. It was really hard for five years, and then things began turning around.

"In 1982 we started something we still do. For a week each summer we take a group of approximately 20 to 25 special-needs people. We just turn the camps over to the residential staff. I cook and clean and everything and they handle the clients. In the fall we have bear and bird hunters and two weeks of deer hunters. Then I stay and do some trapping. In the past I trapped for martin and fisher. Trappers today are catching less martin than in previous years. My feeling is that 95 percent of these so-called trappers are riding up and down the roads, jumping out, and setting a trap here, a trap there. None of the traps are more than 100 feet away from the roads.

But you get back up on a ridge, and you can get all the martin you want. You know what a sable coat is? That's pine martin. They eat mice, squirrels, some carrion, bugs.

"This township supports a plant, the arctic sandwort *(Minuartia rubella)*, a plant of national significance, which grows on the talus slopes of Deboullie Mountain. This particular flower was found in 1980 and is found in only one other place in New England, and nowhere else in Maine. Over on Deboullie, there is a natural ice cave where even in the middle of summer you can reach in and grab a chunk of ice.

"The old Pushineer Dam is the beginning of the Red River. They used to float logs down here and then down the river to St. Froid Lake. And then they'd put them on railroad cars at Eagle Lake. It's called Red River because there is rust formation in certain rocks which causes the river to look red in places. At Crater Pond, over the knoll, you can see the Cliffs of Galilee. They go 500 feet straight into the lake. It's probably the most beautiful of all the beautiful ponds in the area because of those cliffs. There's really just so much that's unique here. We're talking about 23,000 acres our guests can use!"

Peanut "Better" Cookies

> ¾ cup creamy peanut butter, ½ cup shortening, 1¼ cups light brown sugar, 3 T milk, 1 T vanilla, 1 egg, 1¾ cups flour, ¾ tsp. salt, ¾ tsp. baking soda

In a bowl, cream peanut butter, shortening, and sugar together. Add remaining ingredients and stir until combined. If the dough looks greasy, and feels too soft (should be like Playdough), add a little more flour (otherwise the cookie will be too flat).

Drop by spoonfuls on ungreased cookie sheets, flatten with a fork, and bake at 375 degrees for 7–8 minutes.

68. ROSS LAKE CAMPS

AP/HK
OWNERS: Andrea and Captain Donald Lavoie
ADDRESS: PO Box 606, Clayton Lake, ME 04737; 603-320-3208 (cell),
207-695-2821 (radio phone, Folsom's Air Service)
SEASON: Year-round (closed December and April)
ACCOMMODATIONS: Four cabins: one bedroom with loft (studio-style cabins), two outhouses and a shower house, wood heat, gas stove, gas lights, and gas refrigerator; bring your own sleeping bag (AP and HK)
RATES: $65 per person per day (AP); $22–25 per person per day (HK); motorboat and canoe rentals; hunting package rates available

ACCESS: I-95 to exit 56 (Medway). Take ME 11/157 northwest to Millinocket. Go through Millinocket, bear right onto Baxter State Park Road, and go 10 miles to a left-hand turn for the West Branch Region. Continue up Golden Road 18 miles, then take a right-hand turn onto Telos Road. Go 14 miles to the North Maine Woods gate (fee). From here follow camp signs 61 miles on the connecting logging road to camp.

Follow the orange arrows instead of the yellow brick road to Chemquassabamticook Lodge on Ross Lake and, like Dorothy, you'll find lots of adventures on the way—not the least of which is navigating the rugged 3.2-mile camp driveway. The camps, stick built and stained dark brown, are set in a cozy clearing within a stone's throw of Ross Lake.

Don: "I'm from a farming family in New Hampshire, have an agricultural degree, and have spent the last six years as a sports-fishing captain in Key West, Florida. I've hunted and fished in Maine all my life and the 'big woods' here has just held a fascination for me. Andrea's from Ohio and served in the US Navy the last 10 years. We met and married in Florida in '99. Andrea's naval time was up and we wanted to look into living in Maine. We came up to Ross Lake in March 2002 and here we are, six months later, owning the place!

"What happened is the last week in March we were supposed to meet up with three of our friends at Ross Lake. As we were arriving (late because of a series of vehicle-related mishaps while moving back to New Hampshire), they were leaving to avoid a snow-in. Well, we decided to go in and ended up crossing the lake, on snowmobiles, in a white-out. We were so tired the next day we just relaxed. The following day we went out on the lake to fish. Thirty yards from our cabin, I set one tip up, and caught a 16-inch brookie in 20 seconds. Honestly! I just turned around and there it was. This was a good omen because the next fish was a 7-pound togue, Andrea's first togue ever. Well, that was it. She was hooked! Andrea loves fishing; she was the Key West Master Angler two years in a row. That fish is going up on the wall in the lodge. We had three more days of superb fishing—brookies, togue, whitefish, and cusk. The ride home took us 9 hours and by the 7th hour we were discussing how to get enough money together to buy the camps.

"The camps were built in the early 1960s and originally were owned by Bill and Alma Mower. We're only the fourth owners. We also have over 160,000 acres available for hunting with beechnut ridges, clear-cuts, and cedar swamps. I have two guides available for hunting and will be getting my Maine guide's license now that we're here.

"This is one more thing I'm checking off on my life list (of goals): I was a fishing guide in Key West, I have a great wife, and now we're owners of a set of wilderness sporting camps."

Andrea's Peach Cobbler

Don: "This is made with the peaches from my family's farm!"

½ cups sugar, 1 T cornstarch mixed with ¼ tsp. cinnamon, 4 cups sliced peaches (skin can be left on tree-ripened fruit), 1 tsp. lemon juice, 3 T margarine, 1 cup all-purpose flour, 1 T sugar, ½ tsp. baking powder, ½ tsp. salt, ½ cup milk

Heat the oven to 400 degrees. Mix ½ cup sugar and the cornstarch-cinnamon mixture in a 2-quart saucepan. Stir in peaches and lemon juice. Cook, stirring constantly, until mixture thickens and boils. Boil and stir 1 minute. Pour into ungreased 2-quart casserole dish and keep hot in the oven.

Cut shortening into flour, 1 T sugar, baking powder, and salt until mixture resembles fine crumbs. Stir in milk. Drop this dough by 6 spoonfuls onto the hot peaches. Bake 25–30 minutes, or until dough is golden brown. Serve warm with whipped cream: 1 cup whipping cream, ½ tsp. vanilla, 1 T sugar. Beat on high with mixer or with wisk. Stop when peaks form.

69. UMCOLCUS SPORTING CAMPS

HK/AP, SCA
OWNERS: Al and Audrey Currier
ADDRESS: 1243 Oxbow Road, Oxbow, ME 04764; 207-435-8227; e-mail: umcolcus@mfx.net; www.umcolcus.com
SEASON: Year-round (closed April and December)
ACCOMMODATIONS: Six log cabins: one to two bedrooms, porch (some screened), central bathroom and shower house, wood heat, gas lights, gas stove, and gas refrigerator
RATES: $35 per person per day, $210 per person per week (HK); child, group, and hunting rates available; canoes and kayaks available
ACCESS: I-95 to exit 58. Take ME 11 north approximately 50 miles and take the left-hand turn to the town of Oxbow. Go 6 miles to the Curriers' house, on the right, which serves as the town post office and the camp headquarters. Check in at the office in back.

Umcolcus's cabins are arranged in a horseshoe around the family-built main lodge, constructed in 1997. With this handcrafted addition, the Curriers now offer American Plan and "rustic retreats" for groups and organizations. The site is relatively open, looking out on the Umcolcus Deadwaters, with a stream running along a wooded portion of the property and into the clearing.

Al's roots in the area go back a long way: "The site itself is a hundred years old, but the cabins there now are not the original ones. My grandfather was a guide and caretaker for the original camps, which belonged to the Hines family out of Portland, Maine. And as they all got older and the group all broke up, 'for 1 dollar and other valuable considerations' the camps were turned over to my grandfather.

"The name itself is from the Umcolcus Lake. That gets a little confusing because there's an east and west branch to Umcolcus Stream. We are actually on the west branch, which has its headwaters in Cut Lake. The camps are about 5 miles below the lake. There's a big deadwater right in front of camp called Cranberry Pond. Cut Lake is a small lake, shallow, with some trout, so people mainly come in to relax, canoe, hike, hunt, cross-country ski, and snowmobile. We're within 10 minutes of ITS 85."

Audrey: "I got involved in Umcolcus Sporting Camps by being married to Al, of course. We spent the second night of our honeymoon at camp. I had seen the camps once before we were married. His father was running them for hunting season at the time. Then we just started going in on weekends, and as we had children, we'd go in with them. We kept working on the biggest cabin, trying to maintain that as a family cabin. And then, somehow, some hunter and his crew started renting it. We've had the camps since 1972.

"We live full time in Oxbow and our daughters, Tori and Debi, traveled 20 miles to Ashland for school. I'm originally from Ashland, but we've been living here since 1975. I'm also postmaster of the area. The post office has been in this same family and same house since 1917. The mail for the townspeople goes into an antique wooden general-delivery mailbox unit. I put the mail into the small units and hand people all their mail. The population of Oxbow is probably around 80, but I also service 26 general-delivery customer boxes and then there are 14 highway contract boxes in there."

Al shows me an album: "That's my grandfather and that's Jack Dempsey, the boxer. He used to come up with his trainer and go into camp. The old main lodge had two bedrooms, and that's the one we made into a family camp. The old cook's cabin was torn down. One of the other camps was big, with two fireplaces. Dad said it had a hearth so wide you could get right up and lay down on the top section. That camp was struck by lightning.

"So we had a lot of building to do. Fortunately, we've had a lot of help from friends. We felled the logs and took them to a mill where they were two-sided and brought back to the site. Then we built the camps, weekends mostly. You can use white pine, spruce, cedar. I personally like spruce—the original camps were spruce logs. Then we protect the wood with a clear preservative. We've gone away from oakum for caulking and use regular fiberglass insulation. We cut it in strips, lay it on top of the log, staple it, and just keep layering up. You could construct a camp in a month if you set right up to do it. It's quite a process. And then once you go inside and make it into a housekeeping unit, it's like a home. The old camps were on what they called the mud sill. They started right out on the ground, and you

Al and Audrey at Umcolcus Sporting Camps

don't get any ventilation. Eventually the camp would settle and the dead log would be right in the ground. Our new ones are set in a cement slab and then on hemlock puncheons. They're the foundation that the floor stringers for the camp are built on, so we can get under the building and have an air flow. We have some cabins with cathedral ceilings. Inside we framed the bottoms in, put heavy plastic, and then boarded up and down with pine boards. We did the same thing, on a bigger scale, with the main lodge, which in addition has a large fieldstone fireplace.

"Besides building the camps, we also built the road coming in here. It used to be an old tote road for horses, and then we started coming in with old four-by-four army trucks, chains on all four wheels. Over the years I've re-corduroyed sections of the road and bulldozed and graveled to get it to the point where you can get in here with a car or pickup. A corduroy road is a base of wood you lay in a swampy area, where it's just mush. You lay the logs crosswise and cover them with gravel. In the wintertime, I plow for the town of Oxbow and some county roads. I also do land excavation, put in sewer systems, landscape work, so luckily I have equipment to use for the camps. I've been well over 20 years on the camp road. A few years ago we had a logging operation come in and chew up all the work of 20 years. So we're at the road again. It's just the way it goes, I guess."

Audrey: "We work hard to make a nice place for people to relax. And more and more people are coming in to do simply that. They say this peace and quiet just can't be bought."

70. WILDERNESS ISLAND

AP, SCA

OWNERS: Mike and Carol LaRosa

CAMP ADDRESS: PO Box 220, Portage, ME 04768; 207-435-6825

WINTER ADDRESS: PO Box 847, Groton, MA 01450; 508-448-5450; e-mail: islandadventure@themainelink.com; www.islandadventureinmaine.com

SEASON: Mid-May through mid-October

ACCOMMODATIONS: Eight log cabins: one to two bedrooms, indoor plumbing and tub with shower, wood heat, gas lights, limited handicapped-accessible; two cabins with fireplace

RATES: $105 per person per day; canoes, kayaks, paddleboats, sailboats free; child, group, and off-season rates available

ACCESS: I-95 to exit 58. Take ME 11 north to Portage (last supplies or place to call camp). Go left at Dean's Motel and then fork left at the Great Northern Paper Company road (dirt), where there's a sign for the camps. Pay the toll at the North Woods gatehouse. Follow camp signs 17 miles to the boat landing.

Either Mike or Carol LaRosa try to greet every guest at the dock. Such warmth and enthusiasm permeates 10-acre Wilderness Island, formerly known as Zella Island or Fish River Camps. As Mycki McNally, daughter-in-law of the original owners, relates, a woman named Zella Mileau was the first female guest at camp, so they named the island after her. The McNally clan saw this spot as their home camp. Eventually the original lodge just became too small and Mycki's husband, Dana, had a dream one night of a six-sided lodge: "But he realized the corners would be too sharp, so he made it eight-sided, octagonal—that way he could have a wide building but it didn't have to be terribly long. It's 50 feet across by 30 wide. He built a three-sided chimney with rocks from the island. The logs rest on the chimney for support. After a heart attack, he directed construction from a hospital bed until he could get back to work."

Mike: "There are a lot of stories about Wilderness Island. The camps were founded in 1895 and may be the oldest operating sporting camp in Aroostook County. It used to be a stopover. People would come in from the town of Portage, spend the night, and continue on to the Allagash. One of the cabins has the date of 1909 on the wall with all the guides' initials on there. And it's my understanding that where our cabin number 3 is used to be the main lodge. Dana McNally was an architect and he also made all the furniture in the lodge. It's 30 feet from the floor to the top of the fireplace, which is a conversation piece itself. I've looked at the lodge over the years and a lot of those cuts are very difficult to make, the logs in the ceiling fan out from the chimney—it's gorgeous. It had to take a lot of planning before they even started building. I mean, it's really complex. The windows are actually storm windows put in sideways, so you can slide them back and forth. And the windows in our big cabin are 10 feet long by 5 feet high. They brought those up in a canoe, crated, from Portage all the way up the Fish River chain, coming in the east side of the lake. That's 23 miles in a car, but it's a lot farther by boat because the river snakes around so. Trouble is, it takes 4½ hours to get here by canoe without a heavy, tippy load of windows. I love that story, and I hope it's true!

"I'm very prejudiced about Wilderness Island, but there's not a camp in the North Maine Woods I've visited that I wouldn't be glad to stay the night or a week. We used to vacation on Moosehead Lake and were thinking of retiring there. I thought that because I do a lot of woodworking, I would open up a little Papa Geppetto–type shop. Then we went to a real estate office on the last day of our vacation and this place popped up. When I saw it was an island I just couldn't believe it! So we bought it in January 1985. The island is 9.6 acres. When the water's low, it might be even larger! It's shaped like a spade in cards. We can see the landing from the main lodge, and if you drive, we'll look for you for an hour before your estimated arrival and keep looking for you till dusk. If you don't show up, we'll contact the main gate and try to find you." *Carol:* "We have direct radio contact with Wilza Robertson, a retired teacher, who lives in Portage and answers our phone, responds to guest questions, and is our link to the outside world.

"I'm a consultant for computer companies. When we started here, we were trying to restore a business that had eroded over time. So I ended up commuting. I would work Monday through Friday in Massachusetts, drive all night Friday night, work here Saturday and Sunday, and drive back on Monday. Over the course of the time I was here I would work with Mike in the kitchen, training him to cook for this kind of business. And, after two years, I was able to move to another consulting position where I could get more time off. At this point, I'm able to have three months working here. We have three boys, Mike, Eric, and John; this is a family business."

Mike: "Our first year I didn't know how to cook well and I was scared every day. Terrified! I mean, people are paying for what you're cooking, and I wanted it to be really good. I don't think anyone could make me go through that first year again. I'm not proud of doing things I don't like to do, but I am proud of trying to do them well, and I now feel great about the cooking because I know our guests enjoy it. Carol doesn't even need a recipe most of the time.

"For me, the most important thing when you're getting ready to serve a meal is the last 7 minutes, because you've got to do several things at the same time. I cook with a lot of timers and each timer has a different sound. I know all the sounds of those timers, so I know when the muffins are done, when the beans are just about right, when the coffee is done—6½ minutes perked. I've got that all down in my head, and that's the '7-minute challenge' to cooking.

"I've got to show you some pictures of my garden! We've been trying to

The vegetable garden at Wilderness Island

grow a garden here, well, every single season. We have good wax and string beans, peas and broccoli, but they're cool-weather crops, so you expect them to do well. Plus these things would grow in cement, I think! But the soil was mostly clay. So every year we've worked on it. We separate all our garbage, and anything we can put in the garden we put it into what we call the garden bucket. And when that's full we go out and trench it into the soil. We've been doing that since 1985. And then we have horse manure in there, so we have a great-looking garden. I don't even want to harvest it, it's so beautiful! We have guests that come here, Alice, and they get their bucket and little knife and go out and harvest their own beans, and we'll cook them for their supper. They love doing that.

"The way we get our drinking water is interesting. It comes from a spring across the lake, halfway up a mountain. It's all PVC pipe down the mountain, underneath the lake, and back up onto the island, and then up a 40-foot tower—over a mile and a half of PVC pipe. The best part of this system is it's free and it doesn't have to be run by generators, so the camp can be quiet and peaceful. It's probably the purest water you're ever going to drink because by the time it gets to the lake it's run the gamut of rocks and pebbles and really filtered out.

"I'll tell you a cute story about hummingbirds, Alice. One day, in the springtime, when we'd just bought the island, I was walking to the main lodge and something buzzed right by me. I thought it was a bee making a huge noise. When I talked to Carol, she said it had to be a hummingbird. Well, I'd never seen a hummingbird before. The first thing Carol did was go out and buy feeders, and it was just an incredible thing. Here I'd never seen one and now there were 15 to 18 hummingbirds buzzing around a feeder! They are intelligent and aggressive. When they're upset, they fan their tails out for stability. We haven't built the machine yet that can outperform them in the air.

"Before we came here I was planning to retire, but I'm working harder than I did my entire life! I was in the hotel-motel business in Massachusetts. When I first bought this place, people said, 'What's he doing that for? He's not a hunter.' I don't hunt. I don't fish. I don't do any of those things, and here I am in the sporting-camp business. But it's not really the old idea of hunting and fishing, it's really vacationers. Alice, there are two types of businesses when you run a sporting camp, and a lot of people don't understand that. When you come in the main lodge, you're in the restaurant business. When you leave the main lodge, you're in the recreation business. In the main lodge, you're on my turf, and I know how to take care of you. I don't have to be a big sportsman to run a sporting camp. I can get a guide. This is a business of hospitality. Any time you're dealing with people, you're in the business of hospitality. When someone says, 'You're a good host,' my answer to that is, 'I'm a good host because you're a good guest.' And that is absolutely true. When people come into the North Maine Woods, I don't care whose camp they're coming to, they're at your mercy. They really are, because if they don't like your food, where can they go? There's no place around here but Dean's Motor Lodge, which serves good food, but it's across the water and 23 slow, logging-road miles away. If you get hungry at 2 in the morning, and some people do, you're at our mercy again. So I make sure they get plenty of food and that they know where the refrigerator is. Every cabin has a flashlight and they know they can come into the main lodge at 2 AM. They know where the bread and meat is, where all the fixings are, so they can make a sandwich. We say everyone needs a time to retreat, and we want people to relax, unwind, and enjoy. Stress doesn't even make it to our island; it's out there back at the boat landing somewhere!"

Wilderness Island Garden Beans

Carol: "Let me tell you, beans and tarragon are great together." Mike: "We've converted people who don't even like vegetables."

> 1½ pounds wax, green, or romano beans, or a combination, 3 T extra virgin olive oil, ½ tsp. minced garlic, 3 T tarragon or rice vinegar, 1 T chopped fresh tarragon

Fill a large pot half full of water and bring water to a rolling boil. Add the beans (either whole or cut up) and when it comes to a second boil, cook for 3 minutes. Drain the beans. In the empty pot, over medium heat, sauté minced garlic with olive oil until fragrant. Add beans and stir, coating with the garlic oil. Splash in vinegar (if using rice vinegar, add the chopped fresh tarragon). Season to taste with salt and pepper and serve.

Part Three

EASTERN MAINE

This section covers the area east of I-95, bounded on the south by ME 9 ("the Airline") and everywhere else by the Canadian border. It includes the northern Penobscot River watershed to the west and the Grand Lake Stream–St. Croix watershed to the east.

The main cities and towns in this region are Bangor (Maine's second largest city) in the "south," Lincoln as the gateway to ME 6, and Houlton to the north. Calais (CAL-lus), at the end of ME 9 is Maine's busiest border crossing. Just west of Calais is the Moosehorn National Wildlife Refuge, established for the study and protection of regional species, particularly migratory birds, waterfowl, and deer. This sparsely populated section is also an agricultural center for Maine's blueberry and potato crops. In the autumn, the blueberry barrens form an alternative fall-foliage experience. The blueberry stalks turn a bright magenta, while the needles of the softwood "hackmatacks"—that is, tamaracks, or larches—glow golden against the green of evergreens and the brilliant blue skies.

THE NORTHERN PENOBSCOT RIVER REGION

The focus in this region is the Penobscot River—around 250 miles long and fed by over 460 lakes. The Penobscot Indians, the largest tribe in Maine, traditionally claimed all the territory from its source to the sea (the Camden Hills were once known as the Penobscot Mountains). The Penobscot River Basin is Maine's largest watershed and the second largest in New England (the Connecticut is first). The headwaters of the East Branch used to be part of the St. John watershed. In 1841, due to logging competition, dams were built at Telos and Chamberlain Lakes and 270 square miles of Allagash River drainage was added to the Penobscot watershed, which meant loggers could float their logs down to mills in Maine rather than to Canada. The major towns in this region (going south) are Medway, east of Millinocket, where the East and West Branches of the Penobscot join, Lincoln, Howland, and Bangor.

GETTING THERE: Commercial airlines fly to Bangor International Airport, which has rental car services. KT Aviation (207-945-5087) and Telford Aviation (207-990-5555) fly out of Bangor. Driving time (taking I-95) to the Lincoln area from Portland is 3 hours; from Boston, 5 hours; from New York City, 10 hours.

GUIDANCE: For further information contact the Greater Lincoln Chamber of Commerce (207-794-8065).

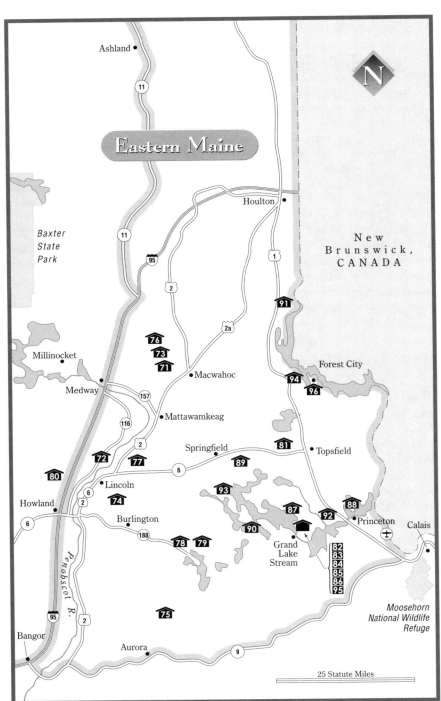

Eastern Maine

Ashland

11

Baxter
State
Park

11

Houlton

95

New
Brunswick,
CANADA

2

1

2a

91

76

73

71

Macwahoc

Forest City

94

96

Millinocket

Medway

157

Mattawamkeag

116

Springfield

81

Topsfield

2

89

72

77

93

80

6

6

Lincoln

74

Princeton

88

87

92

Howland

6

2

Burlington

188

78

79

90

Grand
Lake
Stream

Calais

82
83
84
85
86
95

Penobscot R.

95

2

75

Moodehorn
National Wildlife
Refuge

Bangor

Aurora

9

25 Statute Miles

N

Paul Woodward, © The Countryman Press

71. ALL MAINE ADVENTURES

HK/AP

OWNERS: Ed and Lorraine Harris

ADDRESS: Aroostook Road, Mattawamkeag, ME 04459; 207-765-3955;

E-MAIL: AllMeAdventures@webtv.net; www.uswebx.com/allmeadventures

SEASON: Mid-June through Mid-December

ACCOMMODATIONS: Seven log cabins: one to two bedrooms (some with loft), screened porch, indoor plumbing and shower, electric lights, propane heat; bring towels and washcloths; pets welcome

RATES: $60–85 per person per day (AP); $50–80 per person per day (HK, double occupancy); $250–400 per cabin per week; hunting packages and child rates available

ACCESS: Take I-95 north to Exit 56 (Medway). Turn right on ME 157 and go 12 miles to a blinking light. Take a left on US 2 and go 7 miles. Take the first road to the left (Aroostook Road). Camps are 1 mile on right, office is on the left.

The camp's log cabin compound sits to the right of the road on either side of a cozy main lodge. The office, or 'pow wow' is to the left, along with several boat trailers

Ed: "Our clientele here over the years have all basically heard about us through word of mouth. The camps date from sometime in the mid-1930s. The original gentleman that started them was named Harry McDonald. It started out as one cabin, with a bunch of friends from out of state. And you know how things are when you've got four or five people who are part owners of an operation—more headaches than it's worth. So Harry McDonald bought the place and opened it up as a set of sporting camps. He had it for 10 or 12 years and then sold to a man and woman from New Hampshire, the Harricks, and they had it for 25 years. We bought it, July Fourth of 1976, and are starting our 26th year (in 2002), so we are the longest owners of the place. We both worked for Great Northern [paper company] in Millinocket for 12 years. I also worked for the Harricks as a guide and just loved the hunting and fishing. They were wanting to sell and had let the place go and we decided we wanted to have it. At the beginning I was here and Lorraine kept on at Great Northern to make sure we had an income.

"Where we're sitting now, what we call the 'pow wow,' is new because the old one burned to the ground. It's a one-room building with a little store for hunting and fishing supplies and is something any hunter especially would enjoy 'cause I have 25 whitetails mounted on the walls. I've got five bear, and I've got a 300-pound life-size whitetail. I try to have at least one of everything that runs in the forest around here—bobcat, gray fox, raccoon—so in case someone sees an animal they'll recognize it. For example, a lot of people have never seen a fisher, the Godzilla of the weasel world. A fisher is famous because it's the only thing in the woods that can kill a porcupine and eat it. They can flip the porcupine on its back and rip the stomach out. That's the fisher's main diet. Anything else that tries to eat a porcupine ends up with a mouth and nose full of quills and animals can actually die, because those quills can work their way into the animal. Fisher are very common all through northern Maine. They live in hollow trees. A lot of people don't see them 'cause they're an animal that doesn't really do well around homes and people. But they do enjoy house cats. Back in the heyday of trapping, 40 or 50 years ago, female fishers would go from $400–500 apiece. They were the most valuable fur out there. They were used for trim on coats. They still are a big business, but now females go for, I'm gonna guess, $40 and males $18 or $20.

"The fox population depends a lot on the coyote population because they basically feed on the same small game—rabbits and so on. If a family of coyotes moves into an area—and they run in big packs—they'll decimate the fox population. And the hares, cottontails, and snowshoes run in cycles. This year the coyote population is down and the cats are up, and 90 percent of the rabbits you'll see will be the snowshoes. When you see the snowshoes on the roads all the time you know the coyote population is not that high because even though coyotes do kill deer in the winter and they eat big game, basically their diet is rabbits and field mice, stuff like that. When the coyote got overpopulated around here a few years ago, they got the mange real bad. One coyote with the mange takes it into the den and they all get it—it's a parasite. And if you can feel sorry for an animal, I mean, to see a coyote in January with half the hair off his body, it's tough. They die from exposure. So, it all runs in cycles."

Lorraine: "From bear season through moose season we cook three meals a day in the dining room—so August 'til the first of December. I have help that does the dishes and our oldest girl, Lorrie, has been waitressing for us maybe 20 years. She has a full-time job at the hospital, but plans her vacation time around helping us. Now our grandchildren, Tom and Karen, are starting to help wait tables. We have eight grandchildren, and they've all helped at one point or another. I do all the cooking, which takes 12 to 14 hours a day. We have a certain meal each day. We serve meat-and-potato-type meals. Sunday night we'll have our roast beef dinner." *Ed:* "The only thing exotic we do is we serve lobster every Friday night, with Maine potatoes, Maine corn, and strawberry shortcake. She picks all the strawberries herself, makes all her own jams." *Lorraine:* "I freeze the strawberries so we can serve the shortcake out of season, too.

"I think the best thing about being here is being your own boss. Even though it's long hours from June to December, no break during that time, it's still better to have your own schedule and make your own decisions. I think Ed has it a little rougher than I have because I can come and go, do a few things, but him being a guide, he has a lot to take care of. Ninety

Lorraine Harris and crew at All Maine Adventures

percent of the time, starting the end of August, I'm the only woman around here (outside the girls that work for me)."

Ed: "This might be interesting to you. Molunkus is the Indian name of the area, but for the state we're in an 'unorganized township.' This means our children could go to any school they wanted to 'cause the State paid the tuition. So we have four children who graduated from three different high schools. Molunkus is the name of a chief of the Penobscot Indians. All of the names in this area are Indian names. Mattawamkeag means 'where two rivers meet.' That's where the Mattawamkeag and Penobscot come in together. 'Course the Penobscot River is named after the Penobscot Indians. The closest Indians are at Old Town, at the reservation. There are quite a few people around here that have Indian blood and heritage, but it's back awhile.

"Our business is about 85 percent hunting and 15 percent fishing and family. I mean, we're not on the water, so the camps on the water get more of the fishing business. The only drawback to being on a lake that I can see is that if you have a lodge on a small lake, I would think that after a few days a 2- to 3-mile lake would get a little dry, you know. We do all our fishing on the Penobscot River, fish for smallmouth bass. It's about 10 minutes away. If you don't catch 50 to 100 fish a day, you know you're having a slow day. For our people, when they rent a cabin for a week, we include a motorboat and trailer. They have to have a hitch on their vehicle, but we provide the rest. We have canoes out here too." *Lorraine:* "And he gives everyone a free day of guiding." *Ed:* "Normally I get $150 a day guiding the river for two people, eight hours. But I give everybody that comes in one free day just to show them the places to go. Our business is nearly all repeat, so once I take them to the river, they come back year after year. We just had a party leave; this was their 25th straight year. They spend five weeks a year here. We're the proverbial mom-and-pop hunting-and-fishing lodge. It's basically a two-person operation.

"The fishing in the summer pays the bills, allows us to break even. But our business is hunting. We have a tremendous bear hunting business. I have probably the biggest moose business in the state, numbers-wise. Last year we killed the state-record moose. It goes by the size of the rack; the weight of the moose means nothing. You can have a moose that weighs 500 pounds and has a monstrous big rack, or one that weighs 1,000 pounds, and if he's going downhill, older, his rack will be smaller. Ours was killed with a muzzle-loader, black powder. And it scored 190 total inches—the width, the length, the points; there's 8–10 measurements you make and add those all up. All deer and all moose shed their antlers every year. The rack is what's on them, if it's on the ground it's called a 'shed.' We're in zone 11, and in the last five or six years we've probably taken about 65 moose hunters out. We're in the two-week moose hunting zone; other areas are only one week. In the two-week zone they give out a lot of cow permits to cut back on the herd. Once hunting season gets here I carry a lot of Cronks, a lure made by a big hunting and trapping company out of Wiscasset, Maine. In fact, Edie Cronk is president of the Sportsmen's Alliance of Maine (SAM). I like the Cronks because it is a Maine product. And I carry animal urine, to use to cover human scents. A whitetail's nose is 10 to 15 times better than a dog's, so anything you can do to offset the human odor helps.

With bear, we average 35 to 50 hunters a year. In fact, I sometimes turn bear hunters away because I try to keep it at a certain number each week. This area is loaded with bears. In fact, we're just a few miles from one of the areas where the state does their radio call-ups and testing. Bears are amazing animals. The female doesn't breed until she's somewhere around five or six years old, and then they only breed every other year, because she'll keep the cubs with her the first year. Once they're yearlings she chases them out because she's pregnant again. When she goes into the den she doesn't want to have any offspring with her because male bears will kill baby bears. The reason they do this is that if a male catches a female in June or July and kills the cubs she will come back into heat. So the mothers are very protective of the little bears.

"With deer, this is big woods country up here. This area does have doe tags, but you have to apply for them. We average 100 to 150 deer hunters a fall at our place."

Bass Nuggets

Lorraine: "We practice catch-and-release. I will cook these up for someone once in a while though. They fry up quick, so don't overcook."

2–4 bass (10–12 inches), 2 eggs, ¼ cup flat beer, salt and pepper, pancake mix, butter or margarine

Fillet the bass. Dice into 1-inch cubes. Beat the eggs in a bowl with the beer and salt and pepper to taste. Marinate the nuggets in this for 1 to 2 hours in the refrigerator. Dip the marinated nuggets in your favorite dry pancake mix and fry in butter or margarine until golden brown, 2 to 3 minutes.

72. DAD'S CAMPS

AP/HK
OWNERS: Raymond and Therese Thibodeau
ADDRESS: PO Box 142, West Enfield, ME 04493; 207-557-3237 (cell); 207-732-5309; e-mail: dadscamps@hotmail.com; www.dadscamps.com
SEASON: May through November
ACCOMMODATIONS: Seven cabins (four log, three gray-sided): two to three bedrooms, screened porch, indoor plumbing and shower, electric or gas lights, automatic oil heat, fully equipped kitchens, firepit, charcoal grill, picnic table, free wood; bring linens (or rent for $5 per week), sleeping bag and towels; well-behaved pets allowed ($50 per week)
RATES: $70 per day per person (AP); $40 per day per person (HK); $400 per cabin per week; hunting packages available; motorboats $35 per day, canoes $15 per day
ACCESS: Take I-95 north to exit 55. Turn right and drive 2.4 miles to ME 116. Turn right and go 6.1 miles to camp sign on right.

The cabins are a group of gray-clapboard and log structures on either side of and behind a main lodge and garage area. The place has a lived-in look with a few children's toys here and there. Part of the family arrives from blackberry picking and offers a taste, fresh and fragrant. Family members from different generations come and go.

Raymond: "These camps were built in 1990 on 450 acres, our own property. I own about a mile and a half of river front. It took me five years to build the house, the garage, and three camps. I cut the road [driveway] in from the highway, graveled it. And then the kids and my father helped build the camps. The land itself comes from Kenneth Carver." *Therese:* "As a little boy he used to come here and help Mr. Carver cut wood. And one day he was standing along the river and told Mr. Carver, 'Some day I'm gonna live here.' Mr. Carver always remembered that and wanted Raymond to have the land." *Raymond:* "After he died his widow called and said, 'Are you interested in the land?' I told her, 'Yes, but I don't believe I can afford it.' She said, 'Make me an offer.' I named a price and she right off said, 'Fine, it's yours.' So that's how we came to be here.

"The first cabins were built 35 feet from the water, and now the setback is 100 feet. The Penobscot River here is about 1,000 feet across and we're probably a mile from what they call the Mohawk Rips. It's said that's where the battle took place with the Penobscots and the river ran red from the rips all the way to Howland. We're the only camps situated right on the Penobscot River from Bangor all the way to Medway. It's one of the best smallmouth bass fisheries on the whole eastern seaboard. There isn't a day that we can't go on this river and catch 100 bass, catch-and-release. The Penobscot is just dotted with islands. Within our area there must be 16 or 18 islands and there's rocks here the size of vans, and that's what makes the river so abundant with the bass. The Penobscot Indians do own the islands. If you want to pick fiddleheads on them in the spring, or if you want to hunt, you have to go down to Old Town, to the Penobscot Nation, and get a permit, not to fish, but to hunt and gather on the islands. We do duck hunting on the islands and do get a permit.

"The river's been used for logging for hundreds of years. They drove wood all the way from above Millinocket, from the East Branch and the West Branch, down this way to go to the different mills along the river. The companies would mark their logs with either a certain number or letter, push them on the ice, and then in the spring all these logs would drift all the way to a little above Old Town. And they then had piers that would slow and channel the wood to be taken out to go to the sawmills. The marks on the logs would show each company which was theirs. Between 1952 and 1955 was the last log drive on this river."

Karen McCarthy, their daughter: "I think readers should know it's a good river for families, too. Kids have no patience at all; they just want to catch fish. Here fish bite so much it's fun for them." *Raymond:* "They let the kids fish here with worms. When I was a boy and lived on the river, in Howland itself, the fish in this river was predominately salmon and trout. In the last 50 years it's turned into smallmouth bass. I think it happened because of the water being warmer due to the cutting that's happened all along the rivers and streams inland.

"Like with the moose, Inland Fisheries and Wildlife feel they're responsible for the increased moose population over 10 to 20 years. But really it's the clear-cutting up north and within our area here that's made the food available for the moose, made it more a moose habitat. Being a woodsman all my life, I hate to see the forest decimated, but there's some places that have to be clear-cut. With the root systems that we have here in the State of Maine, once you go in and selective cut, the rest may just blow over. And like on this acreage here a lot of the forest is so mature, if I don't cut it, I'm losing it, so it's not beneficial to anybody. We do moose and deer hunting. For moose we're in zone 18 but most of my permits are in zone 10, which is about 5 minutes from here, and is where I grew up."

Therese: "I worked nine years in a nursing home, and was nine years teaching Head Start, and then for a few years I babysat 12 children. Then I was working taking care of dying people in their homes while we were building here at camp. So I was always with a lot of people, a lot of kids. When we first opened the camp there wasn't going to be any cooking what-soever. But our first guest, a man, didn't want to come in here if he had to cook. So we said, 'Okay, he can eat with us.' Well, word went around and we started getting more and more people and now we do a lot of cooking."

Karen: "My father will go to the sportsmen shows and former guests come up to the booth and brag to people standing around how good the meals are!" *Raymond:* "We do some shows, but it's the word of mouth that really keeps this business going." *Therese:* "When we first started we had just men come, and then they started bringing their wives, and then we started get-ting the kids. I love it when some of the kids get the biggest fish or the most fish. When people arrive we ask them if they have any allergies, or any food on our menu they don't like. It's all you can eat and I never make the same meal the seven days people are here."

Raymond: "You can fish on the Penobscot from the first of April to the end of December. The 15th of October one year I went duck hunting with one guest from daylight until 9:00. At 9:00 I went fishing with him, and we caught 157 bass, catch-and-release, and at 3:00 I was back duck hunt-ing." *Karen:* "You look forward to seeing people come back year after year because they become like family. Sometimes the kids will stay back at camp with us and the parents will go fishing—the parents are really on vacation then!" *Raymond:* "Therese and I have eight kids, four boys and four girls, and 12 grandchildren. Karen's here now helping and my son Raymond Jr. works with us. He takes care of the guiding. He guides himself and he'll employ about five or six guides.

Raymond Jr.: "I'm actually plumber, electrician, carpenter, grounds worker, just about everything. And beyond that, I guide on the water and in the woods. There's about a 30-mile stretch of river you can easily fish to here. We also take people trout fishing up into the Jo-Mary region. For hunting, we have a shooting range, and in the last 10 years we've had 100 per-cent success on our moose hunts. We pretty much ride the roads, and hope-fully find one. The deer hunting's harder in Maine because the woods are so thick. For bear season I use bait the first and second week. Then we hunt with dogs the third and fourth week (with dogs from a gentleman from out of state). We put people on active baits, use 55-gallon drums with rocks on the top, so the only animal that can really push it over is a bear. We cut them up and package the meat for the hunter to take home." *Karen:* "She [Therese] does the cutting, I do the packaging." *Raymond Sr.:* "I am a licensed agent for the State of Maine, so our guests have the option of buying their licenses right here. And we do pick them up at the airport, if they fly into Bangor." *Therese:* "And while they're here, if they'd like to use a vehicle there's always a pickup available." *Karen:* "We offer just about anything you can think of."

Jeanne's Pickled Beets

Therese: "This is my mother's recipe. I was one of 17 children (fifth from the top) and growing up in New Brunswick, Canada, we had a big garden. My grandfather and uncle would prepare the soil. The boys would make the rows. The girls would plant the seeds. And my mother was the one who would cover the seeds with just the right amount of dirt. We put up 200 quarts of string beans for the winter and used 30 cords of wood a year. I usually make up 20 quarts of the beets at a time, but this recipe allows you to make up whatever amount you want."

Wash beets (all sizes) and cut stalks, leaving ½ inch. Put beets in pot and cover with water. Bring to a boil and cook until you can insert a fork (like potatoes). Drain and save the juice. Peel while hot (use rubber gloves). For each quart of beets use:

> 1 cup beet juice, 1 cup cider vinegar, 1 cup sugar. Mix together and heat but don't boil.

While juice is warming up, cut up the big beets, leave the small ones whole, and pack into jars. Pour juice into the jars to cover. Put on the lid (which will seal itself with the heat). These will be ready to eat in four days and just get better over time.

73. DEER RUN SPORTING CAMPS

HK/AP
OWNER: Edith McGovern
MANAGERS: Robert and Darlene Berry
ADDRESS: HC 86, Box 900, Mattawamkeag, ME, 04459; 207-765-3900; fax: 207-765-2400; e-mail: deerruncamps@gwi.net
SEASON: Year-round
ACCOMMODATIONS: Five log cabins: one to two bedrooms, indoor plumbing, central shower house, electric lights, automatic heat; well-attended pets allowed
RATES: $30–45 per person per day (2-night minimum); $200-300 per cabin per week; motorboats $35 per day, $175 per week; canoes: $15 per day, $75 per week

ACCESS: Take I-95 north to exit 56 (Medway). Turn right onto ME 157 and go 12 miles to a blinking light. Take a left onto US 2 and go 7 miles. Take first left (Aroostook Road). Camps are 1.5 miles on the right (sign).

Edith: "We bought this place, in 1965, from Roy and Hazel Richards, who got it from a French man, who got it from a grant in the 1800s. He apparently was quite a character and had oxen and a wooden-wheeled cart to go to town. It's only 7 miles away, but it used to take him the whole day to do his errands. The camps are on a dogleg about a mile and a half from the main lake."

Darlene: "In the mid-1800s it was a logging camp. They cut ice blocks out of the lake, and stored them in the ice house, which is still here. We have some of the original tools they used on display. And there was a sawmill, which is where our dining hall is now. It was run by a one-lunger, steam-powered engine, all belt-driven equipment. They made shingles, fence posts, three-sided logs. The Richards took over and put in some of the buildings you see now." *Robert:* "They were built from the sawmill here."

Darlene: "Then Edith and Ed McGovern bought them. Ed was a pilot for PanAm for 30 years. He put in a landing strip that's our firebreak now. Ed wanted a place that his wife could run and where he could play with his planes. He had some antique planes. They came up from New York, and the runway is the reason they purchased Deer Run. They added the fourth cabin and the little cabin in the woods, the garage. They turned the sawmill into a dining hall so they could offer the American Plan.

"Ed passed away in the summer of '98. And slowly but surely during those last years everything started to deteriorate. I had known Ede and Ed for a long time. I owned my own business in Mattawamkeag, a laundromat, and came here to pick up their camp linens. I offered to give them a hand and in 1999 I closed down my business and came over to work here. At that point we started to restore all the buildings.

"Robert came down the road the following year. The locals call the Aroostook the Benedicta Road because that was the first settlement to survive a winter in Aroostook County." *Robert:* "Ede asked if I could help jack up some of these buildings. I came back the next day to make a deal with her on it, to work on the weekends, but Ede wasn't around. So I hung around all day until she got back and visited with Darlene." *Darlene:* "Following me around while I worked. I was more than grateful to find some extra muscle because by that time I was doing all of it: the buildings, the carpentry, the housekeeping, didn't matter—whatever needed to be done. So the thought of having a guy come down here and pitch in was great. While he was visiting, sitting at Ede's picnic table, he picked a four-leaf clover from underneath her table. I said, 'You just sat there and picked that? I can't believe it! I mean, I mow here all the time!' A few seconds later he picked another one.

"So, by late in the day Ede shows up and traded with him—work for use of a cabin. The next morning, a Sunday, he showed up for work. I was bailing the boats out; it was around 7:30 in the morning. He came down the hill with a beer can in his hand, two four-leaf clovers sticking out of it. Well, now Robert and I pick four-leaf clovers every year. And his son, Chris, has been taught and he now goes out and finds them. We press them and give them away to our customers (we also make up postcards they can buy). They go away with a 'four.' If they're repeat customers we give them a five or even a six-leaf. We've even picked some huge fours for our older guests with poor eyesight! And we do have two rare seven-leaf clovers which we have not dispersed yet. So we're known for our four-leaf clovers."

Robert: "Darlene and I always worked as partners, and I always give her credit for what she did 'cause she worked harder than most men I know. We had been together about three weeks, when we needed to work under one of the cabins." *Darlene:* "I was the only one at the time who could fit under the cabins, so I always did the plumbing work underneath. I went belly-down under the cabin, only from the waist in. The rest was sticking out and he was standing above me. And I called out, 'Everything looks pretty good under here.' And he said, 'Everything looks pretty good out here.' And that was the first time I realized he had any interest in me other than working together. So, it sort of progressed from there, and we got married a year later.

"We had a group of Mexicans in here, and we gave them their four-leaf clovers with a little note in Spanish. We went on-line and got a Spanish dictionary and explained that in America a four-leaf clover represents good luck. We had a lot of fun with them, taught them how to play croquet and horseshoes, taught them how to use paddleboats. They went in circles a lot out there on the lake, but they had a great time, and had a great sense of humor. They do nothing but work up here for seven months, and then they go back to Mexico. They only had three days off, so we tried to give them a real vacation. When they left we gave them a broken croquet set we had. They split it up between them so they each could take something home and so they could make them, and teach their families how to play croquet."

Robert: "The reason they liked it so much was that a lot of people could be involved in the game; the more people the better. They'd never played horseshoes. Before the first game was over, one of them was throwing ringers on a regular basis"

Darlene: "I guess the point is that it doesn't matter who you are, we'll try to accommodate you. We took a 91-year-old woman who was blind. I asked what her needs were, 'cause we're not handicapped accessible—our bathrooms aren't accessible, although we do have a wheelchair here that we can bring out if you need to be wheeled around the lawn. We set her up here, wheeled her around, she was given blow-by-blow description of our bonfire.

"Depending on our customers, whether we have kids or adults, we try to build unusual bonfires. One night it might be pyramid style, another it might be hollow trees that will shoot flames up through the center. Some nights it's just big, 'cause that's what everybody wants. If we have people that like cooking on the coals, like the Mexicans, we just build a low-key fire.

"We had one group that booked the whole place for a family reunion and they wanted a lobster feed for one of their dinners. We ordered 55 pounds of lobster, had it delivered fresh." *Robert:* "Now, thanks to my mother, who owns a take-out business up the road, we have a burner, and buffet units, and big lobster cooking pots." *Darlene:* "We cook lobsters outside and have corn on the cob, potato salad, apple pie. Everything is made from scratch. We did it with that group and we've been doing it ever since. We offer the lobster feed to four or more people.

"About the lake here. It's 6 miles long, shaped like a cowboy boot. We're down in a cove in the toe of the boot. It has pickerel, bass, white perch, brown trout once in a blue moon, and eel (the kids fish for those). They stock it each year with salmon, but the pickerel eat them as fast as the fish trucks put them in. This is a quiet lake, very few camps on it.

"We have great partridge hunting. We have local guides and do primarily, deer, moose, bird, rabbit. We own 200 acres, three-quarters of a mile of waterfront. Ede planted oak trees 35 years ago. So we have the habitat for both large and small game. Because the hunter's cabin is up away from the water, by a grassed-over skidder road and near apple trees, the bucks and does traverse down that road. So they literally are right out the front door of the hunter's cabin. You can wake up in the morning and never have to even put your boots on to get a deer.

"Last year was our first year staying open in winter. We only rent two cabins. There's no running water, just open drains, toilets that flush, and water provided daily to the cabin. We have spigot jugs at the sinks. You can sit right on your porch and watch your ice-fishing flags. The snowmobile trail ends about half a mile up the road.

"Down in the dining room we have a display. We try to recycle where we can, so Robert and I take old blue jeans that people throw away and we make braided rugs, chair pads (he cuts the legs, stitches them together, and I braid and lace them). They last for 40 or 50 years, and they're washable. We recycle our cooked lobster and crab claws, make 'Santa Claws' out of them and offer them for sale to our customers. This is a real family project because you have to sit and stitch the Santa hats, dip the claws in polyurethane, glue on eyes. We made driftwood signs and little birch-bark canoes out of fallen birch bark. We try to recycle everything we can."

Buckwheat Blueberry Pancakes

Darlene: "We use the best buckwheat flour we can find."

> 2 cups buckwheat flour, 1 cup white flour, 1 tsp. baking soda, enough
> buttermilk to make a thin batter (if batter is sticky, beat in 1 egg). If milk
> is used instead of buttermilk use: 2 tsp. cream of tartar and 2 T melted
> shortening.

Prepare pancake batter and ladle onto preheated, greased griddle. Sprinkle the pancakes on the griddle with fresh Maine blueberries, flip, and serve with Maine maple syrup, or favorite sweetener.

74. EAGLE LODGE AND CAMPS

AP/HK, SCA

OWNERS: John and Tami Rogers

ADDRESS: PO Box 686, Lincoln, ME 04457; 207-794-2181; e-mail: eaglodge@aol.com; www.eaglelodgemaine.com

SEASON: May through November

ACCOMMODATIONS: Five log cabins: one to two bedrooms, screened porch, indoor plumbing and shower, wood heat, gas lights, gas stove, gas refrigerator; well-behaved pets ($10 per day). Education center and gift and supply store.

RATES: $70 per person per day (AP); $75 per cabin per day (HK); child rates and guide service available

ACCESS: I-95 to exit 55 (Lincoln). At the US 2 intersection, go straight. At the ME 155 intersection, go left. At the Penobscot Valley Hospital, go right 2.8 miles to a four-corners. Turn left and follow the signs 3 miles to camp.

Even though the town and all its modern conveniences are only about 20 minutes away, by the time you drive along back dirt roads and dip down the driveway to Eagle Lodge and see the familiar sporting-camp log cabins and main lodge you are in "camp mode." Only 50 miles northeast of Bangor, Lincoln has 78 square miles of land, making it the largest township east of the Mississippi. There are more than a dozen lakes and ponds with public access, including the Penobscot River and its bass fishery, within the town's borders.

Tami: "We bought the camps in 1994—looked at them in June, and by July they were ours. We weren't really in search of a sporting camp per se, but it was a meant-to-be situation. In the beginning we worked so hard it was unbelievable. By the time we'd been here eight months, we had a group of hunters that left a $100 tip and we decided it was time to splurge and take the kids, Greg and Courtney, out. So we went to Bangor for dinner and a movie. We were at the restaurant and went into the bathroom to wash up. I met up with John on the way out and we both looked at each other, shocked. Did you see yourself in the mirror? We hadn't looked in a mirror for eight months! But, you know, it was the best winter. We had no radio or TV. We went through one or two books a week, all of us. It was a real connecting time." *John:* "When you don't have a TV or radio, you can hear what's going on around you. We'd listen to the ice—there are air bubbles underneath frozen water that build up and you get this sound we called the heartbeat of the earth.

"The camps are on Folsom Pond, which connects to Crooked Pond, and both are a mile long and wide and have smallmouth bass, pickerel, and white perch. Upper Pond is the headwaters and that has brook trout. The Penobscot River is 15 minutes from here and we fish that—50 to 100 smallmouth bass a day is common.

"We have a lot of hiking trails and do guided rock-climbing trips, even for people who've just learned how to spell 'rock'! We have an excellent hunting season: moose, bear, deer, upland game, and duck." *Tami:* "Yes, we can provide all these things, and more, but what we really offer is nothing. If you want to sit on the front lawn, in the peace and quiet, and watch eagles, that's what you can do."

John: "The camps were built in the early 1920s by a Dr. George Averell from Lee, Maine, who built Lee Academy. The original lodge was elaborate, with flush toilets—this is in the '20s—but it burned and they built another one right off. Teddy Roosevelt was here when he was in Bangor. This was when he was governor of New York.

"The driveway's only been here since the late '60s. Prior to that, they had a set of rollers to crank boats down and every Thursday they'd get to town by boat. The Sharkeys, father and mother and three daughters, bought it in the late '30s. Mr. Sharkey was a schoolteacher who worked two jobs all year so he could take the summer off to come here. If you wanted to stay with the Sharkeys, you'd wait at the railroad station—there was no telephone communication—and they'd swing by to pick you up. One crazy aunt would come in on a float plane with bags of groceries. The three sisters would come in here, without husbands, by canoe at night and lie on their backs and look at the stars and roll down the hill. One sister painted an oil painting of the camps. They come each year; they're hooked forever." *Tami:* "These women have really touched our lives. They've told us wonderful stories about growing up here that have really brought the history to life for us. Their parents finally relented and said they could stay up one hour later, but then went around and set the clocks ahead one hour all summer!"

John: "When the sisters were teenagers and had their cousin around, there were four buddies in town who spent one winter building four canoes, all alike. They called themselves the Four Aces. They put motors on these canoes and would race around the lake trying to get the girls' attention.

Well, Pa had to go to town and there's the guys hanging out in their boats. So he calls to the guys and says, 'I'm headed to town to get reflectors for your canoes.' 'We don't need reflectors,' they say. 'It's for me,' he says, 'so I can get a bead on it to shoot you guys out of the water!'"

Tami: "Some of these guys have been back, one on a motorcycle. He's always loved one of the sisters. The sisters' grandmother died here, and their mother died many years later on the same day. Their father tried to die on the same day but passed away a few days ahead. I believe the passion and love of the former generations for this place is still here in these walls and around us. Magical and special things happen at Eagle Lodge. We have logbooks in the cabins and people write such beautiful things it makes you cry."

John: "On May 3, 1997, we started something that has turned out to be a wonderful and popular addition. That was our first Maine Guide School session. [Both Tami and John are Maine guides.] We get people who come ready to take the Maine guide test. It's rigorous, but they end up prepared and seem to have a worthwhile time. We've had over 500 men and women go through the course and then they can go on to take the test and become registered Maine Guides." *Tami:* "And we're really excited about our two newest ventures: the Sea School and the Wellness Retreat. For the Sea School people come who want to get a 'six-pack' captain's license—which means they can operate 100 tons 100 miles offshore anywhere in the US. Then, I have wellness training, and we're offering a 5 or 6 night retreat where men and women can connect mind, body, and soul, learn to appreciate life, get back to the positive and come into harmony in this beautiful place."

Deep-Dish Moose Stew Pie

Tami: "You can use beef instead of moose." John: "This is so good it makes you want to go out and shoot a moose, even if you don't hunt!"

> 2 pounds cubed moose meat, ½ cup flour, 1 tsp. salt, 1 tsp. basil, 1 tsp. thyme, pinch of five-spice powder, 4-plus cups water, 3 peeled and sliced carrots, 2 chopped onions, 5 medium potatoes, 3 T cornstarch, pastry for single piecrust

Combine flour, salt, and herbs and dredge the cubed meat. Brown the meat in an oiled heavy saucepan. Add 4 cups of water and simmer for 2 hours. Add vegetables and more water if needed. Thicken with cornstarch after the veggies are cooked. Pour into a baking dish and cover with the pastry. Bake at 350 degrees for 20–25 minutes.

A winter scene at Eagle Lodge and Camps

75. GREAT POND WILDERNESS LODGE AND CAMPS

HK, SCA

OWNER: Otis Godley

ADDRESS: 672 Main Road, Eddington, ME 04428; 207-745-6728

SEASON: Year-round

ACCOMMODATIONS: Five log cabins: one to two bedrooms, porch, central shower house and bathroom, wood heat, gas stove, gas lights, gas refrigerator, gas grill; bring sleeping bag, blanket, pillow; pets welcome

RATES: $45–100 per cabin per day

ACCESS: I-95 to exit 48 (Bangor); follow signs to ME 9 east. Take ME 9 east through Aurora and turn left onto Great Pond Road. Go 6 miles to the first right, then go 1.3 miles and turn left. Continue 3 miles to Stud Mill Road. Turn left and go 3 miles. At mile marker 19, turn left and go 2 miles to camp.

Otis: "This place was started in 1904 by a man from Maine called Guy Patterson. He originally had a place on Long Pond and then came over here. It was always run as a sporting camp even though there were logging operations nearby. I've found old logging equipment in the woods around here. I'm the fourth owner in all these years. Ed Musson, on the island across there, owned them before me.

"The camps sit up on a knoll overlooking the lake and all the cabins are on the water. Great Pond is 2 miles long and about half a mile wide, shaped like a boot, with brown trout, pickerel, bass, and some brook trout. There's a big field with a volleyball net and picnic tables as you drive in. We have 300 feet of beach, which is where we have our cookouts at night, and you need sunglasses for our sunsets!

"Hunting is as good as you'll find around here. We have about a dozen deer hanging around camp most of the time. I guide, but if I'm out by myself, I won't shoot a good, big deer anymore—save it to seed the next generation. The property behind my camp hasn't been cut for about 50 years and is the only good place within 10 miles that is natural for the deer. There may be a couple thousand acres in that public lot, owned by the state. We're also surrounded by thousands of acres owned by different paper companies. I own this land, 17 acres, so I have a lot of protection. Moose are a common sight. Many mornings guests look out their front porch to see a moose feeding in the shallow water near the inlet. We're in the southeast zone for moose hunting here.

"I grew up hunting and fishing with my father, and owning and operating a sporting camp is something I've wanted to do for 20 years. But I was in no position to do anything about it because something like this takes a lot of money. I just stumbled into this place when I was out snowmobiling with a friend. It was in a state of disrepair, which is why, in June 1990, I was able to buy it. So I've been playing Mr. Fix-Up. Right now I work for UPS, but this is what I plan to retire to, hopefully within the next 10 years. I'm a Master Guide and have another Master Guide who helps me, Walter 'Butch' Myers. I couldn't possibly do this all on my own. Butch and I and the others in this business for the long haul are here because we like it. It's in our blood. I mean, today practically everyone we know is getting ready to sit down and watch the Super Bowl, but we're out at camp getting things ready for our '98 winter season, when we'll be feeding and fueling snowmobilers. I put in a central shower and bathroom facility, and now we're concentrating on making this a full-service winter snowmobile destination, open 24 hours from Thursdays through Sundays. We're a mile from ITS 84, with a side trail leading right to the lake. Also in '98 we'll be doing bear hunting. It's slow, but exciting, getting closer to the goal of being in here full time.

"This is a great year-round spot. We want to show our guests the beauty of the area, show them a good vacation. Sometimes funny things happen, though, no matter what we do. I remember one time we had a father and son at camp and we'd shown them where to fish. I had to go into town in the afternoon, and when I got back they hollered for me to come over and see the mess of trout they'd caught for supper. Well, I came over, and here they were eating away on chub! I had to laugh—pretty high-bred chub. We also have guided canoe trips on the Machias, Union, Narraguagus, and St. Croix Rivers. In the fall, this is a great place for what we call leaf-peepers. Eagle Mountain is near us, and each year at the height of the fall foliage, we take our guests who want to go up to the top of the mountain for a view of the autumn colors. On the way we go through a place that in the 1800s was a town of over a thousand people, but now is nothing more than a couple of brick ovens by a big spring, some rock foundations, and some old apple trees. It used to be a tannery, but when the hemlock-bark source dried up, so did the town. Marjorie and George Baker wrote a book about the town called Munsungan to the Sea. That's the Indian name for the Passadumkeag watershed we're in. A nice connection is that Marjorie is the daughter of Guy Patterson, who built this place. The book describes how they'd go into their cabins—these were really basic with no windows, and dirt floors—and they'd start a fire to smoke the mosquitoes out. And then they'd go in to go to sleep. Marjorie and her husband used to snowshoe 70 miles a week trapping beaver. That's when women were women, Alice!"

76. LAKE MOLUNKUS SPORTING CAMPS

HK/AP
OWNER: Matthew Ewing
ADDRESS: PO Box 37, Mattawamkeag, ME 04459; 207-944-9974; e-mail: matt@lakemolunkus.com; www.lakemolunkus.com
SEASON: May through November
ACCOMMODATIONS: Twelve log and clapboard cabins: one to two bedrooms,

some with porch, six with indoor plumbing and shower, six use central bath house, gas and electric lights, wood and propane heat, gas stove and refrigerator; well-attended pets allowed

RATES: $31–51 per cabin per day, $150–314 per cabin per week (HK), $62 per person per day, $389 per person per week (AP, parties of four or more); motorboat and canoe rentals and hunting packages available

ACCESS: Take I-95 north to exit 56 (Medway). Turn right onto ME 157 to US 2. Take a left and go 9 miles to first left (Aroostook Road). After about 4 miles it becomes dirt. At the next camp sign turn right into camp.

The camps are a combination of old and newer. Dark-stained log cabins form a semi-circle around a set of gray-sided cabins clumped cozily together where people mingle companionably. A centrally located shower and bath house and large log home (the location of the office) complete the picture.

Matt: "As far as I can tell, the camps began around the 1880s and were built as a logging camp. The main lodge was built and then four or five of the smaller log cabins. Then it became a sporting camp in 1906. The previous owners researched the history of the place and there's only been six major owners of the place (essentially 10- to 20-year owners). And I hope to be the seventh long-term owner.

"The lake's about a thousand acres, roughly 3 miles long by about half a mile wide. Actually, it's shaped pretty much like the country of Italy. We are situated in the northwest corner, the headwaters of the lake. In the late '80s and early '90s it was a salmon fishery in the spring and smallmouth bass the remainder of the year. The salmon have tailed off, so it's primarily bass. It starts in May.

"I purchased the camps in 1998. I worked for the paper company that owns this land, and most of the surrounding townships. I used to stay here, occasionally, through work, on some of the company's projects. I can remember sitting on the lodge's porch, almost every time we were here, thinking, 'I think I'd kinda like to do this.' One thing led to another, and I guess I said that one too many times! And all of a sudden I was here. I don't work for the paper company anymore. I decided if I was going to do this it really needed my full attention. At times it's leisurely, but at other times it's 24 hours a day. But it takes a full commitment to really make it work. I had the background of hunting, fishing, liked to trap and be in the outdoors, you know. I enjoy the guiding part, helping people successfully kill a bear, or hunt deer. I love to take the kids fishing. I try to describe the camps as a make-your-own-fun kind of place. I have paddleboats, kayaks, and canoes. People need to realize that they're on their own at these kinds of places, though. I love to interact, and love having kids in camp, the more kids the better, but it's not an amusement park. Many people come up here and say how glad they are there's no TV; they can't check their e-mail; they

Lake Molunkus Sporting Camps

don't hear a ringing phone. They'll say at the end of the week that they thought their son or daughter might have a tough time without a Gameboy or computer or whatever, but they're usually pleasantly surprised.

"Bear hunting's become big here. The previous owners were school-teachers and they ran it more as a summer business and then November deer season. So I had to establish the client base for a bear-hunting season. And that's been a lot of fun. It's a lot of work. I don't look forward to all the baiting that's involved, but it's so much fun to have hunters in camp. Guys who've hunted all their lives, killed hundreds of deer and consider themselves proficient hunters, I just get thrilled at the way they react when a bear comes in to the bait. They aren't used to the adrenalin that roars through their body. They don't get excited about killing deer anymore, but a 100-pound bear comes in, and they just can't believe it. My clients love to go bear baiting with me. They have no idea what the process is, so I constantly have people tagging along. They'll carry bait for me, carry stands, whatever.

"I don't do a lot of deer guiding. Most of my client base has been here for 30 years, a lot of repeat business, and they all guide themselves and know the area pretty well. It's kind of nice to get through the grueling month of November, the deer season, and then be able to shut the place down and have it to ourselves for a while and then leave for the winter. It makes that anticipation of coming back in April that much greater. It's so nice to get back in here. The kids were thrilled. So that makes it nice, having a break. I lived in here by myself the first three years. Friends would come in, but I lived here throughout the year. I enjoyed it, but you lose per-

244 MAINE SPORTING CAMPS

spective. Everyone comes up, 'What a fabulous place to live. You're so lucky.' Well, it isn't when you live here year-round. I like being here six or seven months and then doing something else. I spend most of my winter trapping beaver. The fur gets auctioned in Canada. It's not a great money-making scheme; it's more for peace of mind. I can get out there and do what I really want to be doing. I usually stay here in camp the month of December and trap around here. December it's open for beaver, and all the other fur-bearers. Actually, I have clients that will pass up deer hunting just to go trapping with me in November when I'll do a lot of martin and fisher trapping. For that you use killer-type traps, so I don't have to check them every day. I'll usually run a 30-mile trap line right around the camps. And I'll check those every two or three days. I use moose renderings for bait. I go to the local butcher during moose season and get buckets full of the waste. Both martins and fishers are weasels. Weasels are the smallest family member, then there's martin, which is about the size of a gray squirrel, only they're reddish-orange-ish in color, and then there's fisher which might go 12–15 pounds. I actually caught three martin in one of my cabins last year. The red squirrels were getting into the cabin eating my bear bait I had left over, and the martin were getting into the cabin eating the red squirrels. Some critters are used for the insides of jackets. I mean you might have a fox or mink and that's obviously on the outside, but the inside might be muskrat. They shear all the hair off of beaver and make hats and gloves. Most of it is foreign trade. Most of your buyers are Russian, Asian. Not much of your fur remains in North America anymore, although that's where most of the supply is.

"Most people that come here from out of state, maybe near big cities. So they live for the one or two weeks they can come up here each year. And I just enjoy helping them experience whatever they can while they're here. It's the little things, like sitting around a campfire, or eel fishing at night. Something they never get to do. With eel fishing, basically you wait 'til it gets dark, throw your worm off the dock, come back to the campfire and tell stories, riddles, jokes, whatever, and check your rod periodically. Sometimes you catch a catfish and sometimes you catch this god-awful, slippery, three-foot, slithering eel. Everyone thinks it's gross, everyone wants to come down and see it, people screaming and yelling. They're pretty nasty critters. Some of the kids want to try eating them. So I show them how to skin them: nail them to a tree, cut right in back of the head, and with a pair of pliers, peel the skin off like a sock. Then you cut them open and clean them out, which is a process. I think half the experience is just the catching and the cleaning and all. People could care less about eating them. But some people are interested in how they taste so you then cut them up, roll them in bread crumbs, and fry them in a pan like you would trout. People think about all this the next day when they're out swimming—there's actually eels in there swimming around. That sometimes becomes a deterrent for a while. I believe eels are still sent overseas. The part-time fishermen, small businessmen, still set up weirs in many rivers. I can't imagine it, but I guess they're a delicacy in some places.

"My 'significant other,' Marie, and her two daughters, Kayla and Darby, have become a big part of the camps in the last year and a half or so. And the girls have never been exposed to anything like this. So this is a real eye-opener for them. And they absolutely love it up here. Kayla turns 10 in August [2002] and she's probably getting a new shotgun for her birthday. She's expressed an interest in hunting. I've had her up on the gun range here, shooting a .22. She and Darby followed me around the woods during bird season, and she wants to go out this year and hunt birds. So hopefully with her, and our new chocolate lab, Cooper, we'll have some luck."

77. NESTING LOON CABINS

HK

OWNERS: Bill and Sheila Fay

ADDRESS: HC 65, Box 3974, Lincoln, ME 04457; 207-794-6002; e-mail: wfay@midmaine.com

SEASON: Year-round

ACCOMMODATIONS: Five log cabins: one to two bedrooms, screened porch, indoor plumbing and tub with shower, central bathroom and shower house (for use in winter), electric lights and refrigerator, gas stove, wood heat; pets welcome

RATES: $30–40 per cabin per day, double occupancy; child and family rates available

ACCESS: I-95 to exit 55 (Lincoln). In Lincoln, turn left at West Broadway, continue on Main Street, then turn right onto ME 6 east. Go 4.5 miles on ME 6; camps are on the left (sign).

Nesting Loon Cabins have a lived-in, year-round look. As you drive in, you pass a variety of winter and summer work and recreational vehicles. Construction is progressing on a number of fronts around the small compound.

Sheila: "The original owner was Gerry Schrite from Pennsylvania, who built the biggest cabin, down by the water, around 1942 or 1943. We've been here since 1994. We liked the place because we could own our own land. It's only 10 minutes out of Lincoln, and within half an hour's drive of 13 lakes.

"We're on Caribou Pond, and only 4 miles to the Penobscot River for bass fishing. The river's been written up in *Bassmasters* magazine. The Indian Nation has rights, I believe, to all the islands in the Penobscot. So it's fine for the public to go fishing in the river, but not to step foot on any of the islands, because that's Indian property. The Indian Nation we're talking about is located primarily in Old Town.

Nesting Loon Cabins

"Our camps are the only boat launch that's available for Caribou Pond, which is one of a chain of three ponds connected by waterways. There's Caribou, Egg, and Long Ponds. They cover about 825 acres and have a maximum depth of 46 feet, with smallmouth bass, white perch, and pickerel. On the pond there's a number of 'floating islands' of aquatic plant life where birds nest and flowers bloom. Our loon logo was designed by wildlife artist Bob Noonan and shows a loon nesting on one of these islands.

"In the fall we have guided hunts for bear, deer, and moose. There's also grouse, rabbit, and duck hunting that's good around here. For the winter, ITS 81 passes close by our cabins and only 4 miles farther east on Route 6 is Mount Jefferson, for all-natural skiing. During the winter, we don't have running water in the cabins, but we provide water in plastic jugs, and our shower and bath house is heated and open year-round."

78. NICATOUS LODGE

AP/HK, SCA

OWNERS: Denise and Gary Betz Jr., Nancy and Gary Betz
ADDRESS: Box 100, Burlington, ME 04417; 207-732-4771;
e-mail: nicatous@midmaine.com; www.nicatouslodge.com

SEASON: Year-round

ACCOMMODATIONS: Eight log cabins: one to three bedrooms, indoor plumbing and shower (April through October), gas lights, wood heat; four lodge rooms (year-round plumbing); pets welcome

RATES: $70 per person per day (AP); $70 (minimum) per cabin per day (HK); motorboats $35 per day, canoes and kayaks $20 per day

ACCESS: I-95 to exit 54 (Howland). Turn right onto ME 155 south. Cross US 2, then pick up ME 188 east to Burlington. Continue east on ME 188, following signs 14 miles to camp.

A gravel logging road bisects Nicatous: On one side is a lawn, complete with raised gardens, which leads to a long, wide dock and boats. An expanse of lake, dotted with islands, beckons beyond the cove. On the other side, perched at the top of a gentle incline, the generous front porch of the log main lodge offers a comfortable welcome. Beyond, nestled in a pine grove and fronting on Nicatous Stream, are the log cabins. The road leads across the stream and to another set of camps within view. It then continues dozens of miles into the wilderness again.

Denise: "Nicatous Lodge has been on this side of the stream and the other, over the wooden bridge, back and forth, since 1928. An old trapper used to live on the other side, at Porter Point, but it wasn't a business then. In 1953 Kate Chamberlain, the great-granddaughter of Horace Greeley, bought it for her husband's anniversary present. The Chamberlains ended up buying Nicatous Lodge. Then it was bought by the present owner of Porter Point Camps, Barry Tyne, who operated Nicatous from 1977 to 1984. Then Pete and Chris Norris had it from '84 to '97. (Pete's the brother of Charlene at Weatherby's and Steve at The Pines.)"

Gary: "The year we bought the place, '97, Jim and Genness Robbins, of Robbins Lumber, purchased the land surrounding the lake, including the islands, and the state ended up buying a 250-foot development easement around the lake. So this whole view is protected. Nicatous Lake is 13 miles long and about 2 miles wide—a shallow, rocky, lake excellent for smallmouth bass fishing. There are a lot of white sand beaches for picnics and swimming. That's what we do, when we've time, go out to a beach, bring a hibachi and some food."

Denise: "Before we came here we'd been working in the hospitality industry. I also worked in a travel agency and cleaned condos—all stuff that leads up to this." *Gary:* "I grew up in a sporting camp, so I knew what to expect." *Denise:* "What a life that was for him. You don't have the TVs and everything kids these days rely on really. And now we have a new little Betz to follow the tradition.

"We haven't changed much around here. I now have a few theme rooms like moose and Indian upstairs in the lodge for guests." *Gary:* "A sporting camp in most people's minds is hunting and fishing, but we're

Snowmobiling is a popular winter activity at Nicatous Lodge.

expanding that a bit. We do the traditional, but branch out and offer rock climbing, cross-country skiing, ice climbing, and mountain biking to diversify our clientele. You can bike a mile or 50 miles on good dirt roads; same with ATVs. In the winter, we're right on ITS 81 and 84 for snowmobiling, and sell fuel, and serve lunch for people passing through. And several lakes around here support salmon and trout for ice fishing. Another thing we get in the winter now is a lot of people flying in for lunch! They're in flying clubs, and come in at least three or four planes at a time.

"We also run specials, like weddings, retreats, seminars, church groups, and family reunions. Recently we had a family game tournament and at the end they gave out trophies and we served prime rib. It was great! And the state group of Ducks Unlimited comes up here each year for their annual meeting. We do a potluck wild game feed and don't know what we'll be cooking until they get here Thursday or Friday." *Denise:* "Last year I marinated some bear in lime juice and Mexican spices, put that in a tortilla with guacamole, lettuce, and tomato, and people were calling it 'Yuppie Bear.' This year our unusual game was Maine porcupine (this is on top of venison, moose, bear, etc.). Last year we also had wild boar and Gary put that right on top of the bean hole beans. It was delicious!"

Bean Hole Beans

2 pounds beans, 1 large or 2 small onions, ½ pound salt pork, 1 cup brown sugar, ¾ cup molasses, ½ cup catsup, ¼ cup Worchestershire sauce, 2 T mustard

Soak beans overnight in enough water to cover—water is mixed with 1 T baking soda. Dig a hole about 4 to 6 times the size of your Dutch oven and split hardwood small, enough to fill the hole twice. Start the fire 1 to 2 hours before you want to put beans in. Burn down to all coals. Drain and rinse beans and put in the Dutch oven. Place sliced onions and salt pork on top. Mix remaining ingredients, pour over beans, and cover with boiling water. Shovel out enough coals to cover and surround the pot. Place the pot in the hole and cover with coals. Cover the coals with dirt so no smoke or steam escapes. Cook 6–8 hours. Variations: Put a roast on top of the beans—bear, moose, deer, beef, or pork—then stir into the beans afterward. Note: The key to good bear meat is to remove the skin and fat as soon as possible. If shot during the August or September hunt, pack in ice right away."

79. PORTER POINT CAMPS

HK

OWNER: Barry Tyne

ADDRESS: Burlington, ME 04417; 207-866-7849; e-mail: tynebb@hyper-net.com; www.porterpointcamps.com

SEASON: Year-round

ACCOMMODATIONS: Five cabins: one to two bedrooms, plus a bunkhouse, indoor plumbing and shower, gas lights, gas stove, gas refrigerator, wood heat; one outpost camp with outhouse, hand water pump, pets welcome.

RATES: $40–75 per cabin per day; $180–400 per cabin per week

ACCESS: I-95 to exit 54 (Howland). Take ME 155 north and then 188 east through Burlington. From Burlington, go 8 miles to the end of the paved road and another 6 miles on the gravel road.

Barry: "I was working as a lawyer with my father in New Jersey in the '70s when I brought my wife, Joan, and two kids, Mike and Jennifer, up to Maine for a vacation. We went to Mount Desert Island and spent 13 days at a campground in a tent and it rained the entire time. As we drove back on Route 2 through Farmington, the sun came out, and it was warm and beautiful. We'd had a great time, in spite of the rain, and I started to think, 'I don't want to go back!'

"By Washington's birthday, we were on a farm in Wilton. A big beautiful place. I was practicing law in a small Maine town. The toughest part was leaving my father. But after a time I found myself peering out the window a lot. One day I was standing at my office window on a sleeting day,

Barry and Mike Tyne of Porter Point Camps

looking at a town road truck go by, and I silently said to the driver, 'You lucky s.o.b.' I really loved working outside. And it was then I realized that it wasn't a change of location, but of avocation, that I was looking for.

"Shortly after that, one Sunday morning in 1976, I was reading the paper and saw an ad for Nicatous Camps, on both sides of the stream, for sale. On Monday we took a ride in and in February 1977 we closed. I sold my law practice and we moved in. Mike and Jennifer went to school from here. I'd drive out 12 miles for the bus each morning and then they'd have another 18 miles to go. It got hectic, with all the sports and no phone communication. Sometimes they'd get home at 9 o'clock. Sometimes I didn't know when they'd be getting home. I always brought a book in case I had to wait hours for them. They were both great students. Mike played football and at 14 left home to board at Maine Central Institute in Pittsfield. From there he went to Dartmouth and Yale Divinity School. He taught a couple of years, wrote a novel, and is now at a seminary in Rome studying for the priesthood. Jennifer went to Smith College and Northeastern Law School and is now in private practice. When they were kids they ran the little general store, which is the cabin nearest the logging road.

"We're on the northern end of Nicatous Lake here, at the outlet where there's a dam and fishway. The lake is stocked with salmon and brown trout, but mainly it's a smallmouth bass lake. Thanks to the efforts of environmental groups, a timber landowner, and the state, the lake and shoreline will remain unchanged forever. It was initiated actually by the Robbins Lumber Company family who had purchased 20-plus thousand acres and recognized the beauty of the area and wanted it to remain undeveloped.

"In 1984, when Brian was born, Joan said, 'I'm out of the kitchen.' The kitchen was really a job. So we sold Nicatous Lodge and retained the housekeeping cabins on the other side of the dam. I have my own set of loyal guests, and over the years they've become real family friends. We home-schooled Brian. Now it's just Brian and me here. Joan passed away in 1994. She was wonderful, a real trouper. She was willing to do anything. When we were all in here together and owned the whole place, it seemed like our own little town. I'd go up and shovel roofs. I'd plow the road at 2 in the morning and see nothing but fox tracks go up the middle of the road. See the moon shining through the glistening trees. It was great! This life is very satisfying, very personal. I'm my own boss, the only one who has to be satisfied with my work."

80. SOUTH BRANCH LAKE CAMPS

AP/HK, SCA

OWNERS: Russ and Cindy Aldridge

ADDRESS: 1174 Cove Road, Seboeis, ME 04448; 207-732-3446 or 1-800-248-0554, e-mail: sobranch@midmaine.com; www.southbranchlakecamps.com

SEASON: Year-round

ACCOMMODATIONS: Eleven log and brown-stained cedar clapboard cabins: one to two bedrooms, indoor plumbing, central shower house, electric lights, gas heat; well-behaved pets allowed

RATES: $80 per person per day (3-day minimum), $475 per person per week (AP); $100 per cabin per day (3-day minimum), $600 per cabin per week (HK); motorboat $45 per day, $225 per week; guided trip rates available

ACCESS: I-95 to exit 54 (Howland). Take 155 into Howland and go left on

The author with Russ Aldridge on the Penobscot River

ME 116 (north) to Seboeis Plantation Road. Go 8 miles to Lake Road on the right and down 0.5 mile to the bottom of the hill. Camp driveway on right.

Though just west of I-95 and thus technically in the "central region," South Branch Lake Camp's water focus is not only its own lake, but also the Penobscot River. The first thing one sees from the wooded parking area is the camp's main lodge and a wonderful "tree sculpture" garden by the office.

Russ: "The story about those carvings is that in '99, right in the heart of June, a storm blew in off the lake and we had a strike of lightning that hit the white pine outside the lodge, grounded out in our water system, blew our pumps out (this is with a couple dozens guests at camp), and basically created a $3,000 weekend for us. On top of that, we had to get a crane in to get the tree removed since it's right next to the lodge. When it got down to about 12–14 feet, I told the tree guys to stop. When they asked me why I said that I'd always wanted a carving and didn't know but that some day I could afford to have it done. Well, it was during bear season that fall that a man named Joshua Sargent, from New Hampshire, was one of my clients. Here was here about a day and asked me, 'What are you planning on doing with all those chunks of wood, including that 12-foot stump that's standing outside the dining room?' I told him about the storm and my hope to have a carving someday. At that point he opened up—he'd been real quiet before—and basically told us that's what he does for a hobby. He went to work and about nine hours later we had three carved bears climbing that whittled-down tree stump! He then went ahead, over the next four days, and carved the owl you see, the raccoon, the rabbit, the other totem pole halfway down the steps to the lake. And at the end of the week, he hadn't spent more than 25 hours on the whole project. They're stained with a CWF water stain, and burned with a torch to give the effect of the hair on the animal, and then there's a colored stain for the "rocks" that have been carved out. In our December [2001] newsletter we told the story of the storm and the carvings and closed by saying, 'If there's truth to the fact that all things have a reason for happening, then ours was this.'

"South Branch Camps, to the best of my knowledge, was built and completed between the years of approximately 1912 and 1920. It was originally built for the loggers who were logging on both Mattamiscontis Mountain and around Seboeis Plantation. A mill was built over on what now is known as 'home shore.' The mill burned in 1973. But back in the early days, there were three log cabins on this point: what are now Skipper and Moose and, on the far side of the peninsula, what we call the 'guide's camp' today was the chef's quarters. The loggers would come down the lake, with their boom floats, in the evening, tie up, come over, eat at the chef's quarters, and then retire for the night in the other two cabins. All the food, all the products that had to come out to this point came by boat. The road in has only been here since about 1990.

"South Branch is a 2,100-acre, spring-fed lake with nine different islands, a beautiful smallmouth bass fishery. It's been known as a bass fishery for close to 45 years now. It's common go out and catch bass in the 3- to 5-pound range."

Cindy: "Part of what brought us here is that Russ is a hunter from way back." *Russ:* "Mom and Dad started me in the woods when I was five. My folks owned a sportsmen's club in Vermont—picture a large-scale shooting range: indoor, outdoor, sporting clays, trap shooting, large and small bore or caliber. And I grew up learning and living all that. I shot for the sportsmen's club rifle team for 13 years and was fortunate enough to have won quite a few state medals, harvested my first deer when I was nine, and have just been hunting and fishing ever since. When Cindy and I got together we were living in a farmhouse in New Hampshire, and I started taking people out hunting. Pretty soon we were filling up the house and started looking for something bigger. We looked all around—even up into Canada, which is where I go with my caribou hunts, both left full-time jobs, sold the farm, and came to do this. Each year the second or third week in December I pack up my gear and head to Canada. From camp it's just over 1,340 miles, one way, 27 hours north of here, about two-thirds of the way up the east side of James Bay. It's wonderful. You'd have to see it to believe it. Every year I offer clients a limited-number hunt. It's a bare-bones hunt and we all work together as a team, so they have to be worth their salt to go. In doing it we have a wonderful time and I've made some good friends, and it falls right in line with the outfitting that we do here.

"Big game animals in general have always intrigued me. It's not so much for the kill of the animal, but for the harvest of something to come— whether it's to have the meat at a later time, being out there for the hunt, as well as taking the animal—all that together. That's a time when I kind of become one with the woods, if that makes sense. Every time I go into the woods, it's just like I've never left. I don't know for sure if I'm going to harvest a deer on a given day, but I do know when I get up in the morning if the conditions are right. When I walk into the deer woods in the morning it could be as small a piece of information as a single row of tracks. I look at those as a potential harvest for the day. Where those tracks take me is the start of my day and I'll continue on them until I find the next piece of the puzzle. It may be as small as a tree rub, or the droppings from the deer along the trail—how the droppings are placed sometimes determines what kind of deer it is. They like 'jack firs,'—small conifers, hemlock, spruce—small trees that act as good cover for whitetail deer. Deer that live in swamps tend to have a little darker hide, and sometimes are a little healthier because they don't get seen as much by people. Gramp and Dad always told me, 'Think like a deer and go where deer go and people don't.' So that's what I try and do. I can go into an area and tell within 10 minutes whether there'll be deer there by the type of browse [buds and forage a deer would feed on] and water available and by the type of cover—whether there is a sanctuary.

"One of the things we do is our wilderness youth program. We have a format: a few questions and criteria, and the kids write us an essay about why they'd like to spend a week at a traditional Maine sporting camp. We look at every one of those essays, whether it was written by a 6-year-old with a crayon or banged out on a keyboard by a 14-year-old, and judge on the intent of the writing. The contest covers all of New England. Then we award that child and a responsible adult a stay here at camp. The only thing we ask is that, one, they spend a day with me, both on the river and on the lake. And two, they meet our local game warden and go to the local fish hatchery. And then, for a week, they get a chance to experience what we see and live every day.

"We have something called 'bragging boards.' Over the years we've taken, or guests have sent us, hundreds of photos. Cindy came up with the idea of putting a nice cork board in every cabin. It's gotten to the point where clients will send their photos after their trip and ask to be placed up on 'their' bragging board in 'their' cabin. The overflow goes on 'the big board,' which is 8 feet by 4 feet, in the main lodge.

"Another camp feature is that Ted Williams, the world-famous base-ball player, spent several vacations here in what is known as Dock cabin, right down dockside. The story goes that, one day after he got back from fishing, Williams asked his guide to stow the rods. After dinner, upon retiring to his cabin, he found that his rods were stored standing up in a corner. He then went up to the lodge, commenced to take a broom from the porch, cut the broom up into pieces in the shop, and made a rod holder. And, to this day, those pieces of broom handle are nailed up down in that cabin.

Monkey Bread

Cindy: "My mother, Teri, is with us here. She worked for around 25 years as a housekeeping supervisor in a nursing home, so she knows clean. When we got here, she went through and washed down the walls in every cabin, and the first year she was basically my housekeeper. I had the bookkeeping to do, other office work, did the shopping for food and other supplies. And she makes all the bread, all the cookies, the desserts. She always encourages kids to come up and sample what she's baking—not only for the American Plan, but for the housekeeping kids too. And what Russ does is before bed, the kids can come up on the porch and have ice cream sandwiches with him. It's a little something extra, and the kids look forward to it."

Basic Sweet Dough

> ⅓ cup shortening, ¼ cup sugar, 1 tsp. salt, 1 cup milk (scalded and cooled to lukewarm), 1 cake compressed yeast, ¼ cup lukewarm water, 2 eggs (beaten), 4 cups flour

Add shortening, sugar, and salt to milk (cool to lukewarm). Crumble yeast in the warm water and let stand five minutes. Combine milk and yeast mixtures. Add eggs and half of the flour. Beat well. Add remaining flour, turn dough in a greased bowl, cover, and let rise until double in bulk.

Bubble Ring mixture

> ½ cup melted butter, ¾ cup sugar, 1 tsp. cinnamon, ½ cup chopped nuts, 1 cup raisins

Punch down dough and roll out to ½-inch thick. Cut into strips ½-inch wide. Cut into pieces about the size of walnuts and roll into balls. Roll each ball in melted butter, then in sugar mixed with cinnamon. Butter a 9-inch tube pan. Layer dough balls into the pan, sprinkling with nuts and raisins between layers. Balls should barely touch each other; use all the dough. Cover and let rise until double in bulk, about one hour. Bake at 350 degrees for 35 minutes. Remove cooked bread and spread with a thin icing if desired.

THE GRAND LAKE–ST. CROIX REGION

A large and interconnecting series of lakes, ponds, and streams makes up what is known as the Grand Lake Stream–St. Croix watershed area, which serves as the focus for a majority of the camps in this region. The unique feature of sporting camps in Grand Lake Stream Village is that they form a close community while maintaining their individuality. Sporting-camp owners have formed their own local association. Thus, guests can experience a village, a community of interconnected camps, as well as an individual camp community. It is the personality of the owners that sets the tone of each camp and attracts kindred clientele. The other feature of this region is its high concentration of Maine Guides. Plying the waters with a Maine Guide is an experience not to be missed.

Many of the camps are close to New Brunswick, Canada, and an annual International Festival in August celebrates the good relations between neighbors. On the US side, there's a Blueberry Festival the beginning of August in Machias, a Salmon Festival the weekend after Labor Day in Eastport, the International Festival in Calais, and the Grand Lake Stream Folk Festival the last weekend in July.

All the freshwater attractions and the ocean are within an easy drive. You can go whale-watching out of Eastport every Tuesday, drive over to Campobello Island, New Brunswick, for a tour of President Franklin Roosevelt's summer retreat, or cruise along coastal villages on the *Bay of Fundy* sloop.

GETTING THERE: Commercial airlines fly to Bangor International Airport, which has rental car services. Bangor to Grand Lake Stream is approximately 100 miles. KT Aviation (207-945-5087) and Telford Aviation (207-990-5555) fly out of Bangor, or you can hire a regular plane to fly you into Princeton airport. If you arrive in a private plane, Princeton has two 4,000-foot runways and is 5–15 minutes from Grand Lake Stream–area camps. Driving time to the Grand Lake Stream area: from Portland is 5 hours; from Boston, 7 hours; from New York City, 11–12 hours.

GUIDANCE: For further information contact the Grand Lake Stream Chamber of Commerce, PO Box 124, Grand Lake Stream, ME 04637.

81. THE BIRCHES CABINS

HK (AP/MAP AVAILABLE)

OWNERS: Gil and Sue Penney

ADDRESS: Route 6, 603 Lakeview Road, Topsfield, Maine 04490; 207-796-

5517 or 1-800-214-9582; e-mail: birches@ainop.com; www.thebirches-cabins.com

SEASON: Year-round

ACCOMMODATIONS: Seven log and wood frame cabins: two to three bedrooms, indoor plumbing and shower ("with an 800-acre tub"), electric lights, gas or electric stove, wood heat; well-attended pets allowed

RATES: $45–60 per couple per day, $295–395 per couple per week; call for AP/MAP rates; motorboat $35 per day, canoe or rowboat $20 per day

ACCESS: I-95 to exit 55 (Lincoln). Follow ME 6 east about 38 miles to sign and cabins on the left.

The Birches, an eclectic mix of cabins on either side of a white main house, range in a semicircle back of a big field off ME 6. The compound itself is on a peninsula in East Mushquash Lake. There are no neighbors in sight.

Gil: "We know that the main house and several of the cabins were here in nineteen-aught-eight. We're not sure how much longer before that. Some of the camps are the old round-log cabins that have stood for just about a hundred years. The large camp uses what's referred to as "standing log" construction, vertical cedar logs, and I built that camp myself.

"East Mushquash Lake is about an 800-acre lake, a medium-sized lake. It's kind of a T-shape and if you went from one end and up to the T it would probably be about 3 miles and probably averages about ¾ mile wide. If we get a northwest wind it can get a little rough, so you'd use discretion about taking a canoe out those days. We have canoes, motorboats, kayaks. This lake is stocked with some real nice landlocked salmon. They have plenty of feed, too. In the summer when it's hot and the salmon go deep, there's a lot of smallmouth bass. And the smallmouth bass are a lot easier to catch than the salmon and they're a lot of fun too. They give a pretty good fight.

"The camps here set about five–six hundred feet off the road with an open field between us and the road. We're kind of set on a point here with the water all around us. We've got maybe 1,000 feet of frontage. Out across from us there's nothing on the back side of the lake. So you look out from your cabin and you're not looking at a shoreline of cabins. It's all wilderness country.

"We've got a large woodlot across the road for people to walk in too. For hiking, the paper companies have put in hundreds of miles of logging roads and they don't mind if you walk or bicycle or use ATVs and all that on them. We've had some mountain bikers in and had some touring bikers too. We just took a reservation the other day from people who are going to fly in to Bangor, rent bicycles, and tour this whole area. They'll stay here for a day or two and then go down around Bar Harbor and come back around.

"We have early spring fishermen, but most of our business is geared toward families. We are set up for housekeeping and provide all the bed

linen and towels, pots and pans, all that. So pretty much all people have to
do is bring their food, bring themselves, and they're ready to go. We do
offer American Plan for hunting season and also offer just the evening meal
if that's what they want (we Mainers call it supper, or "suppah," most people
call it dinner).

"We're both from Maine, originally from down the Sanford area. I'd
worked many years at the naval shipyard down at Kittery and got fed up
with the bureaucracy and the baloney of living down there, so we packed up
and moved. I'm a Master Maine Guide and went back and got my sea
kayaking guide license last summer. I haven't used it much yet, but we're
not that far from Calais and the tidewater comes in there. I'm going to try
to take people down there and paddle out to St. Croix Island, where
Champlain spent the winter of 1604, the first settlement around here. We'd
leave in the morning, take a sandwich lunch, paddle around the St. Croix
River (about 40 miles away), paddle out to the island a mile or so, where we
could stop, have lunch, and walk around maybe (it's about 2 miles long).
They say it was a fairly big settlement. There was a Frenchman in command
(I can't think of his name now); Champlain was the second in command. He
was the mapmaker. People are putting together a big 400-year anniversary
celebration and they're going to open a heritage center in Calais. That winter of 1604 was a very bad winter, and if it had been easier, they may have
made a go of living here. They lost a third of their people, so that when the
spring came and they left, they'd had it, and went down around Bar Harbor,
which is why they've got a lot of French names, Acadian names, there. They
didn't stay there though, as I understand it. They ended up staying in New
Brunswick, Canada, around Port Royal.

"I also do the traditional Maine guided trips out of what we call the
Grand Laker canoes, named after Grand Lake just below us here. You take
people out in the morning, catch a few fish, go in to shore, and cook them
a lunch right on shore. 'Course we bring plenty of other food to eat, too.
There's a lot of different things you can do around this area."

82. CANAL SIDE CABINS

HK, SCA
OWNERS: John and Mary Arcaro
ADDRESS: PO Box 77, Grand Lake Stream, ME 04637; 1-888-796-2796;
e-mail: canalsite@nemaine.com; www.canalsidecabins.com
SEASON: Year-round
ACCOMMODATIONS: Six log cabins: one to four bedrooms, indoor plumbing
and tub with shower, screened porch or deck, gas heat, electric lights; well-
attended pets allowed
RATES: $56–140 per cabin per day, $360–450 per cabin per week; motor-
boats $40 per day

ACCESS: I-95 to exit 45A (Bangor), then ME 9 east. Turn left onto US 1 in Barring. Go through Princeton to Grand Lake Stream Road on left. Go 10 miles to Grand Lake Stream general store and take sharp right onto Canal Road. Camps are on the right (sign).

Canal Side Cabins are on one of the side roads leading to Grand Lake Stream dam. The compound itself is set up on a small knoll with the white main house slightly in front and the cabins ranged in an L behind it. Some of the cabins have tree names (corresponding to the trees near them).

John: "Originally our house here was the lodge. It's from the late 1800s. In 1922 they opened up the first cabin. There's some great pictures of oxen and horses carrying Grand Lakers (canoes) up to West Grand Lake where the guides would hire a paddleboat operator, load their sports into the paddleboat, tie their canoes to the back, and the paddleboat would bring them all the way up to the northern end of the lake. Then they'd take the day paddling their sports back down. When they first opened this place for business in 1922 they were called Brown's Camps, which they were for the longest time, then they went to Canal Site Camps and then, when we took over in '99, we changed it to Canal Side Cabins. People from away don't know what a camp is, and got that and 'site' confused with it being tenting.

"The canal's right below us. It was put in around the mid-1800s. Grand Lake Stream was hosting the world's largest tannery (where the hatchery is now). And what they would do is bring a hemlock log down to the dam, strip the bark off, lift the bark over the dam, and float it down the canal three-tenths of a mile to the tannery, where it was made into tannic acid for the tanning process.

"I've been coming to Maine since I was a kid and fell in love with it. I'd come up for hunting and fishing trips to different areas. One day, me and my son stumbled upon Grand Lake Stream and we just didn't want to leave. Every year we'd come up two or three times maybe. I'm thinking, 'There's gotta be a way for us to stay.' I talked to my wife and we came up to look at some camps. Well, while we were driving around (actually at that point looking for moose), the former owners here just happened to put up a FOR SALE SIGN! Our daughter saw it, called us, and said, 'You've got to come and see this camp.' And it all worked out. I was involved in Boy Scouting quite a bit at the time, and a friend of a friend through Scouting called, asked if we were selling our house, and we sold it right off to him. So it was like we were meant to be here. The past owners are sweethearts, and helped us with any little thing. So here we are.

"At first I tried to hire guides, but I could just never get enough guides. So I thought, well I'll just have to become one myself. I'd rather hire from the outside and keep town people working, but if I can't find anyone and I have someone that wants to fish here, I don't want to ruin their trip because I can't get a local guide. So I became a Master Maine Guide. I'm a camp owner, not a full-time guide, but I fill the void from time to time. Grand Lake Stream has always been known to have the highest concentration of Maine Guides in the state. I'm just trying to think now who's not a guide! Randy Spencer, who's our resident folksinger, and who has a couple of CDs, was taking a guide's class. The question came up, Why did he want to be a Maine Guide? And he looked back at the classroom and said, 'Cause I'm tired of being the only one in town that's not.'

"The typical guide routine is that the night before you spend time getting your cook wood set (we use birch or maple), your cookware together, make sure your canoe's in good shape, you're fueled up. A lot of times we don't know where we're going to go until we pick up our sport. Most of the sporting camps have a lodge area where guides stage and talk, but most of us talk amongst ourselves during the night. Usually we try to get on the water by 8:00 in the morning. We fish 'til about 11:00 or 11:30 and then pick a lunch ground. The Guide's Association has lunch grounds on various lakes that we maintain, with a firepit, couple picnic tables, a work table with a little canopy over it, and we cook 'em up a fine shoreline dinner with boiled coffee. There's 'two schools of coffee.' Mine is I use a medium-sized coffee boiler with around a half gallon of water and about a quarter pound of coffee, to keep them awake for the afternoon fishing, and one medium-sized egg. You mix the egg—yolk, white, shell, everything—with the coffee in a bowl, make a paste out of it, and then put it into the coffee pot that has water boiling. I keep the lid on the pot and take it off the fire, placing it in front of the flames with the spout facing into the fire. As the spout heats, it creates convection and constantly draws the water through the grinds. I let that simmer there the whole time I'm preparing onions, potatoes, fried fish." *Alice:* "Do you have a backup if nobody's caught fish?" *John:* "I have yet to eat onions and potatoes alone! Anyway, you don't want the coffee to boil, you just want to keep it rolling, so you watch and pull it away from the fire a little if you need to. Just about when your potatoes are done and you're about to start your fish—'cause the fish are pretty quick—I take my coffee away from the fire over to a rock, some secure place, and take the lid off. This causes the cool air to hit the top of the coffee grinds, which settles 'em right down to the bottom. Grand Lake Stream guide's coffee, which is the way it's been done forever, is to pour a ladle's worth of Grand Lake Stream water on top, which settles the grinds. Maybe I do it my way because I don't have a ladle!

Mary: "The Fourth of July we have a little parade in town and everybody's mostly in it. Afterward we have a little rubber ducky race down the stream to benefit the locale D.A.R.E. program in the schools." *John:* "Then the last full weekend in July there's the Grand Lake Stream folk art festival.

"In the fall, we have quite a few guests that come up bird hunting and they said, 'Gee, you've got a lot of fishing stuff up on the walls, but no bird stuff.' So I said, from now on when you shoot a nice bird, partridge or ruffed grouse, save me the tail and I'll dry it out and pin it up. (We do have woodcock also, and some duck hunting.) Anyway, you fan the tail out, tack it onto a piece of plywood or foam, and put a little borax or salt on the fatty part of the tail to keep the bugs out. We have a nice set of them in one cabin.

"We do have people who come up here for Thanksgiving, Christmas, or New Years. For Christmas, we set a box of decorations out on the porch and a bow saw. We also set a nice balsam by the side of the cabin if they want to use that. If not, they can take a walk and find one of their own. We have some people that decorate the whole cabin with lights, inside and out, and just have a great time.

"Once we get past the holidays, we're into ice fishing. One year we guided a group of 18 guys from a college fraternity. They had their reunion up here. Four fellows were from Texas and they'd never been on the ice before, never been on a snowmobile, never mind just fishing through a hole! They had an absolutely great time. They were the last to come off the lake, didn't want to leave. There's a lot of ice fishing. February's actually our busiest month. West Grand doesn't open until February first, to protect some of the spawning fish, but the other lakes open January first." *Mary:* "You'd have to see the ice shacks out there, they're like houses. They have stoves, chairs, beds in them. It's like a little village." *John:* "The season lasts until March 31, depending on ice conditions. There are regulations for West Grand Lake: you're allowed two salmon 14 inches or better, two togue 18 inches or better, eight whitefish, and there's no smelting allowed. I'd say 80 percent of our ice fishing is by Mainers. And the other thing is you can take a sled [snowmobile] right from the cabins onto lots of trails. We are the only sporting camp in town that's open all year round." *Mary:* "We've gotten involved in town things because of this. I used to go walking for exercise, but couldn't really get anywhere because I'd see people and we'd stop and talk. So I started an exercise class. And John is a selectman.

"We have really nice people here at camp, and they're always asking about moose. So sometimes I'll say, 'Okay, about 5:00 be ready, and I'll take you moose-watching.' The other thing is when we can we'll sit around our campfire toasting marshmallows, and tell stories and make little cherry pies over the fire. You take two pieces of bread, put some cherry pie filling in between, put it in this two-sided metal toaster we've got, and they love that. Summertime we take the people that really want to do things with us and we go berrying. Then we come back and make pancakes with the blueberries.

Beer Butt Chicken

John: We do a kind of chicken here at camp called (sorry about this) 'beer butt chicken.'
What you do is you get yourself some nice, healthy looking chickens, a six-pack of beer, take

a good swallow out of a beer, and you insert that beer can into the cavity of a well-seasoned chicken. Set the chickens on the side of your outside fire. You want indirect heat, slow roasting. We use a #12 galvanized bucket to put over the top of them to keep the smoke and heat circulating in there. Keep them going for about 4 hours. And what happens is the outside cooks dry and crisp and the inside is moist. The beer seals all the moisture inside. Anything to do with cooking and drinking you'll find most guides there. So after 4 hours, lift the chickens up, take the beer cans out (careful they're hot!), and wrap the chickens up in aluminum foil, and put them in a cardboard box to tenderize for about 20 minutes—enough time to make your french fries—and you're ready to eat.

83. COLONIAL SPORTSMEN'S LODGE

AP/HK

OWNERS: Steve and Pat Takach
ADDRESS: Grand Lake Stream, ME 04637; 207-796-2655; e-mail: takach@nemaine.com; www.fish_gls.com
SEASON: May 1 through October
ACCOMMODATIONS: Five cabins with porches, indoor plumbing and shower, electric lights, automatic heat, satellite TV. Call regarding pet policy.
RATES: $95 per person per day (AP); $60 per cabin per day (HK)
ACCESS: I-95 to exit 55 (Lincoln). Take ME 6 east to US 1 at Topsfield (40 miles). Turn right onto US 1 and drive south 16 miles. Turn right onto Grand Lake Road. Go 10 miles to the village store in Grand Lake Stream. Continue right and go over the bridge where you'll see the camp sign ahead.

Colonial Sportmen's main lodge, a white farmhouse, sits back up on a knoll of carefully mowed grass. Cabins, off to one side and near the trees, head down the hill toward Grand Lake Stream itself, visible and audible from the lodge's long porch.

Pat: "These camps were the first commercial sporting camps in Grand Lake Stream. The earliest brochure I have is from 1908, but before that they took care of the high mucky-mucks when the world-famous tannery was in business. You can see where the chimney was from here. There's nothing left of the building, but it was on the site where our fish hatchery is now. It was originally called Ouananiche Lodge. Ouananiche is the Indian name for landlocked salmon. And they had an outcamp called Sunset Camps on West Grand Lake. It was started by a Mr. Rose and a Mr. Boyton, who belonged to the New York and Boston yacht clubs. They then sold to Weatherby's, and at that point some of the oldest camps or cabins were moved to Weatherby's. The place was then bought by a man named Peabody, who was going to have it as a private estate, and he sold off some more of the camps. The result is we have only three of the original cabins.

"When the camps were first operating, the settlers cut all the trees to build the town. There was basically nothing here except one family—it was the tannery that brought people. Before the town became a 'plantation,' we were what the state calls an unorganized township, which means the state oversees the territory. In the early days a guide used to get $3 for one person, $4 for two, and the rates for camp were $2.50 a day and $15 a week.

"This area is famous for its fishing. Fly-fishing for landlocked salmon in the stream opens on April 1. About the middle of May, the first fly hatches produce top-water fishing with dry flies. In the fall, when the water cools, spawners return. Grand Lake Stream is 2 miles of fast water, boulder falls, and deep pools. Grand Lake, beyond the dam, has been noted for its landlocks since the late 1800s. It is 19 miles long with over 100 miles of shoreline, and most people prefer trolling around it. We also have brook and lake trout, white perch, and pickerel. Plus, you can't find any better fishing for smallmouth bass, especially the first three weeks in June. For those who want saltwater fishing, we are only an hour's drive from the Machias River—which has 60 miles of public water for Atlantic salmon fishing—and from Passamaquoddy Bay and New Brunswick."

An old brochure gives some trolling information:

> With his craft moving about two miles an hour, the fisherman, comfortably seated, pays his line out slowly, till about one hundred feet is in the water. He may get a strike during this process, or he may be in dreamland when the visitor arrives . . . the rod dips suddenly. The reel screams. The old hand snubs his fish for a second to insure the hold, and the game is on.

> The togue tugs hard, shakes his head savagely, rarely breaks water, but fights every moment, making his last spurt when he sees the landing net. His worst trick is to roll over and over at this moment and sag heavily, often breaking tip or line; and, if netted safely, this move is sure to mean a snarl.

> The brook trout is a racer under all conditions. With a free lake, his rush is less dangerous than the spurt for the sunken bush (in a stream); but the pleasure is balanced by the fact that the brook trout run large in the lake.

> The ouananiche is the finished acrobat and strong man, resourceful, almost tireless, and a relentless fighter. When he calls, there is rarely any doubt in the mind of the fisherman as to the nature of his guest. He has evidently spent the winter with a storage battery. An ouananiche may break water a dozen times while on the hook and appreciates the value of a good finish. Woe to the novice who does not watch for that last dip! Once in the net, he is a glory, marked like his lordly cousin, with fine indigo spots on a coat of burnished silver. And, further evidence of fine breeding, he improves on acquaintance. Broiled over the coals, he wins the heart and

stays with you like a man. A few hardtack, a pound of salmon, and a pint of coffee make one fit.

An even older brochure, 1908, asserts:

It is unquestionably true that nearness to nature has an elevating influence upon heart and character. Nature is a school of all the hardier virtues. What, for instance, can impart a more effective lesson in patience than a day's fishing? These quiet places, fortunately, are not beyond the reach of people of moderate means, to whom the "call of the country" means peace and freedom, not the mere shifting of the scene of social dissipation and rivalries.

Grand Lake Cookies

Pat: "I've had this recipe since I moved here. I got it from one of the girls in town and still make them."

2 cups sugar, 1 cup (2 sticks) margarine, 3 eggs, 1 tsp. cinnamon, ¼ tsp. each cloves and nutmeg, 1 heaping tsp. baking soda, 1 tsp. vanilla, 1 package raisins (ground; pulse in Cuisinart), 3¾ cups flour

Beat sugar and margarine, add eggs, spices, baking soda, and vanilla. Stir in raisins and flour. Turn out on floured board and roll out to ¼ inch thick. Cut with cookie cutters. Bake at 350 degrees for 10 minutes or until golden.

84. GRAND LAKE LODGE

HK/MAP
OWNER: Ken Smith
ADDRESS: PO Box 8, Grand Lake Stream, ME 04637; 207-796-5584;
e-mail: lakelodge@nemaine.com; www.nemaine.com/grandlakelodge
SEASON: May ("ice-out") to October 20
ACCOMMODATIONS: Six log cabins: one to three bedrooms, screened porch, indoor plumbing and shower, gas and wood heat, electric lights; well-behaved pets allowed
RATES: $40 per person per day; motorboats $38 per day, canoes $15 per day; family, child, and midsummer rates available
ACCESS: I-95 to exit 45A (Bangor). Take ME 9 east to US 1 north through Princeton. Turn left onto the Grand Lake Stream Road. Go 10 miles to the general store and take a sharp left onto Canal Street. At the end of the street (the dam) take a right turn up a dirt road (sign). (Bangor to camp is approximately 100 miles.)

Ken: "Our place is approximately 300 yards along the eastern shore of West Grand Lake, above the dam. We have a small mooring with canoe and boat rentals. Five of our six cabins are set within 25–30 feet of the lake shore. West Grand is 13,340 acres, but also from here you can go to Pocumcus (known as Cumpus), or up Junior Stream into Junior Lake, around into Scraggly, and if the water's high enough, you can go up to Bottle Lake. It's 20-some miles of waterway you can navigate. And, with short canoe carrys, there are other lakes you can go to. West Grand Lake, along with the stream, which is a very short walk from here, has some of the best fishing and fly-fishing for salmon in the state. As everyone knows, most of the landlocked salmon in Maine came from Grand Lake, from the hatchery. It started out as a federal hatchery and then, in the early 1900s, was converted to a state hatchery. When they started, a certain percentage of the fish were kept for West Grand Lake and the rest were sold or put elsewhere. There's a daily limit of two salmon from the lake, and three or four years ago they started catch-and-release from October 1–15 in the lake and October 1–20 in the stream. The stream closes then after the 20th.

"These camps have been sporting camps since 1946. They were started by a guy by the name of Allen. In 1978 my parents bought them and I've had them since 1986. I grew up in Lincoln. Dad worked in the mill in Woodland and decided that he wanted a set of camps. I had three boys that grew up here. I worked in the mill also, and did these camps besides.

We do a modified American Plan if people need or want it, and we sell resident and nonresident fishing licenses. A nonresident season license—this is for 2002—is $50, a week is $38, a three-day is $21, and a one-day is $9. You can now go on-line and buy your license. The only requirement is you have to do it in time so they can mail it to you before you leave. You go to the Department of Inland Fisheries and Wildlife page. We get a lot of traffic on our web site; that's something that's really changed in this business.

"One of the best things about this place is its location. We're right on the water, and we get a lot of people with their own watercraft. They leave them tied up and don't have to worry about putting boats in and taking them out. We have fantastic sunsets right from the cabins, and then there's the peace and tranquility of it all."

85. GRAND LAKE STREAM CAMPS

HK
OWNERS: Nancy and Gary Betz
ADDRESS: PO Box 17, Grand Lake Stream, ME 04637; 207-796-5562
SEASON: May through October
ACCOMMODATIONS: Five cabins: one to two bedrooms, porch, indoor plumbing, private shower house; wood heat, electric lights; pets welcome
RATES: $26 per person per day

ACCESS: I-95 to exit 55 (Lincoln). Take ME 6 east to Topsfield (40 miles), then take US 1 south 14 miles to Grand Lake Road. Take the right onto Grand Lake Road and go 10 miles to the general store in Grand Lake Stream. Turn left along the stream. At 2 miles, turn right on the road with signs that include the Betz name.

Grand Lake Stream Camps is a cozy compound right along the shore of Grand Lake Stream with a lived-in, homey look. A guest oversees Nancy's refinishing project, Gary putters among the outsized plants in his lush vegetable garden, a guest's dog meanders slowly by while his family prepares for a bike outing. The cabins are a dozen yards from a homemade swinging bridge that spans the gurgling stream.

Nancy: "We've been running these camps since 1973, but we actually started coming here in 1966." *Gary:* "We had a nice little hometown in New Jersey, but two developers showed up and doubled the size of the town. It was too late to save what we'd had, so I had to leave. I was a surveyor at the time and Nancy worked for a pharmaceutical company until we had our family, a boy and a girl. So we bought these camps. I was 29, and my son bought Nicatous Lodge when he was 29!

"The history of the place is that a man named Hill Gould built the original two cabins, Mallard and Teal, around 1927. He was a guide and lived in the farmhouse right down the road. Then he sold to Jack Page, who sold, in 1948, to a Captain Elliott, who was in the merchant marines. Captain Elliott put in the three other cabins and had it 25 years until we bought it. From the stream, we have boat access to Big Lake, so we have the best of both worlds."

Nancy: "The people of Maine almost lost this beautiful area. It all started in October 1992 when the Land Use Regulatory Commission wrote us a letter asking if we wanted a public hearing. Georgia-Pacific Company was planning a 30-lot subdivision right along the stream, if you can imagine! We got other signatures on the petition and had the hearing in the schoolhouse. It was a packed audience and about 30 people spoke. The Passamaquoddy Indians said there used to be a campground for them on our site. And arrowheads and pottery have been found here. The falls area used to be their burial grounds, and they wanted it protected."

Gary: "We were getting ready to put the place on the market because we'd already been through this twice, once in New Jersey and once in New Hampshire, where we used to live in the winter. We knew we wouldn't want to live here with a housing development. We found out a lot of other people in town felt the same way. Most of the people who live in Grand Lake are here for a good way of life. You sell your way of life, what you really care about, and you may get rich quick, but slowly (and sometimes, not so slowly!) you feel real poor."

Nancy: "Anyway, it took the Friends of Grand Lake Stream almost three years to get approval from Georgia-Pacific to buy the land and to raise the money. There are only 180 full-time residents here, but the town gave $10,000, L.L. Bean gave $50,000, the Land for Maine's Future gave $70,000, and about 400 individuals raised more than $90,000. The Maine Coast Heritage Trust was the backbone of the whole effort. The purchase included a 500-foot easement on the other side of the stream. It was incredible. I mean, none of us here had any background with this kind of thing. We honestly didn't know what we were doing at first. But you learn, and it was something that people felt strongly about. We had our celebration in October 1995. We put up a tent at Little Falls and former governor Angus King came, and Leon Gorman, the head of L.L. Bean, and Bucky Owen, commissioner of inland fisheries. Leon Gorman presented Governor King with a fishing rod and the governor caught his first salmon at Little Falls. He is so charismatic—what a speaker. He gave his speech in waders!"

Gary: "It was such a successful grassroots effort that it's become an example for other conservation projects. It would be great if we could do what happened here on a larger scale. I think we should take all the major watersheds in Maine and protect the land around them and the islands in them for future generations."

Nancy: "There's so much history in these places. I've somehow ended up as president of the Grand Lake Stream historical society. In 2000, members and friends raised enough money to purchase the old 1800s Brown Homestead for its new museum. We started fundraising July 17, raised over $80,000, and were able to close November 17! A book written by Minnie Atkinson around 1918 called *Hinckley Township* tells a lot about the village."

She writes that the Passamaquoddy tribe, who live in this region, "formerly used the east bank of Grand Lake, Witteguergaugum, or 'landing place,' as a portage from Grand to Big Lake so frequently that even the rocks are worn." The tribe was able to maintain its obscurity from outside intervention (both Native American and European) by living in "a vast waterway which afforded hiding places." Jesuit missionaries established a spiritual foothold with the tribe, and that religious allegiance was not swayed when the English took over the region in the early 17th century.

However, the tribe took an active part in the Revolutionary War on the American side. After the War of 1812, the region reverted to the English, who planned on making it a Canadian province called New Ireland, but the Peace of Ghent returned it to the United States. The area was called the Hinckley Township after Samuel Hinckley, a probate judge from Northampton, Massachusetts, who paid $9,711.18 for the 30,770 acres in 1811. The first white natives of Hinckley were the children of David "the General" and Ellen "Aunt Nellie" Cass, who came to Big Lake in 1820. In 1810 a dam was built across Grand Lake Stream and "pioneering languished" but logging flourished. Logs were floated down the

Gary and Nancy Betz of Grand Lake Stream Camps

lakes or down the West Branch of the St. Croix River to Milltown, near Calais and St. Stephen, 30 miles away. In 1869, "the turnpike" was built right to the stream to service what was to become the largest tannery in the world. Sportsmen started arriving the very next year, "hiring Indian guides and fishing only the stream." The instant village unofficially took the name of its famous stream and officially became Grand Lake Stream Plantation in 1897, when the village formed its own government. The tannery closed in 1898 and by 1900 the population had plummeted from over 500 to 221. But sportsmen had found their mecca, and the rest, as they say, is history.

Nancy: "People come up here to experience the beauty, be someplace that hasn't been developed, hasn't changed. And these undeveloped places get fewer and fewer. We know. We have kids here right now who were given the choice of Disneyland or Grand Lake Stream and they said they wanted to come back to Grand Lake. It's partly this spot, and partly things like my kidlike husband taking them out in the middle of the night in the Jeep to look for bears! The time just flies here. We love our people, some of them come three times a year. As we say, you either love it or you don't. But if you come here to Grand Lake Stream and love it, you get hooked for life."

86. INDIAN ROCK CAMPS

AP/HK

OWNERS: Ken and JoAnne Cannell

ADDRESS: PO Box 117, Grand Lake Stream, ME 04637; 1-800-498-2821 or
207-796-2822; e-mail: indianrockcamp@nemaine.com
SEASON: Year-round
ACCOMMODATIONS: Five log cabins: two bedrooms, porch, indoor plumbing
and shower, electric lights, wood and automatic heat; pets welcome
RATES: $70–82 per person per day (AP); $30–45 per person per day (HK)
ACCESS: I-95 to exit 55 (Lincoln), then ME 6 to Topsfield (40 miles). In
Topsfield, take US 1 south about 15 miles to Grand Lake Road (right turn,
sign). Go 10 miles to the village of Grand Lake Stream. As you enter the village, look for the CANOE sign on the left by tennis court. The camps' driveway is above a church on the right.

The dark brown log cabins of Indian Rock Camps are in the village of
Grand Lake Stream, but the place feels like it's in a little world set apart.
The porch of the main lodge is full of fishing, historical, and wildlife trea-
sures, and three rooms are set for dining.

JoAnne: "We've had these camps since 1987. Ken and I always fished
and hunted with our dads when we were young. I was brought up in Bath
and Ken in North Windham, on Sebago Lake, so we're both Mainers.
Basically, we found this place by accident. We were on a trip and got lost
driving back roads. We came to Grand Lake Stream and fell in love with the
area. At the time Ken was a mason and I was a hairdresser. We'd raised a
son and he was off and married and we decided before our daughter was off
we were going to do what we wanted to do.

"The camps were started in the late 1800s. They're the third oldest
camp here. It was originally one cabin that belonged to a Mr. Yates and
because of the tannery it grew. It was and is one of the few places with a
barn. The sportsmen who came here originally were rich gentlemen from
the Boston area who had stock in the tannery business. The sporting
camps are really the major industry in town. There are about 85 people
who live full-time in Grand Lake Stream, and it grows to around 200 with
the summer residents.

"We live here year-round and are the only ones who run a dining room
in the winter. After October 20 we do reservations for all meals, but during
our regular season we're very flexible. If guests call ahead, I will cook anything they want off the menu. And whenever they want to eat they tell us
and that's when I'll serve them. We also have a take-out service, so people
who need lunch are welcome.

"Ken is the only Native American registered Maine Guide in Grand
Lake Stream who owns and operates a sporting camp. Grand Lake has a
very active group of guides. In fact, the area has the largest single guides
association in the state. We maintain mountain-biking and snowmobiling
trails; we're right on ITS 84 and have a very active snowmobile association. We just had a bird-watching group in from Texas, and we encourage

hunting with a camera. For gun hunting, the bear, in particular, is good. Many people come up for historical reasons, to see the Passamaquoddy lands and artifacts.

"Ken is a Micmac. The Passamaquoddy reservation surrounds us, and they have concerns about the cutting of ash trees and sweet grass by the sides of the road because they use these for their beautiful baskets. They showed me arrowheads from Mount Kineo, way over at Moosehead Lake, that are here because they were used for trading. There have been an ongoing number of intermarriages between the Passamaquoddy, Micmacs, and Penobscots, but there is still a real sense of their history as individual tribes and as a people. It is a very spiritual culture. The tribes are in the process of getting their own museum here at Indian Township.

"We are very interested in tradition and history and nature. We have the camp checkbook ledger from the 1920s and, on the porch, a collection of natural objects like big wasp and hornets' nests, and family heirlooms. I collect old fishing creels, reels, and rods. For us, this area is like the old Maine. We want to develop it focusing on the natural resources here. And because of this we have people coming from all over the world to see the town that raised its own taxes—we voted down $5,000 and raised it to $10,000—to save our stream from traditional property development. By developing the property in its natural state we are allowing its long-term use by many people.

"Each year we have one very special time called Celebration of Life Week, when we open up, free of charge, to families who have children with cancer. The town is invited to a cookout before the families leave and everyone gets involved. The guides volunteer their time, the townspeople help with cooking and cleaning, our next-door neighbor does magic tricks, another neighbor sings. We started this in 1996 because of our daughter, who has been fighting the good fight over and over for years. She is the bravest person I know. It will always start on August 10, which is when her tumor was found, and is also our anniversary, and go until August 17."

Fall Soup

This is good for any vegetable you may have in the refrigerator, and it tastes even better in a day or two.

2 pounds hamburger, 2 medium onions (diced), 6 potatoes (peeled and cut in chunks), 6 to 8 carrots (cut in chunks), cooked cabbage (cut in chunks), one stalk celery, other veggies you have

Stock: 5 beef bouillon cubes, 2–3 T "kitchen bouquet" herbs, dash Worcestershire sauce, ½ tsp. garlic powder, ½ gallon water

Sauté hamburger and onion in a little bit of butter until hamburger is brown and onion transparent. Place stock ingredients, hamburger-onion combination, and all vegetables in a large, heavy pot. Bring to a boil, lower the heat, and simmer for several hours if possible (or until the carrots and potatoes are cooked). Serves 12 to 15.

87. LEEN'S LODGE

MAP, SCA
OWNER: Charles and Cecilia Driza
ADDRESS: PO Box 40, Grand Lake Stream, ME 04637; 1-800-99-LEENS or 207-796-2929; www.leenslodge.com
SEASON: May 1 through October 31
ACCOMMODATIONS: 10 log cabins: one to eight bedrooms, indoor plumbing and tub with shower, woodstove or fireplace, gas backup heat, electric lights; pets welcome
RATES: $100 per person per day (MAP); motorboat rentals, canoes and kayaks free. Guided fishing and hunting packages; child rates available.
ACCESS: I-95 north to exit 45A (Bangor). Take ME 9 east to US 1 in Barring. Turn north on US 1 north, through Princeton, and turn left on Grand Lake Stream Road. Go about 9 miles. Turn right (sign). The dirt camp road is 2 miles long.

Leen's camps are a family business, owned by Charles and his sister Cecilia and run by Charles and his son, Charles. The camp is located on 23 acres, on spring-fed West Grand Lake. The cabins dot a peninsula and circle a cove. The log main lodge has a large dining room, and the adjacent Tannery Room is a sitting room and gaming area with a whimsical fish mobile. Both rooms have large, west-facing picture windows for sunset viewing.

Charles: "One of my first guests this year, a Mr. A. D. Leavitt, came to visit and informed me that he was the designer and builder of our wonderful fish mobile here in the tap room where we're sitting. It was great to meet him; he's just a wonderful gentleman. He built that, I'm thinking, in the early '60s for Stanley Leen. The camp's got a colorful history. Stanley Leen purchased the camp in 1958, at which point it was called Pine Point Lodge, I believe. And because of Stanley's influence in the State of Maine, and his group of famous sportswriter friends, and nationally renowned baseball players, the place became tremendously famous. A. J. McClane, at the time I believe, the editor for *Sports Afield,* was very good friends with Stanley. He'd written many books, like *The Greatest Hunting and Fishing Lodges of North America,* and included Leen's Lodge in those books. He thoroughly enjoyed fishing here for landlocked salmon, lake trout, and smallmouth bass. And the place has maintained its status as a great sporting camp both for fishing in the spring and for family vacations in the summer.

"Stanley Leen was really dedicated to servicing his clientele. Kathy

Leen, his daughter, was kind enough to spend time with me in 2001, when I first got here, and educate me on some of the operating methods from Stanley's day, which really focused on customer service, making the customer feel as comfortable and relaxed here in the Maine wilderness as they can. My staff and I have really taken her advice in many areas to continue the tradition that Stanley Leen developed.

"We are in a very unique area in the State of Maine because we have so many lakes—about 18—available to us. Because of our exposure, we do get the prevailing westerly winds that get this lake very churned up some days, at which point we'll just bring our clients over to one of the other lakes, to Grand Lake Stream, or the rivers—the St. Croix and adjoining flowages. So we can almost guarantee that we can take people fishing any day they come here. The lake we're situated on, West Grand Lake, is about 15,000 acres. It, in turn, is connected to several other lakes, which greatly expands the acreage of water available to someone to right from our dock. (Anyone who's at all interested in looking at a sporting camp would want to know how many acres their lake is, not mileage.) But from one end of the lake to the other is maybe an 8- to 9-mile boat ride. This area is part of the St. Croix watershed: the water goes through the St. Croix River, which divides Maine and New Brunswick, out to the ocean through the Bay of Fundy. Guests who come here will typically take a day trip to Canada or explore opportunities along the east coast of Maine.

"Our fishing goes until the middle of October, but during that month we also focus on upland bird hunting for grouse and woodcock. The woodcock flights that come out of New Brunswick are of interest to the bird hunters that come here in search of timberdoodles, as they're referred to.

"I've had a passion all my life for fishing and hunting. And I've always dreamed about spending a significant amount of time in this kind of environment. Some of my best experiences in life have occurred in log cabins on lakes. So it just made sense, with my background in fishing and hunting, my interest in cooking, to bring it all together. I'd been researching sporting camps primarily in Maine and the Midwest for about eight years. The beauty of the Maine landscape and the clientele make Maine sporting camps the special places they are. The Midwest, the terrain is a lot flatter, and the clientele was very different. The people who come here are similar to those who visit Alaska. I think they embody a real love of the wilderness experience, especially since a lot of them are coming from the cities. The Midwest doesn't have as much of a distinct difference between the big cities and the wilderness areas. Perhaps the clients who come here appreciate the experience more because it's so different than where they're coming from. But yet, it's close enough to drive here. So Maine, and what Leen's had to offer, was absolutely a perfect fit. I now live year-round in Grand Lake Stream, with my son, Charles (the fourth Charles in the family), who's going to the local high school. He's a big help to me during the summer season.

Leen's Lodge

"I truly believe there's a spirituality about Leen's Lodge in West Grand Lake. The lake is crystal-clear. I think the positive energy about where we are permeates the lodge and the people who come here. I find it fascinating to watch how people will change dramatically during their stay here. When they come, they may be fairly uptight about things, concerned about the service they're going to get. But after two days, we are literally friends. And the environment becomes one of a group of friends. That's why we're offering this place for conferences and retreats. People come here and get to a point of total relaxation and peacefulness.

"It's important to preserve sporting camps because in preserving these places we're preserving the sporting-camp experience, which we're losing to some extent throughout the country. It's like a step back in time. There is some hope because there's a land trust group that's formed and is in the process of purchasing all the land that's contiguous to West Grand Lake for zero future development. I'm the owner of Leen's Lodge, but I see myself primarily as the caretaker of a tradition in an historical place that Stanley Leen started. One of the quirky things about the place, and many of my older clients say this, is that the ghost of Stanley Leen stills presides at Leen's Lodge. I've had several instances of unexplainable events, like lights going on and off, things being moved, that fuel the story. And certainly, I know from being around him this last year, that he's just a very friendly, wonderful man. There never was a bad thing said about him. And I can only hope that someday I'll be the host he was."

Leen's Lodge Wedding Soup

Meatballs: 1 pound ground beef, 2 eggs, 1 cup seasoned bread crumbs, salt and pepper

Soup: two 48-ounce cans of chicken broth, 1 cup of pastina, 2 bags of fresh baby spinach, 2 eggs, Parmesan cheese

Charles: "First you make the meatballs. Mix the ground beef, eggs, bread crumbs, and salt and pepper to taste. Roll into marble-sized meatballs. Put them on a cookie tray and roast them in a 400-degree oven for 15 minutes.

Put the chicken broth in your soup pot. Add the meatballs, 1 cup of pastina (very small Italian pasta), and fresh baby spinach, cut into small pieces. Simmer that for 20 minutes. Right before serving beat the eggs and drizzle them, while stirring, into the hot soup. Serve with Parmesan cheese.

88. LONG LAKE CAMPS

AP/HK, SCA

OWNERS: Sandra Smith and Doug Clements

ADDRESS: PO Box 817, Princeton, ME 04668; 207-796-2051; e-mail: longlake@nemaine.com; www.longlakecamps.com

SEASON: Mid-May through October 31

ACCOMMODATIONS: Fourteen log cabins: one to two bedrooms, porch, indoor plumbing and shower, wood heat, electric lights; pets welcome ($5 per day per pet)

RATES: $80 per person per day (AP); $55–80 per 1–3 people per day (HK); motorboats $40 per day, paddleboats and kayaks $20 per day, canoes $15 per day; child rates

ACCESS: I-95 to exit 45A (Bangor). Follow ME 9 to Barring. Turn left onto US 1 north to Princeton. In Princeton, take a left onto West Street. Go a couple of miles to the camp sign on the right (beyond the airport) and drive 2 miles in to the camps.

Long Lake's cabins sit at the water's edge, their dark-stained logs blending with the tree trunks of the surrounding tall pines. A main lodge (with three dining areas, pool table, and sitting room with VCR and movies) rests, like the hub of a wheel, in the middle of the compound. It may be the large number of cabins, or the location of the main lodge, but one expects kids and counselors to come tumbling out the screen doors. A swimming area, dock, and boathouse full of games and books add to the summer-camp feel.

Sandra: "The history of these camps begins in the early 1940s with Maine Guide Eddy Jones. He described the atmosphere as a 'quiet woods camp with the easy informality that goes with log cabins and wood fires.'

Long Lake Camps

We have the same philosophy and are very laid-back and flexible.

"We bought these camps in May of '97 after spending the past 10 years involved with other sporting camps. We liked these camps because we thought they had a wonderful location, and we thought they were good camps for family vacations because people can do things here or do a variety of things within an hour or so drive. They can go across to Canada (where there's a great chocolate factory) and then, half an hour away, there's St. Andrews, a beautiful coastal community with art galleries and so forth. We're an hour from Campobello Island and the Quoddy Head Light. We have golf courses, hikes, canoe trips, a wildlife refuge, and the village has a couple of tennis courts. There's just so much to do. We're trying to take advantage of this by offering all sorts of specials, like guided kayak and canoe trips and wildlife and bird-watchers' tours, a women's fly-fishing school, a photography workshop. We have all the freshwater attractions, plus the ocean is only an hour away. This is an historically significant area. Also, there's an airstrip right up the road from camp, which makes us easy to get to.

"We're on a peninsula on the south side of Long Lake, which is part of a huge water system—West Grand Lake, Grand Lake Stream, Big and Lewey Lakes, the Grand Falls Flowage, and the St. Croix River. All of the waters from West Grand and Big Lakes drain down through Long Lake through the 'neck' right in front of the camps, which are all virtually right on the water. Landlocked salmon pass through this neck every fall and spring. There are also over 20 miles of interconnected waters that offer some of the best smallmouth-bass fishing in New England. Charlie Moore, from the New England Sports Network, has been at camp three times and made nine TV shows based on the excellent fishing here.

"September is warm days, cool nights, great catch-and-release fishing, a touch of fall foliage—a beautiful month in Maine. October we have grouse and woodcock hunters who can either bring their own dogs or use a guide's. We don't have kennel facilities, so people bring whatever works for them. One mile up the lake on the opposite side is a Passamaquoddy Indian reservation and on one side of us the state owns a site for the University of Maine at Machias, so we have some protection."

Great-Grandmother Smith's Blueberry Cake

Sandra: "I think we may be the only sporting camp that doesn't have set times for meals. We don't wait on our guests hand and foot. They can come in the kitchen if they like. In fact, we just had a guest who cooked us dinner, which was great!"

> 3 T shortening, 1 cup sugar, ¾ cup milk, 2 eggs, 1¾ cups flour, 2 tsp. baking powder, 1½ cups lightly floured blueberries

Cream shortening and sugar together by hand. Add milk and eggs and mix well. Sift dry ingredients together and add and mix. Carefully stir in blueberries. Pour into greased and floured 8-inch baking pan. Bake in preheated oven at 350 degrees for 25 to 30 minutes.

I was taught to cut a piece as soon as it was out of the oven, and to cover the top with butter.

89. MAINE WILDERNESS CAMPS

HK
OWNERS: Charlotte and Bill Bowes
ADDRESS: HC 82, Box 1085, Topsfield, ME 04490; 207-738-5052
SEASON: Year-round
ACCOMMODATIONS: Seven cabins: one to two bedrooms, screened porch, indoor plumbing and shower, wood or gas heat (some with fireplace), electric lights, full kitchen facilities; campsites are available, some with water and electric hookups
RATES: Cabins $70–80 per day, $450–525 per week
ACCESS: I-95 to exit 55 (Lincoln). Take ME 6 east for 34 miles. Turn right at a large sign for the camps and go 4 miles in to Pleasant Lake. Pickup at Bangor International Airport is available.

You emerge from the camp's access road onto an expanse of lawn with unobstructed views of Pleasant Lake. The cleared area is surrounded by 40 acres of forest with footpaths in the woods and a mile of shore frontage. The camps are a mixture of cabins and campsites, which are unobtrusive enough to maintain the traditional sporting camp look. The camps are a ¼-mile portage from the Grand Lake wilderness waterway. The centrally located log main lodge serves as a gathering spot for guests.

Charlotte: "This was originally called the Duck Lake Club, founded in the late 1870s. They had three places: the original one on Duck Lake out of Springfield, this one here on Pleasant Lake, and one down at Pocumcus Lake, which they called the Birches. Guests would be boated down into Junior Lake, Junior Stream into Scraggly Lake, into here and then back, all in one day. The head guide got $2.50 for paddling all day and he had to give $1.25 back to the Duck Lake Club. The other guides got $1.25. The club is gone, the Birches is now private, and we're open to the public.

"The first mention of a building here is in 1917. This main lodge they called the clubhouse and the name of the original cabin is the Gold Brick. This property was all potato fields, and they had a barn, cattle, and a huge bathing beach. Unfortunately, most of the sand is gone now. The club owned this place until 1949. Then Roy Spencer, who was the head guide at all three places, bought it. In '72 it was sold to a retired commander from the Coast Guard who changed it into the Maine Wilderness Canoe Basin and used it for canoeing, biking, and hiking trips. They brought in kids from all over the world. He owned it until '85. Then a couple of retired policemen from Massachusetts bought it and they ran it for one year as the same thing, for the kids. The next owners, Terry and Paula McGrath, bought in '89.

"We bought the camp in '98. When Bill was in the service he lived in Caribou, and he flat loved it. He always said he was going to move back up here. For about four and a half years he looked everyplace: New Hampshire, Maine, Vermont, even Alaska, and this was the one that was the best. We love it, and we'd never leave. We live here year-round. We have quite a few of the old customers. The first year we started out we had 3 seasonals—guests who rented camper sites for the whole season; now we have 10. And we have people who've been coming back for years and rent a cabin for two weeks.

"The camp is at the very beginning of the Grand Falls Flowage. This lake is 1,500 square acres, 120 feet deep. The camps are on 43 acres, and practically all the rest is owned by the lumber company, so there's basically nothing else on the lake. It's stocked with lake and brook trout and land-locked salmon. General law. And there's lots of whitefish in here: white perch. They're a bottom feeder, maybe 16 to 18 inches long, have a really tiny mouth. They're really good eating, have a delicate flavor. Inland Fisheries came up and gill-netted in the lake because they wanted to see how the togue is doing—you can't take togue out of this lake—and they caught a ton of whitefish. It's not too bony and fillets up good.

"This area has always been known for hunting. We have moose, bear, and a little bit of goose and duck hunting, for black ducks, and really good deer hunting. We have people who come from North Carolina to Florida every year to stay here for 10 days to hunt. We're always full for moose season too. We have lots of snowmobilers and ice fishermen. If the road gets too bad, we just don't plow it at all. People park down at the end of the road and snowmobile in. They think that's just the greatest. They stay in the cabins. The lodge isn't heated so we don't use it in the wintertime, just use it for storage after November. The east wing of the lodge has water to it all winter long; we have to shut the water to the cabins off in winter. And we have a frost-free faucet out by the kitchen window and guests just fill four or five buckets, take the buckets into the cabin, and use that for drinking water, washing water, for flushing the toilet. It's all pure water. They keep a pan of water on the stove and that gives them hot water all the time. Ninety-nine percent of the winter people are only here for a weekend anyway, so the water's really no big deal.

"In the summer, one of the things we do is we have dessert night in the lodge. It's usually on a Friday or Saturday night and everyone in this campground is included. It just gives people a chance to sit around and meet everybody. You make new friends and taste a little dessert. I make things like rhubarb or apple pies, or some kind of cream pie, fruit streusel or custard. Also, some of our seasonals are avid fishermen. Sometimes they'll bring us fish and we put it in the freezer. When we've collected a whole bunch we have a fish fry out front for the whole campground. Everybody gets together and brings a potluck dish, and usually Bill and Vic, our handymen, fry up the fish. A good 90 percent of our fishermen, I want to say, are catch-and-release. Or in the fall, if someone gets a moose, we've been known to have a mooseburger party out front too.

"When we got here one of the things we did was build a new rest room and we've filled in and leveled off quite a few camper sites. We bought all new refrigerators for the cabins, and put in new toilets and showers. We have a new one-bedroom cabin down by the pines. And over on the hill we have a remote site that's only accessible by boat. It's a tenting site. Being here was completely different from what we'd been used to. Bill was an animal control officer, I'd managed a bakery and worked in a store. It really has been a learn-as-you-go experience. But I would never ever trade it. We've had trouble with the road, with other things, but we just keep going and it's great really, just wonderful."

90. THE PINES

AP/HK, SCA

OWNERS: Steve and Nancy Norris

ADDRESS: PO Box 158, Grand Lake Stream, ME 04637; 207-557-7463 (cell

phone); 207-825-4431 (winter); e-mail: info@thepineslodge.com;
www.thepineslodge.com

SEASON: May 15 through September

ACCOMMODATIONS: Five log cabins: one to five bedrooms, port-a-potty, sink,
water cooler, central toilets and shower house, gas lights, woodstove; two
guest rooms in main lodge; two HK outpost cabins

RATES: $70 per person per day (AP); $475 per cabin per week (HK); motorboat, canoe, kayak rentals available

ACCESS: I-95 to exit 55 (Lincoln). Travel east on ME 6 through the village
of Springfield. Take right onto South Springfield Road. Go 5 miles and
take right onto a dirt road and follow signs into camp (about 16 miles).
The last mile is a narrow driveway along the shoreline of Lake Sysladobsis.

The Pines has the look of a homestead surrounded by tall pines and log
cabins. The main lodge is a two-story white-clapboard house with a generous front lawn. The cabins are snug at the base of the pines out on the
peninsula or on the wooded side of the front yard. The Norris children,
Vanessa and Matthew, are an integral part of the camp scene.

Steve: "If you talk about the history of this place, it's been in one family since 1938, and they had scrapbooks going back to 1891. The original
builders were the Shaw brothers from Canada." *Nancy:* "It was built to be a
sporting lodge and was fashioned after a lodge up on the Miramichi River
in Canada. Our guest cabin on the point was the first to be built, in 1883,
and then the lodge was the year following. Can you imagine building a
house like this with no roads or anything in here? Boards all flat-sided,
amazing!" *Steve:* "They brought stuff in by a steamer that came down from
the head of this lake (Sysladobsis) to a big tannery in Grand Lake Stream. I
think they employed something like 2,000 people down there, which at the
time was like a metropolis. Now it's gone completely the other way and it's
just a little fishing village."

Nancy: "Anyway, Shaw married a schoolteacher from Pennsylvania. I
bet she wondered what she was getting herself into!" *Steve:* "They raised two
little girls in here. The Shaws had it until the early 1900s. Then the Chase
family bought it and had it nearly 30 years. Then in 1938 the Lewis family purchased it and in '84 a niece of the Lewises' got it and kept it going
until we purchased it in '92. The Lewises were 83 years old when they finished their last season, and in their later years—this is really intriguing—
all the guests would come out back and help with the dishes. So our first
year here a lot of the long-term guests returned, which we really appreciat-
ed. Well, all of a sudden they'd be up from the table, bringing their dishes
out, scraping them off, and we're thinking, what happened?! We weren't
used to that because that was part of our service, you know. But they were
such loyal guests, they wanted to help this old couple."

"Sysladobsis is a 9-mile lake with landlocked salmon in the spring and smallmouth bass the rest of the season. We have a remote pond you can hike to, and there are miles of interconnected lakes which make up what's called the Eastern Maine Canoe Trail.

"As far as our own history—you've heard the names Ruth and Charlie Norris many times, I'm sure. Briefly, Charlie, my dad, was a mechanic at the Boise Cascade mill, but he had a deep love for the woods and was a guide up at Pierce Pond Camps for years. His dream was that someday he'd own a set of camps. He and Floyd Cobb, Gary's father, were close friends and guided together. And old Floyd beat him to the punch by, I think, a day or two at buying Pierce Pond Camps. My dad was crushed. But as it turns out, years later, when he was 52, he decided to leave the mill—with eight children and hardly a penny in his pocket—to go to Kidney Pond in what is now Baxter State Park.

"At the time, 1968, Kidney Pond Camps didn't have the recognition, so it was a real risk. I was 8 years old then, the youngest, so I had the good fortune of growing up in the sporting-camp business. I was there the whole 20 years, except for a couple of years when I took a hiatus and stuck my toe into the outside world and didn't like it. I worked for the Farmers Home Administration—federal government, subsidized loans, forms in triplicate—working out of Caribou and Waterville [Maine]. I went to the University of Maine at Orono, Nancy went to the University of Maine at Farmington." *Nancy:* "That's when we met. Steve's mother hired me as a waitress in '79 and I never left, basically! We got married in '83 at a church in East Millinocket, where I grew up, but we had our reception at Kidney Pond." *Steve:* "We closed camp a day or two early so we could make room for our wedding party. But Nancy organized that whole wedding with no phone, 30 miles from the nearest town, had—I don't know—a couple hundred people up there for the reception. It was great. It was crazy! I got thrown in off the camp dock by my brothers, tuxedo and all."

Nancy: "How we ended up here—it took five years of looking. We've flown, snowmobiled, walked, and driven into places." *Steve:* "We looked at 27 different sporting camps just to see what was on the market at different times. See, in '87 the state chose to revert Kidney Pond Camps, take it back. The family had leased it, so we had no equity. And they just didn't renew the lease, so we were basically left out in the cold. Mom and Dad were retirement age anyway and Dad was ill, but we wanted to be at Kidney Pond. That's why we had put our time in. But it wasn't to be."

Nancy: "We had in our minds just the right place we wanted. We just didn't find it until we found this. We'd heard about The Pines from the previous owners. They were interested in having us manage it, so we thought we might as well go have a look. I said to Steve, 'You know what's going to happen? We're going to drive in and it's going to be the place we always wanted. And it's not going to be for sale.' And that's exactly what happened.

The Norris family welcomes guests to The Pines.

ALFRED J. COOPER

We drove in and it was like, this is it! That was in 1990." *Steve:* "They want-ed us to work for them, but we wanted equity." *Nancy:* "We didn't want to manage for someone else. If we're going to work this hard, we want to work for ourselves."

Steve: "We knew the business, we had clientele, we wanted to find our own place and get the ball rolling. I mean, each year that mailing list would stale on us a little bit more and people would go to other sporting camps. Fortunately, we were able to buy the place from them and start in. One point that's crucial for young couples like us, with limited funds, is that it's hard enough to buy a house, to say nothing of a big business with proper-ty. To go in and buy a property like this and operate with limited revenue, especially seasonally, is really a hard ticket." *Nancy:* "We're doing our win-ter jobs to allow us to do our business in the summer. A lot of people find seasonal jobs in the summer. Our seasonal jobs are really in the winter."

Steve: "I was talking earlier about the problem at Kidney Pond with leasing? Well that's one of the main issues we're tackling with the Maine Sporting Camp Association [Steve is finishing his term as president]. With the old timber companies there was some stability. Now with these new, out-of-state corporations, sporting camps on leased land are in a vulnerable position. Back in 1979 out-of-state people were buying up old sporting camps like crazy and a lot of camps went under. It was one of the most dev-astating times for the industry. That's partly why we all formed the Sporting Camp Association, to try to save the sporting-camp industry. And we're still working at it.

"Our kids' grandparents spent time in here with us. My mother was here several summers and loved it." *Nancy:* "Steve and I spent a lot of good years with her at their Kidney Pond camps. But it's a hard business to be in if you're sick or of retirement age. You have to be pretty self-sufficient being so far out in the woods." *Steve:* "We generate our own electricity with a 10KW generator, solar power—panels and an inverter that changes DC power to regular AC current, and propane for lights, cooking, and refrigeration.

"See this steep stairwell here in the kitchen? It was built back in the 1880s by Bill Shaw, the guy with the two little girls, right? Seems he went up the lake in the winter of 1907, and they found him the next spring, frozen in the ice. Left that family . . . Well, he used to come downstairs this way a lot, I guess. Now, this door here has a nice sturdy latch and all of a sudden, with no wind, no one walking on boards, without anything, it would just pop open. That's serious! We watched it happen couple of years ago for the first time." *Nancy:* "So now every time we see it we say, 'Hi, Bill. How ya doin'?'" *Steve:* "Ever since 1907, first the Chases, then the Lewises, and now us, we've all seen it. I don't know, it's crazy. So now when old Caribou Bill Shaw comes down, we figure, well, here he is to check us out and see if we're running the place right."

Creamy Garlic and Dill Dressing

> 1 gallon mayonnaise, 1 quart buttermilk, 4 cups sour cream, 1 cup vinegar, 2 cups sugar, 1 cup garlic powder, ½ cup dill weed, ½ cup onion salt

Blend all ingredients. Refrigerate.

91. RIDEOUT'S LAKESIDE LODGE

AP/HK

OWNER: Bob Jr. and Jami Lorigan, Bob Sr. and Annie Lorigan

ADDRESS: RR1, PO Box 64, East Grand Lake, Danforth, ME 04424; 1-800-594-5391

SEASON: May 1 through September 30

ACCOMMODATIONS: 22 log and clapboard cabins: porch (on most), indoor plumbing and shower, propane heat, electric lights; HK cabins have gas or electric stove, electric refrigerator; pets welcome

RATES: $75 per person per day (AP); $280–480 per cabin per week (HK); motorboat rentals available, canoes and kayaks free with AP

ACCESS: I-95 to exit 55 to Lincoln, then ME 6 east to Springfield. From Springfield, take ME 169 to Danforth and then go 3 miles north on US 1 to the blue state camp sign and driveway, on the right-hand side of the road.

As you pull into Rideout's you pass under a huge sign spanning the driveway. A little village of red-brown log cabins with green trim is to the right and a large salmon-colored main lodge is to the left, right down at the water's edge and beside an expansive boat dock. Separated slightly from this main compound is a set of housekeeping cabins with their own dock and parking area. The main lodge's honey-colored, log dining room has large picture windows looking out onto East Grand Lake.

Bob Sr.: "We're right in the center of East Grand Lake, at Davenport Cove, and you look out these windows right into New Brunswick, Canada. Larry Rideout was the first owner of these camps. He began work on the place in 1947, and developed 90 percent of what we do today. When he was in business, he catered to a lot of professionals. The president of L.L. Bean would come up frequently. Rideout owned it until 1964, when he sold to George Graham, who had it from '64 to '84, when he sold to us."

Bob Jr.: "Jami and I have microbiology and chemistry backgrounds. We were in EPA-related work for Hewlett Packard in Colorado for 20 years. When our division was separated from the parent company we decided to do something different. And since I was already a silent partner of this, we decided to become active partners."

"We've got a large, relatively undiscovered lake here. We're located on the west side of East Grand Lake about the midpoint of the lake in a sheltered cove. You look out at New Brunswick, which is 4 miles directly across the lake. It's about 8 or 9 miles to one end and about 10 miles to the other end of the lake. We're in close proximity here to the best salmon fishing throughout the year. And because of that we have our guests coming in for a hot lunch in the springtime. Later in the season we provide bag lunches. But not many camps will take the time or expense to provide a hot lunch. People can just zoom in and out from the great fishing in like five minutes. We have really long docks, over 200 feet long, so we can accommodate large boats. And we have 16-foot-long rental boats, rather than the standard 14 feet, with four-stroke motors. People like the fact that there's a bare minimum of smoke and noise from the motors.

"We're nationally recognized for having an exceptional lake for landlocked salmon. We're also recognized for having one of the best bass fisheries in the United States. Our lake is unique in that it's got both of those species in high numbers. On a good day in the spring you can catch up to 30 salmon a day, and when the bass are on their beds and you're sighting with bass probes they can catch over 100 bass a day. We have a lot of people who come here who are accomplished fishermen. They don't want a guide; they don't need a guide.

"Another thing we're unique in is that we have American Plan and housekeeping coexisting harmoniously here. We have large lakefront housekeeping cabins and a group of people who are totally devoted to that sort of lodging. On the other hand we have groups of people who only want the

The dining room at Rideout's

full-meal, full-service plan. They're mixed in the main camp here and then, over at our 100-foot dock we've got housekeeping exclusively. We do allow our housekeeping people to eat dinners on Wednesday and Saturday nights if they would like to take a break from cooking. After the 26th of June every year we let the general public come in to the restaurant Wednesday through Sunday in the evening for dinner, by reservation only.

"We've got the warm, wood interior in the dining room. All these buildings were put up in the 1940s, and it gives you the sense of a real classic lodge when you come in, with the moose heads on the wall." *Bob Sr.:* "We serve Down East cooking and basically the menu hasn't changed in over 50 years—rib-eye steaks cooked on the open fire, roast pork, which I guess we're famous for, because you can't get a seat in here most Wednesday nights, barbecued chicken, baked ham, pot roast, and every Sunday we have a traditional Thanksgiving dinner." *Bob Jr.:* "Our breads, pies, and pastries are excellent."

"In terms of the way we operate around here, we're very laid-back, casual. You won't find a snob within a hundred miles of here. We're very direct, genuine, honest and very accommodating to our guests. People kid around a lot, joke around here. We like to think we're the sporting lodge for family fun up here. We've got 12 kayaks, excellent canoes, guides who take people down remote local rivers; we have mountain bikes; we have a nice little beach."

Jami: "People have such a good time. They're not here just to fish, but to see old friends, and that's a big part of the atmosphere." *Bob Sr.:* "It's like a class reunion. Basically, we think we're reasonably priced, clean, have a good restaurant, and a beautiful spot."

Oatmeal Bread

Annie Lorigan: "This bread recipe has been handed down and doctored up here and there. People come from all around and ask for it. They'll order loaves of it when they come in for dinner."

2 cups oatmeal, 1 cup molasses, ¼ cup sugar, 2 T salt, ⅓ cup oil, 4 cups boiling water, 10 cups bread flour, 4 T dry yeast

Put first five ingredients in a large, heat-proof bowl and pour the boiling water over everything. Stir and let set 45 minutes until lukewarm. Meanwhile, put yeast into ½ cup lukewarm water (it will rise and bubble up). Add this to the lukewarm first mixture. Add the flour and mix well (we use a machine, so 10 cups works for us). Knead until smooth, and place in a greased bowl. Cover or let set away from cold drafts until the dough has doubled in bulk. Punch down, divide into 8 equal balls, and place 2 balls per greased loaf pan. Cover until risen over the top of the bread pan. Bake at 350 degrees for 35–40 minutes, until golden and bread sounds hollow. Take out of the oven and butter the tops of the bread. Makes 4 loaves.

92. SHORELINE CAMPS

HK
OWNERS: Jim and Carolyn James
ADDRESS: PO Box 127, Grand Lake Stream, ME 04637; e-mail: info@ shorelinecamps.com; www.shorelinecamps.com
SEASON: May through October
ACCOMMODATIONS: Ten gray cedar-clapboard cabins: one to three bedrooms, screened porch or sundeck, indoor plumbing and shower, wood stove, electric lights
RATES: $64–90 per cabin per day; child rates and motorboat rentals available
ACCESS: I-95 north to exit 45A (Bangor). Follow ME 9 east to Barring. Turn left onto US 1 north through Princeton to Grand Lake Stream Road on left. Proceed 10 miles on Grand Lake Stream Road and take a left at the Pine Tree Store. Go 2.4 miles to camp sign on left.

Shoreline Camps

Shoreline Camps is another camp in this book that does not have the traditional brown log construction, but has the "right" location and feel. A line of cabins sits on a sandy beach of appropriately named Big Lake. A few picnic tables and outdoor firplaces dot the immaculate grounds.

Carolyn: "These camps were built, one at a time, by Roy Bailey in the early 1940s. He served meals here, and his son Earl and his wife took the camps over when Earl got home from the service. Earl's daughter then took over and ran them for a few years, and that's who we bought them from in 1986. When we bought them there were six cabins sitting down front here on the water.

"We're both from around here, both brought up in Woodland. We had always wanted a camp, just a summer place for us, on West Grand Lake. We were finally able to buy one and moved up there summers. And then we started buying a couple of old camps and fixing them up with the idea to rent them. Of course that's all leased land up there, and they wouldn't let us do it. So we sold them. My husband was out snowmobiling with my father one day, and he came across these, asked about them, and they were for sale. They were very rundown, just about had it, but they were on land we could own. He came home and told me to come see what we'd bought, and I did. Never done anything like this before and wasn't really excited about it at first. They were in bad shape, but he told me we'd fix them up. And that's what we did.

"My dad, my husband, and my son, Greg, did the majority of the work. They had, I think, three done over when Dad passed away. So then my son and husband kept going and we did all the ones down front. Where the house is sitting used to be an old gravel pit, with an old dump out back. We cleared that out, built the house. Then he decided that we really needed some more camps, so he started clearing up back and he's built six new buildings up there. Some of them are big—storage buildings and three new cabins.

"The camps here are located just above where Grand Lake Steam comes into Big Lake. In the spring and fall the salmon fishing is very good, but this lake is really known for smallmouth bass. We have people who come from all over the country to fish here. And it has pickerel and white perch. We've had a few bird hunters come in, and some bear hunters during the season, but we close in October as soon as the stream closes so we don't get a lot of hunters. We don't open the cabins in the winter.

"In the spring and fall we get fishermen, but probably a good 85 percent of our people come back same week, same cabin every summer. We have people who've been here before we bought the camp, and some folks who come stay with us five or six weeks at a time. My daughter-in-law's father does most of our guiding, my son guides, and I can hire guides. My son lives right on the other side of the camps.

"When we first opened the place it was a big job because the cabins all needed to be completely redone. And the grounds were untidy. My husband and I are both neat-freaks. So he has worked long and hard, still is every day, keeping up the outside, and I'm very proud of the inside of the camps. We do provide all the linens, the beds are made, the towels are there, and a lot of other little amenities. Cleanliness is our number-one priority, and we get a lot of complements on the camps.

"I have no desire to put TVs in. Our camp is very quiet. I mean, I like people to laugh and have fun and all, but we don't want parties until two or three in the morning. We have a lot of families, young children. Our three granddaughters have made some great friends because of these camps."

93. SPRUCE LODGE CAMPS

HK
OWNERS: Ron and Kat Bradford
ADDRESS: RR 1, Box 716, Springfield, ME 04487; 207-738-3701; e-mail: alanrokamidmaine.com
SEASON: May through November
ACCOMMODATIONS: Four log cabins: two to three bedrooms, screened porch, indoor plumbing and shower, electric lights, automatic heat, woodstove (in one cabin), gas stove and refrigerator; pets allowed
RATES: $100 per cabin per day; $500 per cabin per week
ACCESS: I-95 to exit 55 and bear right onto the access road (cross the

Penobscot River). At the flashing red light, turn left onto US 2 through Lincoln to the traffic light and monument. Turn left at the stop light. Go 0.1 mile to a fork and bear right onto ME 6. Go about 20 miles, through Springfield. At the top of a hill, at the sign BOTTLE LAKE ROAD turn right. Go 6 miles, then turn right onto a dirt road (at camp sign). Go 2 miles to the camp driveway on left.

Kat: "These camps have been in operation nearly a hundred years. They were called Bayview Camps originally, and we have the old brochure from when Joseph Patten was the owner." A quote from the brochure describes the camps much as they would be described today: "situated on high land on the shore of the lake, and consisting of the main house and several cabins. The sleeping rooms and cabins are all furnished with good spring beds, mattresses and easy chairs.

"Lower Sysladobsis ('Dobsis') Lake is 11 miles long and is part of a huge waterway that was used by the Penobscot Indians when they traveled from the Atlantic Ocean to the Great Lakes. We have lake and stream fishing here with landlocked salmon, smallmouth bass, white perch, pickerel, and some brook trout. The wildlife around here is amazing: loons, eagles, osprey, cormorants, and ducks. Sometimes in the early morning you can see a beaver or muskrat swimming around the docks. Moose are also here, because we have apple trees and berry bushes.

"We have housekeeping cabins, which are great for families—and we get a lot of families. For those who need supplies, Smith's Grocery Store is 8 miles from camp on good roads. In our main lodge we have a mounted rack of what we believe to be the largest white-tail deer ever taken in the State of Maine. It has a modest rack—13 points—but holds the state record and has been written up in the newspaper as holding the national record for the largest deer. Its live weight was estimated at 485 pounds; my husband's grandmother and grandfather got it in the mid-fifties. Also in the lodge we have a telephone for our guests, and we provide daily mail service. We're close to churches, a hospital, and major tourist attractions such as Baxter State Park, and yet we're tucked off here in this corner where it feels peaceful and quiet."

94. VILLAGE CAMPS

HK
OWNERS: Lance and Georgie Wheaton
ADDRESS: HC 81, Box 101, Forest City, ME 04413; 207-448-7726; fax: 207-448-9382; e-mail: lancew@nciz.net; www.thevillagecamps.com
SEASON: Year-round
· ACCOMMODATIONS: Six log cabins: one to two bedrooms, indoor plumbing and shower, gas furnace or wood heat, gas or electric stove, electric lights, well water; well-behaved pets allowed

RATES: $60–80 per cabin per night; $380–480 per cabin per week; motor-boats $50 per day; child and fall and winter rates available
ACCESS: I-95 to exit 55 (Lincoln). From Lincoln, take ME 6 east to Topsfield (40 miles). Turn left at Topsfield onto US 1 north to Brookton (8 miles). Turn right at the sign to Forest City and go 12 miles. Camps are on the left (sign).

The Village Camps line either side of the driveway behind Lance and Georgie Wheaton's white-clapboard house. Dark-stained log cabins lead down to a small, quiet cove where guests can look out to East Grand Lake sunsets.

Georgie: "This place was built as housekeeping cottages in the '50s by a couple of buddies and were originally called the Ed and Don Cottages. We've been here since April 1969. My husband, Lance, was born and brought up right down the road, where Wheaton's is. He's the middle of the three brothers. We'd been married about a year and a half, were working in Connecticut, and had just come back to Forest City from a fishing trip when Lance's folks said this place was for sale. I was young and foolish, so here we are! I knew practically nothing about fishing. I'm from Sherman [Maine], so I do know the out-of-doors, and my brothers were into fishing, but I never was. So when we started running the camps I was doing things like calling fishing rods 'fishing poles' until Lance said, 'Look, if you're going to be running a sporting camp, you'd better start learning what these things are called.' Which I did. And I also learned the names of the various flies right off.

"We raised three daughters here, and it really was good for them in many ways. It's a safe, healthy environment, and they're very people-orient-ed because they've been around a lot of people all their lives. The downside has been that we're so far from 'civilization.' They had to travel 24 miles, one way, to school each day. And they had to miss out on a lot of events. But I think it has made them stronger and more self-reliant. Because we live in an unorganized territory, the state provides tuition for the school of our choice plus gives transportation money, which can then be applied toward boarding a student. This is what we're doing with our youngest daughter now. And Lance is traveling because he's representing Washington County on the advisory committee of the Inland Fishery and Wildlife Council.

"I'm happy that we can offer people the option of housekeeping cot-tages. We have a lot of professional people coming here, so it's not simply a matter of money. Some guests just don't like to be confined by certain eat-ing hours. They figure, if the fish are biting, they don't want to have to hurry back for a meal. For guests going out with a guide, we prepare a shore dinner and sometimes when we have families in during the summer, we'll have a camp potluck supper down by the rec hall cookout area."

Lance: "We're a four-season place here. In the winter we actually have more ice fishing than snowmobiling. I spend my time stocking our ice shacks with wood for guests. It's good fishing here, as always—some of the best anywhere. In the fall there's hunting: deer and moose October through November. In October, I go out and do some bird hunting. We don't kill many birds generally, but we have a lot of fun just wandering around in the woods. I mean, there's more to hunting than killing. It's not like fishing, catch-and-release. There's no such thing as shoot-and-release. So most of us just enjoy the chance to be outside on a nice fall day.

"My grandfather, Arthur, built canoes, and my father built canoes, so I figured I might as well, too. I've been making 21-foot Grand Lakers. I'm old-fashioned and stubborn and never wanted to copy what anyone else had done, so I built a mold myself. But I hated the canoe, the way it handled, so I made a second mold the next winter. I changed it seven times until I got what I wanted. No more changes now, it's a dream—rides well and is safe with a load. I want a canoe that can do the job for the guides, one they can afford and use without a lot of repairs. My canoes are all handmade. The ribs and lining are northern white cedar, the thwarts are ash, the gunwhales are spruce, because they hold their shape, and the heel, stern, and stem are out of white oak. I'll use about 4 or 5 pounds of tacks for a canoe. My bows are indented slightly to split the water in a clean arch. To make it, you 'strake'—or cut, trim, and plane—all the individual pieces of wood to a different taper to lay and fit into the bow. A Grand Laker canoe has a square stern, is generally 18 to 21 feet long, with a 40- to 44-inch beam, and 16 to 20 inches deep. It is rib-built, which means there are pieces of northern white cedar that are bent to go all the way around the canoe for strength. When I take an order for a canoe, I tell my customer, 'I do this because I love to, and I make canoes when I have the time. I know you're on the list, and every time you call to ask me when I'm going to be done, I'll add $100 to the price.' That usually lets me do my work in peace. Then, when I've finished a canoe and hand it over to my client, I tell them with a grin, 'Don't forget, the green side goes down!'"

Lance has been putting down some of his remembrances and someday hopes to compile them into a book. In the meantime, here are two gems:

> One day my father and I were in the shop when a fellow stopped by to say hello. While we were talking, the man looked over to a rack of axes we had on the wall. He said that the ax on the bottom of the rack looked really old, and father said that it had been in our family for over a hundred years. "I've had to change the head on it three times," my father added, "and the handle nine times." The man nodded and left the shop. We don't know if he ever realized that it wasn't a very old ax!

> Another time, I was guiding a couple from New York City and we were out fishing for salmon on East Grand Lake. It was an overcast day in early spring with light mist in the air. The water was flat calm. If any of you have ever fished on that kind of day, you'll know what I'm talking about. The water

Georgie and Lance Wheaton and one of Lance's handcrafted Grand Laker canoes

with the mist had streaks across the top of it. Now, what makes these streaks is beyond me, but I've seen them a million times. About midmorning the lady in the party keeps looking at the lake and finally turns around and asks me, "Lance, what are those streaks out on the water?" Without thinking I answered, "Oh, that's where a car drove on the ice last winter." She looked around for a moment and then said, "Isn't that amazing they would stay there that long." With that I was in so deep, I didn't dare reply!

95. WEATHERBY'S

MAP, SCA

OWNERS: Charlene and Ken Sassi

CAMP ADDRESS: PO Box 69, Grand Lake Stream, ME 04637; 207-796-5558; e-mail: weather@tastelme.net; www.weatherbys.com

WINTER ADDRESS: RR 1, Box 2272, Kingfield, ME 04947-9729; 207-237-2911

SEASON: May 1 through October 1

ACCOMMODATIONS: Fifteen log cabins: screened porch, indoor plumbing and shower, gas or electric lights, gas heat

RATES: $110–140 per person per night

ACCESS: I-95 to exit 45A (Bangor). Take ME 9 east to Barring. Turn left onto US 1 through Princeton and left onto Grand Lake Stream Road. Go about 10 miles to Grand Lake Stream village. The camps will be on your right (sign).

Weatherby's is set back on a knoll in the center of the village of Grand Lake Stream. A gracious white farmhouse with wraparound porch welcomes guests. The cabins, a mixture of shapes and styles, range around the top and one side of the knoll. The camps are within walking distance of the village store, the stream, and the boat landing for the lake.

Charlene: "Weatherby's originally was built because the largest tannery in the world was here in Grand Lake Stream. The tannic acid from the hemlock bark was very plentiful in the area and people would come to Grand Lake to have their hides tanned. Places like Weatherby's, which originally was called the White House in the Birches, were built in the late 1800s to house the people who'd come and have to wait four to six months for their hides to be tanned. They would come and, you know, leave a little bit in the area. The English and Scottish ancestry is strong, although now there's no particular ethnic group."

According to historian Minnie Atkinson's book *Hinckley Township:*

> The tannery was built in 1870 and bark camps were established on the shores of the upper lakes. Two or three hundred men were employed at these camps in a summer season as well as 400 pairs of horses for bark hauling. Forty cords of bark were consumed in a single day as well as 25 barge-loads of imported tan extract per week. Another 200 to 300 men worked at the tannery itself. Sometimes 1200 hides would be finished in a day. On May 11, 1887, fanned by a tremendous wind, four main tannery buildings were flat ruins in 45 minutes and ice in the lake, still a foot and a half thick, was broken and driven to the foot of the lake. In 1898 the tannery was closed. The White House, which had accommodated a few sportsmen, was sold in 1895 to Stephen Yates, son of the first pioneer in the area, and the number of sportsmen visiting increased.

Charlene: "My involvement with sporting camps goes back to my parents, Ruth and Charlie Norris, who were in the business at Kidney Pond Camps at Baxter State Park. Back in 1901, the Balls from Massachusetts bought these camps and put in cabins and a garage. It was called Balls Camps for many years. Then Mr. Rutherford Weatherby from New Brunswick bought it and ran it for 33 years. His son, Beverly Weatherby, the gentleman we bought it from, had it for 25 years. When we first bought the place, in 1974, we didn't have much money. We signed the papers in September and had a couple of weeks' work. But we had no business all winter. None. I mean, no food, nothing! We wondered what we had done. Ken's an engineer and he had dropped all that to go into the woods. It was a little scary that first winter, believe me, living in this big old place, with two kids, and trying to heat it. Our daughter, Jessica, was 12 and our son, Mark, 6 at the time. So it was a little tough for them. They bused 23 miles to the town of Woodland for school. We were just waiting for our first season—couldn't wait to see what would happen!

Ready for action in Grand Lake Stream Village

"That first winter, nobody came to visit. I was shocked! I thought in a little town people would love to meet the new folks. They didn't. I'd stand in the post office and say, 'Isn't anyone my neighbor?' That's the truth! Really, I was terrible. We all laugh about it now. People are very skeptical, you know— new people, oh! Well, the neat part was that we were Mainers. And that's what saved us all these years, even in the town. After a few years they finally accept-ed us, and now we're perfectly accepted. After 30 years, we're part of the wood-work, really, part of the wood. People can't wait to see how the summer will be, because if they work or don't depends on how our business is.

"I do all the cooking. For breakfast, I'll go into my special pastry room, with its baking oven, and start to make muffins and cook bacon or sausage. When we're cooking for 40 and want to get it done, if the guests come right in, I can feed them in 20 minutes—and that's to order, anything they want! After breakfast we have a staff meeting and plan our day. We have to be very organized so that we have time in the middle of the day, because there are no days off. Sometimes we don't know—other than that the menu changes—what day it is! Some weeks I don't go off this lot, and that's the truth. I love to garden. So when everyone's off and I have a few minutes, I go into my flower garden—that's my time."

Ken: "For many years we've had L.L. Bean's fly-fishing school here. They come in on a Thursday and finish up late Monday afternoon. It's for stream fishing mostly—12 to 14 students with four instructors. The school's main focus is to teach people the basics of fly-casting. And most of the time is spent with your fly-rod in hand and studying the motions of your peers, which always brings a smile! A couple of the instructors come up early to see what's going on in the stream, to check the amount of water coming through the dam by the hatchery.

"The Grand Lake Stream salmon hatchery is run by the Inland Fisheries and Wildlife department and is one of the few hatcheries in the state. About half the lakes in the State of Maine are stocked with landlocked salmon from the hatchery here. They run cold water through it, which helps keep the stream a little cooler. I've been working with the paper company to regulate the water flow. Paper companies are becoming aware that they affect a lot of people when they change the flow pattern. As the temperature of the water gets hotter, the trout and salmon become stressed and it's harder to catch them. Fortunately, a few years ago, all the land along the stream was purchased and turned over to the state to remain forever wild.

"We have 25 or 30 registered Maine Guides, the most of any sporting camp. And they all have to be approved by me. Grand Lake is one of the best fishing areas in the Northeast. We have landlocked salmon, lake and brook trout, smallmouth bass, white perch, and pickerel. You can have a pack lunch or go out with a guide in one of our Grand Laker canoes and enjoy a guide's cookout. We have a monument right in town that's dedicated to our guides from Grand Lake, and the last weekend in July we have a folk art festival dedicated to the Grand Laker canoe. In the past few years sports have been catching-and-releasing a number of Atlantic salmon from the stream. Can you imagine fishing for a 20-inch landlocked and catching a 20-pound Atlantic! We do have a fishery."

Guide's Perch Chowder Fritters

Charlene: "This is 'something new for Charlene' and they came out great! One of the guides brought in some leftover perch chowder and I served it to our guests that night. There was still some left so I decided to make fritters. I added some mashed potato, salt and pepper, and scooped them out with a cup and cooked them on a hot skillet. They were beautiful and brown. I offered one to a guide and he said, 'This is perch!' (He didn't know I had used the chowder leftover!)"

Guide's Chowder, Grand Lake Style

4 pieces of bacon, 2 large onions (cut into good-sized chunks), 2 stalks celery (cut up), a few potatoes (peeled and cut in chunks), 2 to 3 cans of evaporated milk, salt and pepper to taste, perch fillets

Fry up the bacon. Add onions and celery and cook until soft. Add potatoes and milk and a little water to thin out the stock. Cook until potatoes are almost tender. Place perch fillets on top of stock, cover, and steam fish until cooked through and flaky. Guides may also have some seasoned salt, hot sauce, or special pepper they like to use. If there is any left over, proceed with fritters as above.

96. WHEATON'S LODGE AND CAMPS

AP, SCA

OWNERS: Dale and Jana Wheaton

CAMP ADDRESS: HC81, Box 120, Brookton, ME 04413; 207-448-7723

WINTER ADDRESS: PO Box 261, East Holden, ME 04429; 207-843-5732; e-mail: wheaton1@hotmail.com; www.wheatonslodge.com

SEASON: May through September

ACCOMMODATIONS: Ten gray-clapboard cabins: one to two bedrooms, screened porch, indoor plumbing and shower, electric light, wood heat

RATES: $92 per person per day; child and midseason rates available; motorboat $45 per day; canoe, windsurfer, kayak, and mountain bike free

ACCESS: I-95 to exit 55 (Lincoln). From Lincoln, take ME 6 east to Topsfield (40 miles). In Topsfield, turn left onto US 1 and go north to Brookton (8 miles). Turn right at the Forest City sign and go 12 miles. The camps are at the end of the road (Forest City).

Dale: "My father, Woodie Wheaton, started these camps in 1952. He was quite a well-known guide and his roots go to Grand Lake Stream. My mother graduated from Massachusetts College of Art and taught painting. You'd never know she was a sporting-camp person, but she was strong on the inside work. Every good sporting camp involves a strong woman—it has to. My mother's sister was Alice Weatherby, and they sold Weatherby's to Ken and Charlene Sassi. My uncle, Bev Weatherby, came up here and guided for my father. I was two when my folks started Wheaton's and I have two brothers. We all grew up in the stern seat of a canoe. So my family's been in the sporting-camp business for what must be 65 years.

"We got on the map in the late '50s by virtue of some articles in *Outdoor Life*. At that time Spednic Lake was regarded as the best smallmouth bass lake in the world. As you market yourself in the accommodations business, you have to carve out what your strength is and specialize. And our strength is fishing. You can get bass one day and landlocked salmon the next. We've been written up by *Sports Afield* as one of the best fishing lodges in North America. A 4-pound smallmouth bass is considered a trophy fish in every state in the union and we catch 25 or 30 at our lodge every year, almost all of which are released. In 2000 we caught the world record for smallmouth bass with a flyrod here. And the exciting news in 2002 is that we're catching big Atlantic salmon. The lake we're on, East Grand Lake, is 18 miles long and flows into Spednic, which is 25 miles long. They're the largest of the Chiputneticook chain of lakes, which forms the boundary with Canada. In the course of a summer we'll fish 10 or 12 different lakes."

Jana: "We met at the University of Maine. I never really went out with Dale until the night before graduation, so it was a near miss. I went on to teach physical education, and he was writing his thesis in economics at the University of Nottingham, England. His folks, when they were ready

A camp breakfast at Wheaton's

to sell, approached all the 'kids' to see if we were interested. At that point, none of us were. We were kind of young and I don't think ready for that kind of responsibility." *Dale:* "The sporting-camp business puts quite a strain on a marriage, particularly if you're young and just crawling out of college, when kids are little." *Jana:* "Anyway, his folks sold to a young couple, and they ran it for three years, and that ended in divorce. At that point, in early '79, we decided we wanted to get into it. The first year was difficult, trying to learn the business, being a manager, and trying to keep everyone happy. There were many nights I went to bed in tears and Dale had to deal with that on top of a day of guiding and all." *Dale:* "There are really only two or three of us with sporting camps that guide full time. It's probably not fair to Jana, but that's my first love, being in a canoe."

Jana: "I guess I'll tell you the story of the blueberry buckle. That was during the hard times, the early years, before kids. Sometimes we'd only have five or six people in camp, but it would run us ragged because the two of us were covering all the bases. Anyway, I was cooking and we had some unexpected company. I had just cleaned the oven and put a blueberry buckle in to cook. I had all kinds of things on my mind and was trying to be cordial to these people. Well, about the time Dale got in off the lake, my blueberry buckle boiled over. All over my clean oven. I was at the end of my rope. Well, I went out on the back porch and chucked that buckle as far as I could chuck it. I mean, blueberry all over everything—the tree, the porch. Then I had a few choice words for Dale. Then I got into our car and went hell-bent for election out the road. Well, I got 5 miles out of town and started feeling sorry for Dale, because dinner was about an hour and a half away and I had left him high and dry. So I turned around and came back. Dale was standing in the kitchen with a cookbook open, wondering how he was going to put a meal together." *Dale:* "We usually have a chore boy, but if something breaks down, it falls back to me." *Jana:* "When he gets in. Otherwise I deal with it, too. For example, we've got regular commercial power. But we were forever losing it—a bird landing on the wire in Canada, where we get the power—it wouldn't take much." *Dale:* "So Jana finally laid down the law: 'I want a generator, I want dug wells. I'm outta here without this stuff.'" *Jana:* "I found that worked nicely. If I threatened to leave and never come back, things somehow seemed to get done." *Dale:* "At least they got way up on the list!

"Jana's got a good crew of six or eight people and most of them have been with us at least 14 years. And I have up to 10 or 12 guides a day. My guides are loyal to me and very competent. One of the biggest roles I do at camp, and one that's obscure, is to match guides to guests. I never assign anyone until I've sat down and talked with people, what their expectations are, what their skill levels are, to see if I can match them in personality with the guide. Some guides are tuned into the fishery, some are tremendous with kids, some are conversant on an intellectual level, and some are happy-go-lucky. If I can match that up, things take care of themselves. Each guide carries his own, as the Indian called it, wanigan bag and his ax. He's self-contained. Most guides nowadays carry a little wood with them, although my father would've kicked my butt until my nose bled if I'd ever done anything like that! In a wanigan bag you've got seven articles—a long-handled, large tin fry pan, a small fry pan, a potato pot with a cover, two broilers or grills, and a coffeepot. The guides cook a full meal every day—steaks, chops, or chicken, plus the fish caught in the morning, potatoes and onions, and coffee. Plus the camp cook makes homemade bread and pie, so it's a big meal. It's a case of pride that the guide cooks fish for his meal.

"You know what the dingle was in the old logging camps? It was the building or shed that went from where the men slept to where they ate, and was where they stored food outside." *Mark Danforth (guide):* "The 'dingle stick' is a long stick that hangs off a campfire to hold the pots and pans. It's made out of a hardwood, mostly green so that it doesn't catch fire. And you make a small, hot fire, not what the Indians called a white man's fire, which was so big you can't get close to it to get warm. The other thing we use is a hookeroon. That's a stick with a branch cut off short at the bottom to pick up your pots when the handles are hot." *Dale:* "You always use the hookeroon to take the grub off the dingle stick." *Alice:* "This is great! So what do you call the thing you use to turn the fish?" *Dale:* "A fork.

"If you're going to be a successful sporting-camp operator, you have to commit yourself for a lifetime. It's your first love. And we've established the Woodie Wheaton Land Trust to protect our beautiful environment around this region. The main point is that everyone has to have a reverence for what's out there, because it will slip away very quickly.

"I think the key to our business is to make it fun. Not just for the people, but the staff, too, and with that kind of attitude you can have a great time. We say with a grin that people come to sporting camps for a change and to rest—the camp gets the change and the guide gets the rest! But it's completely true that people come back here—decades, some—mostly just to unwind and have a good time. Now, I bet your readers would like to know how to earn a small fortune in the sporting-camp business." *Alice:* "Sure!" *Dale:* "Well, first you start out with a large fortune . . ."

Brownie Pudding

1 cup flour, 2 T shortening, 2 tsp. baking powder, ½ tsp. salt, ½ cup milk, 2 T cocoa, ¾ cup sugar, 1 tsp. vanilla, 1 cup walnuts

Sauce: ¾ cup brown sugar, ½ cup cocoa, 1¾ cups boiling water, 1 tsp. vanilla

Mix all ingredients; spread in 8" x 8" pan. Pour sauce over batter in pan. Bake at 325 degrees for 30–40 minutes.

FURTHER READING

Listed below are books and reference materials that were either mentioned to me during my interviews with sporting-camp owners, were available at the sporting camps I visited, or were used in connection with compiling this book.

Anderson, Gareth, and John F. Marsh. *You Alone in the Maine Woods: The Lost Hunter's Guide.* Augusta, Me.: Maine Department of Inland Fisheries and Wildlife, 1983.

The Appalachian Mountain Club. *AMC Maine Mountain Guide.* Boston: Appalachian Mountain Club, 1995.

Arlen, Alice. *She Took to the Woods: A Biography and Selected Writings of Louise Dickinson Rich.* Camden, ME: Down East Books, 2000.

Atkinson, Minnie. *Hinckley Township or Grand Lake Stream Plantation.* Newbury-port, Mass.: Newburyport Press, c. 1918.

Bennett, Dean. *Maine's Natural Heritage: Rare Species and Unique Natural Features.* Camden, Me.: Down East Books, 1988.

Clark, Stephen. *Katahdin: A Guide to Baxter State Park and Katahdin.* Thorndike, Me.: Thorndike Press, 1985.

Coatsworth, Elizabeth. *The Enchanted: An Incredible Tale.* Nobleboro, Me.: Black-berry Books, 1992.

Cobb, Gary, and Alfred H. Fenton. *The History of Pierce Pond Camps* (1992). Gary Cobb, North New Portland, ME 04961.

Cole, Stephen A. *Maine Sporting Camps.* Manuscript on file with the Maine Historic Preservation Commission, 55 Capitol Street, Augusta, ME 04330.

Eckstorm, Fannie Hardy. *The Penobscot Man.* LaGrosse, WI: Juniper Press, 1972.

Farrar, Charles A.J. *Farrar's Illustrated Guide Book to the Androscoggin Lakes.* New York: Charles T. Dillingham, 1881.

Fendler, Donn, as told to Joseph B. Egan. *Lost on a Mountain in Maine.* New York: Beech Tree Books, 1978.

Gagnon, Lana. *Chesuncook Memories.* Greenville, Me.: Chesuncook Village Church Committee, 1989.

Gramly, Richard M. *The Adkins Site: A Paleo-Indian Habitation and Associated Stone Structure.* Buffalo, NY: Persimmon Press, 1988.

Hamlin, Helen. *Nine Mile Bridge.* New York: W. W. Norton & Co., 1945.

Hart, Robert Thompson. *The Nicatous History.* (c. 1978), available at Nicatous Lodge.

Holbrook, Stewart. *Yankee Logger: A Recollection of Woodsmen, Cooks and River Drivers.* International Paper Company, 1961.

Howe, Anne. *Bully, My Third Child, 1985.* Available from Anne Howe, Thorndike, ME 04986.

Huber, J. Parker. *The Wildest Country: A Guide to Thoreau's Maine.* Boston: Appalachian Mountain Club, 1981.

Humphrey, Bob. *Bobby Goes to Maine* (children's book), 1989. Available at Wilderness Island.

Hunt, Harrison and Ruth Thompson Hunt. *North to the Horizon: Arctic Doctor and Hunter, 1913–1917.* Camden, Me.: Down East Books, 1980.

Hutchinson, Doug. *The Rumford Falls and Rangeley Lakes Railroad.* Dixfield, Me.: Partridge Lane Publications, 1989.

Kauffman, John Michael, and Jean Powers Paradis. *Dear Old Kennebago. A Pictorial History of a Maine Lake, 1862–1992.* (1992), available from Kennebago Lake Owner's Association, PO Box 18, Oquossoc, ME 04964.

Kidney, Dorothy Boone. *Away From It All.* New Jersey/London: A.S. Barnes & Co., 1969.

Lansky, Mitch. *Beyond the Beauty Strip.* Vancouver, B.C.: Terrapin Press, 1992.

Libby, Ellen. *Sharing Our Best: Libby Camp Cooks.* Nebraska: Morris Press, 1995.

Lynch, Jim "Grizzly." *An Old Guide's Tales of the Maine Woods.* (1986), c/o Florence Chapman, Portage, ME 04768.

Macdougall, Arthur R. Jr. *Dud Dean and the Enchanted* (also *Dud Dean and His Country; Where Flows the Kennebec; Doc Blakesly, Angler*). Manchester, Me.: Falmouth Publishing House, 1954.

Maine Sporting Camp Association. *Cooking with the Maine Sporting Camp Association.* Kansas: Cookbook Publishers, Inc., 1993.

――――. *The Maine Sporting Camps Association Guide/Flier,* 36 Minuteman Drive, Millinocket, ME 04462.

Marchand, Peter J. *North Woods: An Inside Look at the Nature of Forests in the Northeast.* Boston: Appalachian Mountain Club, 1987.

Martin, Al. *Three Maine Woodland Stories.* Brattleboro, Vt.: A.C. Hood & Co.

McPhee, John. *The Survival of the Bark Canoe.* New York: Farrar, Straus & Giroux, 1975.

――――. *Table of Contents.* New York: Farrar, Straus & Giroux, 1980.

Mithee, Viola. *Living at Katahdin.* Milo, Me.: Milo Printing Co.

Packard, Marlborough. *A History of Packard's Camps: 1894–1916.* (1974), available from Maine State Library.

Raychard, Al. *Trout and Salmon Fishing in Northern New England.* Thorndike, Me.: North Country Press, 1982.

Rich, Louise Dickinson. *We Took to the Woods.* Camden, ME: Down East Books, 1942.

St. Croix Waterway Map, also *St. Croix Management Plan.* St. Croix International Waterway Commission, Box 610, Calais, ME 04619.

Sawtell, William R. *Katahdin Iron Works, Boom to Bust* (also KIW Revisited and KIW III). William R. Sawtell, Box 272, Brownville, ME 04414.

Seal, Cheryl. *Thoreau's Maine Woods, Then and Now.* Hanover, NH: Yankee Books, 1992.

Thoreau, Henry David. *The Maine Woods.* Originally published in 1864. New York: Harper and Row, 1987.

Tree, Christina, and K.W. Oxnard. *Maine: An Explorer's Guide, 11th Edition.* Woodstock, Vt.: The Countryman Press, 2003.

Varney, Susan. *Take a Hike: Featuring the Appalachian Mountains in the Upper Kennebec Valley Region of Maine.* The Forks, Me.: Bread and Water Books, 1990.

Verde, Thomas. *Cornelia "Fly Rod" Thurza Crosby.* Phillips Historical Society, Phillips, ME 04966.

Wight, Eric. *Maine Game Wardens.* (1983), Maine Warden Service Relief Association, available from Eric Wight, Bethel, ME 04217.

RECIPE INDEX

Recipes featured in this book come from the American Plan camps (serve all three meals) rather than those that are primarily Housekeeping (cook for yourself). Maine sporting camps pride themselves on their food, and so they should. The planning, care, and time that go into the preparation of food is prodigious, since most cooks are miles from a grocery store and must cook without the benefit of electricity or modern conveniences year after year. Delicious, simple food—homemade and cooked the slow way—is part of what makes the camps authentic.

Recipes with an asterisk (*) are printed, with permission, from *Cooking with the Maine Sporting Camp Association*.

Dessert

Entrées

Miscellaneous

Salads and Side Dishes

GENERAL INDEX